I0879285

With heightened tensions mounting in the Cold War, President Dwight Eisenhower's request for more accurate intelligence information on the Soviet Union was the spark that ignited the U-2 project. Modified USAF bombers began overflights of the Soviet Union in 1951, but existing lower flying aircraft in the US inventory were vulnerable to anti-aircraft fire and a number of cross-border flights were shot down.

To meet the challenge and improve the survivability, the Lockheed Corporation received approval for their revolutionary design of a new recon aircraft on December 9, 1954. The company began work under a heavy veil of secrecy with only 81 people, including 25 engineers. A test pilot flew the first flight on August 1, 1955, after only eight months of production, a record-breaking result for rollout of a new project, especially one this complex and innovative. A dedicated and inventive group of contractors came together to support the project with partial pressure suits for pilots, high-resolution cameras, and an engine that could carry the aircraft to altitudes of 70,000 feet and higher.

Nicknamed the Dragon Lady, the U-2 has flown over Cuba, Alaska, North and South poles, Vietnam, Australia, Sweden, New Zealand, and Afghanistan. The U-2 is as relevant today as it was 50 years ago. More recently it flew over the hurricane ravaged US Gulf Coast to collect imagery of the destruction over a 90,000 square mile area.

First-person memoirs of many of the men who supported the early US spy plane project are included in this book. They include pilots, maintenance specialists, a flight surgeon, photographic specialists and some family members. The US also trained U-2 pilots from Taiwan and the UK and some of their photos and memoirs are in this collection.

An example of the entries in the book include one pilot's experience on a flight over the North Pole when he discovered his instrumentation was inaccurate due to the magnetic fields and realized almost too late that he was flying directly toward the Soviet Union. Maintenance technicians recalled working long hours to prepare aircraft for historic flights over Cuba. Photographic specialists remembered the difficult conditions in Vietnam, and the care required to download the exposed film of North Vietnamese targets from the cameras in the aircraft. All of these experiences were achieved under Top Secret security conditions and on a "need to know" basis.

Brig. Gen. (Ret.) Gerald R. McIlmoyle
Gerald McIlmoyle enlisted in the USAF in 1951 and completed aviation cadet training in December 1952. He was commissioned a Second Lieutenant and awarded his pilot wings. In August 1957 McIlmoyle reported to the 4080th Strategic Reconnaissance Wing as a U-2 pilot. In 1962 he earned a "spot promotion" to Major and piloted the U-2 over various parts of the world including the North and South Poles, Alaska, Argentina, Australia, Guam, and South Vietnam. McIlmoyle was one of the original group of pilots selected to fly reconnaissance missions over Cuba during the crisis in October 1962. He is a Command Pilot with 4,376 hours flying time, including 47 hours of combat time. Military decorations include the Distinguished Service Commendation Medal, Air Force Commendation Medal, and Air Force Outstanding Unit Award. McIlmoyle currently resides in Venice, Florida with his wife, Patricia, where he is active in community and church activities.

Linda Rios Bromley retired from Federal Civil Service after 33 years employment in such locations as Laughlin AFB, Texas, Charleston Naval Base, South Carolina, USAF Headquarters Europe, Wiesbaden, Germany, NASA and Internal Revenue Service, Houston, Texas. The publication of her first non-fiction book, *Freedom Flight, A True Story* chronicled the early life, entry into the Republic of China Air Force and U-2 flight training of Major Chang-di (Robin) Yeh. Linda was invited to a reunion of the 4080th Strategic Reconnaissance Wing veterans in 2005. At that event, she met USAF and Republic of China veterans and was inspired to tell the awesome experiences of the men who flew and supported the U-2 spy plane. She has been elected to the Board of Directors of the Laughlin Heritage Foundation Museum, in Del Rio.

REMEMBERING THE DRAGON LADY

MEMOIRS OF THE MEN WHO EXPERIENCED THE LEGEND OF THE U-2 SPY PLANE

Brig. Gen. (Ret.) Gerald E. McIlmoyle
and
Linda Rios Bromley

Helion & Company Ltd

Helion & Company Limited
26 Willow Road
Solihull
West Midlands
B91 1UE
England
Tel. 0121 705 3393
Fax 0121 711 4075
Email: info@helion.co.uk
Website: www.helion.co.uk

Published by Helion & Company 2011
This paperback reprint 2013

Designed and typeset by Farr out Publications, Wokingham, Berkshire
Cover designed by Farr out Publications, Wokingham, Berkshire
Printed by Lightning Source, Milton Keynes, Buckinghamshire

ISBN 978-1-908916-93-8

British Library Cataloguing-in-Publication Data.
A catalogue record for this book is available from the British Library.

For details of other military history titles published by Helion & Company Limited contact the above address, or visit our website: http://www.helion.co.uk.

We always welcome receiving book proposals from prospective authors.

Contents

List of Illustrations

Unless noted otherwise, all photographs are from the private collection of the individual in whose story they appear, otherwise © as shown.

List of Abbreviations

A&E	Armament and Electronics Squadron
ADIZ	Air Defense Identification Zone
AEC	Atomic Energy Commission
AEMS	Armament and Electronics Squadron
AEW	Airborne Early Warning
AF	Air Force
AFB	Air Force Base
AFSC	Air Force Specialty Code
AFSWP	Armed Forces Special Weapons Project
AGE	Aerospace Ground Equipment
AMAD	Airframe Mounted Accessory Drive
ANG	Air National Guard
AP	Air Policeman
APG	Airplane General
APU	Auxiliary Power Unit
ATC	Air Training Command
BOQ	Bachelor Officers' Quarters
BX	Base Exchange
CIA	Central Intelligence Agency
CINC	Commander in Chief
CINCSAC	Commander in Chief, Strategic Air Command
CMSgt	Chief Master Sergeant
DCS	Deputy Chief of Staff
DFC	Distinguished Flying Cross
DIA	Defense Intelligence Agency
DMZ	Demilitarized Zone
DR	Dead Reckoning
DROL	Daily Requirements Objectives List
ECM	Electronic Countermeasures
EGT	Engine Tailpipe Temperature
ELINT	Electronic Intelligence
EWO	Electronic Warfare Officer
FAA	Federal Aviation Administration
FAC	Forward Air Controller
FBI	Federal Bureau of Investigation
FCLP	Field Carrier Landing Practice
FEB	Flight Evaluation Board
FMS	Field Maintenance Squadron
GCA	Ground Controlled Approach
GCI	Ground Control Intercept
HASP	High Altitude Sampling Program

IAS	Indicated Air Speed
ICBM	Intercontinental Ballistic Missile
IFF	Identification Friend or Fóe
IFR	Instrument Flight Rules
IP	Instructor Pilot(s)
IPIR	Initial Photographic Interpretation Report
JCS	Joint Chiefs of Staff
JEBU	Jet Engine Build-up
LOP	Line of Position
LSO	Landing Safety Officer
MIT	Massachusetts Institute of Technology
MRBM	Medium Range Ballistic Missile(s)
NCOIC	Non-Commissioned Officer in Charge
NEPHO	Aerial Photographic and Electronic Sensor Maintenance
NORAD	North American Defense Command
NPIC	National Photographic Interpretation Center
NSA	National Security Agency
NVM/NVN	North Vietnam
OIC	Officer in Charge
OJT	On-the-Job Training
OL	Operating Location
OMS	Operational Maintenance Squadron
PE	Personal Equipment
PI	Photo Interpretation
PIF	Pilot's Information File
PLA	People's Liberation Army (Communist China)
PMEL	Precision Measurment Equipment Laboratory
PPC	Photographic Processing Center
PSD	Physiological Support Division
QD	Oxygen Quick Disconnect
R&R	Rest and Relaxation
RAF	Royal Air Force
RAW	Radar Warning
RIF	Reduction in Force
ROCAF	Republic of China Air Force (Taiwan)
RPV	Remotely Piloted Vehicles
RS	Reconnaissance Squadron
RTG	Reconnaissance Technical Group
RTS	Reconnaissance Technical Squadron
SAC	Strategic Air Command
SAM	Surface to Air Missile
SARPF	Strategic Air Relocateable Processing Facility
SEA	Southeast Asia
SES	Strategic Evaluation Squadron
SFERICS	Cover name for electronic countermeasure equipment carried in the U2
SFS	Strategic Fighter Squadron

SFW	Strategic Fighter Wing
SIGINT	Signals Intelligence
SPO	Special Projects Office
SRS	Strategic Reconnaissance Squadrons
SUPIR	Supplemental Photographic Interpretation Report
SVN	South Vietnam
TACAN	Tactical Air Navigation System
TDY	Temporary Duty
TFW	Tactical Fighter Wing
TO	Technical Orders
TTI	Tactical Targeting Information
USAFE	United States Air Force Europe
USN	US Navy
VC	Vietcong, North Vietnamese
VHF	Very High Frequency
VNAF	Vietnamese Air Force (South Vietnam)
VOR	VHF Omnidirectional Radio Range (a radio navigation system)

Preface

Just a word or two about what this book is and what it isn't. It is a compilation of contributed memories by some of those who lived through and participated in the Dragon Lady U-2 Program. Some of the memories here are recorded for posterity by those who have taken their "last flight." Many times there are conflicts between the memories in this book and the various histories written by the historians of the CIA, Air Force, Strategic Air Command and others.

We all remember the disparity demonstrated in the kindergarten game when something is whispered into the ear of a person and they whisper the same to the next person and so on until the last person who speaks the phrase aloud. The first person tells everyone the original phrase and we all laughed at how different the phrases were.

As with that kindergarten game, you will find some of these memories in conflict with one another. The idea that caused this book to be compiled was to record for our children and grandchildren the memories of our participation in this historic program initiated by President Eisenhower during the height of the Cold War. Whenever we who lived it get together, we and our spouses regale each other with our memories of those early days of the U-2 Program and frequently the phrase is heard, "I can't believe we did that!"

The Dragon Lady Program was super secret in its early years. Once when my dad asked me what I was flying at the time, I only replied, "The U-2." He gave me a look only a dad can give and stated emphatically, "You are not going to tell me, are you?" So, you will find humor, comradeship, love, anguish and apprehension all seasoned with a little bit of fear.

Happy reading to you because this program was and is all American, for America, and as such, you were part of it even if you didn't know about it.

Jerry

Brig. Gen. (Ret.) Gerald E. (Jerry) McIlmoyle

Acknowledgements

Throughout this project, we have had the cooperation and support of all the men who told their stories. The stories have been funny, serious and some, downright scary. We wish to thank Glenn Chapman, Bob Ingram, Tony Bevacqua, and Buddy Brown for contributing significantly their time and knowledge of the Dragon Lady's complexities and features. Thanks, guys, for your encouragement and your memories of the old days.

We would also like to thank Nancy Ryan Keeling for her continuing support and editing assistance, Gordon Rottman, and Stan Marshall for their valuable critiques.

We are grateful to all those who felt as we did, that it was time to tell the story from the perspective of those who lived it.

And thanks to Patty McIlmoyle and Bill Bromley for supporting us each day.

Jerry and Linda

From Idea to Reality

"Man's mind once stretched by a new idea, regains its original dimensions."
Oliver Wendell Holmes

A Temporary Unit was Born

4080th Strategic Reconnaissance Wing

The 4080th Strategic Reconnaissance Wing was organized May 1, 1956 at Turner AFB, Georgia, and assigned to the 40th Air Division of the Strategic Air Command. Operational squadrons assigned to the Wing when it was organized were the 4025th, 4028th and 4029th Strategic Reconnaissance Squadrons (SRS). On April 1, 1957, the Wing was reassigned directly to Second Air Force and relocated to Laughlin AFB, Texas. The 4029th SRS and the 4025th SRS were discontinued on January 1, 1960 and June 15, 1960, respectively. The 4080th Strategic Reconnaissance Wing relocated to Davis Monthan AFB, Arizona on July 1, 1963, and was reassigned to the 12th Strategic Aerospace Division. The 4080th Strategic Reconnaissance Wing was retired on June 25, 1966, ten years and one month after it was organized. Aircraft and personnel were reassigned to the 100th Strategic Reconnaissance Wing, a unit with a rich history dating to World War II, which was already established at Davis Monthan AFB.

A New Dimension: Development of the U-2 Program

The U-2 project was initiated in the early 1950s with President Eisenhower's request for more accurate espionage information on the Soviet Union. In 1951 modified bombers began overflights of the Soviet Union, but existing aircraft were vulnerable to anti-aircraft fire and a number of border flights were shot down. At that time the planners imagined a high altitude aircraft hard to detect and impossible to shoot down.

The Lockheed Corporation was awarded the contract with an unlimited budget and a short deadline. The CL-282 AQUATONE was designed as the development name, but the official title took a bit more consideration. The new plane could not be identified with a "B" for bomber nor an "F" for fighter; its purpose did not fit either of those categories. The Air Force decided to call it a utility plane, and the distinctive name was the U-2.

Lockheed received approval for their design on December 9, 1954. The company's Skunk Works, headed by Clarence "Kelly" Johnson, began a grueling pace to meet the deadline. Under a heavy veil of secrecy, Kelly and only 81 people, including 25 engineers, began work on the approved design. The project was so secret that the government's first check was made out to Kelly personally and mailed to his home address.

Pratt and Whitney produced an engine that would perform at an altitude of 70,000 feet and higher. The cockpit was somewhat pressurized to enable pilots to fly for up to ten hours without full pressure suits. Pilots were custom fitted with partial pressure suits to protect them in the event of aircraft pressure loss.

One of the most radical parts of the aircraft's design was the bicycle gear system. The reason for the bicycle landing gear concept was simple: weight reduction. Approximately 2,000 feet of maximum altitude was gained over the more conventional landing gear.

Kelly Johnson, head of Lockheed's Skunk Works, stands beside U-2 N803X. Photo courtesy of Lockheed Martin Co.

However, using one main gear plus a tail wheel for ground handling, Kelly Johnson accepted the fact that landings would be challenging. At that time he only expected to build a few U-2s that would have a short program life.

Outriggers, nicknamed pogos, held the wings level for takeoff and landing. When the U-2 was on takeoff roll, the pogos fell onto the runway from their sockets in the wing. The pogos would be reinstalled after the aircraft landed. The final design was a masterful blend of innovative technology—the successful matching of airframe, sensors adapted for high altitudes, pilot physiological support equipment and a finely turned engine.

Test Pilot Tony LeVier flew the first flight on August 1, 1955 after eight months of production. It was a record-breaking result from contract award to rollout of a new project. Another remarkable aspect of the project was that Lockheed refunded $2 million to the US government making the total cost of each aircraft only $1 million.

An amazing group of dedicated and innovative contractors came together to support the project, such as the David Clark Company of Worcester, Massachusetts, designers and manufacturers of the partial pressure suits worn by the U-2 pilots and future astronauts. The Hycon Company developed the camera for the U-2 making it legendary for the quality of photography produced.

Flying the aircraft was not for the faint of heart; in fact, it was considered one of the most challenging aircraft in the inventory to fly and required a high degree of skill and ability from its pilots. The difficulty experienced by seasoned pilots who flew the U-2 resulted in it being nicknamed "Dragon Lady" meaning the aircraft was extremely unforgiving.

In addition to its uses for military purposes, the U-2 has provided earth resource monitoring, drug trafficking surveillance and national disaster monitoring. NASA routinely performs atmospheric moisture mapping to aid in weather systems modeling. Missions have been flown to both poles from Sweden and New Zealand to measure ozone depletion.

More recently the U-2 has been tasked to perform in peacetime. On September 1, 2005 the Dragon Lady departed Beale AFB, California, to collect imagery of Hurricane Katrina's destruction of the US Gulf Coast for the Federal Emergency Management Agency disaster relief efforts. The optical bar camera, or film based imagery equipment that performed so well during the Cuban Missile Crisis, was considered ideal for photographing large areas with very high resolution. The six-hour flight collected imagery over a 90,000 square mile area.

A Tribute to Our Leader

"You do not lead by hitting people over the head – that's assault, not leadership."
Dwight D. Eisenhower

In Memory of Our Leader

Brigadier General John A. DesPortes (deceased January 14, 2001)
Widow – Peggy

Throughout this book, many of the stories have made references to the memorable commander of the 4080th Strategic Reconnaissance Wing, Brigadier General John A. DesPortes. When first assigned to the 4080th SRW, he was a Colonel, but before his tour was up, he was promoted to Brigadier General.

No matter the rank, he was a great leader and respected by officers and enlisted men alike for his professionalism. General DesPortes knew many of the 4080th SRW support staff by name and never failed to acknowledge them when he visited the flight line. Personal visits by General DesPortes to the homes of 4080th SRW pilots signaled a critical situation about to unfold. During the Cuban Missile Crisis, DesPortes maintained a vigilant watch as his pilots were sent over hostile territory and all but one returned. General DesPortes took a personal interest in his troops' welfare and they returned the kindness with their respect and dedication.

Brigadier General John A. DesPortes. Photo courtesy of Laughlin Heritage Foundation.

The Chosen Few

"We live in freedom because every generation has produced patriots willing to serve a cause greater than themselves."

George W. Bush

The Chosen Few Dragon Lady Pilots

The 4080th Strategic Reconnaissance Wing and subsequently the 9th Strategic Reconnaissance Wing "Dragon Lady" pilots played a major role in the overall security of this nation and the free world. They accumulated an enviable record unequalled by any earlier organizations. Dragon Lady pilots were the first to fly and cruise above 70,000 feet; they were the first to fly with a pressure suit; and they were the first to gather intelligence information in many of the world's hot spots. President John F. Kennedy's appraisal of the 4080th SRW's participation in the 1962 Cuban Missile Crisis recognized the Wing "contributed as much to the security of the United States as any unit in our history and any group of men in our country." President Kennedy's remarks were directed to all the men and women of the 4080th.

I Want to be a Pilot

When I grow up, I want to be a pilot because it's a fun job and easy to do. That's why there are so many pilots flying around these days. Pilots don't need much school, they just have to learn to read numbers so that they can read instruments. I guess they should be able to read road maps too, so they can find their way home if they get lost.

Pilots should be brave so they won't get scared if it's foggy and they can't see, or if a wing or motor falls off, they should stay calm so they'll know what to do. Pilots have to have good eyes to see through clouds and they can't be afraid of lightning or thunder because they are much closer to them than we are.

The salary pilots make is another thing I like. They make more money than they know what to do with. This is because most people think that plane flying is dangerous except pilots don't because they know how easy it is. I hope I don't get airsick because I get carsick and if I get airsick, I couldn't be a pilot and then I would have to go to work.

Authored by an 11-year old

The Chosen Few Dragon Lady Pilots
These are listed in chronological order, by date of certification.

1955
- Tony Levier
- Bob Matey
- Bob Sieker
- J. Ray Goudey
- Bob Schumacher
- Pete Everst
- Lewis Garvin
- Hank Meirdierck
- Robert Mullin
- Lewis Setter
- Bill Yancey

1956
- Howard Carey
- Glendon Dunnaway
- Martin Knutson
- Jacob Kratt
- Carl Overstreet
- Wilber Rose
- Hervie Stockman
- Jim Allison
- Tom Birkhead
- Jim Cherbonneaux
- Buster Edens
- Bill Hall
- Dan McMurry
- Frank Powers
- Sam Snyder
- Frank Strickland
- Barry Baker
- Jim Barnes
- Tom Crull
- Bob Ericson
- Frank Grace
- Russ Kemp
- Albert Rand
- Lyle Rudd
- Al Smiley
- Carmine Vito
- E. K. Jones
- John Shinn
- Jim Abramson
- Jack D. Nole
- Joe M. Jackson
- Floyd Herbert
- Richard K. Nevett
- Howard E. Cody

1957
- Richard A. Atkins Jr.
- Warren J. Boyd
- Raymond L. Haupt
- Joe R. King
- Richard S. Heyser
- Michael E. Styer
- Lloyd R. Leavitt Jr.
- Benedict A. Lacombe
- William L. Alison
- Anthony P. Bevacqua
- Jack M. Graves
- Edwin G. Emerling
- Richard E. McGraw
- John A. Campbell
- Kenneth W. Alderman
- Leo E. Smith
- Ford E. Lowcock
- Linus L. Lee
- Alfred V. Chapin Jr.
- James D. Sala
- Scott G. Smith
- James A. Qualls
- Roger L. Cooper
- Patrick J. Halloran
- Frank L. Stuart
- James A. Black
- Edward C. Perdue
- Roger H. Herman
- Bobbie G. Gardiner
- Marvin W. Doering
- Nathan J. Adams
- Hayden C. Curry
- Forrest W. Wilson
- Roy L. St. Martin
- James R. Bedford Jr.
- Rudolph Anderson Jr.

John T. McElveen
Edward B. Dixon
Harry Cordes
Robert D. Pine
Earl S. Lewis
Wesley E. McFadden
Cozier S. Kline

1958

Donald R. James
Austin J. Russell
Adrian W. Acebedo
John W. MacArthur, RAF
David E. Dowling, RAF
Michael G. Bradley, RAF
Christopher H. Walker, RAF
Robert T. Robinson, RAF
William T. Rodenbach
Robert M. Wood
Robert A. Ginther
Paul L. Haughland
Kenneth R. Van Zandt
Horace B. Reeves
Richard J. Callahan
Buddy L. Brown
John B. Boynton
Andrew J. Bratton Jr.

1959

Ronald E. Hedrick
Harold E. Melbratten
Gerald E. McIlmoyle
William R. Stickman
Richard W. Rauch
Floyd B. Kifer
Shih Chu (Gimo) Yang, ROCAF
Huai Sheng Chen, ROCAF
Tai Yu (Tiger) Wang, ROCAF
Chih Yao Hua, ROCAF
Hsi Chun Hua, ROCAF
T. J. Jackson, Jr.
Charles B. Stratton
Robert J. Schueler
Robert M. Powell
Robert E. Hall
Kenneth R. McCaslin
Jack Carr
Elsworth A. Powell
Junior B. Reed
Raleigh B. Myers

1960

Robert F. Wilke
Robert C. Spencer
Donald A. Crowe
Rex R. Knaak
Anthony Martinez
Henry McManus
David B. Gammons
William W. Wilcox
Leo J. Stewart Jr.
Robert L. Primrose
Edward H. Hill
Joe G. Hyde Jr.
David L. Ray
Clifford H. Beeler

1961

Charles W. Maultsby
Ivan B. Webster, RAF
Charles Taylor, RAF
Charles W. Kern
William E. Lawson III
George M. Bull
Donald N. Webster
Eddie E. Dunagan
John A. DesPortes
Daniel W. Schmarr
John W. Wall
Richard M. Bouchard

1962

Arthur K. Leatherwood
James K. Rogers
Donald R. McClain
Clair A. McCombs
Edmund P. Smart

1963

Victor L. Milam
Ward G. Graham
Chang-di Yeh, ROCAF
Lee Nan (Terry) Ping, ROCAF
Julius H. Baughn
Ronald D. Stromberg
Teh Pei Liang, ROCAF
Shi Chuen (Johnny) Wang, ROCAF
Kenneth F. Somers

Eugene J. O'Sullivan Jr.

1964

Li Yi (Jack) Chang, ROCAF
Hui Chia Yang, ROCAF
Martin E. Bee, RAF
Basil W. Dodd, RAF
Chen Wen (Pete) Wang, ROCAF
Shih Hi (Steve) Sheng, ROCAF
Tse Shi (Charlie) Wu, ROCAF
Theodore J. Paader
John W. Fenimore

1965

Liu Jet (Terry) Chuang, ROCAF
Yu Ching (Mickey) Chang, ROCAF
Jen Liang (Spike) Chuang, ROCAF
Thomas C. McMurtry
Kenneth C. Diehl
Jerry M. Davis
George H. Worley
Arnold L. Strasheim
William B. Copeman
Keith H. Spaulding
Earle K. Smith Jr.
Leslie A. Powell
John D. Amundson
Edward L. Rose
Donald R. Wright

1966

Bob Birkett
Bob Hickman
Harold Swanson
Andy Fan Hug Ti, ROCAF
Billy Chang Hseih, ROCAF
Jim Hoover
Lonnie Liss
Marion C. Mixon
Jim Whitehead
Dave Patton
Sam Swart
Don Aitro
Les White
Richard Woodhull

1967

Tom Hwang Ling Pei, ROCAF
Richard Cloke, RAF
Harry Drew, RAF
Jerry Chipman
Karl A. Larue
Franklin D. Ott
Roy D. Burcham
Bill Park
Art Peterson
Dale L. Kellam
John Shen Chung Li, ROCAF
Tom Wang Tao, ROCAF

1968

Frederick M. Bankis
George V. Freeze
James J. Phielix
Curtis L. Behrend
Gardner D. Krumrey
Ronald R. Williams
Kenneth L. Chisholm
Raphael S. Samay
Jerry R. Wagnon
Stanley A. Lawrence
Lee Po (David) Wei, ROCAF
Denny Huang, ROCAF
Mory Tsai, ROCAF
Mike Chu, ROCAF
Chris I, ROCAF

The Ranch

Known to early trainees as Groom Lake, Area 51, Watertown or The Ranch, this remote desolate area in the Nevada desert was the secret training location for the new U-2 aircraft. Pilots and support personnel were flown from nearby March AFB, California to spend 60 to 90 days TDY learning the new aircraft and all its associated operations. Each weekend a shuttle to March AFB was available for anyone who wanted to leave The Ranch for a bit of relaxation. The site was far from any well-traveled highway and was not depicted on any map preventing a casual observer from stumbling upon the training site. The photos that follow offer a glimpse of the operation.

Trailers were temporary living quarters for Air Force personnel at The Ranch. Photo courtesy of Lockheed Martin Co.

Dining hall at The Ranch. Photo courtesy of Lockheed Martin Co.

Mission planning and tracking. Photo courtesy of Lockheed Martin Co.

Pre-mission briefing. Photo courtesy of Lockheed Martin Co.

U-2 #66708 in flight at altitude. Photo courtesy of Lockheed Martin Co.

Wings of a U-2 have been disassembled and are awaiting transport in a C-124. Photo courtesy of Lockheed Martin Co.

A U-2 fuselage is loaded inside a C-124 for transport. Photo courtesy of Lockheed Martin Co.

Control tower at The Ranch. Photo courtesy of Lockheed Martin Co.

Maintenance operations at The Ranch. Photo courtesy of Lockheed Martin Co.

Technicians work with the camera equipment in the Q Bay below the cockpit. Photo courtesy of Lockheed Martin Co.

Drag chute deployed at touchdown. Photo courtesy of TD-Barnes.com

Flight planning and navigation prior to flight. Photo courtesy of TD-Barnes.com

Inside the control tower with shuttle aircraft in background. Photo courtesy of TD-Barnes.com

Flight line, hangars and control tower. Photo courtesy of TD-Barnes.com

Physiological Support technician checking pilots' flight equipment, including the helmets. Photo courtesy of TD-Barnes.com

A view of the instruments as the pilot would see it. Photo courtesy of TD-Barnes.com

Dragon Lady under construction at the Lockheed plant. Photo courtesy of TD-Barnes.com

The Ranch in the 1960s. Photo courtesy of TD-Barnes.com

Reassembly of the U-2 after it arrived at The Ranch. Photo courtesy of TD-Barnes.com

Security check for passengers boarding the shuttle to and from The Ranch on weekends. Photo courtesy of TD-Barnes.com

Fire truck in front of the control tower. Photo courtesy of TD-Barnes.com

Removal of U-2 tail section for engine maintenance. Photo courtesy of TD-Barnes.com

Drift sight covers installed after flight. Photo courtesy of TD-Barnes.com

Technician checks camera. Photo courtesy of Lockheed Martin Co.

Hangar where photo operations were conducted. Dark room and camera maintenance were below the balcony at the end of the hangar. Photo courtesy of TD-Barnes.com

Chase car follows a U-2 after landing. Photo courtesy of TD-Barnes.com

Anthony P. (Tony) Bevacqua

Yuba City, California
Wife: Marilyn

My Time at the Ranch

After graduating from Aviation Cadets at James Connally AFB, Waco, Texas, I attended F-84 fighter training in 1954 at Laughlin AFB, Texas and Luke AFB, Arizona. I reported to the 508th Strategic Fighter Wing (SFW) and the 468th Strategic Fighter Squadron (SFS) at Turner AFB, Georgia. At the time I came into the squadron, the 508th SFW was transitioning from the Republic F-84G (straight wing) to the Republic F-84F (swept wing) aircraft.

A year later, three other lieutenants, Francis Gary (Frank) Powers, Victor Milam and Wes Upchurch, and I rented a house together in the town of Albany, Georgia just outside the main gate of Turner AFB. I was new to the Air Force, quite naïve and truly "wet behind the ears." Not long after my joining the group my roomy, Frank Powers, disappeared; I mean he just vanished with no explanation, no forwarding address, no phone number, no message to the three of us. I learned later he had resigned from the Air Force. The next time I heard anything about Frank was when I arrived at the training site for the mystery airplane.

Back in those days, TOP SECRET meant just that, TOP SECRET. No one leaked anything to the press or news media. I was completely unaware that Kelly Johnson of the Lockheed Aircraft Company had received the "go ahead" to build the TOP SECRET U-2 spy plane. I had never even heard of Kelly Johnson. The U-2 made its maiden flight only 18 months later on August 1, 1955, just a few weeks before I was promoted to First Lieutenant.

When the Strategic Air Command decided in 1956 to close down its fighter operations, we were all wondering where that left us, where we were going to be assigned and what we were going to fly. Without knowing how or why, I was offered this unique opportunity to fly a mystery airplane. Even mission and the base were part of the big mystery. To this day, I cannot believe some of us signed up for this "pig in a poke." I believe we signed up because this mystery program was more attractive than the prospect of going to bombers or other multi-engine planes or possibly even a Tactical Air Command base that no one liked. As I saw it, the choices then were bombers or this weird program—I chose weird! Maybe that said something about my personality.

Once I agreed and signed on to the program, I was administered an oath that required everything I heard or saw to be treated as TOP SECRET. That meant I couldn't talk about my work to my compatriots in the squadron, my wife or any of my family. Those of us who accepted the challenge looked at each other and at least thought, "I don't know anything to tell!"

Almost overnight we became a small cadre within the Wing that had this mysterious assignment. We were then sent to New Haven, Connecticut, to the Berger Brothers Company, manufacturer of brassieres and corsets. At that time, the Bergers and the David Clark Company of Worcester, Massachusetts were making pressure suits. In the basement of a cavernous building, each of us was fitted with two high altitude pressure suits. We carried our new pressure suits in hand, and went to Wright Patterson AFB, Ohio and Carswell AFB, Texas where we tested the suits in the high altitude pressure chambers. At the Wright Patterson and Carswell pressure chambers, we were informed that we had to pre-breathe 100 percent oxygen to prevent the bends in the event the cockpit lost pressure. I can tell you two hours is a very long time to just sit and breathe.

Now we knew three things: One, it was TOP SECRET; two, a pressure suit was required as the airplane would be flying over 50,000 feet altitude; and three, we had to pre-breathe 100 percent oxygen prior to flight.

As 1956 neared its end, we volunteers were being informed of various aspects of the U-2 program in miniscule bits and pieces. We now knew we were going to be stationed at Laughlin AFB, Del Rio, Texas. No one knew much about Del Rio except that it was 155 miles west of San Antonio and located on our country's border with Mexico. I had been there for T-33 gunnery training in 1954. Housing at Laughlin and Del Rio was almost non-existent and what was available was sub-standard.

On February 21, 1957 orders released me from duty at Turner AFB and assigned me to Laughlin AFB. The orders read "Aprx 75 days TDY e/r at Los Angeles Area, Calif CIPCP purpose to estb an opr cadre in connection with a clas proj." I was further ordered to report to March AFB, Riverside, California on March 18, 1957 and to report to Laughlin, June 1, 1957.

I was told from officers at March AFB I would get further instructions on the training phase in the airplane I would be flying. I still didn't know the name of the airplane or even what it looked like. Since my assignment to March AFB was temporary duty (TDY), I was not authorized by the Air Force to move household goods or family there. My wife went to live with her parents in Phoenix, Arizona.

When I arrived at March AFB, I learned I would be undergoing flight training out in the desert somewhere. Now, how much more mysterious could it get? Our schedule for the training entailed being flown in a C-47 from March AFB about noon on Mondays to the training site and returned to March AFB early afternoon on Fridays. I was happy with the arrangement because it meant I could commute to Phoenix and be with my wife on weekends. Another trainee, Mike Styer, and I teamed up to make that commute. In the mid-1950s, the Interstate Highway system was still a dream. What we traveled on was mostly a two-lane asphalt road through the mountains and desert to Phoenix.

In late February 1957, I went TDY to March AFB/Groom Lake. After we departed March AFB, we got our first glimpse of Groom Lake, commonly known to the trainees as "The Ranch". On the ground at The Ranch my impression was that it was desolate country, truly cut off from civilization. The site was far from any well-traveled highway and was not depicted on any map preventing a casual observer from stumbling upon the training site. There were no nearby towns, no roads. There was only a large multi-purpose building where we took our meals, played pool and cards and watched movies. Groups of four pilots were crowded into one Airstream trailer located adjacent to the flight line. Ground school lasted seven to ten working days prior to the first flight and was held in a trailer or Quonset hut. Everything on that field was new since it was strictly a dry lake prior to it becoming a training base.

My first U-2 flight was on March 14, 1957. The first couple of flights were low altitude *sans* pressure suit; in fact, many of us wore Levis and street shoes while flying. The pressure suit came later. On the third flight, after several touch and go landings on the lake bed, I made landings on the 6,000 foot paved runway. On my first paved runway landing after a nice two-point landing, the left wing tip immediately hit the runway and

Pat Halloran and Tony Bevacqua at Eielson AFB, Alaska, for Operation Toy Soldier.

Major General Montgomery awarding the Distinguished Flying Cross to Anthony Bevacqua, May 23, 1958.

Anthony Bevacqua, July 1, 1965.

Tony and Marilyn Bevacqua, 2002.

the bird turned 45 degrees left even though I had full right rudder. The Mobile Control Officer was God at the time, and even though I added power, wings leveled off, aircraft pointed down the runway, I was told to shut down the engine. I did as I was told and the bird veered to the left again and went off the runway, crossed a tiny creek, and ripped the landing gear off. After the investigation of this incident I learned that particular bird had a history of this problem but no pilot did more than verbally mention the problem. It was verified, I was vindicated and I lost no time in training. I heard the Mobile Control Supervisor was hit with an error due to faulty judgment – better him than me.

I flamed out three times on my first flight. We flew over desolate areas with almost no emergency fields within gliding distance, so I stayed on course, glided down as fast as parameters allowed, restarted, climbed back up to altitude and continued the mission. Two more times, the same thing occurred. I returned to The Ranch two minutes early. The problem was traced to the Cobra fuel control and it was soon replaced on all the engines with a modified unit.

New ideas were always popping up during training. One of those brilliant ideas was that if we would cover our face shield with red plastic while we were pre-breathing and in the cockpit, we could see more clearly. For some reason, this idea didn't last beyond The Ranch because most of our high altitude flights were made at night.

I flew the U-2 from March 14, 1957 until my last flight in June 1965. I was reassigned to Air Command and Staff College at Maxwell AFB, Alabama. My first reaction after learning of the reassignment was to try to remain in the U-2 cockpit, but the upper level brass held their ground and off I went to school. Soon after arriving at Maxwell, I felt relief. I really enjoyed the school and being at home with my family without the worry of TDYs. It almost felt like a vacation after those eight action-filled years in the cockpit.

For immediate delivery to .... referred to in paragraph ....
If delivery cannot be made, return this order to Adjutant, Headquarters Second Air Force, with a statement of facts. For authorized abbreviations see JANAP 169

HEADQUARTERS SECOND AIR FORCE (SAC)
United States Air Force
Barksdale Air Force Base, La.

SPECIAL ORDERS)
NUMBER 108) 4 June 1957

1. Under the prov of para 18, AFR 35-66, and delegation of auth by SACSUP-1 to AFR 35-66, ea of the FNO is apt by auth of SAF as mbr of bd to cvn at Homestead AFB, Fla, to make recm for consideration of Comdr, Second AF, as to whether amn who appear before it should be disch or retained in svc. (Bd apt per para 3, SO 80, this Hq, 24 Apr 57, is dissolved)(* indc Homestead AFB, Fla).

LTCOL FREDERICK F HOLLIER, JR, 5937A, 29th Avn Depot Sq, SAC, *
MAJ JOSEPH KNOPCZYNSKI, 10697A, 379th A&E Maint Sq, SAC, *
MAJ GEORGE E BUCKINGHAM, 6914A, 19th ARefS, SAC, *
MAJ JAMES H MEYER, 11550A, 823d Sup Sq, SAC, *
CAPT JOSEPH P ZAWADSKY, AO2044713, 379th TAC Hosp, SAC, *
CAPT JOSEPH M BENNETT, JR, AO1855642, 823d AP Sq, SAC, *, Recorder without vote.
1STLT JAMES W McDONALD, JR, AO3019739, Hq 823d ABGru, SAC, *, Legal Advisor without vote.

All unheard cases referred for hearing under the prov of AFR 35-66 before bd apt by para 3, SO 80, this Hq, 24 Apr 57, will be heard by bd hereby apt.

2. Cfm VOC, 25 Feb 57, para 9, SO 38, Hq 40th Air Div, Turner AFB, Ga, 25 Feb 57, pert to TDY enroute of FNA, org indc, to Los Angeles Area, Calif, is amnd to incl: "TDY extended aprx 47 days," and: "TDN: 5773400 067-1600 P458-02 03 341-685 and 5783400 087-1600 P458-02 03 341-685." RSPWO.

MSGT JAMES E DUVILLE, AF14474738, 4080th Field Maint Sq
MSGT LEE S CARROLL, AF6980726, Hq 4080th SRW
TSGT AMBROSE V COTE, AF17245969, 4080th Field Maint Sq
TSGT TOMMIE E GAMBLE, AF14417127, 4080th Field Maint Sq
TSGT EDWARD S WHITLOCK, AF34659362, 4080th Field Maint Sq
TSGT DONALD W BAKER, AF11176910, 4028th Strat Recon Sq
SSGT JACK GREEN, AF34973076, 4080th Field Maint Sq
SSGT DONALD G CLIFF, AF15467134, 4080th A&E Maint Sq
SSGT WALTER W GERDIN, AF17313661, Hq 4080th SRW
SSGT FRITON HARPER, AF44038814, 4080th Field Maint Sq
SSGT JOSEPH A HARRINGTON, AF16358462, 4080th Field Maint Sq
SSGT COLUMBUS G HARRISON, AF14432892, 4080th Field Maint Sq
SSGT BOBBY R SMITH, AF14450408, 4080th Field Maint Sq
SSGT DONALD C BUCHANAN, AF14366874, 4028th Strat Recon Sq
SSGT LAMAR COOK, AF14494337, 4028th Strat Recon Sq
SSGT EDWARD L WOOTERS, AF17319990, 508th TAC Hosp
A/1C THOMAS H LEE, AF53039977, Hq 4080th SRW
A/1C AUSTIN B BEAL, JR, AF14076834, Hq 4080th SRW

SO 37, Hq 40th Air Div (SAC) Turner AFB, Albany, Ga 21 Feb 57 Cont

13. FNO 4028th Strat Recon Sq (L) (SAC) this sta
ASSIGNMENT: Are rel from dy sta Turner AFB, Albany, Ga; asg dy sta Laughlin AFB, Tex. No change in org asg. Aprx 75 days TDY e/r at Los Angeles Area, Calif CIPAP purpose to estb an opr cadre in connection with a clas proj.
REPORTING DATA: DALVP not to interfere with rept date. Rept to Comdr 4070th Supp Wg, March AFB, Calif NLT 0800 18 Mar 57. Rept to Comdr 4028th Strat Recon Sq (L) Laughlin AFB, Tex NLT 1 Jun 57.
GENERAL INSTRUCTIONS: Auth: AFM 35-11, Hq USAF Msg AFOOP-OP-02 30311, 13 Feb 57. FNO w/b furn copy of AFP 75-1-1. Med rec will acmp officers to Los Angeles Area. The rqr for the utilization of govt fac are deemed impracticable and will adversely affect the perf of asg dy for pd of TDY. FNO cleared for access to clas mat up to and incl TOPSEC for pd of TDY.
TRANSPORTATION: WP. PCS. TDN. 5773500 048-201 P532-02-03-07 S99-999 (DISLOCATION ALW OTHER) 5773500 048-146 P511-01 599-999. 5773400 067-9400 P458-02-03 S09-608. TPA with 16 days tvl time auth. If pov is not used, tvl time w/b the time of the common carr used.

CAPT BENEDICT A LACOMBE AO1910248 — 1STLT WILLIAM L ALLISON AO2224135
CAPT LLOYD R LEAVITT JR 20257A — 1STLT ANTHONY P BEVACQUA AO3025780

14. SSGT LONNIE O PEACOCK AF14452702 is rel from asg 307th Strat Ftr Sq (SAC) this sta; asg 4028th Strat Recon Sq (L) (SAC) this sta; rept NLT 1 Mar 57. EDCSA: 1 Mar 57. NTI.

15. TSGT ALTON VICK AF14266688 is rel from asg 4025th Strat Recon Sq (L) (SAC) this sta; asg 307th Strat Ftr Sq (SAC) this sta, rept NLT 1 Mar 57. EDCSA: 1 Mar 57. NTI.

BY ORDER OF THE COMMANDER:

OFFICIAL:

Thomas A. Fogarty
THOMAS A FOGARTY
CWO W-2, USAF
Asst Adjutant

F. I. EGLIN JR
Major, USAF
Adjutant

DISTRIBUTION:
25 ea indiv concerned Para 9 thru 13
2 ea amn concerned Para 14 & 15
3 ea Sq Comdr concerned
10 Comdr 340th AB Gp (SAC) Whiteman AFB, Mo
10 Comdr 4th Air Div (SAC) Barksdale AFB, La
10 Comdr 2d Recon Tech Sq (SAC) Barksdale AFB, La
10 Comdr Pnt Sq Sec, 3201st USAF Hosp, Eglin AFB, Fla
10 Comdr 4070th Supp Sq, March AFB, Calif
10 Comdr 4028th Strat Recon Sq (L) (SAC) Laughlin AFB, Tex

2

HEADQUARTERS
40TH AIR DIVISION (SAC)
Turner Air Force Base, Albany, Georgia

SPECIAL ORDERS)
NUMBER 37) 21 February 1957

E X T R A C T

9. CWO W-2 EARL P BAKER AW2203220
ASSIGNMENT: Is rel from asg Hq 811th AB Gp (SAC) this sta; asg 340th AB Gp (SAC) Whiteman AFB, Mo.
REPORTING DATA: 22 days DALVP. Rept to Comdr NLT 25 Mar 57. EDCSA: 6 Mar 57.
GENERAL INSTRUCTIONS: Auth: AFM 35-11, Second AF Msg DPAP 3160, 28 Feb 57. Indiv w/b furn copy of AFP 75-1-1.
TRANSPORTATION: WP. PCS. TDN. 5773500 067-9400 P531.10-02-03 S09-608 (DISLOCATION ALW OTHER) 5773500 048-146 P511-01 599-999. TPA with 3 days tvl time auth. If pov is not used, tvl time w/b the time of the common carr used.

10. 1STLT EDWARD MAJORS AO3018338
ASSIGNMENT: Is rel from asg 811th Opr Sq (SAC) this sta; asg 4th Air Div (SAC) Barksdale AFB, La.
REPORTING DATA: Rept to Comdr NLT 25 Mar 57. EDCSA: 1 Apr 57.
GENERAL INSTRUCTIONS: Auth: AFM 35-11, Second AF Msg DPOP 3374, 19 Feb 57. Indiv w/b furn copy of AFP 75-1-1.
TRANSPORTATION: WP. PCS. TDN. 5773500 067-9400 P531.10-02-03 S09-608 (DISLOCATION ALW OTHER) 5773500 048-146 P511-01 599-999. TPA with 3 days tvl time auth. If pov is not used, tvl time w/b the time of the common carr used.

11. 1STLT HARRY O JACOBS AO2209006
ASSIGNMENT: Is rel from asg 811th Opr Sq (SAC) this sta; asg 2d Recon Tech Sq (SAC) Barksdale AFB, La.
REPORTING DATA: Rept to Comdr NLT 25 Mar 57. EDCSA: 1 Apr 57.
GENERAL INSTRUCTIONS: Auth: AFM 35-11, Second AF Msg DPOP 3374, 19 Feb 57. Indiv w/b furn copy of AFP 75-1-1.
TRANSPORTATION: WP. PCS. TDN. 5773500 067-9400 P531.10-02-03 S09-608 (DISLOCATION ALW OTHER) 5773500 048-146 P511-01 599-999. TPA with 3 days tvl time auth. If pov is not used, tvl time w/b the time of the common carr used.

12. A/2C [illegible] AF12423977
ASSIGNMENT: ([illegible] 3201st USAF Hosp, Eglin AFB, Fla) is rel [illegible] (SAC) this sta; asg Pnt Sq Sec, 3201st USAF Hosp, [illegible] AFB, Fla.
REPORTING DATA: EDCSA: 2 Mar 57.
GENERAL INSTRUCTIONS: Auth: AFM 35-11, Ltr from 3201st USAF Hosp Subj asg of AF Pnt, 12 Feb 57.
TRANSPORTATION: PCS. NTI. 5773500 048-131 P531.8-02-03 399-999.

3

HEADQUARTERS
40TH AIR DIVISION (SAC)
Turner Air Force Base, Albany, Georgia

SPECIAL ORDERS)
NUMBER 47) 8 March 1957

E X T R A C T

19. CAPT WADE C HOOD JR AO590235 4028th Strat Recon Sq (L) (SAC) this sta.
ASSIGNMENT: Is rel from dy sta Carswell AFB, Tex; asg dy sta Laughlin AFB, Tex. No change in org asg.
REPORTING DATA: 30 days DALVP. Rept to Comdr 4028th Strat Recon Sq (L) (SAC) Laughlin AFB, Tex NLT 15 Apr 57.
GENERAL INSTRUCTIONS: Auth: Hq USAF Msg AFOOP-OP-02 30314, 13 Feb 57 and AFM 35-11. Indiv w/b furn copy of AFP 75-1-1.
TRANSPORTATION: WP from Carswell AFB, Tex. PCS. TDN. 5773500 048-201 P532-02-03-07 S99-999, (DISLOCATION ALW OTHER) 5773500 048-146 P511-01 S99-999. TPA with 2 days tvl time auth. If pov is not used, tvl time w/b the time of the common carr used.

20. FNA are rel from asg org indc (SAC) this sta; asg Hq 4080th Strat Recon Wg (L) (SAC) this sta, rept NLT 15 Mar 57, EDCSA: 15 Mar 57. NTI.

Hq 811th AB Gp
MSGT AUGUST KRAMER JR AF6823198
A/2C CLARENCE E KOSCHNICK AF14577484
A/2C NEIL P SMITH AF13551447

811th Opr Sq
A/2C GEORGE W OOGLSBY AF13429892
A/2C EUGENE GRANT AF14547341

21. SMOP 13, SO 37 this Hq as relating to PCS of FNO 4028th Strat Recon Sq (L) (SAC) this sta to Laughlin AFB, Tex with TDY e/r at Los Angeles Area, Calif as reads "TPA with 16 days tvl time auth" IATR "TPA with 14 days tvl time auth".

CAPT BENEDICT A LACOMBE AO1910248 — 1STLT WILLIAM L ALLISON AO2224135
CAPT LLOYD R LEAVITT JR 20257A — 1STLT ANTHONY P BEVACQUA AO3025780

22. SMOP 16, SO 37, this Hq as relating to PCS of FNO org indc (SAC) this sta to Laughlin AFB, Tex with TDY e/r at Los Angeles Area, Calif as reads "TPA with 16 days tvl time auth" IATR "TPA with 14 days tvl time auth".

MAJ JOSEPH E BROOKS AO811537 — 4028th Strat Recon Sq (L)
1STLT JACK M GRAVES AO3005557 — 4028th Strat Recon Sq (L)
1STLT FREDERICK J TIETBOHL III AO2206247 — Hq 4080th Strat Recon Wg (L)

23. A/1C WOODSON N COMBS AF18447602 is rel from asg 811th Opr Sq (SAC) this sta and hon disch eff 15 Mar 57 contingent upon his reenl in the USAF on 16 Mar 57. HOR: 1306 N Allen, Farmington, NMex. 4 days unused ACLV w/b carried fwd IAW AFR 35-22. Auth: SDN 903, Para 38(2), AFR 39-14.

24. SMOP 1, SO 44 this Hq as pert to rel from AD of A/1C EOIL LUDVIGSEN AF13455498 811th AF Sq (SAC) this sta as reads "HOR: Rt #1, Oakland, Calif" IATR "HOR: Rt #1, Oakland, Md".

7

Harry N. Cordes

(Deceased May 10, 2004)

Harry prepared the following document prior to his death and it is submitted here by his widow, Rogene.

The Ranch

In 1948 General Curtis LeMay was disturbed about the lack of bombing accuracy using radar. At this time we had the first generation atomic bombs with 20 kilotons of explosive force. Two evaluation missions were flown with Dayton, Ohio as the simulated target. The results confirmed both navigation and bombing accuracy problems, enlarged and accentuated by 150 to 200 knot jet stream winds at the bombing altitudes of 25,000 to 30,000 feet. General LeMay called a meeting of lead navigators and radar observers at SAC Headquarters to address the problems. I was assigned to rewrite the Radar Bombing Manual for the APQ 13 Radar System of the B-29 aircraft.

Colonel Edward Perry, an experienced lead navigator who was known personally by General LeMay, was selected in 1948 to head a study group of radar observers from the 509th Bomb Wing. Colonel Perry was directed to work with the Air Force Intelligence Staff at the Pentagon in the analysis of maps and charts of potential targets in the Soviet Union. The analysis provided the best estimates of the results that could be expected from coordinated radar bombing. As a member of that team, I became well acquainted with Colonel Perry. I had been the radar observer on the B-29 crew that won the SAC and Radar Bombing Competition in 1948 and from that success, Colonel Perry became aware of my capabilities.

In 1951 Colonel Perry was Commander of a SAC Strategic Evaluation Squadron (SES) that had tested lead crews throughout the Command. By now Colonel Perry and I had become pilots and our crew went through with flying colors even though we were relatively new to the B-50D aircraft. En route to my new assignment at McCoy AFB, Florida in 1954 I visited Colonel Perry at his home in Tampa where he was still Commander of SES. From 1954 to 1956 I flew the B-47 as aircraft commander and flight commander. I amassed almost 1,000 hours of B-47 flight time including deployments to Africa and England. As a Major, I would have been in line for early promotion to Lieutenant Colonel.

At this time the United States was faced with the growing threat from the Soviet Union and its closed society. The Lockheed Aviation Company approached the CIA with a proposal for a new aircraft that could fly at 70,000 feet for 4,000 miles while taking pictures. The proposed aircraft would be safe from all known defenses. The U-2 project, known as AQUATONE, was established with the CIA in charge despite a bitter battle for control between General LeMay and SAC. CIA won the battle and Richard Bissell was put in charge of the project. General LeMay won the right to name the staff and military personnel who would run the flying part of AQUATONE. There would be a SAC training wing with Colonel Yancy in command at March AFB, California, but with duty at Groom Dry Lake in Nevada, later known as Watertown Strip and still later as Area 51. The mission pilots would be screened and selected by the CIA from SAC F-84 fighter pilots with long-range navigation experience. The flying units would be organized into three squadrons known as Detachments A, B and C.

Harry N. Cordes, Deputy Chief of Staff for Intelligence, Strategic Air Command Headquarters, Offutt AFB, Nebraska, October 1970.

General LeMay selected Colonel McCoy to lead Detachment A, Colonel Perry to lead Detachment B and Colonel Stan Beerli for Detachment C. Each detachment commander was authorized to select their military staffs for operations, flight planning, physiological support and engineering officers. Colonel Perry selected several from his staff at SES plus others he had personally known. I received orders to report to the 1007th Air Intelligence Service Group in Washington, D.C. Colonel Perry called me personally telling me a few details of my new assignment.

In February 1956 I swapped our boat for a 1950 Studebaker and got Rogene and the girls settled in Pine Castle, Florida. It was the first home we owned. I had no clue about where I was ultimately going, how long I would be gone, what sort of job I would have or what airplane I would be flying.

Washington, DC and Watertown, Nevada, 1956

When I arrived in Washington, DC, I signed in at Bolling AFB and was given a room in the BOQ. I found the 1007th Air Intelligence Service Group in an old WWII building near Fort McNair. It was then that I learned that I was now a member of the CIA.

Despite my Top Secret Q clearances from Nuclear Weapons training, the CIA insisted I attend orientation classes, physiological tests and interviews and the infamous lie detector exam. I passed all the tests and was admitted to Project AQUATONE. The headquarters for the project was in a super-secure area of the Matomic Building at 1717 H Street in downtown Washington, DC. I met the CIA members of the project who

July 1957, Detachment B, TUSLOG, Incirlik, Turkey, Weather Recon Unit in their "uniforms". Left to right: Harry Cordes, Chet Bohart, Ed Perry, Don Curtis, Unknown pilot, and William Kennedy. Harry was the only U-2 pilot in the group.

TUSLOG, Detachment B, Incirlik, Turkey. Standing, left to right: Francis Gary Powers, Sammy Snyder, Tom Burkhead, Ed Perry, E.K. Jones, Bill McMurry, Bill Hall. Kneeling, left to right: Chet Bohart, Cy Perkins, Buster Edens, Jim Cherbonnoux, Harry Cordes.

were Director Richard Bissell, Executive Officer James Cunningham and the people who would be in my squadron, Detachment B. Colonel Perry had brought his wife and had rented an apartment. Chet Bohart, Cy Perkins, Don Curtis and I rented apartments at 1600 – 16th Street near the Russian Embassy and next door to the Cairo Hotel. We were within walking distance to the Matomic Building.

We studied the U-2 manuals and project documents that had been made up in loose-leaf form. I learned we would be the second U-2 squadron known as Detachment B and following training at Watertown, Nevada we would move to Incirlik Air Base, Adana, Turkey. I would be able to check out and fly the U-2 but only in friendly or neutral air space. The planned overflight missions were operated by ex-Air Force pilots who had resigned their commissions with the promise of future reinstatement depending on conditions at the time. I retained my rank as a Major and was paid by the Air Force. The contract pilots were paid about four times my pay; when deployed, Air Force people were paid $7 per day.

In preparation for the flying checkout, Perry, Bohart, Perkins and I met with Dave Clark of the Clark Clothing Company in Worcester, Massachusetts. The company measured each of us for our custom-made partial pressure suits. In CIA spy fashion, we met Mr. Clark in a non-descript hotel in Washington.

To qualify for the U-2 training, we were also required to pass the comprehensive physical examination at Lovelace Clinic in Albuquerque, New Mexico. This was the same physical that astronauts were given and featured in the film *The Right Stuff.*

I studied the flight manual for the T-33 aircraft, required as part of the U-2 training. While waiting for the training to begin, I made two trips in a C-47 to Watertown. We had unlimited access to requisition office and flight planning materials we needed in Turkey. We were not fully occupied at that time. I used the break to drive to Pine Castle to visit with Rogene and our daughters.

Finally we were getting down to business. We were transferred to Watertown (later known as The Ranch) on April 15, 1956. Our mailing address and emergency contact was a post office box in North Hollywood, California. The schedule for military and civilians there was Monday through Friday at The Ranch. We flew either to Burbank, California, or March Field for the weekend. Occasionally we stayed at The Ranch for the weekend when there was required training scheduled. We returned to The Ranch on Monday morning at 8:00 a.m.

The SAC training unit provided excellent ground school and cockpit checkouts. I checked out quickly and easily in the T-33. The Ranch had a 6,000 foot macadam landing strip and continued for about five miles out over the dry Groom Lake. The runway continuation was marked on the dry lake with Los Angeles and Pasadena traffic markers.

We met our contract ex-F-84 pilots who were now assigned to Detachment B. At that time Lockheed pilots were still testing the U-2. The birds we used for training were the first five or so handmade by Lockheed; maintenance and support were also provided by the company.

Colonel Perry offered his resignation following his physical disqualification from flying the U-2. He felt strongly that the commander should fly the unit's aircraft. In the SAC tradition he felt an obligation to those of us he had brought into this project. So Colonel Perry stayed and was authorized to fly the T-33.

The T-33 was used in the U-2 training program to simulate the floating tendencies of the U-2 during landing. I flew the T-33 down the landing area, set 55% power, half flaps and tried to keep the aircraft at just a foot or less over the dry lake runway. This was remarkably close to the actual feel of landing the U-2. After passing the T-33 and ground school training phases, I put on my pressure suit for my first U-2 flight. Although the first flight was only to 20,000 feet altitude, we still went through the pre-breathing 100% oxygen procedure. I felt like a celebrity pre-breathing with Lockheed's ace test pilots, Tony Lavier and Ray Goudey. My first flight was thrilling, because of the short takeoff roll of 500 to 1000 feet, the great power in the engine and the almost straight up climb to altitude. I had no problems with landing because the U-2 gear was so similar to the B-47 landing gear. On my next flight I went to 70,000 feet and learned about the small margin between low-speed stall and high-speed buffet – the so-called "coffin corner."

My final U-2 checkout flight at The Ranch was a unit simulated overflight mission complete with cameras and designated targets. Takeoff was at night and I was one of the first to use the sextant to measure my rough latitude with Polaris. This mission went west to California, north to Montana, east to the Dakotas, south through Colorado and west back to The Ranch. Total flight time was eight and a half hours. When I landed, I was certified, fully qualified to fly the U-2 and I was the first qualified military pilot in Detachment B. Colonel Perry looked to me as his "alter ego." I was the most direct interface with the contract pilots, one of whom was Francis Gary Powers.

Incirlik Air Base, Adana, Turkey

Our training at The Ranch was completed in August 1956. We then deployed to Incirlik Air Base, Turkey in a C-124. What a long flight that was. We also set up shop while we awaited the arrival of our U-2s via C-124 also. The U-2s were then reassembled by our Lockheed and Pratt & Whitney technicians and readied for flying. Because of my performance at The Ranch, Colonel Perry selected me to perform the first test flight rather than one of the contract pilots. I took the bird to 70,000 feet altitude, shut down the engine and restarted it at 35,000 feet. This became a standard test procedure that I performed on all future test flights and I continued to be the Squadron Test Pilot.

At about the time we arrived in Turkey the Suez Canal crisis resulted in open warfare between Israel and Egypt. Detachment A in Germany flew a few missions over the Mediterranean area to determine what the British and French were doing. Detachment B received its first mission task from AQUATONE Headquarters in Washington on September 11, 1956. Since the mission was over neutral territory, Colonel Perry selected me as the pilot. The targets were British and French fleets and bases and units in the Mediterranean. It was a six-hour mission and I flew it as briefed until I passed Cyprus on the way home. I was flying at 70,000 feet on autopilot when the engine flamed out. My suit pressurized and I descended to 35,000 feet, restarted the engine and proceeded to Incirlik. A short time later Detachment B was tasked to fly almost daily missions over the battle and sea areas of the ongoing Israeli-Egyptian war. Our pilots could actually observe fighting between tanks, units and aircraft through the U-2 drift sight.

For the remainder of 1956 and into the spring of 1957 our detachment had only a minimum of mission tasking, a few Soviet penetrations, a number of peripheral intelligence gathering missions and proficiency flying. I flew a four-hour test mission over

Turkey with weather sensing package aboard. The whole operation at Incirlik became incredibly boring with only periodic breaks to go to Adana. At times that was off limits. Recreation on base was limited; however, the CIA furnished a boat, motor and water skis for us to use at the nearby reservoir.

Colonel Perry thought we were over staffed. He decided to send Bohart, Perkins and Don Curtis home. To pass the time, the remaining pilots did a bit of drinking and playing poker.

In anticipation of future tasks and to relieve some of the boredom Colonel Perry ordered the unit to undergo a simulated deployment exercise in which we packed and cataloged all supplies and equipment we would need at a bare base operations. His foresight was remarkable. In May 1957 we were tasked to move a mobile unit to Lahore, Pakistan, and fly penetrations into the Soviet Union. The preferred base was Peshawar, Pakistan but the runway there was undergoing repairs. Colonel Perry and I moved to a Pakistani air base with weather, maintenance, communications, flight planners and CIA security. We traveled mostly by C-54 through Karachi, but we ferried the U-2 aircraft and a T-33. I used the T-33 to familiarize myself with potential emergency landing sites.

Our Pakistani Air Force hosts were helpful and cooperative. Detachment B personnel lived in a Lahore hotel that had excellent food and service. The menu offered a choice of English or Pakistani selections, the latter being spicier with curry.

Frank Powers piloted one of the U-2 ferry flights; his engine flamed out and he made a dead stick landing on a 6,000-foot runway at Lahore. All of the U-2 pilots had made many simulated flameout landings. Powers landed with no damage to his aircraft, further demonstration of his flying skill.

One of our assignments tasked us to fly out of Lahore. Another covered Tyura Tam Soviet Space and Missile Test Center and recovered to Incirlik. Once we were tasked to fly three missions but we only had two U-2 aircraft. I did the flight plans for all three missions and gave Project Headquarters the option of selection.

In August 1957 the Chairman of the Joint Chiefs of Staff, U.S. Air Force General Twining and a contingent of high-ranking officers, including General William Blanchard, came to Incirlik. Colonel Perry and I were acquainted with General Blanchard. General Twining had been personally involved in the fight with CIA for control of the U-2 program. When I returned to Incirlik, I received permission from Project Headquarters to provide a detailed briefing on our operations. General Blanchard remembered me from the 509th Bomb Wing and he and General Twining were complimentary of my briefing.

Colonel Perry returned to Incirlik and resumed his arguments with Richard Bissell over a number of issues: staffing and lack of meaningful activity, CIA reluctance to turn over photography of Soviet targets to SAC, future project plans and dead ends for military personnel careers. Colonel Perry left Incirlik and the U-2 project in August 1957. I subsequently assumed command when he departed. Richard Bissell didn't trust a Major to command Detachment B and he sent another Major, a Headquarters officer, Major Joe Richmond, to "assist" me. In November 1957, Colonel Stan Beerli arrived from Detachment C in Japan to take over Detachment B. I requested Bissell to return me to the Air Force.

I met in Washington, DC with Richard Bissell in December 1957. I raised all the objections Colonel Perry had brought up plus an additional one about the project organization. His response was the three squadrons would be "permanently" based and adequate quarters provided for families on or near the bases. Bissell and I went to Adana with a lot of money to locate, lease and refurbish houses for our families. I saw the potential for international incidents with automobiles and wives. I tried to caution him about the danger of project compromise and I suggested a concept of operations similar to SAC's 4080th SRW such as permanent basing at a U.S. Air Force base with detachments sent out on temporary duty. Bissell refused to accept my advice or anyone else's. He thought he knew it all.

I left Washington in December 1957 with orders for the Air University. I served on the Air Weapons Staff at Maxwell AFB from January to August 1958 when I joined the Command and Staff School.

Strategic Air Command Headquarters 1959-1965

When I completed Command and Staff School, I was assigned as an Intelligence Staff Officer to SAC Headquarters, Offutt AFB, Nebraska. As a member of the Intelligence Staff, I was cleared for all sources of intelligence including photography taken by the U-2 and controlled by a compartmented system known as TALENT. Spy satellites were just coming into existence. I had access to the SAC U-2 program through the 4080th SRW and my experience of the CIA program. My official assignment was joint duty with the Joint Strategic Target Planning Staff. I maintained my flight proficiency piloting the T-33. I was selected as one of the first Instructor Pilots (IP) for the T-39 Saberliner. As a T-39 IP, I was required to fly any SAC General Officer scheduled on any trip. My General Officer mentor was Major General Robert N. Smith, DCS (Deputy Chief of Staff) Intelligence at SAC Headquarters. I later held that same job as a Brigadier General. General Smith and I made many trips together and it was a pleasure to fly for him.

On May 1, 1960 I received all intelligence reports from the CIA, National Security Agency and Defense Intelligence Agency pertaining to the shoot down and capture of Francis Gary Powers. I defended Powers and his conduct based on my past experience with him at Incirlik and Lahore. My immediate boss at SAC was Colonel Keegan who was well known in the intelligence community for his hawkish positions on intelligence issues. Colonel Keegan considered Powers a traitor for talking to the Soviets, for not destroying the U-2 with the detonator switches and for not taking his own life with the lethal needle concealed in a coin. I maintained a file on all intelligence and open source material on Powers including his imprisonment and trial. Later, these files came in handy when Powers was returned to US custody.

An event occurred in 1961 that had little bearing on my duty at the CIA but confirmed my judgment of Richard Bissell. He had by then been elevated to the position of Deputy Director Plans and Programs for the CIA. Bissell was the main force responsible for the ill-conceived and poorly-executed invasion of Cuba by former Cuban nationals and mercenaries trained and armed by the CIA. This was another example of the arrogance and disregard for the national policy and objectives formed and grown in the CIA under Allen Dulles and his Secretary of State John Foster Dulles. The Cuban invasion as well as Powers' May Day mission were both undoubtedly compromised and doomed to failure from the start. In both cases details were withheld from the military, other intelligence agencies and national command authorities, including Presidents

Eisenhower and Kennedy. The SAC role in this fiasco was an increased alert status, intelligence gathering against Cuba and development of contingency war plans.

It was my understanding that both Allen Dulles and Richard Bissell were fired with Dulles replaced by industrial leader John McCone, whose overall role at the CIA was reduced. It was hard to believe that one government agency could have become so out of control. Part of the CIA arrogance stemmed from some "successes" they had in Central America in the 1950s, including claims of overthrowing and establishing governments in that area.

The Soviet Union determined in February 1962 that Frank Powers was no longer a military, intelligence or propaganda asset. The Soviets were open to swap Powers for Soviet spy Rudolph Abel who was being held in New York on charges of spying in the US. The exchange was conducted on a bridge spanning East and West Germany with CIA Agent Joe Murphy on hand to positively identify Powers. Murphy had been a CIA Security Officer at Detachment B in Incirlik and he knew Powers personally. The CIA flew Powers directly back to Washington, DC where he was reunited with his wife, Barbara. They were put up in the Hunting Towers in Alexandria adjacent to the Woodrow Wilson Bridge.

Because of the intense media attention, the CIA relocated Powers and his wife in the dark of night to Letterkenny Army Depot near Chambersburg, Pennsylvania where they were set up in a safe house.

The CIA still "owned" Powers and they established the interrogation ground rules. The Defense Department was allocated two spaces for the interrogation. John Hughes, an experienced Intelligence Officer, was selected by the Defense Intelligence Agency. The other slot was allocated to the Commander in Chief, Strategic Air Command. General Powers selected me upon the recommendation of Major General Smith and Colonel Keegan.

I flew a T-33 immediately to Washington, DC, and reported to the CIA Project Headquarters. The next morning John Hughes and I, the CIA team, State Department representatives, and White House staff members traveled by unmarked cars to Chambersburg. We spent two nights and three days interrogating Powers.

Frank Powers' reaction to seeing me as part of the team could only be described as joyful. He felt he had someone who would believe in him. We listened to Powers' version of his shoot down, his escape from the U-2, his capture, imprisonment, trial, treatment and the surprise release. I discussed with Frank the discrepancies in his story raised by the NSA analysts and his version correlated with what would have occurred to a U-2 in a near miss with a surface-to-air missile. We returned to Washington on Friday and John and I met on Saturday with the DIA. We briefed the Director, DIA on Powers' interrogation and then we went to the Pentagon E Ring. First, we briefed General Lyman Lemnitzer and the Joint Chiefs, then the Director of Defense Research and Engineering, Dr. Harold Brown. When we briefed Secretary of Defense, Robert McNamara, he expressed anger that Powers continued his mission, despite the autopilot problems. I tried to explain to him the dedication of Air Force pilots to mission completion. McNamara made a scathing reference to "reckless young fighter pilots" and criticized Powers' decision to continue the mission.

I flew back to SAC Headquarters to brief my bosses and General Powers. I returned to Washington to work with John Hughes regarding Frank Powers' request to return to the Air Force and to write a report for the Inspector General.

The Inspector General of the Air Force was the same General Blanchard I had known in the 509th Bomb Wing and the same General I briefed in 1957 at Incirlik. It was his responsibility to decide what to do with Frank Powers. Major Joe Peartree of Air Force Intelligence was assigned to work with me to make a recommendation to General Blanchard. Joe and I examined all the intelligence, press reports and Soviet statements and compared them with Powers' interrogation statements. We reported our findings to General Blanchard at his quarters on Bolling AFB.

Meanwhile, John McCone, the new Director of the CIA, was not happy with the reports he received from the CIA U-2 Staff. He asked retired Federal Judge E. Barrett Prettyman to establish a Board of Inquiry to determine if Powers had acted in accordance with his CIA contract and would be entitled to his back pay. The hearings were informal. Participants were invited to comment and question witnesses. I sat in on the hearings in a dual capacity as a member of the interrogation team and as a representative of General Blanchard and the Air Force.

Dr. Louis Tordello, Deputy Director of National Security Agency and several NSA analysts presented "evidence" that Powers' shoot down story was fabrication. He asked retired Federal Judge E. Barrett Prettyman to establish a Board of Inquiry to determine if Powers had acted in accordance with his CIA contract and if he should be entitled to any back pay. Their recovered intelligence of Soviet tracking led to a scenario of Powers' oxygen problems and descent below 30,000 feet when the Soviets shot him down. I had knowledge of the same information but I believed Frank Powers. When I interrogated him, Powers was the same naïve, country boy I had known so well at The Ranch and at Incirlik.

I asked to speak at the hearing and pointed out several differences with the NSA analysts' findings. The Soviet Air Defense System tended to project target tracks based on predicted tracks. I pointed out a prime example in the Soviet shoot down of an RB-47 in the Barents Sea where the recovered tracking showed the plane circled for 30 to 45 minutes before it hit the water. I also showed them similar incidents during other shoot downs. After my presentation, Judge Prettyman asked Dr. Tordello if he knew about this information. Tordello said he would research it and return the next day.

The NSA team returned and Dr. Tordello acknowledged that NSA's scenario could be wrong and Powers' version correct. Judge Prettyman noted in his report that there was conflicting evidence with Powers' version of the events. Although that version was inconclusive, the preponderance of evidence favored Powers. Prettyman's conclusion was that Powers had fulfilled the terms of his contract and was entitled to his full back pay. This was not the first nor was it the last time I differed with the NSA.

Because I had been on the Powers' interrogation team and had participated in the hearings, the CIA asked me to accompany CIA Director John McCone and senior CIA officials to brief the appropriate congressional committees. Lockheed provided me with a model of the U-2 so I could break it down to show the series of events described by Powers. In closed sessions, we briefed the House and Senate Armed Services and Foreign Affairs Committees as well as the Senate Select Intelligence Committee. Senator Fulbright and his Foreign Affairs Committee were especially critical of the CIA for taking as their own the role of foreign policy. With a non-intelligence background, McCone had to take all the heat generated by Allen Dulles and Richard Bissell.

While I was in Washington, I had one more task to perform. I reported my recommendations on the disposition of Powers to General Blanchard. I reluctantly recommended Powers not be reinstated as a Captain in the Air Force because of the extensive publicity and zealous media interest. I felt his fame and notoriety would seriously detract from his career with any unit he joined. I also recommended that CIA still "owned" him and should use him at their Edwards AFB Test and Training Unit. Lastly, I recommended that Powers receive any future medals and decorations awarded to U-2 pilots and that he be recognized as a prisoner of war.

When I returned to SAC Headquarters, I thought my U-2 days were over. However, when Castro allowed the Soviets to install their missiles in Cuba, I again became involved with the U-2 program. I made several T-39 flights to Laughlin AFB and McCoy AFB to brief the SAC U-2 pilots on what to look for – most especially the SA-2 missile launch site. I personally briefed Rudolph Anderson and Steve Heyser who found the Soviet missile sites on their missions over Cuba. I helped plan the missions to minimize exposure to the SA-2 SAMs. Sadly, Rudolph Anderson was a casualty of the United States' involvement in the Cuban Missile Crisis.

While I enjoyed flying the B-47 bomber, the T-33 and T-39, my most challenging assignment was flying the U-2 in the handmade partial pressure suit.

Richard Giordano

Montgomery, Alabama
Wife: Anita

I had been selected for the U-2 program early in 1956 and had gone through the physical, received my pressure suit and had been though the high altitude chamber tests when I had a T-33 accident on July 19, 1956. That put me in the hospital for seven months. Thanks to Colonel Jerry Johnson, I was assigned to Laughlin AFB in February 1957. I was given a job they made up for me as Executive Officer to Buzz Curry in the U-2 squadron. In between visits to the hospital for continuing plastic surgery I was primarily performing administrative duties in the unit.

Obviously I wanted to return to flying status. The Flight Surgeon said it would be physically possible to return to flying but not in a pressure suit because of the limitation created by the scarring. So I asked to meet a Flight Evaluation Board. It was held on January 27, 1958, almost 18 months to the day after my accident. Given the fact that at that time I looked like death warmed over, I really did not think I had a chance, especially since I had suffered a cardiac arrest during one of my surgeries.

Horace Reeves was the Board President. Members were Floyd Herbert, Leon Steffy, Joe King, Floyd Kifer and Harvey Hertz. Witnesses were Jack Nole, Lloyd Leavitt and Curley Graves. The whole proceeding took about an hour and a half. The Board recommended return to flying status. A.J. Russell agreed and it went to SAC Headquarters. SAC approved it with the recommendation that I not be returned to a combat crew.

I then re-certified in the T-bird. I remember flying guys around for instrument proficiency and even a trip where we took a couple of T-birds to the OL at Ramey for the guys deployed there to practice instrument flying. I thought the trip was unique in that it was the first of its kind and required a stop at Guantanamo, Cuba, where the unit would play a significant role a few years later.

Since my accident was in the T-33, I wasn't particularly crazy about continuing to fly the plane. I asked to get dual qualified also in the U-3A so I would feel more a part of the unit, if only chasing the U-2 around the pattern with a U-2 instructor pilot in the right seat. Nothing exciting there, but I do recall as an instructor pilot, I was almost grounded when I flew too low over Brackettville while John Wayne was filming *The Alamo.* Wing received a nasty phone call about my screwing up their shooting since there weren't any airplanes scheduled to appear in the movie about Texas in the 1830's.

I very reluctantly left in September 1959 for two years in Morocco. I knew I would never have gotten by an FEB as easily as I did had it not been held on my home grounds with fellow pilots and friends. It is something for which I am eternally grateful as it allowed me to finish a 32-year career as an O-6 and Wing Commander. Some of my best friends from that assignment have remained best friends to this day.

Gerald E. (Jerry) McIlmoyle

Venice, Florida
Wife: Patricia

Recruitment into the Dragon Lady Program

It all began 55 years ago, in the spring of 1956. I had just returned to my unit from leave at McCook, Nebraska, my hometown. I was flying the F-84F in the 515th Strategic Fighter Bomber Squadron at Malmstrom AFB in Great Falls, Montana. I didn't think I had been gone that long, but the squadron was abuzz with recent changes. A flight commander myself, I found that two of the other flight commanders, Lt. Barry Baker, Lt. Jim Barnes and the Assistant Operations Officer, Captain Frank Grace had departed Malmstrom to enter a super secret program.

I was disappointed that I had not been included in the selection for the program, but my Squadron Operations Officer, Captain Homer Hayes, told me my name had been on the list of candidates for consideration. The candidates were interviewed at a local hotel in Great Falls. They returned and told our Squadron Commander, Major Robert Keene, that they were resigning their reserve commissions; they were discharged immediately. The three of them were directed not to say anything about where they were going or what they were going to be doing; we just never heard from them again.

It was mysterious and disappointing to me on two levels. I thought Frank, Barry and Jim had been good and close friends. We had all been in Korea together; we partied together, played bridge and poker and camped out together. Christmas rolled around and we received no cards, no phone calls, absolutely nothing from any of them. I really didn't understand why. Subsequently, we have run into each other a couple of times in the past 50 years, but there was no camaraderie, just a handshake and smile, no small talk. I was reminded of the old Pentagon euphemism: those three friends "evanesced".

Scuttlebutt had it that those selected for the new secret program would be flying a new jet aircraft and would be earning about five times our Air Force pay plus bonuses. The rumors seemed to be verified a couple of months later when our squadron commander asked me to lead a flight of four F-84F fighter aircraft to Houston, Texas, to attend the

Gerald E. (Jerry) McIlmoyle.

funeral of Frank Grace, my old friend. We learned during that trip that Frank had been killed during a night takeoff from an unlighted airfield, had hit a telephone pole and crashed. We were directed not to ask any questions about the crash, where, what, how, when, and most especially not about what aircraft he had been flying when he was killed. Frank's wife and children were devastated by their loss, as were we all. Frank had been a good friend to all of us in the squadron, both personally and professionally.

After I returned to the squadron, I learned that Captain Louis Setter of the sister 517th Strategic Fighter Bomber Squadron, was reassigned and no one knew where. It happened rather quickly. Setter was a regular officer and had not resigned his commission, another mystery to the mix. An engineer by education, Setter had designed a small handheld computer for use with F-84 flight planning. The Strategic Air Command (SAC) had jumped to put his invention into use.

All the elusive stories surrounding the Dragon Lady stimulated my appetite to be part of it. After a few months of rumors, the squadron was told that all the fighter bomber wings in SAC were to be disbanded by the summer of 1957 due to the limited range of their fighter aircraft. I was well aware that my four-year obligation to the Air Force would be fulfilled near the end of 1956. I did not want to return to the computer programming job I held before I entered the Air Force and my wife, Patty, wholeheartedly agreed.

I applied for and was offered a job flying for United Airlines out of Denver, Colorado. Flying for a living; I definitely found my niche in life. However, another option surfaced when our Wing Commander, Colonel Murray Bywater, called Lts. Buddy Brown, Hank Macklin and me into his office. He announced that we had proven ourselves to be the class of officer the Air Force needed. He guaranteed us that if we would apply for a regular commission we would be approved. A regular commission was attractive to me if I were to make the Air Force my career because I would not be subject to a Reduction in Force (RIF) which was a possibility as a reserve officer. Patty and I debated about the change and what it would mean to the family. We agreed that I should apply.

Out of the blue, a third choice surfaced. Colonel Jack Nole, the future U-2 Squadron Commander from Turner AFB, came to Malmstrom AFB and I found myself in a room with about ten other pilots. Colonel Nole gave us a sketchy description of a new aircraft President Eisenhower wanted and had funded. SAC needed pilots to volunteer to fly it. The decommissioned SAC fighter wings made available a large cadre of well-qualified pilots from which the still TOP SECRET Dragon Lady program had its choice. We were asked to sign up then and there or depart the briefing room; those remaining would be given a more detailed briefing. Most of us were eager to be part of the new program and raised our hands. The new volunteers pledged an oath of secrecy and signed it. We were now in the program. Patty and I had talked about this program and the possibility I might be selected. We agreed that staying in the Strategic Air Command where we were known was preferable to reassignment to a new command where I would be the "new guy" on the block.

Not even pitiful base housing deterred us from our new post of duty at Laughlin AFB in Del Rio, Texas, just a few miles from the border of Mexico. Still no details on the new aircraft or its mission had been imparted to us. Despite the lack of information, there was a feeling of excitement among the volunteers that our mission was important and the aircraft would be a challenge to fly.

In the spring of 1957 I traveled to the David Clark Company in Worcester, Massachusetts to be fitted for two partial pressure flight suits. Pilots of this new aircraft required extra protection in an emergency loss of cabin pressure. The Clark Company had been a manufacturer of women's undergarments and the founder of the company had been experimenting on pressure suit design with a degree of success. Ordinarily, funding for anything in the Air Force was a major ordeal; however, the CIA was the source of funding for everything related to the U-2 and money was no issue. The fact that we were visiting where the pressure suits were made put us on the edge of the "spook world." We made the trip to Worcester dressed in civilian clothes, no military uniforms were allowed. The trip itself was by a circuitous route and we had no military documents with us. When we arrived in Worcester, we were met at the terminal by a guy with a sign on which our names were written. We introduced ourselves, received a handshake but no name from him in response. On the drive to our hotel there was no conversation from our driver. All he said when we arrived at our hotel was, "I will pick you up here at 8:00 a.m. tomorrow morning."

With the new pressure suits finished, we were sent to a high altitude pressure chamber at Abilene AFB, Texas for testing. The test was to determine the effects of rapid decompression for the pilots and the suits. We went to this chamber because it would be the one used by my future unit's pilots for required high altitude qualification. Once we were inside the test chamber, technicians evacuated the air until the chamber was the equivalent pressure altitude of 75,000 feet. The pressure suits and pilots passed the test.

Volunteers now knew another piece of the puzzle about the aircraft we would be flying; it flew at extremely high altitudes. The highest I had ever flown up to that time was 49,000 feet in an F-86F in Korea. It seemed inconceivable to me to fly at 75,000 feet. It didn't take a rocket scientist to figure out that I would be flying the same plane in a sister program to the one that Louis Setter, Frank Grace, Barry Baker and Jim Barnes had joined eight months earlier. There were other rumors that I associated with those four comrades-in-arms, such as the one about civilians seen taking off in this weird airplane that went practically straight up from US air bases in Germany, Japan and Turkey.

Those of us scheduled to become part of the Dragon Lady program formed a bond that is still firm to this day. We were filled with anticipation of our future flying a new high altitude aircraft and our relocation to Del Rio. The men and women of the 407th Strategic Bomber Wing one by one departed Malmstrom AFB for their new assignments.

My cousin, Colonel Harvey Hertz, was the Flight Surgeon of the 4080th Strategic Reconnaissance Wing. I contacted him and told him I was being assigned to the Wing there. He invited Patty and me to stay with him and his mother (my great aunt) while we looked for a house to rent. Much of the usual anxiety of our new assignment and finding a place to live was relieved by my cousin's generosity.

I reported to the 4028th Strategic Reconnaissance Squadron the first week of August 1957. On that first day at Laughlin AFB, I saw the U-2 for the first time. I was mesmerized by the sleek appearance. For me, it represented a dream come true. It was love at first sight!

What did I feel when I first saw the U-2? It was total, unbridled excitement and I could not wait to get in it and fly. What was it like to take off and climb above 70,000 feet? It was like everything I ever wanted and hoped it would be. It was total euphoria; I was thrilled to the core with absolute and complete focus on what I was doing and making the plane perform. I couldn't get enough of flying this airplane. When I left the U-2 outfit for a staff job after seven years, it caused me real physical and psychological pain to realize I would probably never fly the bird again. Would you believe I still feel that way?

Charles B. Stratton

9 Mile Falls, Washington
Wife: Ann

My First U-2 Flight

There may be some that don't remember their first flight in the U-2, but I sure do. I had flown the F-80A and C, the F-84G and F, the B-57C and the RB-57D. Moving over to the U-2 didn't seem like any big deal. I decided that after checking out in the miserable F-80A that anything else would be a walk in the park. So I was miserable again until my first attempt at landing the U-2.

After the usual ground school, simulated landings in a U-3A, cockpit procedures, briefings, etc., it was time for the first flight. My Instructor Pilot (IP) was Ed Dixon, a really cool, calm confidence-instilling pilot. He briefed me on what to expect in flight and repeatedly emphasized the fact that the bird would not land unless it was held off the runway until it stalled and "dropped" to the runway. Dixon drove home to me the fact that if I touched down above stall, I would be airborne again and "bullfrogging" down the runway. This seemed in conflict with his previous admonition to NEVER, EVER STALL THE U-2! I thought to myself, "Okay, okay, enough already. Let's get on with it. What the hell can be so tough about landing this bird?" I had watched several U-2 landings from the Mobile Control chase car and they seemed normal enough. What I

Charles B. Stratton leaning on the unit's modern speedy Dodge wagon, which served as the mobile control and chase vehicle at Bien Hoa AB, Vietnam, March 1964.

failed to realize was that those landings were by experienced U-2 pilots, and not the new guy on the block that I was.

The takeoff and inflight maneuvers were pretty straightforward without surprises, if anything in the U-2 could be called straightforward. When I had completed my pre-landing familiarization flight maneuvers to get the feel of the U-2, I radioed my IP that I had completed that phase and was ready to enter the landing pattern. Ed instructed me to enter the pattern and reminded me of pattern altitudes. He rechecked my pattern speeds with me and computed my remaining fuel load. My downwind, base, and final approach airspeeds were right on. As I approached the runway, I saw Ed initiating a pursuit curve on me with the chase vehicle.

I passed Ed and he started calling out my altitude above the runway: "10 feet, 8 feet, 5 feet, 3 feet, 2 feet, hold it off, hold it off, HOLD IT OFF!" I held off until it started to shudder and I instinctively released some back pressure, touched the runway and bounced back up. Again I hit the runway and bounced back up. I didn't want to get into a "porpoise," so I added power and took it around. Wow, I got out of that one by the skin of my teeth.

Now, I can guarantee you that the first attempt to land an airplane in a "controlled crash" is a sobering experience. The next approach was similar to the first one, and so was my attempt to land when the bird started to shudder. Again, I couldn't help myself and released some back pressure. There I was "galloping" down the runway. On the next go-around with some one-sided discussion with Ed, I decided to hold that sucker off, even if it crashed. On the next approach, as Ed called off "3, 2, 1 foot, hold it off, hold it off," I kept sucking back on the yoke. The bird started to shudder, so I kept coming back and it "flopped" to the runway. I figured this was a disaster and then Ed called out, "Nice landing!"

My next four or five touch and go's went good, but they still seemed like controlled crashes to me. As all U-2 pilots know, after a few landings, you don't even notice the shudder just before the "crash." After that flight, I really knew the meaning of the pilot cliché, "Well, I walked away from another one!"

Commentary on the First Flights of Republic of China Pilots

by Anthony Martinez

Charles Stratton's account of his first flight brought to mind the critiques I attended as Squadron Operations Officer when the Republic of China pilots were training at Laughlin AFB. The IP was Eddie Dunagan. Fellow pilots knew Eddie sometimes slipped into South of the Mason-Dixon Line lingo when he got real excited.

This particular time, his Chinese student was listening intently to Eddie's explanation of the identical procedure that Stratton described when the bird is one foot above asphalt. Eddie said, "I don't want you to start "crow hopping" from main gear to tail wheel or you're going to be in real trouble. Do you understand?" The ROC pilot answered with a puzzled look, "What do you mean, 'crow hop'?" I not know what is 'crow hop'." Then Eddie proceeded to demonstrate with his hand bouncing up and down on the table. We all looked at each other and had a good laugh. The ROC pilots had learned much of their flying talk from the one and only "Muddy" Waters. He and his wife, Marty, really made those young ROC pilots feel at home while they were with us.

Carmine Vito

(Deceased August 27, 2003)
Widow: Barbara

The following is summarized from the *Austin American Statesman,* Saturday, August 30, 2003.

> For decades, the world knew nothing of Carmine Vito and his covert U-2 missions over the Soviet Union. That changed in 1998 when the Central Intelligence Agency declassified the details of the spy flights and their contributions to the Cold War.
>
> "I want to say a special thanks to the pilots, from Carmine Vito, to the U-2 pilots of today," CIA Director George Tenent said at a 1998 symposium on the U-2, the high-flying surveillance plane that debuted in 1956.
>
> "The courage that Carmine and his colleagues showed made an enormous difference to the security of our country," Tenent said. "These men allowed generations of Americans to live in peace and prosperity."
>
> Vito, who flew 65 spying missions for the CIA, was the only American pilot to fly a U-2 reconnaissance mission directly over Moscow. That flight, on July 5, 1956, collected critical information about the Soviet military capacity. Vito's U-2 hangs from the ceiling of the Smithsonian National Air and Space Museum in Washington, along with the Tutti-Frutti gum that he left beneath the canopy.

The CIA flew 24 missions over Russia between 1956 and 1960, when the loss of Francis Gary Powers' U-2 plane halted the flights.

Glen Dunaway, also an Austin resident, was one of the first group of six pilots, along with Vito, to operate the U-2. Dunaway remembers Vito as an ebullient and thoughtful man who was always ready to fly. "It was a huge deal, and everybody knew it," Dunaway said of their missions. "They also knew the dangers of a mission when you fly in somebody else's back yard and they don't like it. You have to treat it with maximum respect and professionalism."

The photos taken from the U-2 provided the first verifiable data about the Soviet Union's military capacity and was used to debunk rumors that the Russians were much stronger than they turned out to be.

"It was the beginning of a program that allowed the US to have a much better understanding of what was going on in the Soviet interior," said Jeffrey Richelson, a senior fellow with the National Security Archive at George Washington University. "Accurate information about the Soviet military laid the groundwork for future arms treaties," Richelson said.

Vito met Barbara at CIA Headquarters where she was an administrative assistant. They married in 1960 and had four children. Vito spent the remainder of his career in the Air Force, retiring as a Colonel.

Tightly wrapped U-2 is unloaded from a C-124. The U-2 was partially disassembled for transport and then reassembled at the destination. Photo courtesy of Lockheed Martin Co.

Pilot is being prepared for a mission. The houdah or portable canopy is used to temporarily protect the pilot and cockpit from the elements prior to takeoff. Photo courtesy of Lockheed Martin Co.

Flying with the Lady

"Once you have tasted flight, you will forever walk the earth with your eyes turned skyward for there you have been and there you long to return."

Leonardo da Vinci

Julian Anderson
Vashon, Washington

My crew was flying our last B-29 training mission the day "The War" ended. In November 1945 a large portion of the crew was transferred to Roswell AFB, New Mexico to be discharged or reassigned. I considered my options at the time; I was 5 feet 5 inches and pilot requirements for commercial airlines were 5 feet 6 inches. Employment as a commercial pilot did not seem to be a viable option for me. I decided I would stay in the Air Force and I became an Administrative Officer in the Base "Pool" Squadron until I received an assignment. I was finally assigned to the 393rd Bomb Squadron, 509th Bomb Wing as a co-pilot when it returned to Roswell. After 18 months, I was upgraded to Aircraft Commander. A great deal of my Air Force career was subsequently in aircraft safety where I participated on a number of aircraft accident investigations.

In August 1948 Jack Nole was assigned as the Deputy Commander of the 393rd Bomb Squadron. We were deployed to Goose Bay, Labrador for a short TDY. Our new squadron commander had a friend who had been assigned to the Wing and to my crew for that TDY. He was designated as the Wing Fly-Away Kit Officer. The Kit Officer was responsible for insuring that anything required for support of the squadron aircraft on TDYs was stowed in the bomb bays until supply lines could be established. Not only did I fly a combat crew, but I was also the Squadron Technical Supply Officer and Fly-Away Kit Officer. For that scheduled flight, I already had a substitution of other members of my aircrew when the Squadron Commander requested that his friend be assigned to my crew. The friend was to have flown the "test hop" of our aircraft, B-29 S/N 44-86383 on Wednesday, August 11, 1948. However, he did not show up for the flight which was flown with another crew member as co-pilot. On Thursday, August 12, prior to takeoff I briefed the Squadron Commander's friend on his responsibility on the takeoff. I specifically briefed him on the "flap retraction procedure." I explained what the procedure was and why I would call for "flaps 10 degrees" after the aircraft was established in a climb. The last 10 degrees of flap retraction in the heavyweight B-29 would lose a lot of its lift so we would then gain more airspeed. To ensure we had a climb re-established on the flight before retracting the last 10 degrees of flaps, I called for "flaps 10 degrees." About the time I felt the aircraft losing lift, I heard the co-pilot say, "Uh-oh, I forgot to play their coast." A quick glance at the co-pilot's instrument panel showed the flap indicator almost at "zero." My efforts to stop the aircraft from settling were almost successful but it was not enough. The two inboard propellers on the B-29 were six inches lower than the outboard propellers, a fact which played against us that day. I saw a flash of fire and instantly knew we had struck the ground. I concentrated

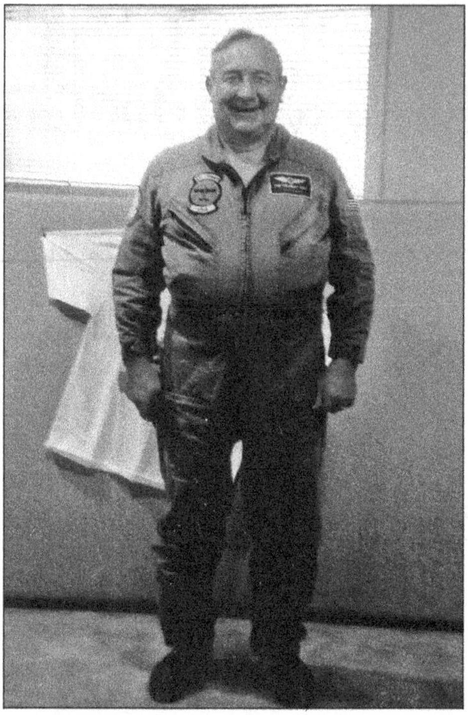

Julian Anderson awaiting his flight with Air Combat USA, 2005.

Julian Anderson checking the scheduling board for his flight, 2005.

on keeping the wings level and the nose slightly elevated for the next impact. The crash came with such devastation that only eight of the 21 crew on board survived. After the aircraft hit the ground, my left leg extended with the rudder pedal to keep the wings level and I sustained a fracture at the knee joint. I sustained head injuries that I can only attribute to my good fortune and a Guardian Angel to have survived. I was off duty for three months recovering from my injuries. I was fortunate to be among the eight, but to this day I remember those who lost their lives.

Following my recovery and return to flight duty, I attended Air Tactical School and Air Force Instrument Instructor Pilot Training. I transitioned into the B-50s as the 509th Bomb Wing was being converted to the B-50 aircraft. Then the B-47s came into operation and I volunteered to be reassigned to that aircraft. The original intent was to have the B-47s operated by a three-man crew and all qualified as navigators/bombardiers/radar navigators. The plan was to have the crew members rotate in each of the positions; however, the headquarters decision makers never implemented it.

After a year of training schools, I was assigned in 1951 to the 376th Bomb Wing at Barksdale AFB, Shreveport, Louisiana. I flew the B-29 until our unit subsequently received their B-47s. I was offered a job on the Wing Staff but I declined in order to refresh my proficiency in the aircraft. Part of my flying included testing the newly devised Minimum Altitude Bombing Technique for the SAC War Plan procedures. After transitioning into B-47s, I became an Instructor Pilot (IP) in the B-47 and accrued 1,000 hours. Later I was selected as the Wing Director of Safety under the new Wing Commander. Part of my new duties was to fly the Wing Commander whenever he wanted to go in a B-47.

One day a B-29 crashed while attempting a three-engine emergency landing. It occurred away from the airfield in the Special Weapons Storage area at Barksdale, but it did not impact the storage bunker. Crash equipment was routinely positioned alongside the runway at regular intervals for easy access in case of emergency. As the aircraft burned, the crash recovery crew had to travel a circuitous route to get to site. There were no survivors of that emergency.

I was a member of the investigative board proceedings for this accident. I recommended to SAC that procedures be revised. The recommendation was—if a B-29 pilot was making an emergency three-engine landing, once he descended through 500 feet altitude above the ground, he was then committed to land the aircraft, hopefully on the runway or within the confines of the landing area where the crash recovery vehicles are positioned, making it more probable for crew members to be safely rescued.

As a result of those recommendations, I learned that Brigadier General Austin Russell, Commander, 4th Air Division at Barksdale was impressed with the accident investigation. Another accident involved a B-47 from Eglin AFB, Florida that crashed in the Mississippi River. The pilot was attempting to "get on top" of a line of thunderstorms en route to Edwards AFB, California. I learned again that General Russell was pleased with the board's investigation of the accident.

The 376th Bomb Wing was relocated to Ohio and the Strategic Evaluation Group (SEG) came to Barksdale from MacDill AFB, Florida. It was considered to be a SAC Headquarters assignment and I was assigned as Director of Safety for the SEG.

When it came time for the relocation of the 376th Bomb Wing to Ohio and the SEG to Barksdale, General Armstrong, Commander of Second Air Force at Barksdale made his first visit to the 4080th Strategic Reconnaissance Wing at Laughlin AFB, Texas. The day General Armstrong arrived at Laughlin, his plane was delayed from landing due to a crash of B-57C right on the runway. It took two hours for the crash recovery team to get the runway cleared to permit General Armstrong's plane to land. Rumor was that General Armstrong returned to Barksdale and immediately phoned General Russell and said, "A.J., you are now Commander of the 4080th Strategic Reconnaissance Wing at Laughlin. Get down there and straighten them out."

I recall a conversation with our Personnel Officer who had just returned from Second Air Force Headquarters. He said, "You know what is going to happen to you, don't you?" I replied that I was to be Director of Safety for the SEG when they arrived from MacDill. The Personnel Officer told me he had seen my name on a message from General Russell at Laughlin saying he wanted me as his Director of Safety in the 4080th. I knew what General Russell expected of me; he expected regular visits, even if it were only to have a cup of coffee.

I was assigned to Laughlin AFB from Barksdale AFB in January 1958. My B-47 experience enabled me to be checked out in the B-57C.

A ground incident occurred in the 4028th SRS Physiological Support area. Due to the extreme altitudes involved with these flights, high-pressure oxygen bottles were included in the pilot's equipment. While handling one of those bottles, one of the technicians inadvertently dropped it. When the bottle hit the cement floor, the valve was knocked off and the bottle became a flying missile, passing through a solid wood door two inches thick. Fortunately, no one was injured, but the incident sure got everybody's attention.

A ground accident occurred during the servicing of the forward wheel on a U-2. Due to the high altitudes the U-2 flew, the wheels had to be serviced with high pressure gas rather than air. The gas was in a two-bottle wheeled cart. The valve system required the sequential adjustment of two valves to put gas in the tire without allowing too much pressure to build up. Sadly, the valves had not been adjusted properly and the unlimited buildup of pressure disintegrated the tire and severely injured the young Crew Chief working on it.

On August 3, one of the Republic of China pilots encountered an engine flameout at 70,000 feet. Rather than bail out, he began descending above an undercast layer of clouds. From 35,000 feet to 17,000 he made four unsuccessful attempts to get the engine restarted. As he approached the top of the clouds at 14,000 feet, he saw an opening and spiraled down through the overcast. As he broke out, he noted the lights of Cortez, Colorado in the distance and the flashing/rotating beacon of the Montezuma County Airport. He retracted the landing gear and the speed brakes to help lengthen his glide distance. He was successful in getting to the vicinity of the airport trying to land on the runway in a southerly direction. He was not quite aligned with the runway so he touched down and skipped a short distance, turning about 135 degrees and slid backwards off the runway where he came to a stop.

Major Mike Hua got himself disconnected and out of the cockpit, retrieved his identification papers, removed his helmet and walked over to the terminal where he found an agent on duty. Major Hua said, "I yust crash land an aircraft on your airport." He then presented his identification papers to the agent who called Kirtland AFB, Albuquerque, New Mexico. The agent told Kirtland a foreign pilot had crashed an aircraft on his airport and presented a packet of papers. The agent asked, "What should I do?" The person at Kirtland replied, "Do what the papers tell you to do" and he hung up.

As soon as the 4080th received notification, plans were made for the accident team to depart the next morning to pick up Major Hua and the U-2 engine. I was onboard the aircraft that day and recalled it was my fifteenth anniversary as a rated pilot. When we arrived at Montezuma County Airport, we met Major Hua and he said repeatedly, "I sure lucky, I sure lucky."

That was the last accident investigation team I participated in with the 4080th SRW. I have many fond memories of my service with that organization and the many life-long friends I made.

An RB-57D accident in the 4025th SRS occurred when one of the most professional pilots I knew was at the helm. With many years between then and now, unfortunately I can't recall the pilot's name, but I think it was Bob Schuler. However, he could always be counted on to touch down in almost the same spot on each of his landings, which resulted in him being awarded a Spot Promotion to Major. On this particular flight, the pilot took off but the nose gear failed to retract. After consulting with the Command Post, he was directed to land. He flew his usual landing pattern and touched down in the same spot. As the weight settled on to the gear, he continued his roll, but the left wing failed at the outboard side of the left engine.

General Russell was on the scene immediately and I was summoned from my U-2 Field Training class. Upon investigation, I saw indications the wing spar had cracked. I told General Russell of my theory of the wing spar crack and recommended that we recall any other RB-57s in flight to check for the crack. My counterparts at Second Air Force Safety told me I was nuts because the wing spar could not have been cracked. When the results came back from Wright Patterson AFB Testing Lab, they proved that the wing spar was indeed cracked.

General Russell left Laughlin in early 1959 and was replaced by Colonel A. J. Bratton. I then tried to get reassigned to a KC-135, hoping it would help me obtain employment at Boeing in Seattle after retirement. I had already purchased property on Vashon Island in order to be near my wife's parents. I had a friend in SAC Headquarters who was trying to guide my application through the Personnel channels. We thought we had it made but one day while my friend was out of the office, a "Hawkeye Sergeant" looked at the application and put the skids on it. He said, "This guy has B-29, B-50, and B-47 bomber experience. He can't go to KC-135s; he has to go to B-52s. It was already in concrete before my friend was able to do anything about it. I was due to leave for transition at Castle AFB, Sacramento, California in early September 1959. I was assigned to a B-52 wing at Sheppard AFB, Wichita Falls, Texas from 1960 to 1965 at which time I was transferred to Yokota AB, Japan as Director of Safety. I checked out in the North American Sabreliner T-39. Part of my job was to fly the Air Division Commander to visit tactical squadrons stationed in South Vietnam and Thailand as well as Japan, Korea, Okinawa and Philippines. I had two TDYs to Vietnam flying the Scatback Sabreliner operations that transported personnel and classified materials.

At Fuchu Air Station, Japan I served as Director of Safety for Fifth Air Force. During my briefing for Lieutenant General Seth McKee, a messenger summoned the General to the Command Post for an emergency. The USS Pueblo had just been seized by North

Korea. I was directed to report to Osan AB, Korea as Director of Safety until the Pueblo situation was settled to the satisfaction of those in command in Washington, DC.

After my tour in Japan, I was reassigned as Assistant Deputy Commander for Materiel at Udorn, Royal Thailand Air Force Base for my last year of active duty. The Wing there consisted of two F-4 fighter squadrons, two RF-4 squadrons and an intelligence C-130 in addition to the base flight group. Our R-F4 squadrons were the first to receive the new laser cameras.

Following my reassignment stateside, I retired from the Air Force on September 1, 1969.

Buddy L. Brown
Knoxville, Tennessee
Wife: Nancy

My Greatest Ass Chewing

This is a short story about a long ass chewing, which I rightly deserved, by my Detachment Commander, Colonel Forrest W. "Whip" Wilson. I would like to state that the nickname "Whip" was really a term of endearment. He was by all accounts a great leader, an outstanding pilot and most importantly, an officer and a gentleman.

Whip Wilson was one of those dedicated pilot/commanders who, if he had his way, would extend the day from 24 to something over 26 hours. He was our Maintenance Officer at Laughlin AFB, and a Detachment Commander when we were deployed.

The story starts at Barksdale AFB, Louisiana. The Cuban recon program had been moved from McCoy AFB, Florida to Barksdale to operate the U-2 out of a SAC base and to provide better support. The Detachment Commander, Whip Wilson, was assigned four pilots, including Yours Truly. We were flying Agency (Central Intelligence Agency) "C" Model U-2s for several reasons; we could get to higher altitudes and could have an updated defensive system.

It was the middle of August and Louisiana was hot, muggy hot, sticky and nasty and humid. On that particular day I was primary mission pilot. I completed the normal mission planning and briefing in our Operations hangar monitored by Colonel Wilson. I left the Operations building early to start my crew rest for a 3:00 AM scheduled takeoff. This was normal takeoff time for the Cuban mission out of Barksdale in order to arrive at the target area with the right sun angle (approximately 30 degrees) and before the thunderstorms built up over the island. My wakeup call, pre-mission and maintenance briefings all went according to schedule. Colonel Wilson was in attendance during the briefings. I was dressed by the PSD (Physiological Support Division) folks and transported out to my aircraft.

Before I climbed up the ladder to get into the cockpit, a couple of the maintenance guys came up to me and asked if I would do them a favor. Without hesitation I said, "You bet." The maintenance guys said they would all have their cameras out on my return from the mission and would like for me to make a pull-up for them. I thought about this request for a couple of seconds and said, "Okay, have your cameras ready." I would be making my first approach at about 10:30 a.m. I had said "Okay" because I knew that Colonel Wilson was never out on the ramp or runway during a recovery, so I felt confident I could pull this off.

Buddy Brown

I was strapped into my bird, went through the challenge and response checklist, taxied out to the runway and was cleared for takeoff. My takeoff was on schedule and I headed across the Gulf of Mexico for Cuba. For about three hours I photographed targets and flew my return flight back over the Gulf arriving at Barksdale right on time for my 10:30 recovery.

I called Barksdale Tower and requested a low approach prior to landing to verify my gear was down. The Tower approved. I also requested a pull-up over the base to approximately 10,000 feet and again the Tower approved. I started my approach, gear down, flying down the active runway at about five to ten feet altitude. I approached the midpoint of the runway. All the troops were in several of our maintenance vehicles, cameras ready. When I was just opposite of where they were standing, I called the Tower and stated that I was going to make a pull-up over the field to 10,000 feet. I requested re-entry to traffic for a full stop landing. Again the Tower approved.

I flew opposite the maintenance folks, pushed the power to full throttle and pulled the aircraft to a vertical attitude. With only 200-300 gallons of fuel remaining, the thrust of the J-75 was more than the weight of the aircraft. At 10,000 feet I recovered to level flight attitude and requested a pattern entry for a full stop landing. Again the Tower approved.

I flew my approach, was chased by Mobile Control and stopped on the runway. The maintenance guys ran to install the pogos, the manually installed gear that held the wings level on the ground. The Mobile Control Officer stated that Colonel Wilson had watched my pull-up. That was my clue that I was in hot water. After the pogos were on, I taxied back to the hangar. As I stopped the aircraft and was unhooking my equipment, I saw a steaming Colonel Wilson standing at the base of my ladder. I could tell by his expression he was almost over the top angry. I thought, "Colonel Wilson never came out for a recovery, but this time he did. Just my luck." I knew I was in for a big time chewing.

I climbed down the ladder and Colonel Wilson ordered me into a "brace" at full attention, eyes forward, no speaking. Remember, it was August in Louisiana and I still had my pressure suit on and it was hot, hot, hot. Colonel Wilson began to chew. The maintenance folks knew what was going on; they looked a little startled when I glanced their way. The chewing continued for what seemed like hours; actually it was probably only about 10 to 15 minutes. Sweat was running down my face and inside my suit. Colonel Wilson was also sweating from the hot sun and from the fierce tirade he was delivering.

There was no regulation against a fly-by pull-up for a gear check, but clearly this was not the reason. Colonel Wilson pointed out during his lecture that grandstanding like I did out there would not be tolerated. His primary concern was that I was returning from an operational mission over Cuba. I had a load of exposed film to be removed and processed immediately. I believe his exact words were something like, "When you return from an operational mission, you land the aircraft and download the film. You do not show your ass flying around the flagpole." He was absolutely right on every count. It was really a dumb mistake on my part to make a pull-up like that.

Whip finally finished chewing me out and said, "What do you have to say for yourself?" I was still in a brace. I said, "Colonel Wilson, you are absolutely right. I really enjoyed it, but I would never do it again." And I didn't.

When he cooled off, Colonel Wilson told me later that he just about had a heart attack because the J-75 engine makes a lot of noise. He didn't realize when I started my level-off at 10,000 feet I had pulled the throttle back to "idle." The level-off went from a tremendous volume to absolute silence. He said he thought I had flamed out. I think that ticked him off a bit more.

For a couple of days, I received some hard looks from Colonel Wilson, but after a couple more days, our dialog was back to normal. Colonel Wilson was later awarded the Koligan Trophy for his outstanding airmanship in a critical emergency during an operational mission out of Eielson AFB, Alaska. By the way, I repeat, that chewing I received from Colonel Wilson was well deserved.

Comments by Anthony Martinez

I liked this memory of Buddy Brown's "debriefing" by Whip Wilson. I was especially fond of Whip. He was my backyard neighbor in base housing at Laughlin. Whip had the most spacious lawn of anyone on base and he manicured it weekly. As testimony to his fastidious nature, his hangar at the Operational Maintenance Squadron was a showplace at any hour of the day or night. He had set the standard and one by one the other buildings started to look better.

I had the opportunity to spend a week with Whip in 1963. Colonel DesPortes, 4080th Wing Commander, appointed us to survey several SAC bases for the purpose of relocating the McCoy AFB, Florida Cuban Surveillance Operation. We set out in a Lockheed T-33 (T-Bird) with about a week's worth of skivvies. At Barksdale AFB we received the royal treatment from the 2nd Bomb Wing Commanding Officer. The Base Commander there gave us the run of the base and agreed to give us two huge enclosed nose docks for our Physiological Support Division, pre-takeoff kitchen, pilots' briefing room and administration and operations offices. Whip got us all the necessary Aerospace Ground Equipment and vehicles; we were in business in short order. Last time I saw Whip was in Laughlin for the 4080th SRW reunion about ten or more years ago.

Richard (Dick) Callahan

San Antonio, Texas
Wife: Sharon

It was an uneventful takeoff and initial cruise on my fifth or sixth training flight in the U-2. There had been an unusual amount of emphasis on the possibility of a flameout, the U-2 being a single engine aircraft. At an altitude of 70,000 feet the U-2 can glide approximately 250 miles with a dead engine. That being the case, finding and getting to an airfield is really no problem. We were constantly reminded to be aware of where we were in relation to a suitable landing strip.

I had not yet had my final training flight and Stand Board (Standardization Board) check flight so I was ensuring that I did everything by the book. Every procedure was new, to say nothing for the perspective of viewing the earth and navigating from an altitude of 70,000 feet.

The usual western training route was over El Paso, Texas to Phoenix, Arizona and then north. But on this particular flight that route was not open for NEPHO (photographic) training. Everyone always flew north to Salt Flat then west. Not this time, thanks to Jack Moon, Harding Smith and Ray Pierson who managed to stretch the string and find some NEPHO targets for my training flight. They also planned my day celestial training leg coming back west so that when I finished, I would be close to my letdown and landing at Laughlin AFB, Texas.

Everything was going great. I was experiencing some new and different NEPHO runs other than the usual El Paso, Lordsburg, Tucson, etc. I had finished my NEPHO run over Hot Springs, Arkansas. I turned south for my last run heading towards Shreveport, Louisiana where I would start my celestial navigation leg.

In 10 years flying Air Force single engine jet fighters, I had never experienced a flameout, but my luck had just run out. This was to be my first flameout. I know we had practiced this and had even shut the engine down on an earlier training flight. We talked about the U-2 being prone to flameout at high altitudes, but if you just keep your cool, the aircraft can be restarted.

To restart the engine, I knew I needed to keep the airspeed up, the engine windmilling at about 35 percent on the tachometer and electrical power to the battery. There is definitely no restarting without power. I notified FAA of my emergency, stopcocked the throttle, and set up my glide for Barksdale AFB, Louisiana. Air start altitude was 35,000 feet. I could see Barksdale in front of me so I knew I would arrive over the runway with plenty of altitude in case I wasn't able to restart the engine.

I attempted my first restart at 35,000 feet, with no indication of an air start when the engine tailpipe temperature (EGT) did not come off the stop. With a sinking feeling in my stomach, I recalled how "everyone" had assured me that flameouts were common

Richard and Sharon Callahan.

and after air start, "they said" you just climb back to altitude and continue the training flight. Again I reviewed the restart checklist precisely, carefully checking each and every point. After several attempts, it became apparent this bird was not going to restart.

I was approaching Barksdale and requested FAA permission to go to the Barksdale Tower radio frequency. I informed the Tower that my U-2 had flamed out and I had not been able to restart the engine. I requested permission to make a dead engine landing on their runway and asked them to notify the 2nd Air Force Command Post of my situation. Barksdale Tower gave me clearance for a flameout landing on Runway 12 and advised me their winds were light and variable. Passing through 20,000 feet, I informed Barksdale that I was continuing to attempt air start as I descended over the runway. The Tower had me in sight and informed me that they observed something streaming from my aircraft, probably fuel. Needless to say, I ceased attempting air start.

I set up my flameout landing pattern with left hand orbits over the landing approach for Runway 12. As I descended, the Tower advised me there was construction equipment off the left side of the approach to Runway 12. Since winds were light and variable, I requested and received permission to land on Runway 30 so construction would not be a factor. I arrived at high key over the end of Runway 30 at 1,700 feet above the runway. I started my turn for the left hand pattern and everything seemed ideal until on final. "Oh, shit! I'm going to be short," I yelled aloud to myself. I checked my airspeed and saw it was seven to eight knots high. Whew! I bled off my airspeed to the desired amount and crossed the end of the runway with altitude to spare. I landed 1,500 to 2,000 feet down the runway with no mobile chase car to call off my final few feet of altitude to me, another first for me on this flight. I already had more of those then I needed.

After stopping on the runway, I was suddenly surrounded by more full colonels than I had ever seen before. I turned off all the switches and inserted my seat ejection safety pins, opened the canopy, disconnected my oxygen supply, shrugged out of my parachute and prepared to exit the aircraft. Those terrific maintenance guys put up a ladder to the cockpit. I climbed out and took off my pressure suit helmet. Someone asked if I needed anything. I replied, "We usually are medically prescribed two beers after every high flight." Sure enough, they sent someone to get me a beer.

The Barksdale maintenance guys were unfamiliar with the peculiarities of the U-2. They wanted to put a huge rope around the nose wheel and tow the U-2 clear of the runway. I told them that was a definite "no, no." We would have to unlock the tail wheel and push the aircraft. They did exactly that and parked my bird next to a hangar. Maintenance cordoned off the plane and stationed a guard next to it.

A maintenance team arrived from Laughlin AFB. They found and repaired a ruptured fuel line. I flew the bird home the next day, but I didn't get credit for my celestial training leg and had to do it over. Fortunately, there was no flameout on the next flight.

Orville Clancy

Portland, Oregon
Wife: Betty

Orville submitted the following as a summary of a story written by Ray B. Sitton in the *Aerospace Historian*, June 1978.

> In the early morning hours of the late 1950s, a Republic of China Air Force (ROCAF) pilot was on his first night navigation training mission and experienced an engine flameout over southwest Colorado. He went through his emergency procedures and descended to the altitude for an engine restart. As he descended closer to the mountain peaks below, he continued several unsuccessful engine restarts. The pilot decided to descend through the cloud cover and hopefully make a successful emergency landing.
>
> As he broke through the cloud cover, he saw lights of the small Cortez, Colorado Airport, the only airfield for many miles. Without radio contact, he circled the field in preparation for an emergency landing. As he turned on final approach to the runway, he determined that he had sufficient hydraulic pressure to lower the landing gear. With the gear locked into the down position, he then realized he had lined up with the lights of Main Street, Cortez and not with the airfield. He raised the gear and turned toward the field. He tried to lower the gear but was unsuccessful this time. The U-2 continued to descend silently, unannounced and undetected, to a belly landing at the Cortez Airport.
>
> The ROCAF pilot disconnected all his cables, hoses and harnesses, a task usually performed with help from the PSD guys. He exited the aircraft and walked toward the lighted airport office in his pressure suit and helmet.
>
> To the shocked night manager and a friend who was visiting, the ROCAF pilot appeared like a space alien from the movies. In the excitement of the moment, the pilot had difficulty with his command of English. However, he remembered

his instructions concerning security of his aircraft in the event of an unscheduled landing. So he yelled, "MAXIMUM SECURITY! MAXIMUM SECURITY!"

The manager's friend knocked over his chair and ran for the back door. The manager shouted, "COME NO CLOSER! COME NO CLOSER!"

After both the airport manager and the pilot regained their composure, they were able to arrange for security of the U-2. The pilot called for a USAF recovery crew at Laughlin AFB to retrieve him and his aircraft. The following day, the U-2 and the pilot departed Cortez inside a C-124 transport with many of the residents of Cortez on hand to witness the departure.

Ward Graham

(Deceased May 8, 2004)

The following was submitted by Ward prior to his death.

My Flameout Landing

September 22, 1965 was a day that has remained etched in my memory. The deep blue sky was peppered with cumulus clouds. It was a vision of tranquility contrary to the imminent danger that I faced. My black, long-winged airplane silently approached the runway at Flagstaff Pulliam Field, Arizona. I circled once and headed in for a dead-engine landing on Runway 21, almost 7,000 feet of asphalt. I glided my Black Dragon down from above 70,000 feet to this field on the high mesa of Arizona, 7,014 feet above sea level.

The probabilities of a successful U-2 landing on such a short runway at such high elevation without power was slight. I thought at the time the odds were against me as I was considering I did not have flaps, speed brakes, drag chute nor communication from the Control Tower. I did not even have communication from another U-2 pilot in a Mobile Control chase vehicle about wind direction and speed.

About 40 minutes prior to this landing, I had been on a celestial navigation leg westbound about six hours into a routine training mission. I had completed a series of sextant shots on the sun and was recording data on my map. I noticed the shadows changing on the chart. I looked up and discovered the airplane in a 60-degree left bank. The autopilot had disconnected. I reached for the controls to roll back to level flight, and I heard the sound no jet pilot wants to hear--the spooling down of the engine. The extreme bank angle had caused a flameout.

My pressure suit inflated and my face piece fogged over. I began to shut down systems in the airplane to conserve battery power for an expected air start of the engine in the denser air below 40,000 feet. I made an emergency call but I received no response from Phoenix Center. I began to make large spirals around a town I saw on the ground. I descended through 40,000 feet, and initiated one of several air start attempts on the normal and the emergency fuel system. With a sinking feeling, I discovered that the engine was not going to start. I was down to 30,000 feet and noticed an airfield that was just south of the town I had been orbiting. I did not know what town this was nor the length of the runway, but leaving the "bird in hand" was not an option. Due to the celestial navigation leg and the confusion of the first few minutes following the flameout, I had become lost, something few pilots like to admit. I had no idea how far it might be to a longer runway.

Praying hard to the Lord for deliverance, I continued to descend toward the town's runway. By this time the battery was dead and no communication with the ground was possible. I guessed at the altitude for high key and tried to get some action from the flaps and speed brakes. There was virtually no hydraulic pressure available to operate these systems. The U-2 has no backup hydraulic system. I knew that with the engine dead, the chance was very slim of a successful drag chute deployment.

By what I can only attribute as help from the hand of God, I made a normal, no flap, flameout pattern. I touched down on the first 1,500 feet of a rather short runway at Pulliam Field, the civilian airport at Flagstaff, Arizona. There was no convenient taxiway on which to turn off so I stopped on the runway. After I landed, some firemen and mechanics came to the airplane. We were able to move it off the runway and prop the wings up on 55-gallon drums in one of the hangars on the field.

I had an interesting two days in Flagstaff staying with the firemen at the local station and being interviewed by a reporter from Phoenix. Investigators found a valve had failed in the fuel control. The failure was such that the engine would continue running in the air, but once fuel flow was interrupted it could not be restored. The real mystery to me was why the autopilot disconnected with no previous warning.

Three days later I flew the airplane back to Davis Monthan AFB without further incident. As a result of this flight, I was selected as Strategic Air Command "Pilot of the Month" and received a Distinguished Flying Cross. More importantly, I have been able to credit God for saving my life.

Patrick J. Halloran
Colorado Springs, Colorado

Loss of Oxygen at 63,000 feet

After I finished my initial U-2 checkout in mid-1957 at Laughlin AFB, I proceeded through the advanced training in long-range navigation and photo run sorties. Missions of this type were normally six to eight hours' duration and usually involved a number of visual runs on photo targets using pilotage navigation, followed by an extended celestial navigation leg on the return flight.

On one such sortie I departed early in the morning from Laughlin AFB and I climbed to altitude in a northern direction towards Dyess AFB at Abilene, Texas. After reaching an initial cruise altitude of 62,000 to 63,000 feet, I began to concentrate on visual navigation to my first set of photo targets in the panhandle part of Texas. All was going well when I became aware of an increase in my rate of breathing to the point of obvious hyperventilation. This would sometimes occur during the period of pre-breathing preflight preparation while wearing the pressure suit. I think most pilots experienced a degree of claustrophobia and hyperventilation at one time or another in their early days in the pressure suit. For all who did have this experience, it was a very uncomfortable period of anxiety and difficult to control. Definitely it was a "mind over matter" situation. I had been bothered by this phenomenon a few times, but immediately recognized the indications when I encountered it this time in flight – a cold, clammy feeling on the skin.

The recognition of hyperventilation gave me an immediate surge of adrenaline and an awareness that something was drastically wrong and required my undivided

Marking the one millionth foot of film shot over Cuba in 1963 are, standing left to right: Colonel DesPortes, Major Halloran, Jim Combs (Hycon Tech Rep), CM Sgt Max Burns, CM Sgt Willie Haynes; kneeling left to right: Airmen Jim Lobig, Jim Manis and Joseph "Rooster" Robinson.

Laverton RAAF Station Australia 1965, celebrating 1000 hours in the U-2 for George Bull. Left to right: Ray Pierson, Line Chief Okie Barnes, Crew Chief unknown, Ed Purdue, Pat Halloran, George Bull.

Beijing, China, 2004. Pat Halloran standing alongside the U-2 flown by Jack Chang, ROCAF. Chang was shot down by an SA-2 missile on January 10, 1965.

attention. I began a quick mental review of my situation and attempted to force myself to return to a normal breathing rate. This procedure normally worked on the ground, but I suddenly felt the breathing bladder of my pressure suit helmet collapse around my head. I knew that I was in serious trouble. I was at 29,000 feet cabin pressure and was OUT OF OXYGEN.

I frantically checked the primary and secondary aircraft oxygen system gauges and valves but everything indicated "normal". My mind was racing to find a fix or an alternative plan but nothing was making much sense. My hyperventilation, while attempting to breathe through the anti-suffocation valve in the helmet, was increasing to the point that I was becoming aware of serious hypoxia symptoms, the "old gun barrel" view of the world as my vision narrowed.

I went through a mental process of looking for a means of immediately getting to a lower altitude. I knew that I couldn't "fly" the aircraft to a meaningful, lower altitude as it would take too long and I wouldn't retain consciousness. I discarded a plan for an autopilot descent. That would take too long and would probably result in a flameout if I wasn't capable of making throttle adjustments. I remember considering either stopcocking the engine and attempting an emergency descent or bailing out. There was no ejection seat then. I realized that both options would have immediately moved my physiological altitude from 29,000 feet to about 63,000 feet. Survival would be unlikely. I probably went through this review process in seconds. The time of useful consciousness at that altitude is short and I could tell I was running out of time.

I was frantic and tried to think of an alternate plan. I reached for one of the cockpit mirrors to check my faceplate. My vision was seriously deteriorating and my physical actions were getting a bit spastic. I reached to adjust the mirror; my arm jerked and I hit the mirror with my hand so hard that it grabbed my attention. The mirror was now aimed at the lower right side of my body where the oxygen hose cluster on the pressure suit was located. Looking in the mirror I was startled to see in the shadows that my faceplate breathing hose was disconnected from the cluster and was dangling free.

With all the concentration I could bring to bear, and with an awareness that this was going to be my last shot, I managed to twist around, and with both hands, reconnected the breathing hose. Relief was immediate as my helmet filled with oxygen pressure and my sight and breathing returned to normal. I had an overwhelming sense of relief that I could continue the long training mission without further difficulty. When I landed seven hours later and relayed the incident to the Lift Support and Safety folks, I was roundly criticized for not aborting the mission and returning immediately to the base. At that stage of our training, what did we know?

The problem, as I learned later, was the procedure for connecting the individual hoses to the cluster. It was a simple "press to insert" and then twist to drop the "dog ears" into a retaining slot. My hose had not been twisted far enough to drop the "ears" into the locking slot. It remained in that intermediate, though still functional position, until my cockpit movements popped it loose. Subsequently, the little spring safety clip was added to the assembly. It could not be installed unless the hose was in the fully locked detent position.

For some reason, I didn't think of activating the emergency oxygen bailout bottle because if I had thought of it, I'm sure I would have done it. However, it wouldn't have been any help because no oxygen would have gone to my helmet anyway. I've had a chilling thought of that incident if I had not been able to correct the problem. I was on autopilot, on a western heading with enough fuel to fly several thousand miles before the plane would have flamed out. I wonder what part of the Pacific Ocean that would have been! The Safety Office would have had one hell of a time trying to figure that one out.

This one scared the hell out of me after the fact, but in those early days in 1957, I suspect that there were lots of incidents like that which didn't get publicized too much. It was part of the "development" of the system I guess, so when someone had a major problem, they just said, "OK, we'll fix that and let's press on."

Roger Herman

(Deceased May 23, 2010)

The following was submitted by Roger prior to his death.

Wouldn't this burn you up?

During the last years the 4080th SRW was located at Laughlin AFB, we were tasked with a project to map a number of areas in the upper Midwest. The project name eludes me but, as best I can remember it, it was in the area of Ohio, Wisconsin, Minnesota and maybe some of the fringe areas next to those states. Clear weather that would provide fine photographic reconnaissance was always a problem in these northern states. Consequently, whenever the weather forecast was favorable, any pilot scheduled for a long duration training sortie would be tasked to plan a NEPHO Run (photo recon) to take high-resolution photographs of as much of the not-yet-photographed area as possible.

On this day I happened to catch such a mission. However, the weather was only forecast to be somewhat favorable early in the day. Therefore, I was scheduled for a takeoff several hours before daylight. I rolled out of bed at "O Dark Thirty", (translation: very, very early). I departed home in the black starlit night en route to the quiet Laughlin flight line. I had my usual medical check from the Flight Surgeon and then my high protein breakfast of steak and eggs. I always looked forward to that because the cooks in the PSD always sent us off with a wonderful meal designed to last many hours. The PSD personnel helped me into my pressure suit through pre-flight by the Mobile Control Pilot and PSD hookup and check of my life support equipment and system after I was in the U-2 cockpit. Engine start and takeoff were on schedule.

The "as planned routine" ended almost immediately after takeoff when "you know what" hit the fan. I heard a "whoop" followed by a loud "whoosh" and a rush of very warm air. I reached down and placed the pressurization switch to Ram Air. That stopped the rush of warm air, but it also left me without cabin pressurization. That's because pressurization and cockpit heating come from a bleed valve that siphons compressed air from the sixteenth stage of the J-57 engine. My switching to Ram Air shut off that system entirely. Of course, it solved one problem but created another. Without pressurization, I couldn't go to altitude. Recommendation from Ground Support was that I return the pressurization switch to Normal. So, I did that, and it was a really BIG MISTAKE. The extremely hot air was still flooding the cockpit. The air conditioning system had swallowed its bleed air-mixing valve. This meant that no air-conditioned air could be mixed with engine bleed air. I immediately returned the switch to Ram Air but now that did not correct the problem. Within a couple of seconds, I knew the cabin pressurization and heating system was now stuck in full hot bleed air from the engine. Believe me, it was really hot! I couldn't remember the temperature of the bleed air as it comes off the compressor section of the engine, but I believe it was in the 200 degree range. The goal was to maintain absolute minimum power to reduce the bleed air as much as possible. There was no putting down the landing gear, opening the speed brakes and trying to burn off fuel to get to landing weight pronto. Even absolute minimum power produced unbearably hot air.

It was still several hours before daybreak and ground support decided we would try to hold off on the over-weight landing until it was light. About 20 minutes into the flight, most of which was at a near idle power setting, Operations suggested I try stuffing my gloves into the air outlet ducts that were accessible. If I had been able to do it, the hot air probably would have burned up the gloves. But I never got that far. When I took my first glove off, I found the yoke already too hot to grip with my bare hand. Fortunately, I had not taken my face piece off. But, even with my face shield in place, my face was still extremely warm. However, thankfully, I was being cooled somewhat and breathing the cool oxygen from my life support system.

I informed the Mobile Control Officer and Squadron Operations about how hot I was feeling. After another 20 minutes, following a discussion with the Supervisor of Flying (SOF), the Flight Surgeon and other consultants, we arrived at the conclusion that it might not be safe, physiologically, to wait another hour or more for a daylight landing. So, even though I still had in excess of 1,000 gallons of fuel, the decision was made to land as soon as possible. Usually the computations of flight speeds for the landing pattern and final approach were computed from the fuel remaining reading and done with little effort by the pilot. On this day, I had a lot of help determining my landing pattern, base leg and final approach speeds. Fortunately, I accomplished a rather smooth landing. During the landing rollout after touchdown, every circuit breaker in the cockpit popped! As soon as I stopped my roll, I opened the canopy. What a relief to feel that cool, early morning Texas air. When my pressure suit was removed, the outsides of my ankles were extremely red. If they weren't considered burns, they were the next thing to it and remained that way for another 10 days. Afterwards, I consumed about a quart of orange juice.

All's well that ends well and I could look forward to my next "exciting" U-2 flight.

Anthony Martinez

Clio, California
Wife: Jeannine

Early Days at Laughlin AFB

I was one of the original members of the 4080th Strategic Reconnaissance Wing (SRW) assigned to the 4025th Strategic Recon Squadron (SRS) recently arrived from Turner AFB, Georgia in June 1957. A month later, the first U-2s that formed the 4028th SRS arrived from The Ranch. The two squadrons parked their aircraft at opposite ends of the ramp. Although we knew most of the pilots of the 4028th, the mission of the U-2 was not discussed openly with us 4025th guys.

The well-known cover story was contained in the official designation of the 4028th Strategic Reconnaissance Weather Squadron. When the 4025th SRS was deactivated in early 1960, some of us had the opportunity to transfer to the 4028th SRS. The fellows who were transferred there with me were Chuck Stratton, Deke Hall, Vic Milam, Bob Schueler, Dave Gammons, and a few others.

My training in ground school and flight phases was supervised by two instructor pilots, Roger Cooper and Bobby Gardner. These two excellent pilots had been with the program from the early days, and they were very helpful in getting me ready to fly the U-2. By May 1960 SAC had established a formal training syllabus for checkout as well as combat ready status. Everyone who flew the aircraft, both staff and crews, were required to undergo the training.

I made my first solo flight in May 1960. It may not seem much of an accomplishment to some folks; however, just flying the traffic pattern, approach and landing were critical, all the more challenging with the instructor pilot in the twin engine chase plane on my wing chewing in my ear to maintain the correct airspeed. Then landing the U-2 was another matter. Crossing the runway threshold, the ground mobile control in the chase vehicle took over and advised me of my height above the runway. The ideal attitude for the airplane was to touch down with the main gear and tail wheel in a two-point attitude. Then the challenge was to keep the wings level as long as possible on center line to stop on the runway. Everyone who checked out in the airplane went through the exact same routine on their first landing.

OL20 Bien Hoa, October 1964 - 4080th SRW compound, hutches on the right.

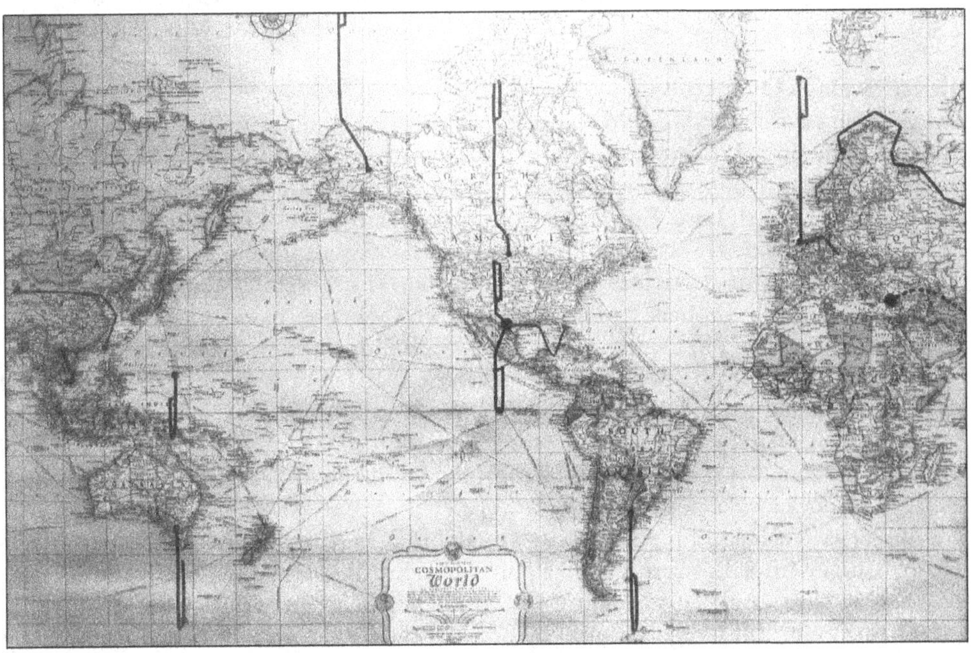

Maps showing routes of high altitude air sampling.

Aerial view of OL20, 4080th SRW compound at Bien Hoa, October 1964. Hutches are to the left, trailers to the right.

OL20, Bien Hoa, October 1964. Left to right: Capt. Jim Rogers (pilot), Capt Birk (Intel), Capt Ray Lodin (nav), Major Don Webster (pilot).

Thirteen Days Over Cuba

The thirteen days of October 1962 have been chronicled by many writers over the years. I can relate one side of the story that started the evening of October 12, 1962 at Laughlin AFB. Three of our pilots, Steve Heyser, Rudy Anderson, and Gerald McIlmoyle were transported to North Base, Edwards AFB, California, to check out in the Agency (CIA) C model of the U-2. It was equipped with the J-75 engine and its power management during climb was of particular importance. That same evening the Commander in Chief SAC General Thomas Powers arrived in a VC-97 command aircraft with Major General K. K. Compton, Deputy Chief of Staff SAC Operations, and Brigadier General Robert Smith, Deputy Chief of Staff Intelligence. The SAC generals transported our team which consisted of Colonel John DesPortes, 4080th SRW Commander, Lt Col Frank Shipley, Deputy Commander Maintenance, all the maintenance, operations and physiological support team and me as commander of the 4028th squadron to McCoy AFB, Orlando, Florida.

We departed Laughlin AFB in time to arrive at McCoy for the recovery of Major Heyser's flight from Edwards AFB. Upon our arrival General Compton immediately proceeded to the Agency Detachment Command and Operations Center where he informed Lt Col Bill Gregory that, "By order of the President, effectively immediately, the Cuban mission has been turned over to the Strategic Air Command." Prior to the

Lt Col Anthony Martinez, OL20 commander, October 1964.

OL20 Bien Hoa, September 1964 - two of our sergeants in the uniform of the day.

directive, the Agency had the lead in the Cuban crisis. Our operations staff moved in and occupied the facility with the exception of the Agency Communications Center.

We prepared the flight line with the necessary equipment for Major Heyser's arrival. He departed in his Agency U-2 from Edwards AFB at midnight on October 13 and arrived at McCoy at 9:20 a.m. on Saturday morning. He had already made a pass over Cuba and photographed part of the island. As soon as he landed, Heyser was promptly sequestered for the classified debriefing by General Compton and General Smith. Heyser, still in his partial pressure suit, related his observations while the film was downloaded. A USAF T-39 waited to ferry some of the film to the 544th Reconnaissance Technical Group (RTG) at SAC Headquarters, Offutt AFB, Nebraska; the "B" configuration camera film went to National Photographic Intelligence Center (NPIC) in Washington, DC.

The developed photos Heyser took of the western portion of Cuba were on President Kennedy's desk the following morning. For the next thirteen days we received as many as five mission routes on a daily basis from the Joint Reconnaissance Center. The Center was part of the Joint Chief of Staff (JCS) in the Pentagon. The missions were sent to us at McCoy from the SAC RTG with the JCS receiving copies as information. Each mission brought back additional evidence of the military buildup on the island.

The daily mission schedule came to a climax on October 27 when Major Anderson was lost over northeast Cuba near the town of Banes. The thirteen days ended after the shoot down; however, we continued to fly over Cuba for many years even after the blockade ended and the missiles were removed.

OL20 Bien Hoa, October 1964 - Major Roger Herman, pilot with pet monkey.

Cuban Mission from Barksdale AFB, Louisiana

Toward the end of 1962, as the crisis over Cuba was winding down, it became necessary to move the U-2 operations out of McCoy AFB. It was less critical to maintain the detachment at McCoy, and SAC Headquarters elected to relocate us to relieve the congestion in the airspace over southern Florida. Colonel DesPortes appointed me and Lt Col Forest (Whip) Wilson to check out several SAC bases east of the Mississippi River to find a suitable base that could accommodate the Cuban mission. We took a T-33 and over a period of six days surveyed and briefed our requirements at several SAC bases.

We found the most suitable facilities at Barksdale AFB, Louisiana where the Second Bomb Wing was stationed. We were offered a B-47 nose dock with adequate operations office space, a maintenance area as well as rooms for the Physiological Support Division, crew kitchen and operations planning. I was the first operating location (OL) commander at Barksdale. The crews were Capt George Bull, Capt Charles Kern and Capt Joe Hyde.

We flew two or three sorties per week with the three aircraft assigned. It was on one of these sorties that Joe Hyde was lost as he descended from altitude over the Gulf of Mexico south of the Florida panhandle. He had experienced an equipment malfunction. The Barksdale operating location continued for several years as we continued to monitor the island.

OL-20 Bien Hoa, South Vietnam

Following the Gulf of Tonkin Resolution in 1964 the squadron was ordered to deploy three U-2s to Bien Hoa Air Base, South Vietnam. Our compound consisted of three air conditioned trailers which housed the crews and our flight surgeon who was in charge of the physiological support unit with medical facilities and partial pressure suit storage. In addition, a fourth trailer contained our secure communications and flight planning section. Maintenance personnel and non-crew staff were quartered in hooches (tents) on another part of the base. Our entire compound was surrounded with chain link fencing and topped with concertina wire.

My tour was September through November 1964. On Halloween night, October 31, 1964, at about midnight we were awakened by the sounds of mortar fire on the base. The sirens and lights were going off. In the pitch dark night we all grabbed our weapons and scrambled into our sandbagged bunkers adjacent to our trailers. We were welcomed to the bunkers by huge rats and various other crawling critters. The mortar fire continued for another thirty minutes. We could hear explosions coming from the vicinity of the flight line area. A few days before, a DC-130 had arrived with the Lightning Bug reconnaissance drones. Ken McCaslin was the commander of the unit. He and I took our government vehicle and made our way to where our aircraft were parked to assess any damage. In the meantime, the mortars were falling less frequently. Fortunately, we found that none of our aircraft was damaged as our parking areas were a considerable distance from the main flight line. The day before the mortar attack, one of our pilots, Don Webster, had completed his tour and headed into Saigon for his return home. After the mortar attack, Don made the decision to stay at Bien Hoa one more night.

HASP High Altitude Sampling Project

During the years 1957-1965 the 4028th SRS was involved in flying out of several operating locations in support of Armed Forces Special Weapons Project (AFSWP). The locations were Ramey AFB, Puerto Rico and Plattsburg AFB, New York to start the program. Over the years other locations were added: Eielson AFB, Alaska; Anderson AFB, Guam; Ezeiza Airport, Argentina; Howard AFB, Panama; East Sale RAAF Station, Australia; and Mildenhall AFB, United Kingdom. Every Tuesday and Thursday we launched an aircraft on a seven-hour roundtrip flight from the OL to an altitude of 60,000 to 65,000 feet collecting gaseous and particulate samples from USSR nuclear detonations onto special equipment. Each pilot was equipped with a personal dosimeter to measure any radiation encountered during flight. If the flight encountered a "hot cloud", as indicated by the dosimeter, the aircraft was isolated and decontaminated before downloading the samples.

At some OLs we flew in coordination with the WB-57s of the Weather Service. The WB-57s flew our identical route at an altitude of 30,000 feet. Upon landing we combined our package with theirs and it was all shipped out together. Flying out of Eielson AFB, Alaska, which was typical, we flew north to the geographic North Pole. After departing Point Barrow, we used celestial navigation, as the magnetic variation at those northern latitudes render the magnetic compass unreliable. When summarizing the hazards encountered during the sampling missions in all parts of the world, it is not a stretch of the imagination to state that the flights were conducted over shark-infested waters and uncharted wastelands.

Gerald E. (Jerry) McIlmoyle
Venice Beach, Florida

Low Fuel Warning Light
Night celestial navigation training was another challenge in learning to fly the missions of the U-2. It was exciting to enter the navigation training room managed by Lt. Col. Don Todt. In those days there were no navigation aids in the areas of the world in which the reconnaissance missions were flown.

In some respects we were like Christopher Columbus, venturing into the unknown and using celestial navigation to get us into the sky and back to earth. I was excited about knowing how well I would be able to learn and apply godly navigation directly related to mission accomplishment and my own personal survival. Contemplating flying the U-2 on 3,600 nautical-mile flights without navigation aids really got my attention. I understood that celestial navigation would be critical to successful mission completion.

Jerry McIlmoyle receiving an award, 1960.

I felt inspired as I entered the navigation flight planning room. I had dreamed of flying since I was in elementary school. I was learning a navigational device that has not changed much from the days sailors used it more than 600 years ago. Quentin Stokes taught me the fundamental heavenly navigation techniques. I was lucky because "Quent" knew his technology. He included the underlying philosophy of celestial navigation and the technique of a good instructor.

Quent was, and still is, a happy, easygoing guy with a ready, wry grin. I sometimes had to give him my "double take" to determine whether he was telling me something factual or if he was pulling my leg. In any case, Quent-the-Expert, taught me well, from basics through sophisticated application of the navigational system. Quent went the extra mile with me, too. He would meet me at night at the squadron to take hand-held sextant fixes on stars from our fixed location. We knew that the U-2 on autopilot was seeking the set airspeed and heading. This "seeking" had a sine wave curve of approximately two minutes' duration. Quent taught me to be patient. We had to keep the star centered in the bubble for a two-minute period and then average out the elevation readings recorded by centering and aligning the sextant's indices.

I never was able to shoot a star and have my reading be precisely my location, no matter how hard I concentrated. Quent's indoctrination made me realize what he was teaching me; my celestial star shots were going to yield my "most probable position" but not my exact location. He thus convinced me that the best navigation approach was a three-star fix with one of the three stars as close to my line of flight as possible. He said this would give me a good speed line. The other two stars should be preferred so that their Line of Position (LOP) formed as close to and equal to lateral triangle as possible. The small triangle derived from dropping a perpendicular from the apex of the triangle to the opposite side would be my most probable position and close to my real location.

Left to right: Jerry McIlmoyle, Danny Schmarr, Ray Lodin and Ed Dixon, November 1963.

I don't know why but, to me, this navigation technique was exciting, intriguing and fascinating. I would have the knowledge of being able to navigate anywhere in the world by lining up with the stars. Of course, this gift of navigation was basic to our squadron's mission of flying over the North and South Poles. I could span the oceans of the world and stretch my U-2 over the Amazon jungle. I could traverse the periphery of the Soviet Union, China, North Korea, North Viet Nam, anywhere.

On this special night of flying the U-2, I was "charged up." I was going to test my first attempt to navigate using three star fixes on two separate night celestial legs. Before the flight I had a relaxing dinner with my wife, Patty, and our two children, Patrick and Ruthie. I left them about three hours before takeoff. Most of the squadron was flying or supporting our celestial training this particular night, including the Squadron Commander, Hayden (Buzz) Curry. The wives were going to play bridge into the wee hours of the morning. I had to wait for the heavens to get dark. I told Patty as I left, "If I ever get reincarnated, I want to come back as an Air Force pilot's wife!" Patty laughed. She knew who had the fun job and it wasn't her.

My first stop after leaving home was the Physiological Support Division (PSD), the Flight Surgeon's domain. The Flight Surgeon and coincidentally my cousin, Colonel Harvey W. Hertz, gave me my preflight physical. Harvey gave me the thumbs up and sent me to the dressing room to begin my two hours of pre-breathing oxygen. This pre-breathing oxygen process removes as much nitrogen from the body as is reasonably possible. It prevented the "bends" in case of cabin depressurization at altitude. I walked from PSD carrying my portable oxygen supply to the waiting PSD transport van that drove me directly to my assigned U-2. My aircraft had already been preflighted by a fellow pilot and was set for takeoff. As I stepped out of the PSD van, I noticed the unique Texas night sky. It was clear and cloudless, with a million stars forming an enormous black dome over Laughlin AFB. What a sight for a celestial navigational flight in this high-flying airplane. I was "wired" and I was anxious to get airborne.

Everything had gone so smoothly; I anticipated a flight that would be satisfying in every respect. On climbout, I started trimming up the U-2 so I would have the best possible platform for my celestial training. I was approaching 45,000 feet altitude and was ready to turn on the autopilot when the fuel warning light lit up – a bright orange glow. What the hell? A quick glance at the fuel counter told me I had used 45 gallons of fuel since start engine. The light was correct. I had 40 gallons of fuel before flameout. I immediately retarded my throttle to idle, turned back towards Laughlin, notified FAA and declared an emergency.

Once informed of my traffic and cleared to Laughlin, I cancelled my clearance and dialed our squadron radio frequency to inform Mobile Control of my problem. My eyes were set on the red fuel button; I was down to 35 gallons of fuel. I radioed Control that I intended to set up a flameout landing pattern and land. The calm, controlled voice of the Mobile Control pilot talked to me in a monotone voice—always a monotone voice for emergencies. "Winds are light and variable, no traffic in the pattern and you are cleared to land Number 1."

When I arrived at high key for my flameout pattern, I estimated I had remaining 20 gallons of fuel. I thought to myself, "No sweat! I've got it made." I concentrated and focused on making as smooth a landing as I possibly could. I was at maximum gross weight for landing; U-2 pilots considered that a "no-no." We thought of the bird as being made out of aluminum foil. Touchdown and rollout were smooth and I breathed a grateful sigh of relief. I brought the aircraft to a stop and the engine quit; it was a flameout from fuel starvation. My fuel counter indicated I still had another 5 gallons of fuel. Well, maybe not!

Opening the canopy, I anticipated exiting the aircraft and receiving praise for my absolute skill and cunning. I brought the bird back on the ground without damage, right? But, right then the Squadron Commander jumped above the cockpit railing with a pissed-off look on his face. In a pissed-off voice and similar demeanor, he asked me, "Why did you shut it down?" Through the yelling, he told me emphatically, "We will have to close the runway while we get a tow vehicle out here to tow the airplane back to the ramp." I replied, "Sir, I did not shut it down. The plane flamed out all by itself."

Without comment the Commander's head withdrew and the roar diminished. Was I ever glad that a maintenance inspection found the fuel shutoff valve in the OFF position. I had taken off with only 95 of the 1335 gallons of fuel normally onboard. As I rode my bike home that night, I felt proud of myself for getting the bird back on the ground undamaged. One of the pilots in the squadron burst that bubble the next morning when he informed me, "That's your job!" From then on the maintenance inspection plate was left open and checking the fuel shutoff switch in the "ON" position became a pre-flight checklist item.

Erratic Airspeed Indicator

I had just taken off from Laughlin AFB at about 2230 hours on a night celestial navigation training flight. As I was climbing out, I set up the aircraft so that it was in trim and holding 160 knots indicated airspeed. The string outside the canopy was centered with the airflow indicator line and was aligned with the longitudinal axis of the aircraft. It was just an old simple string on this sophisticated aircraft. The wings were level and the aircraft was holding its airspeed and heading, flying hands off with only a gentle correction now and then.

As I passed 45,000 feet indicated altitude, I engaged the autopilot, checked that my VOR indicator was tuned to the Cotulla VOR and the pointer was dead on the nose of the aircraft. By then I passed about 50,000 feet and started to set up my sextant for taking my first heading star shot. The indicators pitched down. I usually flew with one hand on the aircraft control yoke. I over controlled the autopilot, then disconnected it and did a rapid crosscheck of the instruments. Everything was normal, aircraft attitude OK, vertical velocity OK, but the airspeed indicator was rapidly vacillating between no airspeed and exceeding limits. The altitude and vertical velocity indicators work off the same pitot static system and were indicating normal. Within a few seconds, I decided that I did not want to climb higher. I cut the power back and started a descent, turning back toward Laughlin.

Precise trimming the aircraft was to me critical to a successful flight. It aligned the aircraft so that it flew straight through the air and not sideways. Trimming in the U-2 was even more important because all those aircraft were handmade. None flew straight unless trimmed for straight flight. Trimming enabled the autopilot to better maintain a heading and a Mach number. It also made the indicators from the sextant celestial readings more accurate. Trimming also affected the gravity flow of the fuel stored in the U-2's wings. An out of trim aircraft resulted in uneven flow of fuel because the high wing's fuel drained to the sump pump near the engine faster than to the low wing. A truly simple solution was devised to align the longitudinal axis of the aircraft with the direction of flight. A white line was precisely lined up with the longitudinal axis of the aircraft and then finely etched into the top of the cockpit canopy from fore to aft. Yes, an ordinary string was attached so that when in flight the airflow across the canopy would cause the string to align with that airflow. If the string was not aligned with the line etched in the canopy then the rudder trim tab was used to align the aircraft with the airflow and the string would indicate alignment with the canopy line. A simple string was used to give pilots clear assurance that the aircraft was flying straight through the air and not sideways.

When I contacted the Squadron, the first advice I received after reporting my situation was, "Try not to stall it or exceed 220 knots Indicated Airspeed." Although it wasn't a laughing matter to me, I said to myself, "Shit, I already know that!"

The next problem was how to land without stalling or exceeding aircraft limitations. As I passed 45,000 feet altitude in descent, I engaged the gust control to give me an extra margin of safe airspeeds I could fly. It was a clear night with light winds so turbulence was minimum. As I approached Laughlin AFB, Squadron Commander Buzz Curry came on the radio and asked me to describe my situation. I explained my circumstances and we discussed burning off some fuel at 10,000 feet so I would have time to eject if the aircraft became uncontrollable. We decided that was my best option and they would get the U-3A launched. By the time Curly Evans was airborne in the U-3A, I had reduced my fuel load by half and we decided to attempt to land my U-2.

As I made my approach to landing, Curly was to fly formation with me and call out my airspeed. I was afraid of that approach because of the delay in reaction time, and I was uncertain that his airspeed would be precisely the same as mine. I requested to fly formation on his U-3A right down to landing. Curly was to fly five knots above our computed landing speed based upon my fuel load at that time. I also wanted Curly to rendezvous with me, not me with him. That way I would always know my airspeed in descent. I could get out of gust control and set up for landing. It all worked like a charm and we got my bird back safely on the ground. On postflight inspection our maintenance guys found a small flake of rust in the pitot tube.

The next day "Goog" Boyd, from Maintenance, made a formal presentation to me of the offending rust flake. It was only slightly larger than the head of a pin. It was hard to believe something so small could cause such an enormous problem, but it sure did.

Crosswind Landing

Crosswind landings in the U-2 were a real challenge whenever the component was above 15 knots. After reading about crosswind landings in *Plane and Pilot*, I recalled a crosswind landing I made in a U-2 at Plattsburg AFB, NY in 1959. I was returning to base from an air sampling flight near the North Pole only to find a crosswind of 15-20 knots, gusting to 35. The U-2's maximum crosswind tolerance was 25 knots because of the tandem landing gear. The main gear, located just below the cockpit, and the rudder-linked steerable tail wheel, were in line and on the aircraft's centerline.

My ground controller had computed the crosswind right at 25 knots and reviewed the landing procedure with me, the danger being weather vaning upwind. This was due to the high, large vertical stabilizer, rear center of gravity and lack of tail wheel traction (only six inch hard rubber wheels).

The technique was to land with full flaps on the downwind side of the runway in a combination crab and slip to kill the drift. Once I touched down, I was to immediately put the downwind wing tip skid on the runway and hold it with full down wind aileron deflection and full downwind rudder. Luckily, Plattsburg had a significantly crowned runway center which helped counter the weather vaning. I was able to stop my aircraft on the runway though it had slightly weather vaned. My U-2 and I had crossed the centerline and were headed for the "boonies."

I have landed many places in the world, but I still remember every single second of that landing. A crosswind landing in a U-2 can be a memorable event when it is successful.

Jack D. Nole

(Deceased June 8, 1996)
Widow: Celeste

The following was submitted by Robert Ingram.

> Colonel Jack Nole, commander of the 4028th Strategic Recon Squadron, had the distinction of landing the first U-2 aircraft at Laughlin AFB. He also earned the

distinction of the first military pilot to safely bail out of a U-2. He recorded the highest altitude parachute escape in history on that ejection.

On September 26, 1957 Colonel Nole had been airborne approximately 35 minutes. He was on what was to have been a routine test flight following maintenance performed on the flight controls and the engine. He was nearing 53,000 feet altitude. Colonel Nole was in contact with Laughlin tower as he began his checkout of the various systems. Without warning the aircraft nosed over and began plunging toward the earth. The flap position indicator showed the flaps to be fully extended but he had not selected that position. Corrective action had no effect on the falling aircraft. The tail section separated from the fuselage. He reported the condition to Laughlin tower and their response was "Bail out, bail out!" He thought, "I wonder what they think I am trying to do."

Ejecting from the U-2 was no simple process. Each hose, tube and connector had to be individually disconnected, including the shoulder harness and radio connection. Nole had shut down the engine when he first observed the trouble. His pressure suit had inflated and further restricted movement in the cockpit. He struggled to release himself from the various connections then released the canopy and exited the aircraft.

He faced another problem after he had ejected from the aircraft. At this altitude, he had two choices. One, he could pull the cord to open his parachute and allow himself to get oxygen from his emergency tank. Two, he could free fall and risk suffocation. There was a possibility of freezing to death if he opened the parachute at such high altitude. He remembered his training—any action was better than no action, so he pulled the ripcord.

As he descended, he was swinging alternately face up then face down. For the first time in his 17 years, in the cockpit, he became violently airsick. When he landed, he came down on his seat pack on his bottom. Investigators said it would have broken his back without the pack.

As a result of Colonel Nole's incident, many changes were made in the U-2, the most significant being the ejection seat. The first U-2 was designed without ejection seats, but "the decision makers" soon decided to install one in each aircraft. Quick disconnects were also incorporated for all systems and harnesses.

Colonel Nole's successful ejection contributed to the future survival of countless other pilots.

Chris Pocock
Uxbridge, United Kingdom

The following is an article that first appeared in the *United States Air Force Yearbook*, 1997. Chris has authorized use of this article.

Riding the Dragon Lady

We had been airborne for almost 50 minutes before I really appreciated just how high we were! As we cruised steadily across California's San Joaquin Valley, I glanced down and to the right. Way below, an airliner leaving a thick contrail was intersecting our flight track. As it passed underneath us, that jet seemed no bigger to the naked eye, than if I had been looking up at it from ground level.

Chris Pocock shown after his own U-2 flight to high altitude.
Courtesy of Chris Pocock and Schiffer Publishing Ltd.

In fact, this was no illusion. The airliner was at 35,000 feet; whereas, we were above 70,000 feet!

We were 50 minutes out of Beale AFB, and I was riding backseat in the U-2ST trainer 80-1064, call sign "Pinon 72". From the front cockpit, my Instructor Pilot (IP), Major Brandon King, explained that the Pinon grows at higher elevations than any other tree. The U-2 Dragon Lady is similarly found at higher altitudes than any other flying machine, except the occasional SR-71 Blackbird from the same stable, Lockheed Martin's famous Skunk Works.

The enlarged and improved U-2R model which first flew in 1967, proved to be an unrivalled platform for a new generation of reconnaissance sensors. It offered a stable environment for sensitive, long-range side looking cameras, radars and signals-gathering devices. They could listen and look further from the U-2's lofty perch than if they were carried on more conventional craft. Most importantly, the U-2 could hang around—operational flights usually last for more than nine hours. Blackbirds, satellites and unmanned aerial vehicles come and go, but no one has yet devised a more cost-effective method of airborne intelligence gathering.

Such are the rewards of long-endurance, high-altitude flight. But there are also penalties, and I was wearing one of them, the S1031 pressure suit and helmet. It's bulky and inconvenient, forty pounds of cumbersome restriction to the everyday movements that one takes for granted (including bodily functions). It's also a virtually complete barrier to sensible communication with the outside world, save through the intercom system. But if you want to survive a cockpit depressurization at high altitude, you don't leave the ground without it.

U-2 pilots learn to live with it, and I seemed to be coping quite well too, thanks to the previous day's very thorough induction into the strange world of pressurized protection at Beale's Physiological Support Division (PSD).

Following a stringent medical, I had first been introduced to the S1 ejection seat. This is a zero-zero device for low-altitude escape, but if a high-altitude ejection is ever required, it is designed to descend from the heavens with its occupant still attached, who thus benefits from a continuing supply of oxygen for breathing and suit pressure from two emergency cylinders. At 15,000 feet, aneroids automatically command release of the body-restraining straps, and one floats free as the parachute deploys.

Then I was invited to change into long white underwear, and don the suit itself. This procedure requires the active cooperation of two PSD technicians who do most of the tugging, stretching, attaching and zipping. From the inside out, the suit consists of a nylon inner layer, a polyurethane-coated pressure layer, a restraint layer of adjustable mesh-patterned nylon, an immersion layer and an exterior cover of yellow-colored nomex.

Supervised by Dick Cook, a veteran PSD supervisor, my assistants pulled on my boots and clip-fitted the gloves to the suits' rigid metal attachment rings. Then I squeezed my head with some difficulty into the goldfish-bowl helmet. This too was attached to the suit, and now I was ready to go "on the hose". I flopped into a semi-reclined leather chair next to the oxygen console.

Nothing really prepares you for the sense of detachment which ensues once the faceplate has been latched down and the oxygen starts flowing. People carried on conversations a few feet in front of me, but I couldn't hear them. They sometimes moved out of my limited field of vision. I found that I could only follow them by raising my arms to the helmet and physically pushing or pulling the helmet sideways. The sound of my breathing was amplified through the built-in headset and soon became monotonous.

According to Major King, some prospective U-2 pilots never get past this initial suit up. A member of the 1st Reconnaissance Squadron (Training), King manages the recruitment of the 20 or so pilots who join the Wing each year. "One in ten of them feel uncomfortable and get claustrophobic. They become disconcerted hearing their own breathing. We call it the Darth Vader Syndrome," he told me.

My indoctrination at PSD continued with a visit to the altitude chamber. I was positioned in the chamber and the "climb" began. At 20,000 feet, Cook invited me to remove the faceplate for a demonstration of the insidious effects of hypoxia. Then the ascent continued to 70,000 feet, then down to 55,000 feet, whereupon Cook simulated an explosive decompression. The chamber fogged over, though I could still see the glass of water which had been placed on a nearby ledge and which was now boiling vigorously. My body fluids would have met the same fate had I not been protected by the pressure suit which had now inflated to hold my arms and legs in a vice-like grip. I wondered how a U-2 pilot could physically manage flying the jet if this should ever happen for real.

Still, Major King gave every reassurance when we met later to discuss the next day's flight. After discussing my few essential tasks (pulling the pins, sealing the canopy, etc.), he proffered some culinary advice. On long flights, U-2 pilots take sustenance by squeezing pureed food up a tube inserted into the helmet through a pressure port. King recommended "Peach and Pear" and suggested that I also take at least two bottles of liquid along to help prevent dehydration.

The day of the flight dawned, cloudier than I had hoped. At the office, King introduced me to Captain Steve Reed, another 1st RS pilot who would be our "Mobile" today. He would preflight the black jet while its two prospective pilots were suiting up and pre-breathing. He would also assist the heavily encumbered King and myself into the aircraft and generally supervise the ongoing flight.

Off we went to suit up. A one-hour period of pre-breathing is necessary to reduce the proportion of nitrogen in the blood and prevents decompression sickness. King demonstrated a useful procedure for passing the time: He fully reclined his chair and fell asleep! When the appointed time came, our oxygen supply was switched to portable containers, and we waddled out of PSD onto the van which took us to the flight line.

After negotiating the steps up to the cockpit with some difficulty, I gingerly lowered myself inside, one leg either side of the huge, old-fashioned control column. A long process of connecting man with machine ensued—oxygen hoses, communications cord, seat harnesses, boot stirrups and so on. According to standard procedure, I was a helpless spectator throughout the process which was carried out by two PSD technicians and Captain Reed.

In the four dual-control U-2 trainers, the rear cockpit occupies the space known as the Q-Bay on operational aircraft where cameras or other sensors may be carried. The instruments are conventional with a large attitude indicator at center front. Unfortunately, I was denied the use of a unique U-2 feature, the drift sight which affords pilots a splendid view of the territory beneath them. Shielded by a rubber cone protruding from above the attitude indicator, the viewing optics for this are at head level, but in the two-seaters, only the front cockpit is so equipped.

With some difficulty thanks to the heavy helmet, I glanced down and sideways. Throttle and trim wheel to the left, with radio and oxygen controls aft, next to a recess where Reed had placed my food tubes and drink bottles. Navigation and some environmental controls were to the right. Somewhere behind me were a whole raft of circuit breakers, which could surely only be manipulated by feel.

On the intercom, I heard Major King call for engine start. The brand new General Electric F118-GE-101 turbofan wound into action. We set off for a holding point on the taxiway which intersects Beale's 12,000-foot runway at the halfway point. No need to take the full length in this bird! The departure performance is so impressive that each mission is said to "launch" rather than "take off". And for today's two-hour flight, we would be launching with only a half fuel load.

We taxied onto the runway and paused to allow the ground crew to extract the locking pins from the outrigger wheels known as "pogos". Then King selected 80% power, released the brakes and we surged forward. In no time at all we were rotating into a steep climb that took us to 6,000 feet before we reached the end of the runway!

King had prepared me for this, but it was still breathtaking to watch the altimeter wind up at such a rate. We passed 20,000 feet after only three minutes, and King soon engaged the autopilot in pitch mode. The 30-degree climb attitude seemed more like 60 degrees to me as we turned north to our first waypoint above the Sierras.

As we neared 50,000 feet, King decreased the pitch so that we could establish a speed schedule of Mach 0.72, then re-engaged the autopilot. We were about to enter the cruise-climb, and henceforth the aircraft would rise steadily but more slowly as fuel was burnt off. King bid goodbye to Sacramento control and checked in with Oakland Center on a special frequency which had only another U-2 flying from Beale to keep us company. After 18 minutes of flight, we passed through 60,000 feet.

We turned south over Reno, Nevada, and I caught a glimpse of Lake Tahoe below as the overcast thinned. Right now, though, it was more interesting to look above and to the side. The sky had turned darker as we climbed, and directly overhead it was now almost black, with stars visible. The blue had retreated towards the horizon where it resided as a thin line separating earth from sky. This horizon seemed a long way distant and I could now discern the curvature of the earth quite clearly.

It was all rather peaceful and beautiful, but my reverie was interrupted as Major King invited me to take the controls. I accepted a trifle reluctantly, having heard plenty and written some about the dreaded "coffin corner" or "throat". This is a condition known to all high fliers as they approach the top left hand corner of the envelope. Put simply, the slowest that the aircraft can go comes close to the fastest that it can go, as the margin between stall speed and Mach buffet steadily erodes.

In the original, smaller U-2 versions, that margin could be a mere five knots under certain conditions. Right now our margin was a generous 30 knots, but King warned that we were only a few knots from overspeed, and he told me to maintain 100 knots indicated airspeed, Mach 0.71. I tried a few gentle turns, and the big winged bird responded well. It seemed at home up here.

Now King fell silent on the intercom, and my sense of isolation grew. I could not actually see him in the cockpit forward and below mine because the interior was obscured by its large black sliding sunshade. Some minutes later, I learned that his microphone was malfunctioning intermittently. In the meantime, though, I began to experience something of the "out of this world" feeling which has been described by so many U-2 pilots.

In order to re-establish some relationship with Mother Earth, I peered downwards over the canopy rail. The altostratus had cleared and we were approaching our next turn point at Monterey on the California coast. I had a superb view all the way up the San Francisco Bay. King re-established contact, and after we rolled out of the turn he checked our fuel balance. Soon it would be time to start the descent.

The U-2 is the only flying machine where you routinely extend the landing gear at 70,000 feet, plus the speed brakes. The throttle is brought back to idle, the flaps are set to the gust position, and with luck, the aircraft may now be persuaded to quit the heavens and start a slow descent. King set a direct course back to Beale, but although the base was more than 100 miles distant, we weren't coming down quickly enough. A lazy 360-degree turn helped us lose 15,000 more feet.

As we passed through 30,000 feet, I took control again. In contrast to its earlier performance at altitude, the aircraft now handled like a truck in the thick lower air. I handed it back to King, and since we were now safely below 20,000 feet, unlatched my faceplate and turned the oxygen supply off. For the first time in this entire exercise, I could smell real airplane!

At 5,000 feet, King retracted the speed brakes, faired the gust control, and trimmed the bird for landing. This can be the most challenging phase of flight, especially for novice pilots. The correct procedure is to cross the runway threshold at 10 feet and the correct speed for the aircraft's configuration. With 600 gallons remaining, our T-speed today should (would, dammit!) be 76 knots.

Our Mobile came up on the radio, ready to talk us through the landing and chase us down the runway in one of those ostentatious five-liter Ford Mustangs. We arrived overhead the field and turned downwind at 105 knots. Flaps and speed brake were extended once again.

The "powers that be" had rejected King's request to perform a touch and go, so we performed one low approach before repositioning for a full stop landing. King told me that on hot afternoons in summer, strong thermals rising from the cornfields surrounding Beale can wreak havoc with even the most carefully flown approach. No such drama today, though. With the appropriate adjustments for yaw, pitch and power, we reached the threshold in good shape.

King flared for landing. "Five feet, four, two," called Reed from the Mobile. As we touched down, King retracted flaps and speed brakes, but continued making yaw and pitch inputs until the aircraft slowed to near walking pace. Ground crew re-inserted the pogos, and we headed back to the ramp.

A small reception committee awaited. Later, I was required to seal my initiation into the world of the "high flyers" by drinking a yard of ale in the so-called "Heritage Room". A less distinguished flying outfit would merely describe this place as their bar. But no other wing has a drinking establishment which can boast wall plaques listing every pilot who has ever qualified on type. Even after all these years, the U-2 drivers are still a select band.

Chris Pocock is the author of *Dragon Lady, The History of the U-2 Spyplane; The U-2 Spyplane, Toward the Unknown;* and *50 Years of the U-2.*

Francis G. (Frank) Powers

(Deceased August 1, 1977)

The following was contributed by Frank's son, Francis G. (Gary) Powers, Jr., Director of the Cold War Museum, Washington DC.

Frank Powers joined the USAF in 1950 and flew the F-84 with the 468th Strategic Fighter Squadron at Turner AFB, Georgia. He was recruited by the CIA and was a pioneer in the field of U-2 aviation. He resigned his officer commission in the USAF in 1956 in order to fly with the CIA.

Francis G. (Frank) Powers. Photo courtesy of Lockheed Martin Co.

Most of the U-2 pilots flew their secret missions with little notice from the Air Force and the country. However, Frank Powers' entry into the history books came on May 1, 1960. His plane was the target of a surface-to-air missile over the Soviet Union. He survived the crash in the Soviet Union and was convicted of espionage. He was sentenced to three years' imprisonment and seven years of hard labor. However, 21 months after his capture, he was exchanged in Potsdam, Germany for US-held Soviet KGB Agent Rudolf Abel.

Following his extensive debriefing by the CIA, Lockheed and the USAF, Powers appeared before the Senate Armed Services Select Committee. During the analysis following Powers' testimony, the NSA acknowledged he had followed orders, did not divulge any critical information and conducted himself "as a fine young man under dangerous circumstances."

Subsequently, Frank left government service and was employed by KNBC television station in Los Angeles. On August 1, 1977, while working as a helicopter reporter, he died in a crash caused by a malfunctioning fuel gauge that was repaired without his knowledge.

Daniel W. (Danny) Schmarr

(Deceased December 9, 2005)

The following was submitted by Danny's widow, Kay.

Danny was in the cockpit approximately 22 years, including pilot training, and he absolutely loved every minute of it. His favorite years flying were in the F-4 although he had been in the U-2 for four years with the Air Force and five years with the CIA. He was the epitome of the fighter pilot, and the F-4 filled those needs in him. He served as Squadron Commander during the Vietnam War at Ubon, Thailand, with the Night Owls. It was the only squadron to do the "dirty work" at night and it was his proudest time.

Danny was the USAF Operations Officer aboard the USS *America* aircraft carrier when the U-2R qualified on the vessel. They were out of Edwards North Base. He reported the landings on the carrier by the U-2 as a hair-raising experience. However, it was more interesting to watch the sailors when the U-2R took off rolling mere feet before being airborne.

I was so fortunate to have such wonderful life-long friends at each location we were stationed. When the men were TDY, we wives checked on each other frequently, shared rides to the commissary and held our families together. Everything about the U-2 program was so "hush hush" and I knew that Danny couldn't talk about it at home. Like most of our friends, Danny and I had no close relatives nearby; our Air Force friends became our family.

After Danny retired, we had a little Cessna for our own personal travel. He also worked with KHQ Radio/TV in Spokane, Washington. He did traffic reports

Daniel M. Schmarr in the cockpit preparing for a flight.

and became quite the local celebrity. He always said, "When I become rich and famous…" and he laughed because he had become a local celebrity. He never quite achieved the "rich" part except in the many blessings from above.

Robert M. Wood
Gig Harbor, Washington

My first landing in the U-2 at Laughlin AFB was successful and I felt good about it. The only comment by the Mobile Control pilot was "After touchdown, hold your yoke back to keep your tail wheel down."

With those comments in mind, I took off and prepared to make my second landing. Approach and landing were normal with tail wheel down as the Mobile pilot had instructed. After touchdown, I brought the yoke back. The next thing I knew, I was airborne again at a very steep angle! The power was in idle and my left wing started to drop. I hit the power to maximum to recover from a most difficult position and to save the aircraft, to say nothing for saving my own butt.

My thoughts at the time were that I had just "bought the farm" and this was it. I was holding back the yoke trying to pick up the left wing to keep it from hitting the ground and the aircraft turned approximately 45 degrees to the runway. So in this nose high, left wing down position, I said to myself, "Where in the F--- is all this power that I have been hearing about?" Just in the nick of time, before impact, the power did kick in and

Robert M. Wood relaxing at his home in Gig Harbor WA, 2006.

the aircraft started to fly. Then it became a matter of a vertical wing over recovery 200 to 300 feet altitude with a 20 percent power reduction.

The final landing for the day was normal. Debriefing comments by General Russell were, "About average first landings, Captain Wood. You have a nice weekend."

U-2 #66954 ready for takeoff. Photo courtesy of Lockheed Martin Co.

U-2 #66721 ready for touchdown with only a few feet off the runway. Photo courtesy of Lockheed Martin Co.

U-2 #66722 in flight. Photo courtesy of Lockheed Martin Co.

It Took a Dedicated Team ...

"What the human eye observes casually and incuriously, the eye of the camera notes with relentless fidelity."

Bernice Abbott

What is NEPHO?

When the Lockheed U-2 was conceived, it became obvious this aircraft would be the most technologically advanced reconnaissance system ever devised. It was not until the advent of the CIA A-12 and the USAF SR-71 that this high tech equipment was updated beyond that of the U-2. The A-12 and the SR-71 no longer fly, but later generations of the U-2 are in the air today. Currently, the U-2S is the primary manned airborne reconnaissance system the US has in its intelligence-gathering inventory.

Jim Baker, an optical engineer from MIT and Edwin Land, developer of the Polaroid camera, were tasked to design the camera system for the unique aircraft. The specifications seemed impossible to meet: capable of photographing ground areas from altitudes in excess of 70,000 feet, weigh less than 500 pounds and compact enough to fit inside the equipment bay. Baker and Land worked with the Hycon Company of Monrovia, California to develop the camera known as the Hycon 73B, or simply the "B" configuration.

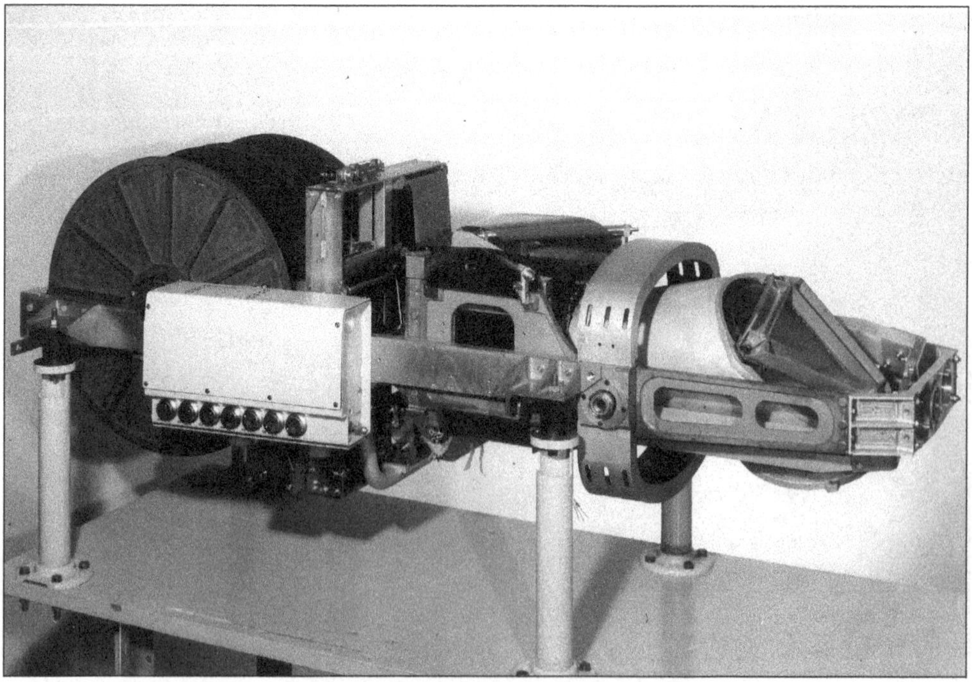

Itek optical bar camera used in the U-2.

Baker and Land knew that the most important part of this camera would be the lens and they turned to Perkin-Elmer of Norwich, Connecticut, for the optical lenses. With the precision optical lenses from Perkin-Elmer, the team set about to design a camera that met all of Lockheed's requirements and specifications. Together, Baker and Land engineered a photographic system for the U-2 that made it a success in every corner of the globe the U-2 was directed to fly.

The Hycon 73B camera or B configuration held two sizes of film: two 4,000 foot rolls or two 6,000 foot rolls. The length of the mission was the determining factor for the film selected. One spool fed from the front of the camera to the take-up spool at the rear of the camera; the second spool operated in reverse. This process was critical for the balance requirements of the aircraft. A unique feature of the camera was the film it used. The image on the film would produce a picture 18 inches square.

The purpose of the T-70 Tracker camera was to help the Photo Interpreter quickly find the most important imagery (target). The Tracker also eliminated the need for the interpreter to go through 6,000 feet of B configuration film. The T-70 Tracker camera used a Perkin Elmer prism that scanned from horizon to horizon in order to get a panoramic view of the area below. The Perkin Elmer "split prism" resulted in extremely high-resolution photography.

The secret nature of the photography spawned a language spoken by all who were involved in the operation and maintenance of the cameras. NEPHO became the term used to describe the camera and film equipment used in the U-2. TOP SECRET security clearances were required for all personnel who were assigned to the NEPHO operation.

Glenn R. Chapman

Tucson, Arizona
Wife: Sylvia

Glenn and the Flight Line Badge

Back in the good old days in 1958 at the 4080th SRW when I was just A2C Glenn R. Chapman, I was a young Nephographics troop in Armament and Electronics (A&E) Squadron. I learned early on the definition for nephography was "study of the clouds." When I first joined the outfit, I had only a SECRET security clearance, but a TOP SECRET clearance was required to work on the U-2. Only a year and a few months earlier the U-2s came to Laughlin AFB at Del Rio, Texas. While waiting for my clearance to be approved, and like many other two-stripers, I was assigned to the A&E coffee bar. I was far removed from the activities that were going on all around us. I spent six weeks there until I finally got cleared for TOP SECRET work.

The Nephography Shop was where all the action with the RB-57D and U-2 cameras took place. My Squadron Security Officer gave me the official "Shut Up and Burn Before Reading" TOP SECRET briefing. He said in no uncertain terms that outside this shop not a word was to be said about what we did or how we did it. Security was so tight and important in Hangar 2 that even the other shops seemed to be in the dark about what NEPHO did. The same attitude went for us at "SFERICS" which was Electronic Countermeasures.

Everyone knew the primary part of our security was the little piece of plastic-laminated paper called a flight line badge. Not only did it allow us into certain parts of the flight line, it also authorized our entry into specific areas, such as NEPHO, SFERICS, Operations, etc; or, rather, DID NOT allow us into certain areas. The badge had a picture of the individual on the front along with a multitude of numbers indicating areas of authorization. Numbers were either visible or punched out prior to lamination. The numbers remaining on the badge were the designation for areas where the individual was authorized entry. The reverse of the badge contained ID information, signatures, and a round, funny looking red inked circle that seemed not to have been inked properly. These "un-inked" properties were intentional and none of us knew what they meant. However, the Air Police, or "Sky Cops" as they were called, knew what those spots on the badge meant.

There were quite a few Sky Cops out on the flight line, each providing security for designated aircraft. When we went out on the flight line, the badge was clipped to the collar or pocket on our fatigues. When we came off the flight line and entered a non-secure area, the badge came off and went into the shirt pocket securely buttoned up. It was each individual's responsibility to take good care of the badge, or else it was "doomsday" for them with the Security forces.

After a year of being cleared for TOP SECRET, I was pretty confident of the procedure. About the same time, the Squadron Security Officer was replaced by a Captain named, you guessed it, Chapman.

One day, Bob Archey, a co-worker in NEPHO, and I decided to go for a cup of coffee so we cut across from the NEPHO Shop in Hangar #2 to A&E Squadron. Normally, the line badge didn't need to be worn on this part of the ramp, but we all wore it. Halfway across the ramp, one of the Sky Cops walked up and grabbed the line badge

Glenn R. Chapman and his son Joseph Michael Chapman, a U-2 crew chief at Beale AFB, California with Oscar, the Crow Flight mascot.

off my collar. What he held in his hand was only the badge clasp, no badge. This was cause for three blasts on his whistle which summoned just about every Sky Cop on base. I was ordered to "assume the position" on the ground face down, hands over head. A short time later Captain Chapman showed up and I was ordered to stand and answer his questions. It was over almost as fast as it started, and I was turned over to Captain Chapman. We went together to Pass and ID for my new badge. Then another problem surfaced. When they asked for my ID data, I gave them my last name, first name and middle initial. They asked what was my middle name and I told them that I had no middle name, only an initial. The Pass and ID staff really came unglued with that answer. Captain Chapman told them that he knew me well and I was not lying about the middle initial. Then Captain Chapman, still chafing from his humiliation of one of his troop's negligence in proper care of his Flight Line badge, looked me straight in the eye and told me in no uncertain terms: "Chap, one of us gotta change our names and it ain't me!" No, I didn't have to change my name either.

Another memory I have of the Sky Cops was with a three-striper named Ross. I got to know Ross off duty as well as on duty. He was a very nice, gregarious person, but Lord help the individual who crossed him during his official duty.

One day at the base cafeteria, Ross came in and asked to see my badge. He had seen it earlier and something struck him wrong about it. I gave it to him and he asked when I got it. I told him the date and he told me what the problem was. I didn't have the red-inked circle on the back of the badge. It took me a while to convince Ross that there had been a mistake made when I got the pass. He wrote out a citation for me to have the problem taken care of. I went straight to Captain Chapman and he made a few phone calls. The reply he got was that there were a few badges that were made that same day that didn't get the proper stamp on the back. I went back to Pass and ID for the red-inked stamp.

One of our longest serving and most revered 4080th SRW Wing Commanders was Brigadier General John DesPortes. We enlisted guys, depending on whatever outfit we were with or whatever the circumstances, usually were extremely sorry or very glad to see a "Wing King" leave and get replaced by someone else. There was always hope when a commander left that the new Colonel Someone Else would be better than the last or the fear he could be even worse.

Sometime after DesPortes assumed command, somebody in the Wing came up with the name of "Big John" for him. We came to know him as a hard but fair commander who somehow came to know just about everybody in the 4080th by either first name or nickname. This kind of congeniality was the only time in my entire Air Force career that I experienced it. When he learned who the drift sight guy was, he called me "Chap" like everybody else in the unit did.

The drift sight was an upside down periscope placed in the U-2 aircraft so the pilot could view downwards to check a target on the ground. It was a lousy hunk of junk, but I was one of only two or three guys that liked working with the drift sight. I became very good at working on it. Every one of us was extremely competent on systems (Bobbie

Black on the 73B camera, Jerry Fogel on the Tracker, Bob Archey on the A-2 camera configurations). Maybe I just wanted to do my best for "Big John". I thought the world of him and still do. Like all the other guys, he was always "Big John" but I never even came close to saying "Big John" where he could hear me.

A few years ago, I wrote a book about my U-2 experiences titled *Me and U2: My Affair With Dragon Lady*. I had volunteered to conduct a course about the U-2 to a local senior citizen group. One of the attendees was a gracious lady who introduced herself to me as Peggy DesPortes. I had a pleasant conversation with her and I decided I should tell her about the "Big John" nickname. I let her know that it was just a nickname someone came up with because we liked him so well. She told me that DesPortes knew from the first day that we called him "Big John" behind his back because he came home for lunch or dinner and told her, grinning, "They are still doing it!" Peggy said he just loved it, because he knew he was doing things right and that we appreciated him.

A few years ago we lost Big John to Alzheimer's disease. It was a sad ending for one of the greatest guys I ever served. He was a great humanitarian and a good old southern boy. God love and protect you, Big John, from all of us in the 4080th SRW.

For the Chapman family, the tradition of working with the U-2 has continued with my son, Joe. He was sworn in to the Air Force on the same day as my own father and I. I worked on the U-2A through the U-2F and Joe has worked on the U-2R and the U-2S. Joe was with the 9th Recon Squadron at Beale AFB and the 5th Recon Squadron, the Air Force Black Kats at Osan AB, Korea. I was with Operation Crow Flight, the High Altitude Sampling Program. The same program was renamed Project Olympic Race when Joe worked with the U-2 at Beale.

Alexander R. (Alex the Old) Dulevitz
Spring, Texas
Wife: Ann

My early exposure to the U-2 was in 1959 when I was living in Incirlik, Turkey. My father, Alexander Dulevitz, was a civil engineer providing contract support to the USAF units assigned to the base. I was a dependent son who took advantage of my father's foreign employment to see a part of the world that I had not seen, and at age 19 there was a huge world out there. Having lived on US Air Force bases all my life, I was reasonably confident I could identify most, if not all, aircraft in the United States' inventory. I noticed an unusual looking aircraft and I was curious about its location--always on the "other side" of the base. I started asking a few questions about the aircraft and its mission. Upon reflection, I realize I was fortunate that not more was made of my inquiries, but I was told it was a "weather" aircraft. I watched it take off several times, and the sight of that aircraft zooming so quickly into the air was breathtaking and a most memorable experience.

During my stay in Turkey, I met some airmen on the base and bowled with them in their off-duty time. I learned that a unit associated with the aircraft was Detachment 1010. At the time there were three detachments: A in Germany, B in Turkey and C in the Far East. There were veiled references to Detachment 1010, although the official line was that it was all weather related. Knowing the people who worked there did not give me any confidence that they were in the weather business, but I did not suspect that they were "spooks," either. Later I learned that it was the support unit for the mystery aircraft and a temporary home of the photographic interpretation unit and the collected imagery. At this time the US was using the U-2 to over fly not only the Soviet Union but China as well. Actually, I didn't learn the full story until five years later when I was a young Air Force lieutenant assigned as an imagery interpreter to Headquarters United States Air Forces Europe (USAFE).

When I was commissioned in the Air Force, I passed the physical exam for flight school. For most Air Force officers, the ultimate goal was to be a pilot, but I don't like airplanes. I know it is unusual to be in the Air Force and not be in love with airplanes. So there you have the honest answer. I recall meeting the "motivation board" and they asked me what type of aircraft I wanted to fly. The correct answer was, of course, a fighter. I responded that I would like a bomber. When asked by the board why I wanted to be a bomber pilot, I answered, "Because they have more engines." That answer told the board all they needed to know and they sent me into something less glamorous. Someone decided I might be interested in Intelligence and there my career unfolded.

I was first introduced to the unique capabilities of the U-2 in 1963 as I assisted with the development of tactical targeting materials used by the tactical units in Europe. The materials were used to develop attack routes to targets in the former Soviet Union and Eastern Europe. In 1965 the imagery was still within the realm of sensitive controlled information, but we followed procedures for release of some imagery at the SECRET NOFORN (No Foreign Nationals) level. The Tactical Targeting Information (TTI) sheet used the printed imagery and specific data about the target. Given that much of the Soviet Union had not been photographed by the U-2, we also used German World War II imagery with a much lower resolution and no explanation for the changes that occurred over time. The TTIs were of limited value, but gave the pilots some sense that there was a real target at the end of their penetration route. Obviously, it was better when the TTI contained U-2 imagery.

Within the imagery interpretation process, there were generally considered to be three phases. The first was the "initial" in which the imagery was reviewed for coverage of intended targets. The product of the application was called the Initial Photographic Interpretation Report (IPIR). The secondary phase was the review done for any number of reasons, but actually involved the more complete use of the imagery for target/installation review and update. The product was called the Supplemental Photographic Interpretation Report (SUPIR). The third phase was generally considered to be the in-depth review done for specific installations. For example it could include detailed reporting on the launch complex at Tyura Tam or the flight test range at Akhtubinsk-Vladimirovka or the Surface-to-Air missile test facility at Sary Shagan where the Russians eventually developed their missile test range. The folks who did the third phase were indeed the experts such as the man who taught antenna configurations at NPIC.

I was stationed at USAFE from 1963 to 1967 at Lindsey Air Station, Building A-17 which housed the Headquarters Deputy Chief of Staff for Intelligence, my home away from home for three of those four years. Most of that time I spent as a briefing officer, or "talking dog," as the common title was known. I briefed the air attachés on a recurring basis, several ambassadors to the Soviet bloc countries and Senator John McCain's father,

Admiral John S. McCain, prior to his taking command of our Pacific Forces. Admiral McCain made a tour to get an appreciation of the European threat and I was available to brief him. I recall the event primarily because of the timing of his trip near the Christmas holidays.

My primary duties involved briefing the National Intelligence Estimates on Soviet forces, both offensive and defensive forces, in addition to developing other staff briefings of interest to the Headquarters staff. I also worked with the Headquarters Foreign Technology Detachment and provided imagery support on such topics as the new Soviet aircraft unveiled at the Domodovo Air Show in Moscow when the Soviets allowed us glimpses of the aircraft they were developing.

One event has remained in my memory on how interesting my briefings were to civilians. One day I was told I would be briefing the Ambassador to Turkey, and I pulled out my briefing slides and awaited his arrival. The briefing room had a huge mosaic from imagery covering East Germany, a rather impressive backdrop. The Ambassador, Parker T. Hart, was a career diplomat who served as our ambassador in various Middle Eastern countries, including Turkey, Saudi Arabia and Kuwait. He arrived in the mid-afternoon, and I proceeded with the briefing which was about one hour depending on the number of questions asked. Mr. Hart sat quietly through the briefings and at the end asked only one question: "Are you related to Duley Dulevitz?" I replied he was my father. Mr. Hart nodded, thanked me for the briefing and left. I reflected that out of all the information provided, he was most interested in my name tag.

In 1967 my tour in Europe ended and I was reassigned to Southeast Asia (SEA) and again ran across the U-2. The aircraft was then flying its primary routes and target areas developed to provide information and photography for the National Intelligence Community, a term that refers to certain three-letter agencies in Washington, such as CIA, NSA, etc. At one time, there was a National Intelligence Board comprised of all intelligence agencies and the Director of the CIA served as titular head of the group.

The tasking for the U-2 in SEA focused on possible Chinese road building in the northern area of Laos. It was estimated the roads were being constructed to provide the Chinese access to the eastern provinces of Thailand. By 1967 the increased sophistication of the North Vietnamese defense environment made U-2 overflights impossible. That chore was assigned to other "air breathers" including the A-12. The term air breathers referred to aircraft that flew within the atmosphere using that same air as a prerequisite for their combustion engines. They were a great deal cheaper to operate than the more expensive satellites.

Additionally, the weather over SEA was abysmal, often cloudy, so it was less expensive to use an aircraft rather than a satellite with limited film supply. Our primary intelligence focus remained the Soviet Union and China. Therefore, our aircraft continued to be a practical and affordable alternative.

When the A-12 passed from CIA control to SAC and became the SR-71, it was modified for a two-man crew. In addition to the U-2 and A-12, we had the remotely piloted vehicles (RPV), little Firebee drones that were launched from beneath the wing of a modified C-130 transport aircraft and flew over North Vietnam. Some of the most startling imagery from that war came from those little drones which, at times, were no higher than 50 feet above the ground.

When I arrived in SEA, the U-2 was tasked with covering portions of Laos and the transportation network known as the Ho Chi Minh Trail into Vietnam. The resolution of the imagery collected by the U-2 was so superior that even camouflaged trucks could be detected as they traversed routes into South Vietnam. Unfortunately, given the jungle environment and terrain, much of the film was of tree canopy.

I used a loupe (same as jewelers use to view gemstones) and on a light table viewed a large roll of film showing the tree cover. The method at the time was to rapidly look over the image for features that were not normal and then, if necessary, use high-powered stereoscopes to magnify the image for detailed study. This would suggest that the imagery was being well analyzed, but I observed interpreters working late at night actually fall asleep as the imagery slowly moved beneath their eyes.

Once again I found myself in the role of "talking dog." As the 7th Air Force intelligence briefer, I briefed the strike and reconnaissance results daily to a range of people, occasionally including civilian officials. I briefed the images that were of interest to the attendees such as successful strikes on convoys, air combat showing successful kills, and often what we called "happy" snaps that gave various general officers a feel for what we were seeing. The U-2 photos were useful because they provided very high quality images of trucks destroyed by US aircraft. At times we even had pictures of bicycles moving equipment down the Ho Chi Minh Trail. The most popular images were from the RPVs which at times flew so low that they captured the facial expressions of the startled North Vietnamese.

One day I was briefing several civilians at the request of the Deputy Chief of Staff for Intelligence. They had been introduced to me by another civilian as "controlled American sources." As it turned out, they were Germans who were going to penetrate into East Germany. I had been tasked to brief them on the installations and terrain of specific areas. During the course of the briefing, one of the men spoke to another in German. Colonel Opper, DCS/I, observed my reaction and told me to continue. Later he told me that we were supporting the Chief of Station in Bonn.

Initially, the U-2 film was sent to the Strategic Air Relocateable Processing Facility (SARPF), a group of specially configured trailers where specialists processed the raw images and several trailers for interpretation. When I arrived in Vietnam, the SARPF was located at Tan Son Nhut. The U-2 film was initially processed by a SAC detachment and then shipped to the US for further analysis at the National Photographic Interpretation Center in Washington, DC. The SARPF was returned to the US in 1967 for refurbishment. When the SARPF left the theater, the imagery then went to the 6470th Reconnaissance Technical Squadron for interpretation and that unit then morphed into the 12th Recon Technical Interpretation Squadron. Primary emphasis was on analysis of imagery from tactical reconnaissance platforms, gun camera film, SR-71 film and the RPVs.

When I was later assigned to SAC Headquarters, I researched the office responsible for the SARPF. I was surprised to learn the extent of the damage to the unit as a result of weather and corrosive chemicals used in the photo processing. The refurbishment costs exceeded the original development costs.

The lack of emphasis on the U-2 imagery within the theater resulted in a real cost. In February 1968, most of the interest was focused on the Battle of Khe Sanh and the recapture of Hue. It was then that North Vietnamese Army units using PT-76 tanks overran a Special Forces camp. I was the 7th Air Force command briefer and I recall the furor that ensued regarding the strike and reconnaissance results. We were taken completely by surprise. We were totally unaware that the North Vietnamese were introducing armor into the battle for the South.

To say General Momyer, Commander of 7th Air Force, was irritated was an understatement. He asked me time and again where the tanks had come from and why we had not known about them. Unfortunately, I was unable to give him an answer. I knew that there had been rumors of armor for several months, but we had been unable to confirm them from the imagery. I subsequently reviewed a great deal of film and was unable to find any evidence of the tanks prior to their introduction at Lang Vei. In 1971 I was assigned to the Air Staff on Project Corona Harvest, an evaluation of air power in SEA. I found a report completed by the NPIC that traced the route of the tanks as they moved down the Ho Chi Minh Trail to Lang Vei. The report, using U-2 imagery, was not distributed outside the Washington, DC intelligence community. I was surprised and then chagrined as I reflected upon the fact that we had the imagery but had failed to use it wisely. The result was the unnecessary loss of American lives.

During my assignment as briefing officer at SAC Headquarters, I was frequently in front of various staff officers, such as the DCS/Intelligence or DCS/Operations. I had a relatively close working relationship with General Philpott, 7th Air Force Intelligence chief, his successor, General Keegan, "Crazy George," and other generals at headquarters. I was a friend of Colonel John Craig, the Commander in Chief's (CINC's) Executive Officer, who picked me to write the narratives for several general officer awards. That assignment gave me special access to the CINC's office, but it also resulted in headaches when things were done discreetly. When I went to the Pentagon, I had relationships with the Director of DIA as one of his budget "pukes" and was honored on my last day of service in 1985 when the director, General Williamson, came to my office to express his appreciation and to wish me good luck.

Following the SEA tour, I was assigned in September 1968 to SAC Headquarters where I became the Collection Requirements Manager for imagery from SAC-operated platforms. It included the SR-71s, RPVs and the U-2s. The 544th Strategic Intelligence Wing operated a "contingency exploitation branch," a small group tasked with assisting in the development of imagery "boxes." Imagery boxes were mosaics made from the imagery acquired by the U-2 or other platforms to assess the success of the B-52s in keeping their ordnance within specified "boxes." This allowed the interpreters to count the number of bomb craters within the box to assess the effectiveness of Arc Light strikes. Arc Light was the project name given to the cells of B-52s operating from Andersen AFB, Guam. There were normally three B-52s within a particular cell. U-2 imagery was regularly used and interpreted to determine the traffic flow south on the Ho Chi Minh Trail and to detect changes in the routing. This same imagery was used to provide targeting for the B-52 strikes on the truck traffic.

The same contingency group worked the Olive Harvest imagery in 1973 collected by the U-2 over the strip between Egypt and Israel following the 1973 War of Atonement. The protocol was established by the US State Department with photos from the missions to prove to the Israelis and Egyptians that each side was abiding by the cease-fire agreements.

The bulk of my time was spent providing a daily listing of requirements objectives to the planners in the Strategic Reconnaissance Center. The listing included the target name, coordinates, priority rated from 1 to 5, requested frequency of coverage. When I started, there were only a few priority targets, but as the war intensified, we faced a listing of over 100 different targets. To discriminate, we used frequency of coverage as a metric. That, too, began to inflate and we had to use other metrics, such as quality of coverage, to provide a sense of real urgency. It was appropriate, I realized, that the target listing we provided was called the Daily Requirements Objectives List, or DROL. If it had been my choice, I would have found another word beginning with "L" to make the title complete.

There was one event, during the Christmas bombing of Hanoi and Haiphong during 1972 that stood out from all the others. It was the very first time the President had authorized the use of B-52s to bomb Hanoi and Haiphong. The CINCSAC, General Meyer, immediately tasked his recon platforms with assessing the damage his aircraft inflicted. At the same time, we were getting multiple requests from Washington, DC for specific coverage of various targets. The 7th Air Force Commander, General Lavelle, demanded we focus on his targets. Since CINCSAC owned the aircraft, they first satisfied his needs and then the Washington needs. General Lavelle sent a scathing message to CINCSAC demanding better treatment. I was asked to draft a response, not to General Lavelle, but to the Joint Chiefs. I developed a message that clearly demonstrated that our coverage had addressed our Command's needs very successfully as well as those of the Joint Chiefs and the civilian community. Colonel Jerry McIlmoyle signed the message for the CINC since he was the intelligence head of the Strategic Recon Center.

Perhaps what Jerry did not know was that my Directorate Chief, also a colonel, was furious with me for developing the message. I was astounded by his reaction because I had coordinated it with him, but apparently he assumed that either the CINC or the Deputy Chief of Staff/Intelligence, a general officer, would sign the message. He gave me an hour of his time and a significant piece of his opinion of me, and it was hardly favorable. Fortunately, DCS/I, General Brown had also seen the message as I coordinated it within the Headquarters Staff and the DCS/Operations; they were all pleased with it. I'm not sure what lesson I was to draw from this experience except that it is difficult to please all in a crisis environment.

I left the Intelligence career field for about six years and served in the 90th Strategic Missile Wing in the Minuteman program. There I ran across Jerry and Patty McIlmoyle again. During that time an injury I sustained in Vietnam changed my physical profile and I was released from Operations to return to the Intelligence field. I attended the Post Graduate Intelligence Course in Washington, DC where I was awarded a Masters in Strategic Intelligence. Subsequently, I was assigned within the Defense Intelligence Agency as a program analyst supporting the General Defense Intelligence Program staff.

I was tasked with assessing the U-2 portion of the Intelligence budget as a Budget Program Evaluator. The most amazing thing about the U-2 is its durability, from both acquisition and budget perspectives. I doubt that I have the same attachment to the aircraft as its pilots and crew chiefs. However, looking at the U-2 from an Intelligence view, it was one of the most expensive single items in our Intelligence inventory. Despite its mystique, the U-2 is increasingly vulnerable to intercept by the world's fighters, a factor that limits its use in a modern environment. For that reason and its increased operational costs, Deputy Secretary of Defense, Frank Carlucci, decided to cancel the

U-2 program. The Air Force argued strongly to retain the program, but the numbers reinforced the decision to cancel the program.

General Jerome O'Malley, former commander of the 9th Strategic Reconnaissance Wing, home unit of the SR-71 and the U-2, launched his own effort to save the U-2. He visited with friendly members of Congress, briefed them on the value of the program and lobbied for its continuation in the modern Air Force. O'Malley's action resulted in the reversal of the Program Decision Memorandum and his own subsequent reassignment to command the Pacific Air Forces.

It is interesting to note here that General O'Malley's opposition of the Deputy Secretary of Defense's decision was bold, yet it was supported by various members of Congress. With that said, his career was effectively ended with his reassignment. It was in the tradition of the best leaders willing to risk all to support what he considered to be a valuable program. General O'Malley would be the first to point out that the U-2 served to fly the missions over the "no-fly" zones defined at the end of the First Gulf War. Effectively, he was proven right and the detractors of the U-2 proven wrong.

Gary (Shorty) Erdman

Lake Hiawatha, New Jersey
Wife: Ann

After graduating from Patterson Central High School in Patterson, New Jersey in 1960, I considered military service as a career option. At 5"2", I had always been nicknamed "Shorty" but I had tall ideas. Two of my three brothers were in the Navy, but I didn't like the idea of being on ships or submarines. I preferred having the earth beneath my feet. So I approached the Air Force with my own career goal in mind; I told the Air Force recruiter I wanted to become a butcher. The recruiter told me, "You want to be a butcher, we'll make you a butcher." I realized in a minute the recruiter probably told everybody exactly what they wanted to hear.

Gary Erdmann 1961.

Prior to entering the US Air Force in July 1961, my only photographic experience was with my mother's old Kodak Brownie camera. There really wasn't a lot of skill involved. I was the photographer for family gatherings. I never dreamed photography would become a career for me.

Once in the Air Force, I realized I would be doing something much different from meat cutting. Actually, I figured out there were no butchers in the Air Force because all meat is pre-cut. I took the placement tests and I was surprised to learn I had a knack for photography.

After basic training, I was assigned to the 4080th SRW at Laughlin AFB, Texas. I trained in all the photographic equipment of that time from 35mm single lens reflex and 16mm movie cameras to studio cameras. When I had all the appropriate security clearances, I was assigned to the photo lab and developed some of the film taken over Cuba by pilots of the U-2. I remember thinking at the time as I saw the missile sites in the completed film, "It looks like we got 'em." The resolution of the film was so precise that we could identify considerable detail.

During this busy time, all of us photo technicians slept in the lab when we were able to catch a couple hours of sleep. Technicians were required to be available immediately for processing the film when it came in with the returning U-2. Most of us in the lab were oblivious to the severity of the crisis because we were confined to the lab without communication of radio, television or newspapers.

I remember CIA agents always watched over the shoulders of the lab technicians. During much of the Cuban Missile Crisis, developing the film took about eight hours. We made five copies of the film and I know one copy went directly to President Kennedy. I believe other copies were sent to various intelligence units for analysis.

4080th SRW Photo Lab, Laughlin AFB, Texas August 1962. First row left to right: C. Cook, F. Robinson, R. Dobbleman, E. Branning, Lt G. Baker, Capt R. Duggan, W. Williams, E. MacGil, L. Dillon, J. Lyons. Second row left to right: R. Barfield, B. Burge, B. Brewer, W. Duette, H. Warrick, J. Hendricks, L. Pincombe, L. Ames, H. Reed, H. Wayman, G. Gwilliams, S. Andrews, A. Robertson. Third row left to right: G. Stoddard, G. Erdmann, B. Payne, A. LeDuc, L. Oberlander, B. Davis, C. Davis, G. Garcia, T. Presnell, H. Eaves, C. Hunt, R. Hall. Fourth row left to right: B. Nuckolls, L. Dennison, L. Robertson, D. Techman, T. Lee, E. Hinojosa, L. Small, J. Montano, P. Lindke, G. DelaGarza, B. Casterline, D. Smith, R. Heintzleman.

4080th SRW Photo Lab, Laughlin AFB, Texas, August 1962. First row, left to right: G. Stoddard, B. Casterline, G. DelaGarza, C. Davis, G. Erdmann, E. Branning, L. Oberlander, B. Nickolls, T. Lee, D. Smith, C. Garcia, J. Montano, A. LeDuc, P. Sharp. Second row left to right: T. Presnell, C. Cook, D. Techman, B. David, L. Dennison, L. Small, Lt G. Baker, Capt R. Duggan, L. Dillon, E. Hinojosa, B. Payne, L. Robertson, C. Hunt, H. Warrick, H. Eaves, K. Bartly. Third row left to right: A. Robertson, J. Lyons, E. MacGil, H. Wayman, R. Dobbleman, W. Williams, L. Pincombe, L. Ames, B. Brewer, B. Burge, F. Robinson, D. Jacob, H. Reed, J. Hendricks, W. Duette, P. Lindke, R. Barfield, S. Andrews, D. Davis.

4080th SRW Photo Lab. Left to right: Gary Erdmann, Larry Oberland, Everett Owens, Tom Presnell, kneeling: M.K. Bevz.

4080th SRW Photo Lab. Front row, left to right: G. Hinojosa and wife, P. Brazee, C. Davis, C. Hunt, G. Erdmann, T. Lee, D. Smith, M. Riles, D. Techman, E. Owens. Back row, left to right: T. Presnell, H. Eaves, L. Ames, H. Reed, D. Sharp, L. Pincomb, G. DelaGarza.

Gary Erdmann 2010.

My next assignment was also photo related, but with greater risk than I experienced at Laughlin. In late 1964 I was assigned to Tan Son Nhut Air Base, South Vietnam. I flew aboard a C-123 and photographed the area for mapping the extensive tunnel network used by the North Vietnamese. I was so scared that bullets would penetrate the aircraft I sat on my parachute for extra protection.

I enjoyed my time with the Air Force. Specifically, I liked my service with the 4080th SRW. I met a lot of guys who became as close as brothers with me. Everett Owens was my first roommate at Laughlin. He currently lives in Connecticut and we stay in close touch. Larry Pincombe and George Gwilliams IV were also friends from my 4080th days and we remain in contact now.

Gerard (Jerry) Fogel

Sun City West, Arizona

The early days of the 4080th SRW were filled with power and mysticism, something awesome to behold. Sometimes the mere mention of the organization opened doors otherwise sealed shut.

While on temporary duty at Barksdale AFB, Louisiana in 1963, I was the Non-Commissioned Officer in Charge (NCOIC) of the NEPHO Section when Don Armstrong got sick with some kind of flu bug. We took him to the base hospital for admission and during sign-in, the admitting nurse asked for his medical records. I told her we did not have the records because we were there TDY. Remaining strict in compliance with her procedures, she insisted all incoming patients must have medical records. We were getting into a loud argument when a doctor came by and asked what the problem was. I explained we were trying to get Don admitted for treatment of his illness. His only question was, "What outfit are you with?" When I told the doctor we were with the 4080th he said, "Bring him right on in."

Another time at Hickham AFB, Hawaii in 1961, I went to the Hydraulic Shop to get fittings for nitrogen bottles since my gauges would not fit without an adapter. The nitrogen was used to purge the drift sight to remove any air with water vapor to prevent fogging. When I asked the airman in the Hydraulic Shop about a fitting, he wanted some kind of written authority. I requested to speak with his supervisor. The supervisor looked at me strangely and asked what outfit I was with. I told him I was with the 4080th and he said, "Take whatever you need." When I said I would return the fittings, he told me to keep them.

We literally took everything we needed to launch the U-2 at the remote site when we went TDY. We took yellow jeeps, a blue staff car used as a chase vehicle, fuel and plenty of spare parts. We understood the base personnel had been briefed not to ask us questions about the U-2 and most importantly, not to take pictures of the bird. So there we were going to the BX in our yellow Jeep dressed in fatigues with the 4080th A&E Squadron patch on the right side and the SAC patch on the left side, with an A&E baseball cap on our heads. It seemed everybody we saw looked at us furtively and whispered to each other. Of course, that made us strut a bit more. We were all young guys and so full of ourselves. After all, we were with the U-2 spy plane, the most secret plane in the AF at the time. It was a great time with lots of fond memories.

In March 1964 I was at Bien Hoa Air Base, Vietnam supporting the NEPHO Shop for the U-2 missions. We were instructed not to take any personal photos of the flight line at the base. A message came from SAC Headquarters back in Omaha, Nebraska.

The message was that SAC wanted some photos of Bien Hoa to see what kind of facilities we had – where we lived and worked.

Jim Combs, our Hycon Tech Rep, suggested we take a Perkin Elmer Tracker (70mm, 3 inch focal length camera) and photograph the base. We loaded a tracker in a pickup truck with two 12V batteries and covered it with canvas, leaving only the bubble exposed. Bob Ingram and I sat in the back of the truck and held the tracker on a box. B.C. Fowler and Jim Lobig drove the truck slowly up and down the flight line and all over the base. At one point during the ride, an Air Policeman stared at our glass bubble and rotating prism. He didn't approach the truck with any questions though.

We returned to the shop and shipped the film directly to SAC Headquarters. The next day, a couple of Air Police came around looking for the truck with the glass bubble. We told them we didn't know what they were talking about.

Three weeks later a message came in from SAC. The message said, "Thank you, thank you. The pictures were beautiful. We now know what kind of conditions you live and work under."

2005 4080th SRW Reunion. Left to right: Al Defilipis, Horace Tanner, Bob Zint, Bobbie Black, Jerry Fogel, James King, B.C. Fowler and Bob Ingram.

One day we were sitting around in the NEPHO Section office of the A & E Squadron at Laughlin drinking coffee and telling war stories. A call came in from the base hospital that one of our NEPHO men, Harry Magill and his wife, Dixie, had tested positive for hepatitis. We were advised that anyone who had contact with Harry should report to the base hospital. We looked around at each other. Bob Ingram exclaimed that we all had contact since Harry's greeting was a handshake. Tom McClung, the Perkin Elmer Tech Rep yelled out, "Yesterday Harry had a sip of coffee from my personal coffee mug!" So we all went to the base hospital. At the hospital, we were told to drop our pants and a very painful gamma globulin shot was administered to all. As you can imagine, I hold fond memories of that event. Thanks Harry.

At Davis Monthan in September 1964, I was NCOIC of the trackers. After major maintenance, it was customary to test the camera. We made sure the camera was operational before sending it out on a mission. We placed the camera on its side on a portable bench and took it outside the NEPHO Shop. The camera faced the parking lot and the runway. This procedure had been done many times before. On this particular day, we received word that Bob Primrose had crashed on approach to the runway. When we realized that the camera was pointing in that direction, Ron Kupan, the Perkin Elmer Tech Rep who replaced Tom McClung, shouted that maybe the camera had recorded the crash. We terminated the test and rushed the film to the Photo Lab. Sure enough, the crash was recorded and it showed the problem to be the gusting crosswind.

B. C. Fowler
Toccoa, Georgia
Wife: Blanche

My R&R in Germany

I was a young A2C two-striper assigned to the 4080th SRW as a NEPHO repairman in A&E. In January 1959 I went TDY to RAF Brize Norton, to support the RB-57D-2. The RAF base was located near Oxford University, quite a spectacular complex. Col William J. Gregory was the detachment commander. We had been working daily for about a month when Col Gregory gave us a stand down weekend, no flying planned. Everyone was free to go and do whatever they wanted. Most of the fellows went to London. I was one of the few who stayed at the base. Col Gregory and some other officers had plans to go to Wiesbaden, Germany, and he asked if we wanted to go. Several of us accepted his offer to see some new country. We dressed warmly in civilian clothes and flew into Wiesbaden Air Base. When we arrived at Wiesbaden, Col Gregory had arranged for a bus to take us to the American Arms Hotel. It was a lovely hotel located in the local community for US field grade officers and above. (Remember I said I was a young two striper?) The only instruction Col Gregory gave us was, "Don't wear your uniform downstairs in the hotel." It was the dead of winter in Germany, cold, foggy and miserable. We had a great time, rested a bit for the coming week, did a little sightseeing, and enjoyed chatting with the officers in the snack bar downstairs.

Don Cinnamon (left) with B.C. Fowler (third from left).

Don Cinnamon (left) receiving an award.

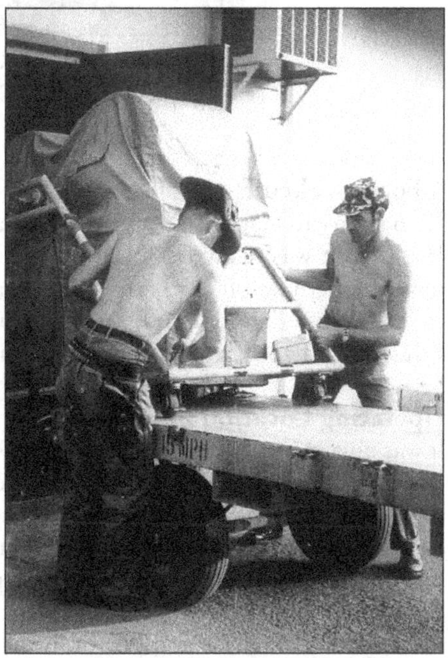

Silas Lewis (left) and B.C. Fowler loading a camera for a flight in Vietnam. Note the sidearms.

Lester Herling, Crew Chief (left) and Ed Stewart, SFERICS systems. A jokester had covered the unit shield with black panties.

A Foggy Takeoff

We had an early launch at a northern location, and the area was blanketed with dense fog. The aircraft was ready for takeoff at the end of the runway. The pilot called the control tower for permission to take off which was granted. Two or three minutes later, the tower called back to the pilot and stated he was given permission to take off. The pilot replied, "I did take off and right now I'm breaking 10,000 feet and climbing."

Operating Location 20 (OL-20)

It was quite a feat setting up OL-20 in 1964. We island-hopped in the Pacific for a couple of weeks or more awaiting permission to enter our destination country. A few missions were flown during the time. It was difficult, mainly because of the lack of facilities, such as adequate darkroom for the photography equipment. We arrived at our destination, but we found a primitive base. Our living quarters were tents that accommodated twelve men. The building we found suitable for a shop was quite a distance from the hangar where we installed the equipment in the aircraft. We learned to be inventive. We had to haul the heavy equipment on a trailer behind a pickup truck. Two airmen rode on each side of the equipment to keep it stable and to keep it covered. Our biggest problem was getting it on and off the trailer. Si Lewis and I struggled with that problem more than once.

Joe Franklin
Whitesburg, Tennessee
Wife: Lola

One of my favorite anecdotes about my U-2 association was at Turner AFB, Albany, Georgia. Colonel Beauchamp was the Base Commander and lived in town next door to my own rental house. One Sunday morning he came out onto his front porch and threw a phonograph record off into the distance. One of the other neighbors witnessed this; he then retrieved the record and gave it to me. Well, it was Elvis Presley's "Hound Dog." I kept the record and after about a month in Texas, I dropped it off at his office, telling the secretary that he had left this in Albany. I never followed up but I did get some secret pleasure from resurrecting what was probably the Colonel's overdose of "Hound Dog."

When Lola and I arrived at Barksdale AFB, Louisiana from Ramey AFB, Puerto Rico, the place was abuzz with the news that some airman had been working as a disk jockey at a late-night radio station. He considered himself quite the comedian and would fill in time with jokes and comments on local events. He made the mistake of commenting on the personal appearance of our Base Commander who was helping direct incoming traffic during a SAC alert exercise. The airman's name was George Carlin. He was discharged and for years went on to use that event as his prime comedic delivery.

In September 1955 I was promoted to Master Sergeant and was sent to the 2nd AF NCO Academy. It was a course aimed at improving leadership abilities, and it did just that. I graduated tenth in a class of 120 students and was runner-up for the Commandant's Award. The following day I received orders assigning me to the 4080th Strategic Reconnaissance Wing at Turner AFB.

I had been at Turner less than a week when Gary Powers returned from his induction into the CIA. Everywhere he went, he was surrounded by a covey of "suits." I met him and knew his mother-in-law, a cashier at the BX. On May 1, 1960, almost five years later, I was waiting for him to land.

The entire Wing was transferred to Laughlin AFB in Del Rio, Texas. The big secret about the 4080th was the U-2 aircraft. One Sunday morning I was herding my family, Lola, Donald and Lela, into the Base Chapel. The first U-2 wobbled onto our lonely runway. Minutes later, one by one, U-2s were all over the place. That day church services were delayed as everybody wanted to get a glimpse of the new aircraft.

Laughlin AFB did not have family quarters when we arrived there. Most married personnel lived in the Hunter subdivision on the east side of Del Rio. Captain Roger Cooper and his family shared the other half of my duplex. Our next door neighbor was Colonel Jack Nole, Wing Commander.

From my back yard, I could see to the north and east for what looked like a hundred miles of cacti and stones. My family and friends would watch the wild pigs, called

Lola and Joe Franklin.

javalinas, grazing and arguing. Quite frequently jack rabbits were also spotted in the scrub brush.

My parents drove all the way from Tennessee to spend a week with us. Dad was a busy contractor. We took them across the Rio Grande to Mexico for a dinner at Mrs. Crosby's Restaurant and then to see Judge Roy Bean's little hamlet at Langtry, Texas.

One Saturday afternoon, Tim and Sandy Nole came rushing over to our house asking for my son, Don. They blurted out, "Dad has just bailed out of a U-2 from over 60,000 feet!" I asked where their Dad was and they said he had just arrived home. I ran to his house to find him sitting in an easy chair, one bandaged leg propped on a hassock and a glass of bourbon in his left hand. He was noncommittal about the whole affair.

I was NCOIC of the Mission Evaluation Unit. In normal times it would be described as Photo Interpreter Unit, but the word "photo" was not spoken and the unit was officially a "weather" squadron. We worked among the birds in a small building down on the flight line. We were a group of five with Captain Bill Ming and Lieutenant Fred Tietbohl. Then came Captain Niemciewich, an ex-Marine we called "Nemo," who was always in hot water with the Base Commander over his beer-guzzling stunts at the Officers' Club. Ming was a Baptist preacher who refused to even join the Officers' Club. He took a dim view of Nemo's antics. All of the photo and electronic intelligence stuff was processed in our building. The few high-risk missions flown by our pilots were planned in Major Ogglesby's shop. On occasion I was called to help with issues related to our operation.

On Thanksgiving Eve, 1958, I departed for Yokota, Japan. Due to the political turmoil threatening an invasion of Taiwan, my family was unable to travel with me. However, they joined me later.

Before we left Del Rio, John Wayne had erected a movie set of old San Antonio for his movie, *The Alamo*. This was located north of Brackettville, a few miles east of Del Rio. How lucky we were that Wayne was on the same flight with my family and traveled with them all the way from San Antonio to Los Angeles. He gave my daughter, Lela, his autograph. John Wayne had a soft spot in his heart for servicemen and their families.

I was at the 6594th Recon Technical Squadron at Westover AFB, Massachusetts during the Cuban Missile Crisis. We worked with satellite coverage when we received U-2 B configuration film for processing. It had come from Homestead AFB and was escorted by a Brigadier General. Sometime during the film processing, the lab chief feared the film was "fogged" and he asked me to look at it. What I saw was the ocean floor off Cuba where the water was transparent and only the sand dunes at the bottom were visible. I had flown over that area in 1954 exactly where that blue hole appears on the ocean floor. When I explained this to the lab chief, he was really relieved. Just then a frame came into view from the processor that had a "Star of David" SA-2 site on the Cuban mainland. This shocked me because my brother was on standby awaiting call on the base with his EB-47 and crew. When he came over to my house for supper, I was really torn apart because I was not allowed to mention what I had seen. As it turned out, my fears were short-lived.

Was that the film from Major Anderson's U-2? Jim Combs, our Hycon Tech Rep, told me the film was retrieved from Anderson's crash site. Jim had taught me how to measure image resolution at Laughlin. Six months after I retired to Bossier City, Jim came to my house and asked me to give him some "slant-range" data because the mission profile for recon was being changed. He took me on base where I met Major Tietbohl who had been a First Lieutenant in our Photo Interpretation shack at Laughlin. The Image Motion Compensation cams on the camera bed had to be redesigned and they needed slant/range data before grinding them. I was back into the picture as a civilian working for AIL, EW specialists where I did the threat profile for the B-1 under Rockwell International in 1966.

I have worn many hats in my career, but somehow they all seem to be related over time.

Robert H. Ingram
Greensboro, North Carolina

The Beginning
For seventeen exciting, memorable years I supported the U-2 program assigned to NEPHO (aerial photographic and electronic sensor maintenance). From 1956-1960, I maintained the camera systems, hand control and drift sight. From 1960-1966, I was supervisor of the camera systems. I was honored to be selected to attend factory training at Perkin Elmer Corporation and Hycon Corporation, manufacturers of the optics and

Bien Hoa AB, standing in front of a hut that served as living quarters. Left to right: Charlie Couch, B.C. Fowler, Jim Lobig and Si Lewis.

Air Force attendees at Stanford University IRIS camera training sponsored by the ITEK Company. Left to right: Bob Ingram, Instructor unknown, Photo Specialists Jenkins, Goudy, Johnson, Rodriguez, Washburn, McDowell and Cook.

camera systems. From 1970-1971, I was assigned to the Special Projects Office (SPO) at Robbins AFB, Georgia.

During World War II, MSgt Bill Dyche flew as an aerial photographer in a B-26 over Germany from a base in England. He had to hold a long focal length aerial camera between his legs in the forward oblique position. There was not enough room for him, the camera and a parachute in the tight space so he left the parachute behind.

Bill was my non-commissioned officer in charge (NCOIC) at MacDill AFB, Tampa, Florida. We were assigned to the 306th Bomb Wing and maintained the B-47 Stratojet camera systems. With only thirteen men in our shop, we supported 45 B-47s between 1955 and 1956. Bill was an expert teacher for us young guys learning the ropes, and every Wednesday he taught a class for our shop personnel. He instructed us on optics, electronics, aerial photography, film processing and chemistry. What a mentor! I learned so much from him. In 1956 he was transferred to Turner AFB, Albany, Georgia where he would work with the RB-57s.

One Saturday morning in August 1956 Bill showed up at my front door with a smile on his face and a confidential announcement. He owned a home in Tampa and came there from Georgia to visit his family. We went into a back room and closed the door; I was definitely curious. He said, "I can get you in a new program. I can't tell you what it is, what you will be doing or where you will be stationed." He said the program was Top Secret, and he knew it would enhance my career. I had a lot of respect for Bill and confidence in his judgment. "Yes," I told him, "If you say it will be good for my career, I will put my faith in you." He cautioned me not to fight a transfer to a weather station in the desert. I was definitely intrigued; there was certainly an air of mystery in Bill's message. My wife, Barbara, recognized something was stirring, but she didn't say any more. She was a model Air Force wife.

An Unusual TDY

In October 1956, I received a call from an administrative officer at Sixth Air Division Headquarters, MacDill AFB. The lieutenant said he had a Top Secret message from Strategic Air Command (SAC) Headquarters, but because I only had a Secret clearance, he could not let me read it. The only thing he could tell me was that I would be sent on TDY immediately, followed by a permanent reassignment. I told the lieutenant I definitely wanted to accept this TDY. His final comment was, "You know all about this, don't you?"

Personnel had arranged my transportation to Norwalk, Connecticut. I was directed to wear civilian clothes and the Air Force would pay for them. That was not the least of the unusual requirements. My instructions were to call a Mr. Ore Heath for further information at a number I was given. Orders directed me to Norwalk, but there was a significant amount of information omitted on the orders.

At the Finance Office, a master sergeant stared down at me; he must have been well over six feet. He bellowed, "Who the hell do you think you are? We are not going to pay for this. I'll just take this to Finance Officer Major R. L. Griffith and let him decide." The reply from Major Griffith was that he would pay $16 per day per diem, but no civilian clothes.

Housing for South Vietnamese Air Force personnel.

Jim Combs, Hycon Tech Rep (foreground), with Jim Lobig NEPHO specialist (far right) at Bien Hoa AB, Vietnam 1964.

I had lived in Florida for two years and did not have adequate clothes for the considerably colder fall weather in New England. And I was specifically directed to wear civilian clothes, no military uniforms. Credit cards were not available in those days, and credit in a clothing store for a military person was impossible.

It was 5:00 p.m. on Friday and I had to be in Norwalk on Monday morning at 8:00 a.m. Desperate, I returned to the lieutenant at Sixth Air Division. The lieutenant called SAC Heaquarters; fortunately, Omaha, Nebraska was on Central time, one hour behind, while we were on Eastern time. While I waited in the lieutenant's office, he connected with someone at SAC Headquarters and said, "I'm calling in reference to Project Dragon Lady." That was the first I heard the name of the project; it sounded big. He explained that I did not have funds to purchase civilian clothes that were required for the TDY. The person at SAC said he could call back in ten minutes, and when the call came, the lieutenant looked across the desk at me and gave me a thumbs-up sign.

The lieutenant hung up and called Major Griffith at his home. He told the major that "SAC Hq said if TSgt Ingram was not in Norwalk by 8:00 a.m. Monday morning, the major could report to General Curtis Lemay (Commander in Chief, SAC Headquarters) and explain why." Amazingly, Major Giffith had a friend from the local Lions Club who owned Janses Clothing Store in Tampa, Florida. He called the owner and cleared my purchases. When I arrived at the store, the owner asked, "Who do you know?" I felt very special indeed, but it was a secret project so I said nothing.

Riding the Pullman train from New York City to Norwalk was an experience I could have done without. The change of stations in New York allowed sufficient layover time to tour Time Square and the Empire State Building. While I was in Time Square, news flashed across the billboard that Russian tanks had moved into Hungary. It was October 1956.

I returned to the train terminal and went to the Information desk to ask where the Connecticut train would leave from. In a voice guaranteed to humiliate, the desk clerk said, "Can't you read? Gate 36. Everybody knows that." *Everybody but me.* A crowd had already started to form at Gate 36, and when it opened, everybody ran. I thought it would be more dignified to walk. When an old lady passed me, I decided it was time to run, too. I soon discovered why everyone ran to the train; there were not enough seats. There were two reasons why I stood out in the crowd on the train. First, I carried a suitcase; no one else did because this was essentially a commuter train. I had a Florida tan, and most of them were chalky white.

Once in Norwalk, I took a taxi to the motel where I was directed to check in. I called Ore Heath at the number I was given; it was his home. He instructed me not to talk to anyone and he would be at the motel lobby at 8:00 a.m. the next day. Heath was there at 8:00 a.m. on the dot and I met George Jewell who was also there for the same project. He became my life-long friend. B.M. Dennis came from Lake Charles AFB, Louisiana and I had met him at MacDill. Jewell was the only one who had driven from Savannah, Georgia.

Heath told Dennis to ride with him, and I rode with Jewell as we followed behind. Our destination was the Perkin Elmer plant, the world's largest optical company.

Our training began on the 70mm tracking camera, drift sight and Mark II hand control. The drift sight was a periscope, and the hand control was the electronic device that controlled it. The hand control was still in production when we arrived. There was still no mention of any aircraft. We learned there were others who had been at the plant before our arrival, but names were not revealed. More interesting, we did learn they were with the Central Intelligence Agency (CIA).

Our training was conducted by the engineer who designed the camera and its systems. After two weeks training, we returned to our home bases, and returned to Norwalk for additional training in December 1956.

Once back at the 306th Armament & Electronics (A&E) Squadron at MacDill, I was the source of curiosity. All the guys wanted to know where I had been. One interested captain took me to lunch and grilled me on my TDY. I never told him anything. It was still a Top Secret project; however, at that point there was not a lot to tell anyone.

In December 1956 I returned to New York City and caught the same train back to Connecticut for an additional week's training. This time I outran the little old ladies and scored a seat. Training ended the week before Christmas, and a return flight to Tampa was not available. I rode with George Jewell to Norfolk, Virginia, his destination for the holidays.

There was not even a bus with an available seat out of Norfolk. Five Navy fellows and I decided to hire a cab to take us to Durham, North Carolina. I got a standby flight from Durham to St. Petersburg/Clearwater, Florida. From the Clearwater airport, I took a limo to Tampa and the driver even drove me directly to my home. It was 11:00 p.m. on Christmas Eve, but I was happy to be home.

The Ranch

In January 1957 I received reassignment orders to Turner AFB, Albany, Georgia and at the same time, TDY orders to March AFB, Riverside, California. Now it was getting interesting. My family was in Florida, I was assigned to a base in Georgia, and I was going TDY to California for four months. Later I would end up in the Nevada desert.

My friend, George Jewell, met me at the bus station in Tallahassee, Florida, and we drove together to March AFB at Riverside, California. When we arrived at March, we reported to the 4070th Support Wing (SAC). The 4070th was one barracks with only a lieutenant and a civilian secretary. The following morning we returned to the barracks where we waited with 35 other airmen. Two Air Force buses took us to Base Operations where we boarded a C-124 Globemaster, destination unknown. I could tell we were flying east, and we landed an hour later on a dry lake bed; it was designated as Groom Lake on a road map. Through the windows I could see a paved runway, hangars, mess hall and barracks and on the paved ramp, six silver gliders with jet engines. That was my first glimpse of the U-2. I was learning fast that this area nicknamed, The Ranch, had tight security and even the name of the aircraft was classified Secret.

Our group was escorted to the mess hall, and there was a smiling MSgt Bill Dyche. Bill welcomed me to The Ranch. He and six other airmen had gone to training on the A-1, A-2 and "B" configurations at Hycon Manufacturing Co. in Pasadena, California for six weeks. Col Jack Nole was our commander and one of the finest officers I knew throughout my Air Force career. Lt Col Joe Jackson was Col Nole's deputy and was himself a very fine officer. (Lt Col Jackson was later awarded the Congressional Medal of Honor, the highest military decoration awarded by the US government, for his heroic action in Vietnam.)

In our introductory briefing, Col Nole cautioned us, "No writing home about where you are working and absolutely no photos will be taken here. This place is referred to as simply The Ranch." It was controlled by the Atomic Energy Commission, including our security. When a bomb was detonated on the other side of the mountain, we had to leave the area temporarily. Our work schedule was Monday through Friday with weekends off. On Friday an aircraft was available to take us back to March AFB and it returned to The Ranch on Monday. There was absolutely no driving in or out of the area. We were on per diem of $16 a day with no charge for housing. Meals were excellent, and only cost $1 for a meal such as steak, salad, potato and drink.

One weekend I stayed at The Ranch. The mess hall showed movies at night and weekends, but after a boring two days, I decided to depart on the next Friday. George Jewell and I stayed at the YMCA in Pasadena, California for only $3 for a two-man room. We went to Hollywood, Santa Monica, Disneyland, Sea World and Knott's Berry Farm. I felt guilty going to Disneyland without my daughter, Stacy, who was four years old, but our family toured the park in 1959. I used direct dialing for the first time on a public phone when I called Barbara from Pasadena.

Our work at The Ranch was to become acquainted with our new camera systems and have them ready when we returned to our home base. CIA had personnel there, too, but they didn't interact with us. They referred to us as Blue Suiters because we were Air Force personnel who typically wore blue uniforms at our home bases.

Lockheed, the designer and builder of the U-2, had a large number of employees at The Ranch. The aircraft was built at Lockheed's Skunk Works plant in Burbank, California, disassembled, wrapped in canvas and loaded on a C-124 for transport to The Ranch. When it was reassembled, Lockheed pilots tested the plane then turned it over to the Air Force when it was determined to be airworthy.

Most of the flights from The Ranch were day missions and camera configurations were set accordingly. On one memorable night-time mission, the pilot experienced a flameout and had to dead stick (glide without power) to Kirtland AFB, Albuquerque, New Mexico. The U-2 pilot had to personally deliver a letter to the base commander who was attending a formal event at the Kirtland Officers Club. The letter gave directions for securing the U-2 including covering it with canvas, and placing armed guards at the tail, each wingtip and nose while it was on the ground. Further, the base was to be evacuated until the aircraft was airborne. The letter, signed by President Eisenhower, contained a $100 bill. Needless to say, the partygoers weren't too happy to break up, and some thought the base commander was playing war games. A Lockheed tech rep was flown to Kirtland; he repaired the U-2 and flew it back to The Ranch without the knowledge of anyone there.

Col Nole offered to get an airplane if any of the married guys from Turner wanted to return for four days to visit their families. It didn't take long to have the C-47 Gooneybird fully occupied. The Gooneybird was made famous in World War II, and the TV series *Band of Brothers* used the same model plane. We took off at March AFB dressed in a variety of work clothes. When we landed at England AFB, in Alexandria,

Louisiana, folks there thought we were some sort of security team. Base security forces came out and surrounded the C-47 with weapons drawn. Col Nole explained with limited information who we were and why we were there.

While our aircraft was being refueled, we ate dinner and a short time later took off for Turner AFB. I took a commercial airline flight to Tampa, Florida where Barbara and Stacy lived. After being away three months, we had a happy reunion. It was a short four days; I returned to Albany, Georgia to meet my group for the return flight to March AFB.

Relocation to Laughlin AFB

In June 1957 our crews were divided, half went to Laughlin AFB, Del Rio, Texas, and I stayed with the other half at The Ranch. One week later we launched our U-2s from The Ranch to Laughlin and shipped the remainder of our equipment to Del Rio.

George and I returned to March where he collected his car for the drive to Del Rio. At Indio, California we encountered the mother of all sand storms. It was so severe that it removed the paint from George's car and sand blasted the windshield. When we arrived in Del Rio, George dropped me at the bus station for the trip to San Antonio where I boarded a commercial flight to Tampa.

Barbara and I sold our house and shipped our household goods to Del Rio. We drove with Stacy in our 1953 blue Ford station wagon to Georgia to visit my family. Apparently I was the talk of the town; family and friends were eager to know what I was involved in. They said the Federal Bureau of Investigation (FBI) had been talking about me to a lot of local people. I could only say I was not in trouble and I would tell them someday.

En route to Arlington, Texas to visit Barbara's family, we encountered a tremendous storm in Louisiana. We didn't realize it was hurricane strength until we arrived in Arlington. Barbara's family told us we had just driven through a hurricane, but there were no television warnings in those days.

We arrived in Del Rio on July 4, 1957 and the next day I reported to the 4080th A&E Squadron First Sergeant. He said excitedly, "Ingram, we didn't know you really existed. I've had your name on my morning report since October 1956." He welcomed me to the squadron where I would be assigned for the next six years.

One of my interesting memories occurred in March 1958 when we deployed to Eielson AFB, Alaska for the U-2 to fly high altitude radiation sampling over Russia. Captain Michael Styer flew a mission that took him over Siberia. At the time Russia was testing atomic bombs above the earth. After the Russians exploded a bomb, Captain Styer flew directly through the cloud.

When he landed and taxied in, the U-2 was so hot with radiation, he had to stay in the aircraft for another two hours while the ground crew washed down the aircraft. He then opened the canopy, jumped out and ran to the building. At debriefing he said his Geiger counter went off on his return flight coming out of Russian airspace at 30,000 feet. He reported that two F-89 Alaskan Air Defense planes had him on radar, but could not see him. They ordered him to identify himself or they would shoot him down. Captain Styer said he was on radio silence. He hit the U-2 throttle, pulled back on the stick and shot up to 50,000 feet. At that altitude he circled around the F-89s and landed at Eielson.

When we finished our post-flight work, we caught the base bus to the mess hall. The bus radio was on. Suddenly the radio announced, "Attention, two Alaskan Air Defense fighters encountered a UFO at 30,000 feet. Then the UFO shot off to outer space." We smiled at each other as we listened to the radio with the others in the bus. When we left the bus, we had a good laugh; we all knew what the UFO really was.

For our work during that TDY, a few days later, the photographic laboratories in New Jersey notified us, "Congratulations. The data you sent was of great value to our national security."

One day in 1960, I was told to get two men, three "B" configuration cameras and be ready to depart in three hours. I chose Bobbie D. Black and John Washburn, the best technicians we had. I went to my home on base and Barbara helped me pack. I didn't know where I was going or how long I would be gone. I gave her the checkbook, kissed her and our daughter, Stacy, goodbye.

When we got to the flight line, a KC-135 Stratotanker was being loaded with cargo and the refueling tanks were being filled for the U-2s. The KC-135 loadmaster asked us how much the U-2 fuel weighed. None of us knew; we were all camera guys. He said he would have to guess at it and pulled out his slide rule to do some calculations. The temperature on the runway at Laughlin AFB was a stifling 115 degrees Fahrenheit. As most Air Force personnel knew, jet engines did not perform well in high temperatures. Colonel T. J. Jackson, Director of Operations, told the ground crew to remove the over-run barrier to allow more runway for takeoff. The KC-135 developed radio problems and our takeoff was delayed three hours.

Finally, it was a "go" and we rolled out to the end of the 8,500 foot runway; the point of rotation was 7,000 feet. That meant no stopping once we started the takeoff roll. At the end of the runway, we were still on the ground and hit the dirt over-run. It was like driving a car at 100 mph on a paved highway and suddenly hitting a dirt road.

Three backup U-2 pilots were onboard our KC-135. One of them jumped up and yelled, "We're not going to make it!" Dirt and small bushes flew by the windows. We lifted off, clipped some small trees and were airborne into the blue Texas sky. We breathed a collective sigh of relief.

Shortly after noon that day, Barbara and Stacy, went to the base swimming pool located on a hill overlooking the runway. As they observed the KC-135, everyone at the pool remarked that the airplane was having trouble with the takeoff and all ran to the fence for a closer look. Barbara said confidently, "I'm glad my husband is not on that plane. He left this morning, three hours ago." She did not know the full story until I returned two months later.

On our return flight from Kadena AFB, Okinawa, the KC-135 was again full of cargo and fuel. Over the Pacific west of Wake Island, the navigator had fallen asleep when we hit a violent storm. Suddenly all the cargo started shifting and the wings of the airplane were flexing like a bird's wing in flight. John Washburn's face turned deathly white. He turned to me and said, "Bob, we are not going to make it."

Negrito village chief, Philippines, 1964.

Bunker for protection against rocket attacks, Bien Hoa AB.

Bien Hoa Air Base, South Vietnam, 1964.

A C-130 at Clark AB Philippines with a volcano in the background.

The pilot pulled back on the controls, and after fifteen long minutes, we got above the storm and landed at Wake Island. When we exited the plane, we observed 90 percent of the SAC insignia and the AF blue stripe on the KC-135 fuselage were missing. The pilot said it best: "Men, we are not supposed to be here." He then moved the radar indicator where he could monitor it for the reminder of the flight to Laughlin.

In 1960 I was Chief Master Sergeant (CMSgt) assigned to the NEPHO Shop (Sensors), the aerial camera of the U-2. My Squadron Commander, Lt Col F.M. Shipley, headed up the 4080th Armament & Electronics (A&E). Col Shipley's family and my family attended St James Episcopal Church in Del Rio. I was aware that he was diabetic and I knew how to read his moods . When his diabetes was not well controlled, he would have some bad days. If his face was red and flushed, I kept my mouth closed until he spoke. I also knew I certainly did not want to be the bearer of bad news when he was having a bad day.

Lieutenant Dennin was assigned to our shop, his first assignment in the wing. He was directed to shadow my daily activities in order to learn the operation of maintaining the camera configuration.

When a camera system malfunctioned, Col Shipley summoned me to his office and I explained the problem. Lt Dennin followed me each time like a puppy tracking my every move. Once in the colonel's office, the first thing I would do was check his complexion to assess his mood. If his face was red and flushed, I held any comments until he spoke. On these occasions Lt Dennin seized the opportunity and rushed to respond to the colonel's questions, always eager to impress. As a result, Col Shipley chewed out Lt Dennin like a drill sergeant in basic training. When I was requested to respond to the colonel's questions, I was always treated professionally.

After a few months of this routine, on the walk back to our shop, Lt Dennin said to me, "I don't understand it. Col Shipley chews my ass when I explain the maintenance problem, and he treats you with respect when you explain the same problem." The lieutenant was reassigned to Beale AFB a short time later, and I never revealed my clues about the colonel's mood. Lt Col Shipley was an outstanding leader and a great friend.

Supporting the Crisis

In September and October 1962, the 4080th SRW flew missions over Cuba from McCoy AFB, Florida. Major Richard Heyser was the first to find the Russian missiles on the island. We flew one mission every three to four days.

One morning at 1:00 a.m. Col Shipley came to my barracks and woke me. He said, "We have received orders to fly five sorties today. Can we do it?" I said with absolute confidence, "Yes, sir." We had five U-2s and five Hycon "B" cameras, 36-inch focal length, and five Perkin Elmer 70mm tracking cameras. My team and I started to work.

Missions were scheduled at two hour intervals, flying off the coast of Cuba at a high oblique angle of the camera lens. The sun angle was critical for each aircraft to capture the best photography. Then we discovered we only had four sets of mounts to hang the "B" cameras in the Q-bay of the U-2. There was not enough time to fly a set of mounts in from Laughlin on one of the T-33s. The way the flights were scheduled, the first aircraft landed when the fifth aircraft took off. When Col Shipley stopped calling me "Bob," and started calling me "Sergeant Ingram," I knew I was in trouble.

We decided not to tell Colonel DesPortes, the wing commander, about the camera mounts until the last minute. He was known to have a short fuse. Jim Combs, the Hycon Tech Rep, saved the day. He took a set of mounts to the McCoy Field Maintenance Squadron; duty personnel there called a sergeant from home at 2:00 a.m. Jim asked if the sergeant could duplicate the mounts which he did with the raw metal on a lathe. They weren't pretty, but they were just what we needed. Jim gave the sergeant $50 cash and asked his commanding officer to write a letter of commendation.

We installed the mounts, closed the hatch and operated the camera to make sure it cleared the heater ducts behind the windows. The new mounts worked perfectly. We never had to tell Colonel DesPortes. The last time I saw those mounts was in a box at Davis Monthan AFB, Arizona. There was a lot of stress over those mounts and a vivid memory for a few of us.

Across the Pacific

In late 1964, I was called to the 4080th A&E Maintenance Supervisor's Office. I was told I would be going TDY, but I was not told where or how long. Jerry Fogel, Charlie Couch, Si Lewis, BC Fowler, Jim Lobig and Jim Combs, the Hycon Tech Rep, were also selected for the same TDY.

I went home, told Barbara and she helped me pack. Once again I said goodbye to her and Stacy not knowing when I would see them again. Saying goodbye to my family was always the hardest part of my military career.

Our instructions were to prepare three "B" Hycon configurations, 36-inch focal length cameras, and load them in the doghouses. In addition, we prepared three 70mm tracker cameras in their cases and three "B" configuration lower hatches with windows.

On this deployment we took three U-2s and six pilots. Three pilots flew the U-2s and three backup pilots traveled in one of the two KC-135s. The KC-135 carried a full cargo load of fuel and maintenance personnel to support the operation. We were designated Operating Location 20 (OL 20) and our commander was Colonel Kenneth McCaslin.

The flight from Laughlin to Hawaii was uneventful. The KC-135 had to land prior to the U-2s in order to recover the aircraft, install the pogos and assist the pilots in disconnecting the gear and exiting the aircraft. After refueling the U-2s on the ground, we launched again with three backup pilots.

The next stop was Clark AFB, Manila, Philippines. I was excited to be in the Philippines for the first time. We NEPHO troops had unloaded our cargo, doghouses, test equipment, film and support supplies into a big hangar at Clark. Once we were established there, we only flew training flights, no aerial reconnaissance missions were flown.

As I got adjusted to the area, one scene that caught my eye was the huge mountain on a flat plain twenty miles from the base. The mountain I learned was an active volcano, and years later it erupted and destroyed Clark. I was happy God's timetable wasn't set for the volcano to erupt when we were there.

We learned through the rumor mill the American Ambassador had directed us to leave the country. A short time later the ambassador flew nonstop on a KC-135 to Washington, DC, briefed the administration and returned to the Philippines. It had to have been an exhausting trip for him. The result was we were allowed to stay in the Philippines.

One of the most interesting off-base trips I took was to a local Negrito village. The Negritos, Aborigines of the Philippines, were only about five feet tall, had very black skin and lived in grass huts elevated about seven feet off the ground. I talked to the Negrito chief, whom I found to be quite an interesting fellow. He was dressed in casual western style slacks and short sleeve shirt. The remainder of the tribe dressed in colorful costumes like they were in a Hollywood movie. The chief said his people were employed by the base as guards. Besides their pay, they had a choice of medical care at the base or exchange privileges. They usually chose the hospital care. I was surprised to learn from the chief that his son was a medical doctor and an officer in the US Navy. Looking at the village resembling something from the Stone Age, it was hard to believe his son was an officer in the Navy. I didn't ask the chief how his son made the transition from the village to the Navy.

Theft was rampant at Clark, and I asked the chief why he could not stop it since he was in the security business. He replied, "I could, but the base commander turned me down when I asked him for a truck to haul away the culprits."

All of us bought blowguns in the village, actually a hollow tube from a plant with a dart inside. Other souvenirs were bows and arrows. I bought a $2 machete, sixteen inches long made from an auto spring with water buffalo horn handle. I still have that machete; I use it to cut up boxes for recycle. BC Fowler became quite proficient with the blowgun. However, when he returned to Arizona, he said the blowgun tube and the bow and arrows had split in the dry Arizona climate.

I was in the Base Exchange when a crew chief came in and shouted the President of the Philippines had ordered us out of the country. We had four hours to pack up and leave. We did some fast packing of all our gear and loaded the two KC-135s. The crew chief of the KC-135 I was assigned to fly on told Colonel McCaslin he had a load of JP-4 fuel onboard for a training flight with a fighter scheduled for that night. As a result, the plane was overloaded. McCaslin ordered, "Dump it, we have to go." We taxied to the end of the runway, pointed the refueling boom toward the jungle and shot JP-4 out of the boom. What a scene! The colonel shouted, "Let's go, we are out of time and I don't want an international incident." The boom operator said, "I'm not finished." The pilot headed the aircraft down the runway spraying JP-4 as we went. Later, I asked Col McCaslin why he moved to the jump seat. He laughed and said, "I wasn't sure we were going to be able to takeoff."

On to Andersen AFB, Guam. We stored our equipment in a hangar at Andersen. The base housed all the enlisted men in two-story brick barracks in the jungle at Maroboro, Guam, about ten miles off base. Near the barracks was a small store that sold beer and snacks; it resembled a country store back home. Each day we went to the main base to check in. There was really nothing for us to do, but eat, sleep and drink beer for two weeks. What a life!

Between Maroboro and Andersen was a span of thick jungle. I often wondered if there were any Japanese still hiding in the jungle. When I expressed this to one of our men, he told me I was nuts because the Japanese had been gone for years. World War II had been over for nineteen years. Would you believe it, two years later, two Japanese came out of the jungle and surrendered on Guam.

Colonel DesPortes flew from Laughlin to join us on Guam. He had a yellow envelope with him and he announced, "Here it is, boys. Our orders, but I can't open it until we are airborne." We loaded the KC-135 with our cargo and were ready to go. Colonel DesPortes learned there was a Russian trawler two miles from the end of the runway monitoring planes taking off from Guam. He said, "We can't have that." A local KC-135 offered to get rid of the trawler for us, and he took off with a load of JP-4 fuel. He flew directly over the trawler and started yelling, "May Day! May Day!" As was planned, the boom operator sprayed the deck of the trawler with JP-4. The pilot reported he last saw the trawler headed out to sea with the crew washing down the deck.

The runway at Andersen was 10,000 feet and ran downhill to a low area then uphill again. At the end was a 200 foot cliff with jagged rock, and the blue Pacific Ocean beyond. The pilot started down the runway and the plane began sinking; it shook and vibrated so much I felt I had double vision. Si Lewis was in the boom operator's seat where there was a large window. He reported, "The blue Pacific Ocean came up at us, and I felt I could reach out and touch it." I exhaled and the pilot leveled the aircraft and climbed to higher altitude.

I was sitting next to Colonel DesPortes when he said, "Let's see where we are going." He tore open the large yellow envelope and announced, "We are going to Ben Ho-ey" which was actually Bien Hoa Air Base, South Vietnam.

It was March 1964 when we landed on a brand new concrete runway at Bien Hoa. A short time later I asked the flight surgeon when we would get our plague shots. He said rather sarcastically, "Ingram, the Bubonic Plague has been eradicated for years."

A local base captain drove up and said they only learned we were arriving an hour earlier. Headquarters had told the captain we had Priority One orders, and they would give us whatever we needed. Colonel DesPortes turned to me and told me to go with the captain to set up the NEPHO shop. The NEPHO guys and I hopped in a pickup truck headed for the hangars. Bien Hoa was built by the French, taken over by the Japanese in World War II, returned to the French after the war, and now the South Vietnamese had custody. The hangars were a sad sight, rusty metal thick with red mud; grease and dirt covered the floor. I told the captain this hangar would not work for us. We needed a 20 feet by 30 feet air conditioned room for our systems and film.

The captain replied that the only air conditioned building on the base was the NCO Club and Base Communications. I asked to have a look at the Base Communications building. It was a brick building with large green doors. The captain pounded on the doors, and a staff sergeant dressed in a nice, clean 1505 uniform appeared. The captain introduced me and explained we needed a shop for our operation. The sergeant said, "Well, we can't give up our office." The interior was divided by a wall creating two equal size rooms. The captain asked what I thought about the space and I responded, "This is it!" The captain called to the staff sergeant and ordered him to move out. We moved our doghouses into the hangar and our film equipment into the Base Communications building. When we saw him again, the sergeant was stripped to the waist, sweating profusely and sending us a "Go to Hell" look. We flew 33 successful missions before one "B" configuration failed.

Now about the rats; I learned that Southeast Asia is home to an extremely large population of enormous rats. They were about fourteen inches long excluding the tail and weighed up to eight pounds. At night some of the guys would trap a rat in a wire cage and spray paint them different colors each day. The rats only came out at night, and once they actually did trap the same rat a second time. One night we heard a loud, horrific scream from the next hut; we learned one of the rats had found its way into the bed of one of the troops. The poor airman almost tore the hut down getting out of there. Two days later, we were all told to report to the flight line for our plague shots. I said to the flight surgeon, "Hey Doc, I thought you said the plague had been wiped out." He smiled and shouted, "Next!"

One day Colonel DesPortes came to our shop and said he had been ordered to go to Bangkok, Thailand to brief Robert McNamara, Secretary of Defense, on our operation. The colonel was slightly inebriated, well, really tight as a banjo string. He was obviously nervous about the McNamara briefing. Jim Combs, our Hycon Tech Rep, went over everything Colonel DesPortes needed, and by the time they finished their preparation, a whole bottle of booze had been emptied.

Three days later Colonel DesPortes returned with a smile on his face. The briefing went well. He had news that I was glad to hear. In May 1964, Fogel, Couch, Lewis, Fowler, Lobig and I rotated back to Davis Monthan AFB, Arizona. As we left Bien Hoa, I thought to myself how glad I was to leave. Little did I know that I would be returning later with Bobbie Black to support the Drones. On that TDY we were there for Thanksgiving, Christmas and New Year, and we saw the Bob Hope road show. I left Vietnam in January 1965 and vowed, "This is it for Vietnam." Once again I returned to Vietnam in 1966 on permanent change of station orders.

The Next Chapter – Special Operations Office

In late 1969, Lt Col Warren Boyd came to our shop from the Special Projects Office (SPO) at Robbins AFB, Georgia. I had first met him at The Ranch when he was a 1Lt U-2 pilot. He was now second in command at the SPO, and he asked if I wanted to transfer there. I told him I would talk to my family and get back with him. Barbara, Stacy and I discussed the transfer and all were in agreement to go to Robbins in January 1970.

The SPO was located in a large building at Robbins behind what was called the Green Door. Colonel Peter Economy was our boss, a quiet man who had a gift for languages and musical talent. Everyone in SPO had to have a Black Clearance which is higher than Top Secret. Part of the mission of the SPO was to interface with vendors who had contracts with the Air Force. My vendors were in Palo Alto, California, Norwalk, Connecticut, Boston, Massachusetts and Davis Monthan AFB, Arizona.

One day Col Economy came to my office and announced the Under Secretary of the Air Force, John L. McLucas, would be at SPO the next day, and I was designated to brief him on the camera system in the U-2 program. The colonel told me to wear my blues and look sharp. The Under Secretary had a doctorate in physics and had been president of Penn State University.

When I went home that day, I thought about what Under Secretary McLucas might ask that I don't know about our camera systems. I wasn't stressed or nervous. The next day Col Economy stuck his head in my office and said, "Bob, you are on."

When I walked into the large conference room, I discovered it was wall to wall with generals, colonels, GS-15 civilians, one Lt Col and two Majors. I was the only enlisted man in the room. The Under Secretary was about six feet tall and looked every bit like the PhD that he was. He shook my hand and politely said, "I'm happy to meet you, Chief." He asked a lot of good questions, easy ones for me to answer. After about twenty minutes, he shook my hand again and said, "That was a very good briefing, Chief." He announced he was ready to leave and the entourage left the room like a vacuum had sucked them out of the door. Col Economy commended me on the briefing. Hal Benton, a civilian GS-15, asked where I learned all that information. I replied, "After fifteen plus years, if you don't learn something, then you're pretty dumb."

I want to thank the Air Force families, my wife Barbara, my daughter Stacy and the many friends who supported us during our separation. I am proud to say I can still call many of those fellows my friends today.

Jose F. (Lops) Lopez

Los Angeles, California
Wife: Irene

Lightning Bug Mission

I was on my second TDY at Bien Hoa Air Base, Vietnam (known as OL-20) in 1966. Somehow I was "volunteered" to go to DaNang Air Base to help with a couple of missions for the Lightning Bug Project. The project consisted of a Firebee reconnaissance drone that was air-launched and controlled from a DC-130 aircraft. The Firebee drone was flown on low-level photographic missions over North Vietnam. Following the drone's recon flight, it was directed to a recovery area where its parachute was deployed. The

Getting ready for a mission launch.

Promotion party celebration - Jose Paz (A2C to A1C) (left), Jack Owens (second from left) and Jose Lopez (fourth from left).

Left to right: Jack Owens, Chuck Dreiling, TSgt Dan Reyna, Jose Lopez.

Our main transportation to the town of Bien Hoa.

Firebee was then recovered from the landing location, on land or at sea. It was my job working out of the NEPHO shop to be part of the recovery team to remove and safeguard the film magazine from the camera attached to the drone.

On one particular mission, the Firebee was launched toward North Vietnam. A squad of US Army soldiers and I boarded a CH-3C helicopter. I carried my tool bag in one hand and my AR-15 on my shoulder. Our chopper was escorted by six Huey helicopter gunships. We flew from the base over thick green jungle. After we were airborne for a time, our pilot received information from the C-130 regarding the landing location of the drone and we headed in that direction. The remote guidance systems in those days were slightly less than exact. The drone we were chasing landed in a small village in the middle of the jungle instead of a large safe area as planned.

The pilot found a small clearing to land our helicopter and some of the Army troops jumped out and set up a defense perimeter. The remainder of the troops and I headed to the village where the drone had landed. The Huey gunships stayed overhead and circled our location for our protection. We cautiously scanned the village area for VC but the only people we found were a few scared villagers yelling and running around in panic. We found the drone; it had landed in a fenced area near a villager's hut. I went directly to the drone and removed the film magazine while the soldiers attempted to calm the villagers. We returned to our helicopter and headed back to DaNang. The chopper pilot reported that while we were in the village he heard a radio transmission from a flight of

B-57s asking the Huey pilots if they had VC's trapped in the area. The B-57s were itching to level something with all the ordnance they had onboard. The Huey pilots replied they had not seen any VC and the B-57s continued on while we returned to the base.

One of the Army soldiers reported the village chief claimed our drone had killed one of his pigs, but I never saw any dead pigs. The chief demanded payment for the pig and one of the officers took care of the payment. Once we were back at DaNang I handed over the canvas bag with the film magazine to a waiting officer; my mission was complete. I was now free to enjoy a cold Ba-mi-ba (33), a Vietnamese beer.

James D. Manis
Waikoloa, Hawaii

During our deployments, one of the U-2 pilots usually flew a C-54 that carried many of us of the NEPHO Unit to our destination. On one deployment to South America, Captain Charlie Knapp was the navigator. He was charged with mapping the flight plan for the pilot, Major Ed Emerling. To pass the time of the long flight, I played cards with some of the guys. We did notice that the plane was circling a lot. Major Emerling called for Captain Knapp to come to the cockpit for a consultation. When Captain Knapp returned to the cabin, I asked him if there was a problem. He rather sheepishly responded that he had mapped the flight over Cuba instead of the destination in South America. That was at the time when there was already quite a bit of activity in Cuba. We wanted no part of that. Captain Knapp had probably mapped quite a few flights to Cuba in previous months. Prior to becoming officers, both Major Emerling and Captain Knapp had been enlisted men. When we landed, in the presence of all of us on the flight, Major

2005 4080th SRW Reunion, left to right: Jerry Fogel, Al Defilipis, Horace Tanner, B.C. Fowler, Jim Manis and Bob Ingram.

Jimmy D. Manis.

Emerling asked Captain Knapp, "I know how you got to be a Captain, but what I want to know is how you became a Staff Sergeant?" Of course, all of us who were witness to this had a good laugh at Captain Knapp's expense.

We were at McCoy AFB, Florida during the Cuban Missile Crisis. When a U-2 pilot landed, he was instructed to remain at the end of the runway while we installed covers on all the windows. On one memorable day, Mobile Control had stopped its van next to the U-2 on the ground while the cameraman raced to install the covers. The cameraman was near the main gear when the Tower called to see if it had cleared the runway. They had another bird on approach. Mobile Control responded to the Tower to let the bird on approach "go ahead." A series of mixed messages unfolded about that time. Seeing the scrambling cameraman trying to get away from the U-2 where he had installed the window covers, Mobile Control shouted to the pilot of that aircraft, "Not Clear." The aircraft on approach heard "Not Clear" which he thought was meant for him. He was told to abort his landing. In his haste to pull up and go around, he almost clipped another U-2 in the pattern. What a close call that was!

While I was at Edwards North Base in 1960, the US trained Taiwanese pilots to fly the U-2. The Taiwanese pilots were housed in mobile homes on the base. They were not permitted to leave the base. On a training flight over Canada, an excited Taiwanese pilot called back to base that he had experienced a mechanical problem. There were a number of remote landing sites that had been used for training flights such as this one. The pilot was directed to the nearest remote runway and a KC-135 took off to locate and recover the U-2. North Base was unable to contact anyone at the remote site tower. The pilot landed his U-2, disconnected himself and walked to the nearby tower building. Seeing this most unusual sight appear at his tower so frightened the operator that he raced out of the building, jumped in his car and sped away to town. The KC-135 landed, repaired the U-2 and everyone took off. The next day, the local newspaper headlines read "Martian landed, area secured by Air Force."

William L. Ming
New Braunfels, Texas
Wife: Virginia

I supported the U-2 program from the time I joined the 4080th SRW at Turner AFB, Georgia, in 1956, following the unit to Laughlin AFB, Texas, through my assignment at Tan Son Nhut Air Base, Vietnam in 1962. My job at Laughlin was the Assistant Officer in Charge, Intelligence Photographic Evaluation.

The OIC of our operation was Major Harry Oglesby who was later replaced by Lt. Col. Frick. Our team included Captain Carothers and Captain Glen Furbish, and our enlisted staff included Technical Sergeant (TSgt.) Joe Franklin, SSgt. Walter E. Davis and Airmen Green and Reid.

I never got used to going to the base in the morning and then during the day being instructed to go home and pack my gear to go TDY. I would phone my wife to start

William Ming receiving an award from Col Bratton, 1958.

packing for me. I rushed home, finished packing, rushed back to the base, boarded a KC-135 and departed for an unspecified period. England or Alaska were my most frequent destinations.

The TDY to Alaska was the best. The mess hall treated us as if we were royalty. Anything we wanted, we received. Once a week, the Officers' Club served King Crab, all we could eat for $1.25!

There was a nice side benefit of going to Alaska. The U-2s would come up to Eilson AFB configured for their mission. When they were to return to Laughlin, they were "light." We would load the empty bays with frozen King Crab which would stay frozen all the way to Laughlin. When the U-2 was about an hour out, Base Operations called the wives and simply said, "Mrs. Ming, will you come out to Base Ops and pick up a package?" She would pick up her frozen crab and happily head for home.

This was an exciting time and we were working with a classified aircraft. Challenges abound. The camaraderie was great and we knew we were gathering intelligence for a purpose.

Loomis L. (Robbie) Robertson
Oxford, Mississippi

When I reported for duty to the 4080th Wing Lab in April 1958, I was one totally confused and rather unhappy airman. I was "hand-picked" by my former supervisor to go to Laughlin AFB, Texas. The only thing he told me was I would be working in a "Weather" organization. That didn't make any sense because I didn't know anything about predicting weather. I was very happy with the 70th Recon Tech Squadron at Little Rock AFB, Arkansas. I was asked to volunteer, but since I didn't want to leave, and I didn't find going to a weather outfit very exciting, I refused to volunteer. Well, you can guess the rest of the story. The Air Force was kind, however, and since my wife was six months pregnant, she was allowed to stay in Little Rock and she was given an additional 90 days to recuperate. My son was born on January 14, 1958. To the day I was on my way to Laughlin exactly 90 days later.

I arrived at Laughlin and I was told that I couldn't go to work because I would have to have additional clearances. That was confusing because I already had a TOP SECRET clearance. In the meantime I would be working on the Tower just below the Air Traffic controllers photographing with a motion picture camera all the takeoffs and landings of two types of aircraft. One of the aircraft was a B-57D, but the other didn't have a name. I was just told to be on the lookout for something that slightly resembled a glider. The Major doing the briefing told me how important the job was, but I still wasn't excited. He also told me they had never had a crash on takeoff or landing, but he said, "If they do and you don't get a record of it on film, you might as well jump off the Tower, because you've had it." That got my attention, but then I thought, "How difficult could this be?" and for the most part forgot the matter. I was still trying to figure out how "weather" factored into it.

As it turned out, it didn't take long for things to get exciting. I reported for duty the first morning at my makeshift office one floor beneath the Tower room. I saw a B-57 starting its roll, so I panned it until it was airborne. With one eye on the runway and the other on the sky in the direction of approach that morning, I turned the camera off and relaxed. Later the B-57 came home; I caught him as he broke the horizon and panned him until he almost stopped. Then I caught a glimpse of this weird-looking apparatus on approach, and I thought, "Yep, that's got to be the glider." I caught him in the same area as I did the B-57 and panned him until he was safe on the ground and had completed his roll, I thought. I reached over and picked up my cigarette and was feeling pretty good about the whole picture taking thing when all of a sudden I looked at the runway and this weird thing was lying on its side! I just about had the "big one" as I vividly remembered what the Major said about missing a crash. I thought before jumping off the Tower, "Let me check with the controllers and see if they can tell me what happened."

I rushed inside the Tower room and asked them, "What just happened?" First they looked confused, and then I pointed to the "thing" lying on its side. In unison all of them started to laugh. They explained about the "thing" not having any wheels under the wings and they let me know that was normal. They even mentioned something about "pogo sticks," but I didn't know what they were talking about. I was happy to know that I had not missed anything. Of course, I wondered if this thing that flew was somehow connected to this weather outfit.

Three months later I got the clearances I needed to work the job and was given a tour of the Wing Lab. I knew what was going on; it was exciting and everything was new. I had never seen any of the equipment and never heard about the film. Even with the newly granted clearances, I was told not to ask too many questions. I finally understood and I couldn't thank my former supervisor enough for handpicking and volunteering me for this obviously challenging job. I was told, "Don't ever mention the word 'photo' in the same breath as the U-2." As I look back over the years, it seems that I was told something to that effect on countless occasions.

I never did anything with the program that I didn't find both rewarding and challenging. There was plenty of excitement that came packaged with every assignment. It seemed to me that "professionals" just came out of the woodwork. One super person would leave and be replaced by another equally proficient professional. I can truly say that I have been blessed beyond measure to have the opportunity to work with the U-2 program and its myriad personnel.

Like most of my friends, I did not like being separated from the family on some of the long TDYs. I firmly believed what I was doing made a difference, so I gladly made the sacrifice. My wife didn't like the TDY's either, but she still raised the family and supported me 100 percent. Hats off to our officer cadre who did an excellent job of instilling the importance of the Wing mission to all the troops.

I still maintain contact with several of the old troops, and many of the officers from the program. Tony Bevacqua and Pat Halloran are just a couple of the dear friends that I've known for years. The camaraderie with this organization was unequalled with any of my other units.

Joseph (Rooster) Robinson

Tucson, Arizona
Wife: Barbara

I was assigned to the Nephographic Shop of the 4080th SRW at Laughlin AFB in April 1959 and the equipment at this duty station was new to me. Before Laughlin I was

Joseph "Rooster" Robinson with trophy awarded for Airman of the Month.

with a recon wing at Little Rock AFB, Arkansas. I needed to have a Top Secret security clearance with complete background investigation. (That meant some investigator would be knocking on doors all over my hometown.) I was a stranger in the NEPHO Shop for a while. I was allowed to work on the RB-57 aircraft assigned to the unit until my clearance approval came through.

Once my clearance was approved, I was busy learning the ins and outs of the new photographic configurations flown on the U-2. My first TDY with the U-2 program was in 1962. I received a call about midnight instructing me to report to duty immediately and to bring all my mobility gear in preparation for a short excursion. I boarded a C-123 transport with other members of my unit for a mission at an unknown destination. Our instructions were not to ask questions, do as we were told on a need to know basis, which was actually very little. I was at Homestead AFB, Florida for three days before I knew where I was and what our mission was. I was there in support of the Cuban Missile Crisis.

It was a sad day in my life when one of the pilots from our wing, Major Anderson, was shot down while photographing over Cuba. That was the second time I was in the area when a U-2 was lost. In 1960 I was TDY at Incirlik AB, Adana, Turkey with the RB-57s when Gary Powers was shot down and captured over Russia—another sad day.

The thing I remember most about the Homestead TDY was the day President Kennedy came to visit. All of the aircraft were on static display, the U-2 parked among them waiting for the President's arrival. Our commander, Colonel DesPortes, had to briefly leave the area but he said he would return soon. He gave me explicit instructions that absolutely no one was allowed to view the inside of the cockpit until he returned.

Shortly after Colonel DesPortes' departure, a staff car drove up with the most generals I had ever seen. They said they wanted to look into the cockpit of the U-2. There I stood, an Airman First Class, telling a group of generals that I had instructions from my commander that no one, including the President, was to look into the cockpit until he returned. Fortunately, Colonel DesPortes wasn't gone long, but it seemed a lifetime. When he returned, the Colonel congratulated me in front of the group of generals for standing my ground and following his instructions.

The planes were readied to depart Homestead after viewing of the aircraft on display. Right then a young Major passed by and made a comment that the C-124 aircraft that he flew could beat the U-2 off the ground on takeoff. At that time the big lumbering Douglas C-124 Globemaster II was the largest transport in the aircraft inventory. Getting that fully loaded aircraft off the ground took all available runway. The brash comment was overheard by one of the U-2 pilots and the challenge was on. The U-2 pilot accepted the challenge and told the Globemaster pilot to stick around and see how quickly the U-2 would be off the ground. The pilot of the U-2 instructed the crew chief to remove all the fuel from the wing tanks and get the bird ready for a max takeoff. Word spread. The U-2 was going to put on a show and that is just what we witnessed. The ground crew hand launched the aircraft shortly after rolling a few hundred feet down the runway. The pilot pulled up, sped toward the heavens and went completely out of sight. It was a beautiful. Several guys there found it hard to believe what they had seen that day. The C-124 pilot stared with surprise as the U-2 disappeared above the clouds only seconds after liftoff. That C-124 pilot was probably grateful he had not bet a lot of cash on his aircraft.

Joseph Robinson standing fifth from right with his unit.

I had always enjoyed sports and I played on several teams at Laughlin. Sports passed the time because there wasn't much for a single airman to do off duty. On a TDY to Carswell AFB, Fort Worth, Texas I joined the basketball team. One of the Carswell players made a comment that I ran up and down the court like a proud rooster. The following year I was on another TDY and was unable to participate in the game against Carswell. They asked about the "Rooster" but the Laughlin team didn't know who they referred to until a photo was produced and I was then identified. From then on everyone started calling me Rooster and the name stuck. Some people I worked with actually thought that was my real name. To this day, some of the guys from the old days still call me Rooster.

I had a great 26-year military career, several years in the 4080th and the 100th. I traveled all over the world with the U-2 group, sometimes not even knowing where I was. I always managed to meet people and made a lot of lifelong friends. As a result of those friendships, I could get almost anything I needed to get a job done. I could get a piece of equipment up and running or a case of steaks for a cookout at a TDY location. It's who you know. People asked how I was always able to come through, but I kept a tight lip about my connections as I did about my job. For me it was always important to maintain trust and confidence from the people I worked with.

I often found it difficult not being able to tell my wife and kids about my job in the Air Force. All they knew was that I worked around the U-2. When folks asked about my job, I would jokingly reply, "If I tell you what my job is, I'll have to kill you." That usually put a stop to further questions.

The people of the 4080th were a very special group. Our normal situation at Laughlin found us typically understaffed when half of our unit was away on TDY. A routine day could change quickly and we had to prepare for another TDY. The camaraderie and professionalism in the 4080th were unequalled in other units and I am proud to have served with these men.

Charlie Rogers

Montgomery, Alabama
Wife: Myrtle

I was fresh out of basic training and I arrived at the 4080th SRW at Laughlin AFB when Brigadier General DesPortes headed the organization. My first assignment was in A & E with SFERICS and camera NEPHO. One of my memories during that time was the quality of the leadership; I considered this leadership to be the absolute best. Two of our young airmen and I were summoned to General DesPortes' office to receive an award. The General, being from North Carolina, learned that I was also from the South and he offered good naturedly to "translate" whenever I needed help with the language. We both smiled.

I was married with a young family living in Del Rio. Stretching my airman's pay was always a challenge. For a time I worked nights washing dishes at the Officers' Club and walked the seven miles to my house in Del Rio when the club closed.

I was in the Air Force 30 years and consider it some of the best years of my life and my time with the 4080th a highlight.

Gene Stoddard

Schenectady, New York
Wife: Virginia

As an enlisted photographer, I did get to see a little more of the total operation than the average aircraft mechanic. I covered a variety of official events, newsworthy items and routine base photo duties.

I joined the Air Force as a 17-year-old high school dropout in November 1959. After four weeks basic training at Lackland AFB, Texas, I went by train to Lowry AFB, Colorado. At Lowry I attended the Still Photography School and in June 1960 I arrived at Laughlin AFB assigned to the Base Photo Lab.

The Base Photo Lab NCOIC was Master Sergeant Eric McGough, a no-nonsense Georgia native with a thick southern drawl; next in rank was SSgt Jack Dempsey Lyons from Florida. Both were later reassigned to the Wing Photo Lab, as were most of the airmen there at the time. The base lab was the place to be while awaiting TOP SECRET clearances required for work at the Wing Photo Lab.

Others I recall at Laughlin were Airman First Class (A1C) Mike Bevz, A1C Ernie Libertore and the remainder, like me, were junior airmen in training. Some of those in the group were Alfred Robertson, William Duette, Jimmie Hendricks, Larry Ames, Paul Sharp, and Gustavo DeLa Garza. Some who joined the lab later remained after Air Training Command took over support functions. TSgt "Nick" Nickerson did join us at the Wing Photo Lab, but Cecil Dean, Eugene Monaghan and ex-Marine Richard Thrun remained at the Base Lab along with Bevz and Libertore.

During a night alert, one of our U-2s went down in the desert area near the base. A1C Jimmie Hendricks was on duty that night and accordingly had the job of photographing the crash area. Upon returning to the lab, he took the initiative to call for help. Together Jimmie and I worked through the night processing film and making finished "contact" prints which were on the Wing Commander's desk by the start of the workday. Jimmie did a bang-up job. The Colonel was pleased enough to send a Letter of Commendation for us. Of course, the Colonel didn't have our names so the letters somehow found their way into the promotion packets of two other airmen. Jimmie deserved to be credited with a great job at a crucial time.

Jimmie told me that while he was photographing the crash site, at one point he needed to stand in the cockpit to shoot the instrument panel. The officer in charge of the site cautioned Jimmie not to move "because the idiot didn't replace the pin in the ejection seat." I didn't have any idea who the officer in charge was or the "idiot" he referred to. I guess the pilot had thoughts of ejecting and then changed his mind. I'm sure the officer in charge didn't really think the pilot was an idiot but it was one of those times when everyone was very excited and stressed.

There were so many camera assignments it is difficult to single out any one as a career highlight. However, there was one I considered as less than stellar. I had been sent to record the return of our birds from a TDY in Australia. I went out with standard equipment for a daylight shoot. The arrival was delayed and when the planes finally came in, it was almost dark. My assignment was to photograph the returning pilots beside their aircraft with their families and friends. I only had flash bulbs suitable for fill work and they were not very powerful. The result was photos that showed the people and

Gene Stoddard 1961.

Photo specialists at Bien Hoa AB 1964, standing left to right: John Washburn, Larry Wachter (Tech Rep), Sgt McDowell, Airman Rodriguez; kneeling left to right: Airmen Salisbury and Clampit.

planes reasonably well but with a completely black background. To my horror, three or four photos made the front page of the *Del Rio News Herald,* the local newspaper, with my name as the photographer.

I enjoyed my assignment in the Photo Lab and I was giving serious consideration to my career after the Air Force. Photography seemed like a very real possibility for me until President Eisenhower visited Laughlin on October 24, 1960 while in the area to meet Mexican President Lopez Mateos. The occasion was to mark the opening of the new international bridge that spanned the Rio Grande between the two countries. On the previous day, I had photographed the arrival of Secretary of State Christian Herter. For me that was a life-changing experience because I decided then not to pursue a career as a news photographer. It was an unpleasant side of the news world as the "pros" jockeyed for position.

When our TOP SECRET clearances were approved, most of us were then transferred to the Wing Photo Lab where the precision processing of aerial roll film was done. The lab itself was in a windowless building near the flight line with a convenient walkway to the flight line coffee shop. At times an armed guard would be posted at the main entrance of the building, such as during the Cuban Missile Crisis. Admission to the building was strictly controlled.

The Officer in Charge of the Wing Photo Lab was Captain Roy B. Duggan, a real interesting character. I was told he was a survivor of a WWII paratroop platoon and his rank was established through a field commission made permanent by Act of Congress. My account of his record is strictly hearsay. His confidence was perhaps evident by one half of a phone conversation I overheard. It involved a dispute with a superior officer regarding base policy of additional duties for lab personnel, such as kitchen patrol or KP. It negatively affected the ongoing lab operation during the Cuban Missile Crisis. I can still see the Captain as he tipped back his chair, put his feet on the desk and drawled, "Well, Colonel, that's not the way it's going to be." I believe he was talking with the ATC base commander, Colonel Byerts. The end of the story was that Captain Duggan did indeed get his way.

During the Cuban Missile Crisis, two state-of-the-art prototype Kodak machines were installed to speed up processing of duplicated films. After October 1962 we were extremely busy until we stood down for removal to Tucson in 1963. At times we operated for long periods without sleeping, the longest such period I recall was 52 hours. There were breaks and catnaps, but no bed rest. All of our equipment was pressed into service, including the mobile unit, which we had taken to Hawaii for Operation Dominic. We also had a contingent of extra TDY photo personnel from other bases to help handle the heavy workload. Two of the TDY personnel were Stanley Knutson, whom I'd met in photo school and Eugene Mock.

One of my additional assignments was filming U-2 training flights. I never saw any of the movie film I shot; I can only assume it was okay because I never heard a complaint. The idea was that the pilot trainees could see and evaluate their landing and takeoff skills. The filming was done from a level-on position below the control tower.

A few highlights of our off duty life came as improvements were made to the base recreation facilities. The addition of a bowling alley, Airmen's Club and library probably created havoc in the economies of Del Rio and Ciudad Acuña bars. The new swimming pool was directly across from my barracks and was a Godsend on some of those brutally hot summer days. Even when we were not at the pool, we could enjoy some of the more attractive female swimmers a short distance across the road.

I was assigned a TDY as part of a large operation called Joint Task Force 8, also known as Operation Dominic. It took place in late spring of 1962 and the objective was in support of atomic tests over Johnston Island in the Pacific. For this operation, a large, unused section of Hickam AFB, Hawaii was opened for our use. We lived in pre-WWII barracks that boasted patches covering the bullet holes from the Japanese attack on Pearl Harbor and Hickam Field. Surprisingly, the barracks had small individual rooms, rather than an open bay construction.

There was one detonation over Johnston Island that I watched with others from the ridgepole of our rickety old barracks. The remaining operations were delayed and then cancelled. After several weeks in beautiful Hawaii, we packed up and went home ahead of schedule. I never visited the Arizona Memorial, something I regret to this day.

One fun thing at Hickam was a design spray painted on our shirts. Oscar the Crow, a four-foot cigar-chewing model of the Old Crow Distillery symbol, became the mascot of our Crow Flight detachment. One of the flight line crew was an artist and he had devised a set of stencils with a special version of Oscar the Crow in native attire. The shirts caused something of a stir at Fort DeRussy and Waikiki. I'm afraid my shirt disappeared after my discharge.

In September 1962, I was sent to Guam on another TDY. The announced purpose of the TDY was support of high altitude weather sampling, but who knew. Two of us were sent out. Our only function was to set up a field photo lab from standard field issue. This would be done only in the event we were sent to an un-named forward position. My only duty was to inventory my equipment and wait.

Once we arrived, Airman X (as I refer to him here) and I had no real functions but were assigned "make-work" duties. I was assigned to an air-conditioned Quonset hut where our pilots suited up. All I had to do was drive the pilot to his plane in the air-conditioned truck. Most of my time was spent drinking coffee and playing cards with our private cook, Airman Arby, who had been temporarily assigned from the main mess hall. As I recall, he made perhaps the world's finest coffee.

Guam was beautiful, the climate was ideal, and I had a great duty assignment. Then Airman X struck and the tides turned. He was a unique person with a Bronx, New York, attitude and an abrasive personality. I figured the Wing Lab had probably sent him for the express purpose of being rid of him for a while. He had been assigned to do errands for Lt. Col. McCaslin and the Operations Center staff. I'm not sure what he did to irritate Colonel McCaslin or the staff, but he certainly messed things up for me. The upshot was he got my cushy job and I got his in the hot, un-air conditioned operations building with no cook and no world-class coffee.

Lt. Col. McCaslin was a tall man who barely fitted in the cockpit of his U-2. I was told his head was in a forward position and his helmet contacted the canopy when he flew. He seemed an affable person and I never experienced a problem with him or anyone else. I concluded then that Airman X had been at fault. My new duties then became mainly the destruction of classified data and making up the weekly football pool.

An interesting side note concerning Airman X—before we departed on that TDY, we were both issued some travel equipment. Among the items was a B-4 bag. On his B-4 bag was the name of the previous user, Second Lieutenant (2Lt) Powers, Francis G.

While on this beautiful island, I purchased my first 35mm camera and began taking some personal photos. I swam at Tarague Beach, played pitch and generally enjoyed the scenery. There were inter-service football games and even cheerleaders.

An interesting feature of our rooms was a live gecko-lined ceiling. They became a little noisy but in general caused no problem. In fact, their presence significantly reduced the bug population. The shower and other facilities were conveniently located between two bays. The rooms had no windows, just louvers. The barracks building was three stories high, built of sturdy concrete, which would shortly be put to the test with Typhoon Karen.

One evening in October we received a general alert. Everyone was to report to their duty station immediately. There was a mad scramble and for a time it looked as if we would soon learn the location of that un-named forward area. Our gear was put on transport planes that were loaded and idled on the runway. We were lined up and given shots for some unusual destination. Luckily, the alert status was changed and not only had I been fortunate to miss the shots, we were not leaving for a combat zone. We learned later the reason for the alert was the discovery of missile sites in Cuba.

A couple of weeks later we were warned of an approaching storm. It turned out to be one of the most powerful typhoons ever recorded for the area. November 11, 1962, Typhoon Karen came ashore with devastating effect. As I recall there was no loss of life on Guam, but there was tremendous loss of property.

After the initial storm warning, Lt. Col. McCaslin informed the area commander that our two U-2s were incapable of taking off if the winds reached a certain velocity and evacuation would then be impossible. The evacuation order was delayed and later the storm trackers predicted a direct hit. By that time, wind velocity exceeded the U-2's limitations. The planes were put in a hangar by the runway. Unfortunately, the storm

Photographic Lab, Group I.

destroyed the hangar and the planes inside were too badly damaged to fly. After some scary work removing twisted and swinging girders, we removed the U-2s, crated them and flew them home on transports.

Without planes, our operation had ended. We didn't leave immediately and therefore, we enjoyed the pleasures of post-typhoon life, such as K-rations, no showers or potable water. The storm had changed weather patterns and it didn't rain for several days. When it finally did rain, most of us rushed out on the lawn with a bar of soap. Although we could see the Pacific Ocean, the beach was off limits due to dangerous and poisonous creatures washed ashore in the storm.

Only slightly more pleasurable than my rain shower was my first cup of Hobo coffee. It was produced on a paint-can stove and boiled in a #10 can mooched from the mess hall, along with the coffee grounds. As much fun as this had been, we packed up and left for home.

Things were pretty much work and sleep for a while when I got back. We were processing film hot and heavy. Although I never knew many details, there was no doubt from the film of the existence of missile sites in Cuba. The only breaks we had were the results of too much cloud cover over the target area and no film to process. Sadly, we learned one of our pilots, Major Rudolph Anderson, was shot down over Cuba while filming those same missile sites. May a grateful Nation never forget him.

Another unforgettable character was Headquarters Squadron First Sergeant Russell Field. He was a powerfully built man who was a serious weight lifter. I was told he had once competed in the Mr. California Competition and came in second to Steve Reeves of the Hercules movie fame. Perhaps this was an exaggeration, but I never knew for sure. I do know that nobody messed with the "First Sleeve" in our squadron. While I'm sure it wasn't strictly legal, Sgt Field would make small, short-term loans of 5 for 6 on payday. Everybody always paid up. I'm almost sure he made more in his "loan" business than the Air Force paid him.

Sadly, the only time I was ever in the Base Chapel was on a photo assignment. I did occasionally attend the Lutheran Church in Del Rio where a youthful Reverend Ahlert J. C. Strand had a way of making me feel I was the subject of his sermon. Perhaps it was my conscience working on me, as it might well have been, but I think he was really a very good preacher. No fire and brimstone mind you, just strong lessons in personal conduct.

Between TDY's in 1962, I played on the lab's slow pitch softball team led by TSgt LeDuc and SSgt Loomis Robertson. While we lost every game, a good time was had by all. One game started off with a bit of excitement when a small rattlesnake was killed at home plate.

Events eventually wound down and I received an early discharge due to the 4080th SRW's move to Tucson. Had the move not forced an immediate decision on my part, it is quite likely that I would have re-enlisted and made the Air Force a career. That being said, I took the other fork in the road.

John W. Washburn

(Deceased December 12, 2006)

The following information was submitted by John prior to his death.

> I was with the U-2 program for 12 years and thoroughly enjoyed the camaraderie of the men I worked with. I was assigned to the NEPHO unit and worked with the cameras that were installed in the U-2 for the photo recon missions. During many operations, we worked around the clock to prepare, load and unload the cameras. I made a lot of life-long friends during that time, too many to list. Like all the other fellows, I went on TDYs with the unit but I felt badly being away from my family for long periods.

Buck A. Young

Baytown, Texas
Wife: Claire

On April 1, 1957, the 4080th SRW moved from Turner AFB to Laughlin AFB, and the first U-2 arrived at the base on June 11, 1957. I watched the plane land, but even as the Base Information Services Officer, I did not know what to make of this unusual plane. I certainly had no idea about its mission.

My wife, Claire, and I had made arrangements for Space No. 29 at the Rio Vista Trailer Park off Gibbs Street in Del Rio where we set up our Hicks mobile home. Rio Vista in English means "River View" but there was no river within sight of our home. In fact, the railroad ran behind the trailer park. I didn't have a clue how to set up a mobile home, but fortunately for me, there were a number of Air Force personnel already living there. Everybody pitched in to help get our mobile home connected, propped up and leveled. The wives brought over a pot-luck supper while the men worked on setting up our home. We immediately felt welcomed into the trailer park.

My job as Information Services Officer at Laughlin got off to a fast start. Colonel Willard Beauchamp summoned me for a staff meeting. I had the competent assistance of A1C Reginald "Dub" Lawley who had been best man at our wedding. In addition, my staff included SSgt. Larry Miller, A1C Dick Oakerson, and four airmen fresh out of basic training: Roger Newell, Alfred Warjas, Bill Hillard and Dewey Griffith and photographer TSgt. Jasper (J.J.) Derouen. This staff was responsible for publishing the eight-page tabloid called *The Laughlin Recon* printed by contract at the local newspaper, the *Del Rio News Herald*.

I was also responsible for community relations and with Colonel Beauchamp attended monthly meetings of the Good Neighbor Committee in Del Rio. In the summer of 1957, the Committee decided to hold a fundraiser for the planned October Festival. The fundraising event was to be a "bloodless" bullfight in Acuña, Mexico, across the border from Del Rio. Colonel Zemke, the Wing Commander, his Deputy Commander Colonel Nate Adams and Colonel Beauchamp joined six local citizens in the bullring at La Macarena to taunt, poke, provoke and generally intimidate the bull before running from it. Jim Thatcher and I were the wheelbarrow and shovel crew to clean up after the bull. The predictable result was that the bull was declared the winner, but it was a fun event enjoyed by all who attended.

1/Lt Buck Young 1958.

Supervising preparation of the base newspaper, November 1957. Left to right: A3C Roger Newell, A3C William Hillard, 1/Lt Buck Young.

In March 1957, almost a year after my arrival at Laughlin, I was reassigned to Sondrestrom Air Base, Greenland.

My first opportunity to return to Laughlin some 41 years later was the 2005 Reunion of the 4080th SRW. I attended with my daughter, Lila. It was an enjoyable weekend renewing old acquaintances and showing my daughter where we lived so many years ago.

Dressing Up and Stepping Out

"Experience teaches slowly and at the cost of mistakes."

James Frounde

The Development of the Partial Pressure Suit

David G. Clark started working with a knitting company in the 1930's and later left the company to start his own business manufacturing two-way stretch fibers used in women's girdles. Although his formal education ended at age 15 when he left school to work full time, he attended evening schools for courses in accounting and business at the insistence of his father. He earned no diplomas or degrees after grammar school, but he had an insatiable interest in science. By age 39 he had been granted six patents for items related to the knitting business.

Through his friend, E. J. Baldes, head of Biophysics at the Mayo Clinic, David Clark began research into the development of "G" or pressure suits. The pressure suit, required for flights above 65,000 feet were vital in saving a pilot's life if the aircraft lost pressure. Without a pressure suit to provide supplemental oxygen, the pilot had 60 seconds maximum before he became incapacitated. During his research, Clark became acquainted with a Navy flight surgeon stationed on the aircraft carrier USS *Franklin Delano Roosevelt*. He was asked by the flight surgeon to make an ear protection device for the men on the flight deck of the carrier; they had nothing but their hands covering their ears to keep out the jet engine noise. Through that contact, Clark pursued his production of the pressure suit and the company began blitz production for the Navy.

When the end of WWII came, the company anticipated an order from the Navy to cease production. However, the order was, in fact, just the contrary and the Clark Company continued production of the pressure suit.

In 1946 the Air Force became interested in the pressure suit for its own pilots. The future of aviation had a special niche to be filled by the David Clark Company. With a budget of $20,000, the Air Force ordered 20 pressure suits from the Clark Company. Through much trial and error and reviews by Wright Patterson, a final pressure suit was approved. With modifications over the years, the Clark Company has continued to make pressure suits for the Air Force and NASA.

Until recent years, all pilots went to the Worcester, Massachusetts factory to be measured and fitted for their custom made pressure suit. Now the company has 12 standard sizes of patterns for the suits with the exception of a couple of female astronauts who had to be custom fitted due to their petite size.

The Clark Company also designs and manufacturers helmets and ear protectors with microphones. Their ear protectors are in use by military and civilian aviation pilots and flight line support personnel.

4080th SRW Physiological Support Division

The Physiological Support Division (PSD) consisted of two groups to support the U-2 pilots in their flight preparations. The Personal Equipment Group consisted of about 30

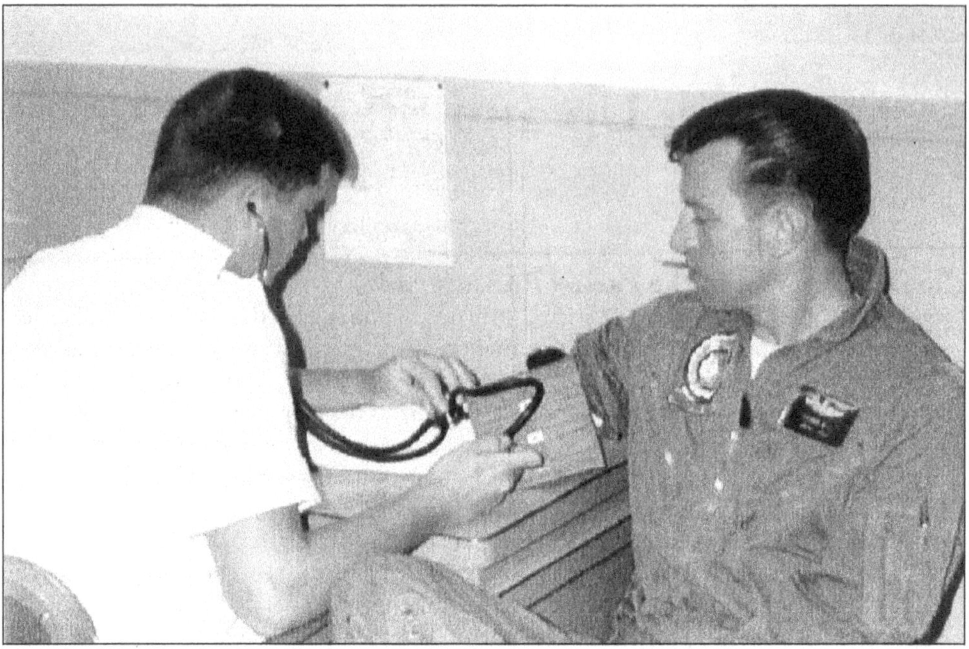

Buddy Brown beginning pre-flight physical exam with the Flight Surgeon.

technicians and the Medical Group consisted of about 25 fully qualified flight surgeons and medical technicians. The technicians in both groups were cross-trained to support each other on TDYs. It was not unusual for only four Personal Equipment technicians to be on duty at Laughlin when all others were on TDY.

Pilots scheduled for flights were given a physical by the flight surgeon on duty. (See the section Dragon Lady Doctors for additional information.) PSD operated a fully equipped kitchen and supplied the high protein meals each pilot ate prior to flight. Steak and eggs, the most common meal, was cooked on the spot and served to the pilots.

When the pilots were cleared to fly by the medical team, they came to the Personal Equipment unit where technicians assisted them in suiting up. Each pilot was assigned a locker for storing his gear—the long johns, pressure suit, parachute and helmet. Each parachute received an inspection every 90 days and was rechecked once a year.

Fully suited up, the pilots went to a room with recliners where they pre-breathed 100 percent oxygen for one hour. Once suited up, the pilot carried approximately 35 pounds of gear. The medical technicians were on hand to monitor the pre-breathing process and connected each pilot to a portable oxygen bottle for the van ride to the aircraft. When the pilot was seated in the cockpit, the technician disconnected the portable oxygen supply and connected him to the aircraft system. Then the technician went through an audible checklist to ensure that all hoses, belts, and connectors were at the appropriate settings. When the checklist was completed, the technician patted the pilot's helmet, climbed down the ladder and was replaced by the Mobile Control Officer to perform his checklist with the pilot.

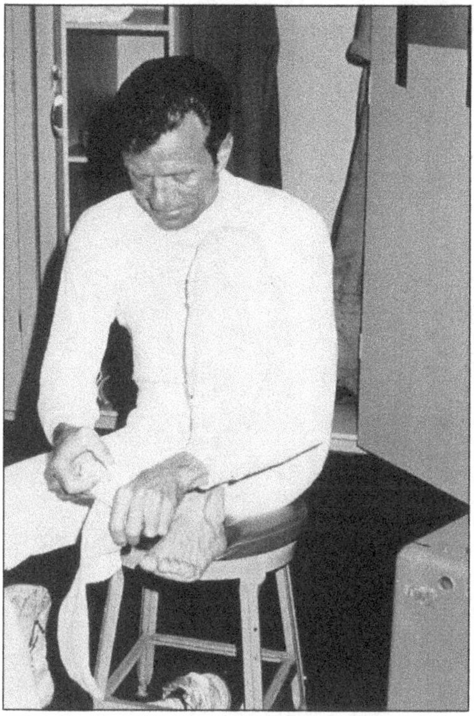

Buddy Brown dressing in the long underwear worn under the partial pressure suit.

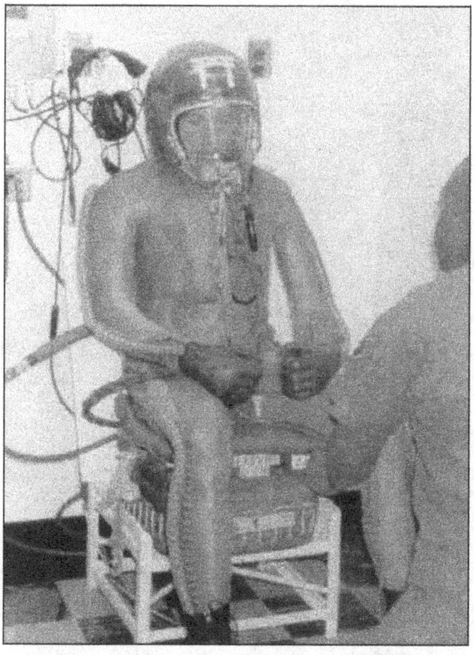

Buddy is hooked up by PSD Specialist Jessie Gamble to the seat kit system. Next procedure is pre-breathing 100% oxygen for one hour.

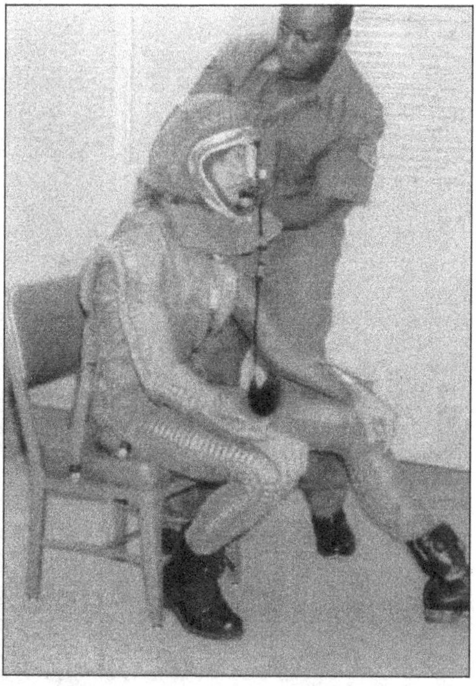

PSD Specialist Jessie Gamble assists Buddy with his partial pressure suit.

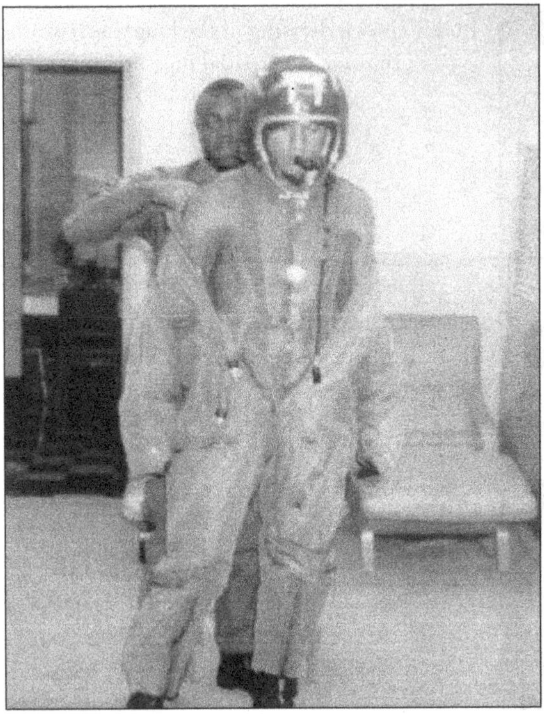

PSD Specialist Jessie Gamble assists Buddy with the outer garment which protects the partial pressure suit.

Buddy in the cockpit going through pre-flight check with the Mobile Control Officer.

A pilot is prebreathing oxygen while the flight surgeon performs a check of his vital signs. Photo courtesy of Lockheed Martin Co.

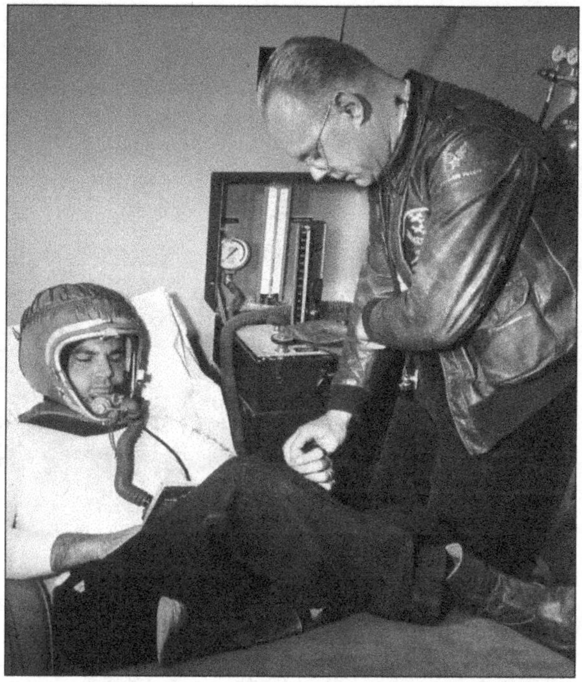

Technicians help the pilot secure connections on his pressure suit in preparation for the flight. Photo courtesy of Lockheed Martin Co.

A pilot arrives at the aircraft tethered to a portable oxygen tank. Once in the cockpit he will be connected to the aircraft oxygen. Photo courtesy of Lockheed Martin Co.

James W. May

Mesquite, Texas
Wife: Patricia

Naturally, all of my time at Laughlin AFB was not spent on base. I recall a fishing trip I went on with a Del Rio friend, Gordon McGonigle. The Air Force had a recreation facility at Lake Walk where we could rent boats.

Gordon really knew where to find the best fishing holes, but this particular time was rather scary. There was an upper dam and lower dam on the lake and we went to the upper dam. On the right side of the dam was a discharge tunnel about 10 or 12 feet wide, with water rushing from it into the lake. Gordon headed the boat at full speed into that dark hole in the dam. The water flowed so fast we inched our way inside about 20 feet. Our lantern was bright and Gordon tied the boat to what looked like hitching post rings on the walls. We had to use very heavy weights on the fishing line to compensate for the swift current. I had watched Gordon a few nights before make the weights from the lead in busted up old car batteries. He melted the lead and poured it into a large spoon.

We did catch a bunch of fish that time but I never wanted to go into that hole again. I don't know what Gordon does now but I heard his brother is a fishing guide at Lake Amistad. That love of fishing must run in the family.

I went fishing with a bunch of guys on the Devil's River before Lake Amistad was built. I liked to fish next to the old steam plant where the water was the clearest and cleanest I had ever seen. I caught bass, perch, crappie, catfish, garfish and even an occasional green turtle. When we got tired of fishing, we would go hiking around the countryside and look for wild javalina hogs running in packs.

James W. May, 1962.

After two years at Laughlin AFB, I was fortunate enough to meet and marry a Del Rio girl, Patricia Tabor. After a one-year courtship, we married at her preacher's home and was that a story worth telling. Sgt. Hand and another sergeant I worked with showed up drunk and crying, "James don't do it. You're messing up your life." The preacher made them stay in the kitchen during the ceremony.

After the ceremony, we headed out on our honeymoon to Dallas. We had gotten 31 miles to Brackettville when Pat said she'd forgotten her straw hat. It went with a certain outfit, so she made me turn around and go back for it. That's 31 miles driven, 31 miles back to get the hat and 31 miles again to Brackettville, a total of 93 miles for a bonnet. Was that what Sgt. Hand was trying to tell me?

We were married one year before my discharge from the AF and in that year, I went TDY to England for four months. TDYs were rough on the married guys and families.

On days off from Laughlin AFB, everyone learned by word of mouth where to go for fun. Paul Arnold and I played billards at a pool hall next to the City Café on Main Street. We also spent time at the bowling alley. Then there was the Rita Theatre in town or the Gay 90 Drive In Theatre on the highway to the base. Between paychecks, when money was short, the trunk of my car could hold three guys who would sneak into the drive-in. I guess the theater ticket seller thought I drove a "low rider" but we never got caught. Having a car made it nice to hang out at the local restaurants that had drive-in service such as Ceasar's or the High Hat.

Another fun place I found near Del Rio was Garner State Park which had a pavilion with a large outdoor dance floor. That's where I learned the Texas two-step.

On one three-day pass Clem Francis and a few of us guys rented a cabin on the Nueces River north of Brackettville. We spent time fishing and had a big fish fry on our last night out. During that weekend we stopped at the Devil's Sink Hole which wasn't a state attraction yet. The guys lowered me and another small guy by rope into the huge, deep natural hole. It was approximately 40 yards across and over 1000 feet deep. I was last to be brought back up, but at first the guys couldn't lift me, so they tied the rope to the rear axle of the Jeep Wagoneer and I was up and out fast. Before the Jeep was brought into the mix, I made a lot of promises to the Lord as I was hanging in space. I probably haven't kept all of them.

While on a stop over in Hawaii en route to Australia TDY, we were assigned to set up and receive our U-2s coming in to Hickam. We were all told the bad news that one plane had a "flameout" over the ocean about 500 miles out.

As the story was told to me, the pilot was asked for his coordinates so any ships in the area could do a rescue. To their amazement, he said he was coming on in. Now, I call that gliding! He would only make one pass to land which he did with all of us watching. You don't forget stories like that.

Hawaii was beautiful. A couple of guys and I went to Waikiki Beach, wearing our swimsuits under our jeans, and swam in the clear waters of the Pacific Ocean. Then donning our jeans over wet swimsuits, we went into town for a couple of very expensive beers. It was still a fun experience though.

When we departed Hawaii, we were island hopping; first to Cantoon and then Fiji. I have a very scary memory of Cantoon. The runway there is very short and with our fully loaded C-130 Globemaster, it took three attempts to get airborne. Each time the pilot would rev up the engines for a long time then the big giant would shoot off like a race car. Twice he hit the brakes with a lot of smoking and groaning from them. We would stop, turning around only a few yards from the waves coming in. After that experience, I am convinced – you pilots have brass ones!

After a fuel stop on beautiful Fiji Island, we reached our destination of East Sale, Victoria, Australia, about 200 miles southeast of Melbourne. We arrived at the end of winter and beginning of spring, October and November 1960. Their seasons are opposite of ours.

The people of Sale treated us very well. It was embarrassing being asked for an autograph. Some of their customs are a little different from ours. On my first day in town, another airman and I learned one such custom. We went into a pub for a cool one (no "cold" ones there). Before finishing our mugs, two more were set in front of us, courtesy of some blokes at a nearby table. The bartender said it was a custom to buy them one in return which we did. To make a long story short, we kept this exchange going until I'd had 7 or 8 mugs. I'm still unclear how that 19-year-old got back to the barracks. From then on, I was more careful with the ale.

Before our tour called Crow Flight VI was over I went to a sheep ranch for a big cookout of lamb chops, naturally. A local farmer took me kangaroo hunting. It was neat to see the kangaroos bouncing over fences.

Later I went on a two-day R&R to Melbourne. What a great city! There was an open house on the RAAF station for the local community, Royal Australian Air Force personnel and the press. My contribution to the event was to suit up in the high altitude pressure suit and helmet for a four-hour demonstration.

I thoroughly enjoyed that TDY; for me, it was a sad day when we packed up and returned home.

Late one day down at PSD the last U-2 pilot landed and was brought in to be undressed from his pressure suit and debriefed. Before he landed, the pilot, whom I refuse to name, was still airborne and needed to relieve himself most urgently. He got out the "pee" bottle, unzipped the flight suit but couldn't find the opening in his long-john underwear. After trying several times with no luck, he got out his survival pocketknife and cut a hole in the underwear. That's needing to go bad.

While we were undressing him, the large hole in front of his underwear had blood all around it. In his haste to take care of business, he had cut the end of his "you know what." He insisted on no stitches and a medic just cleaned the wound and put a band aid on it. I guess that's why he got hazard pay.

My second TDY was quite different; I spent four months at Eielson AFB, Fairbanks, Alaska. I have never been so cold or seen snow that deep in my entire life.

We arrived in the middle of March and returned home in the middle of July. That's really a good time to go there because we had an opportunity to see winter, spring and part of their short summer. Experiencing 24 hours of darkness and then 24 hours of daylight was strange.

On my one day off, I went up to the ski lodge to learn snow skiing. On the bus I talked with a guy who wore a big leg cast. He said he had broken his ankle a couple weeks back when he tried to ski for the first time. That's all I needed to hear and I no longer wanted that adventure.

One day while on duty, I had to go with the pilots to watch a survival film. The film actually showed how to build an igloo by cutting snow blocks. If the weather was bad, the film said to just dig a hole in a snow bank resembling a bear den and close up the hole. The film reassured us help should be on the way. I know that our country owes a lot to these pilots for all the dangerous places they fly.

Late one day, I noticed something was causing the pogos to stay on the wings of the U-2 on takeoff. To avoid aborting a flight because of the pogo problem, I was told to hold up one wing and another airman would hold up the other wing. As the pilot started his takeoff, we were to run like h--- with him until he could balance it. We only had to run about 15 or so steps before "Kitty Hawk" took off.

When we were leaving for home at the end of the TDY, we loaded aboard the C-130 for a nine-hour flight to Seattle, Washington. Every time I looked out the windows, all I saw were snow-capped, wicked-looking mountains. About three hours out, we had one engine catch fire. The pilot shut it down, and we continued on to Seattle.

After one more hour, an engine on the other side started smoking and it was shut down. We then returned to Fairbanks. We never unloaded the plane; we slept in chairs in the base terminal while a dozen engine techs overhauled both engines for about eight hours. One of the techs showed me a burned valve from one of the engines. I asked him, "What if two engines were lost on the same side?" He said it could still fly but would need to have the load lightened.

James and Patricia May, 2004.

I was a little nervous getting back in that old C-130 so quickly, but we flew on safely to Washington and then to Laughlin. I was returning to marry my fiancé, Pat Tabor. I thank all those pilots and engine technicians for knowing and performing their jobs so well that day.

Down at the Physiological Support Division, better known as PSD, after all the flights were in, one of the U-2 pilots asked us not to undress him. He said he wanted to see if, in a survival situation, he could get himself out of it.

Well, we all stood back, gave him some room and watched what kind of looked like Houdini getting out of a straight jacket. After about 20 minutes and a lot of sweat, he asked us for help. Since this was a serious matter to him, no one uttered a chuckle until the pilot was gone.

Many unusual things happened after the U-2 pilots came in from their flights. On one occasion, a pilot returned from a flight and was getting undressed as usual. Poor fellow must have had a stomach virus because he had completely soiled his pressure suit.

I was on duty that day but I got lucky because Senior Master Sergeant Clem Francis picked my roommate, Bob Wilson, to take the suit into our latrine and clean it. The outrageously expensive suit could not be laundered. Bob cleaned on it for quite some time but Clem smelled it and sent Bob back for more cleaning. Three checks of the suit after attempted cleaning and Clem finally said, "Condemn it!"

One lazy Sunday while I was on duty alone down at PSD where we stored the parachutes and flying gear, I was called and told to hurry up and bring out 25 parachutes to our C-123 cargo plane. The plane was carrying our baseball team somewhere for a game that day.

It took me a while to get them loaded into the van and out to the flight line to the C-123. Since they were in a hurry, the ball team was told to help me get them loaded in the plane. How was I to know they thought that metal D-ring was a carrying handle? As I recall, they popped open about six parachutes before they learned that the D-ring was not a handle. I returned to PSD for more parachutes and finally sent the team on their way.

Lewis C. Nelson
Hudson, Florida
Wife: Doris

My Early Days
In November 1952 I was assigned to the 305th Bomb Wing, 366th Bomb Squadron at MacDill AFB, Florida as a personal equipment technician for the B-47 and the RB-47 Stratojet. It was my home for the next four years, and temporary duty assignments (TDY) were quite routine during that time. On one TDY I went to Sidi Slimane, Morocco, North Africa for 90 days and on another 90 day TDY to RAF Brize Norton, England. Both TDYs supported B-47 recon missions over Europe and the Mediterranean Sea in the cat and mouse game of the Cold War; some of the missions even flew over the Soviet Union. Occasionally an aircraft strayed over the border; the cat would show its teeth, and the mouse would run for home.

In those days, the aircraft did not reach altitudes greater than 40,000 feet. The pilots wore a regulation flight suit, carried a survival pack, and cold weather gear, all maintained by the personal equipment section. MacDill AFB played a big role in the Cold War activities. Strategic Air Command (SAC) had B-47 wings in various parts of the US and TDYs were coordinated among those units. SAC aircraft were airborne 24/7 and armed with destructive devices ready for any situation. However, if the mission was uneventful, it was still considered to be a good training opportunity. Our B-47s flew into history and were replaced by the B-52 Stratofortress in 1955.

In November 1956 I was scheduled for reassignment to Turner AFB, Albany, Georgia. I knew a fellow who had recently relocated from MacDill to Turner; I called him and decided to drive to Albany to look around. My friend and I talked about the operation at Turner; I was interested to learn what aircraft was flown there. It was quite a surprise to learn the entire unit at Turner was scheduled to be transferred to Laughlin AFB, Texas. I thought it a bit odd I was assigned to a unit that was soon to be relocated. But those decisions were made above my rank, and my job was to do as ordered.

My orders for transfer to Turner came in January 1957 and indicated the unit designation was the 4080th SRW. I reported to the building noted on the orders. After I furnished a copy of my orders, the clerk said he knew the colonel would want to talk to me. The colonel was on base that day, but according to the clerk, he was usually at

The Ranch. Throughout my Air Force career I had heard a lot of unusual names and designations, but I had never heard of anything called The Ranch.

I was ushered into the Colonel Jack Nole's office; he was still wearing his flight suit. He welcomed me to the 4080th Strategic Reconnaissance Wing and the Dragon Lady program. Col Nole was a handsome guy, like one of those stereotypical photos of a jet pilot. He was easy to talk with and I felt quite at ease. He very thoughtfully asked about my family and if they were with me. I replied they were setting up housekeeping in Albany.

Col Nole knew I came from a bomb wing, and he said he was going to send me to a program across the flight line called the Black Knights, part of the 4080th SRW. The 4025th Strategic Recon Squadron flew B-57s. The colonel told me I would see equipment I had never seen, and he instructed me to absorb as much as I could in the next two weeks. We were scheduled for a TDY to California, but I had no idea what we would do there.

The following day I went to the new unit across the flight line. As Col Nole instructed, I rang a buzzer for access to the building. I met another new airman, James Childress, awaiting entry also. James had come from Gunner AFB, Alabama and said he had worked at the altitude chamber there. If this assignment was related to the altitude chamber, things were going to be interesting; I had never been through the chamber.

Inside the huge building, I saw a large board with names and a checkmark to indicate they were out of the unit. Their destinations were indicated as Yokota, Japan. James said he knew one name on the list, Harold Pfeiffer, whose destination was indicated as The Ranch. James said Pfeiffer had left Gunner six months earlier, but nobody knew where

Lewis Nelson (right) with Joe Jackson (left) at the 4080th SRW Reunion, 1987.

he went. There it was again, that mysterious name, The Ranch. Nobody had yet said what The Ranch was, where it was located or what went on there. All the enlisted men I met in the building were helpful and congenial; I saw some men sitting in lounge chairs hooked up to oxygen hoses. I would learn more about that in the weeks to come.

The B-57s would fly to altitudes above 40,000 feet and pilots were required to pre-breath 100 percent oxygen to remove the nitrogen from their systems. I observed the techs in the unit as they assisted the pilots with their pressure suits. For the next ten days, James and I took our turns at helping the pilots with their partial pressure suits. We joined the pilot and the personal equipment specialist in the air conditioned vehicle for the trip to the flight line. The specialist helped the pilot climb into the cockpit, connected all the hoses and transferred the pilot to the aircraft oxygen system.

After two weeks observation in the squadron, the orderly room clerk called that orders were ready for me, James Childress and another new man, Michael Rodriguez, to report to March AFB. As James and I cleared the base, we met an Air Policeman who also had orders for the same base. He was driving to March AFB in his new Ford Country Squire Station Wagon and invited us to ride with him.

In February 1957 the US interstate highway system was still a dream; we drove the famous scenic Route 66. The journey took four days through some beautiful country as well. When we arrived at March AFB on Friday, we checked in at the front gate and the AP pointed where our building was located. However, he said the building was completely empty. We drove to the building to look it over and sure enough it was not only empty but also locked tighter than a jail. James and I were on per diem and could not stay at the base. We spent the three nights at a motel outside the gate in Riverside and returned to the base on Monday morning.

The building we had observed to be empty on our first visit was now a beehive of activity with a group of men waiting outside. Some men were in fatigues, some in civilian dress. The door finally opened and Col Nole, who I had met at Turner, welcomed everyone. He called names from his list and said, "Fall in with your bags." The colonel called my name, James, the AP and Rodriguez. A bus pulled up, and we climbed onboard bound for a C-47 Skytrain on the flight line. Col Nole instructed the group to put our bags onboard, we were going for a ride. The aircraft held 27 people, and when everyone was onboard, Col Nole walked to the cockpit. I thought, "This is interesting; the colonel is going to fly the C-47." I noticed most of the people onboard wore civilian clothes, some guys even wore Levis. I was in fatigues.

Col Nole taxied and took off without a hitch. He flew in one direction for a while; I observed the sun on one side of the aircraft. Then we changed direction, and the sun was on the other side of the aircraft. The colonel was trying to gain altitude to get over and through a gap in the Sahara Mountains. From my window, I looked down and saw huge black spots on the ground. I did not know at the time we were flying over Camp Mercury in Nevada where the Atomic Energy Commission (AEC) had conducted atomic bomb testing.

Col Nole started his descent, but I still could not see any sign of life. When we landed, I saw a mountain range in the distance. Our aircraft had landed on a runway at the edge of a dry lake. The colonel taxied a short distance and shut down the engines.

The back door was opened, and I could tell we were in for an adventure. Two men in blue coveralls met us as we exited the aircraft with our bags. One of them said,

"Gentlemen, welcome to Groom Lake. You are on part of the Atomic Energy test site. Please follow my colleague into the building. You can leave your bags because nobody will bother them here." No one was allowed on this facility without approval at the highest levels of security.

Inside the building, another man in blue coveralls told us that photos and badges would be made immediately; badges were required to be worn at all times. If we were discovered without the badge, well, that was another story. This was a place of extreme security. We were told, "What you see, you forget." There was only one person we were authorized to talk to about our work, the man we worked with. Even mail was subject to inspection, and garbage cans were checked daily for any written material that was discarded.

Now to the important stuff. We were taken to the mess hall facility where our guide announced we would be fed by AEC personnel. I heard some men express their concern about being around the AEC site, but it didn't bother me. I can definitely say the AEC fed us well. We were assigned to quarters in permanent buildings, four men to a room. I roomed with James Childress, Harse Perkins and Mike Rodriguez. That evening when we went to the mess hall, James saw Harold Pfeiffer who had disappeared from Gunner. Pfeiffer promised to meet us the next morning, and take us to the units where we would be working.

As we approached the building the next morning, I commented on the brand new station wagon parked there, and Pfeiffer said it belonged to us. I later learned the real purpose of the station wagon. Pfeiffer, one of the members of the first group to work at The Ranch, told us there were no scheduled flights until the following day. He took us to an equipment storage room; everything was very different and new to me. We took care of Lockheed pilots the same as we did Air Force pilots. Some Air Force pilots would be arriving later to check out in the aircraft.

Pfeiffer took me to the personal equipment shop, and introduced me to Andy Eloff, a tech rep from Firewell Co. of Buffalo, New York, manufacturer of the oxygen regulator. It had many functions, but if the aircraft lost pressure, the regulator would kick in and deliver oxygen to pressurize the pilot's suit. Without the pressurized suit, the pilot would die in ten seconds. Eloff instructed me on the regulator while the other men worked with the pressure suit.

Four flights were scheduled for the next day; the other three guys in my group were required to be there because they were already familiar with pressure suits. I was not yet trained on that aspect of the job, but I would soon learn more than I ever thought possible about the partial pressure suit.

Next stop on our tour was the flight surgeon's office; James and I looked at each other, "Why do they need a flight surgeon?" I knew the flight surgeon took care of the pilots in the hospital on base, but the presence of one at this unit was unusual. However, neither of us was brave enough to express it on the first day. Until now, the name or type of the aircraft to be flown there had not even been discussed.

The next morning when we arrived at the building, everyone wore civilian clothes with no visible sign of rank, and only first names were used. Wearing his helmet, a Lockheed pilot was the first to arrive for his preflight processing, and I watched as Pfeiffer hooked him up on the oxygen lines.

I worked with Eloff on the pilot's survival pack; I was familiar with the B-47 survival pack, but this one was a new ballgame. We went over everything repeatedly; I was certain I didn't want anything to fail on my watch. During a brief period of relaxed conversation, Eloff told me he had commuted between The Ranch and his home in Glendale, California for several months. Every Friday he took the Lockheed C-54 from The Ranch to Burbank and returned on the same plane on Monday morning.

Pfeiffer took the pilot off the oxygen, put him on the walk-around bottle, and escorted him from the building to the new station wagon for the drive to the aircraft. When Pfeiffer returned, he took me to the hangar to see the aircraft. I thought it was probably a modified B-57. An armed guard was stationed at every building and badges were carefully scrutinized. Finally granted access to the hangar, Pfeiffer stood aside and said, "There it is." It was like no aircraft I had ever seen, and I'd been around a few years.

Pfeiffer said the aircraft, called the U-2, was classified Top Secret and a new language had sprung up to describe many aspects of the operation. For example, the U-2 was called an "article" not an aircraft and pilots were called "drivers." Bringing the article to The Ranch had been a covert operation of the first order. It was disassembled and ferried to The Ranch from Lockheed's Skunk Works plant in Burbank on a C-124 Globemaster. When it arrived, a huge canvas-covered cart was wheeled out and connected to a Jeep that pulled it directly into the hangar. Inside the hangar, the two wings and the fuselage were uncovered.

After the article was reassembled, Lockheed was responsible for testing it and resolving any discrepancies before it was assigned a number and turned over to the Air Force. While the article was visible on the ramp during engine testing, it was immediately returned to a hangar to prevent casual observation. Pfeiffer and I looked into the cockpit under the supervision of a Lockheed mechanic. As I walked around the article, I asked Pfeiffer about the part hanging under the wings. He explained they were called pogos the pilot would jettison after takeoff, and they would be reattached after landing. However, for training purposes, the pogos were retained throughout the short flight.

Then we watched as a Lockheed pilot launched in a U-2. After he dropped the pogos, he went almost out of sight in mere seconds. It was spectacular to witness. The Air Force pilots were not that far along in their training for a takeoff of that magnitude, but they would be soon.

I got to know some of the Lockheed personnel, Ray Gotti, Schumacher, Seiger, and four of the Lockheed test pilots, all great fellows and completely dedicated to the project. The next day, an Air Force pilot was scheduled to begin check out, training first in a T-33 Shooting Star. He had to hold the aircraft just above the dry lake bed at only 18 inches off the ground as he would have to do in the U-2. The Air Force pilot flew the T-33 several times to ensure he had learned the holding procedure well enough to move on to the real thing, the U-2. I thought it was a procedure not for the faint of heart.

A U-3A, the military version of the Cessna 310, was used as a chase plane with an instructor talking to the pilot of the single cockpit U-2. The Air Force pilots sometimes bounced the bird around, but for the most part they caught on fast. When given the go-ahead signal, they could pull the pins to release the pogos. Maintenance technicians in a leased Jeep raced to collect the pogos for reattachment after landing. All the vehicles at The Ranch were leased with not a single military mark on them, and all had civilian license plates from the State of Nevada.

Every Friday afternoon a C-47 flew to March AFB and on to Burbank with anyone interested in making the trip. March and Burbank were about one hundred miles apart. I could not stay at March AFB because I was on per diem and paying for a motel every weekend could get expensive. The mess hall facility at The Ranch transformed into a movie theater on weekends. Food at the mess hall was exceptional. A couple times a week we had steak with all the trimmings; breakfast included eggs cooked to order and bacon or sausage, toast and plenty of coffee. At first I didn't think there would be much to do there on weekends, but that opinion was quickly dispelled. Several guys notified the AEC guards they wanted to go hiking in the mountains surrounding The Ranch. The guards took the hikers' names and watched them with binoculars the entire time. No chance of getting lost with the guards watching.

Jack Nole came to the personal equipment shop a couple of times and asked me if there were any parachutes that needed to be repacked. When I told him we did have some, he said we would go into town the next day, town being his way of saying March AFB. After I stowed the chutes in the U-3A, he called the tower and off we went across the runway. Thirty minutes out of March AFB, he called the tower, requested a VIP slot on the ramp and asked that a colonel friend of his be notified of his arrival. When we landed, a "Follow Me" vehicle led us to the designated slot where an Air Force staff car drove up and a colonel stepped out. Col Nole introduced me to his friend who told me to put the parachutes in the trunk, and he drove us to the parachute shop.

I took the chutes inside the shop and explained to the NCOIC we needed them to be repacked as soon as possible. The sergeant commented the parachutes were quite dusty and asked where we were from. I told him I could not discuss that. The sergeant casually took the chutes and told me to come back tomorrow to collect them. I returned to the staff car and reported when the sergeant said the chutes would be ready. The colonel then went in the shop and asked the same sergeant how long it took to pack a parachute; the sergeant replied about thirty minutes. Since there were three parachutes, the colonel said he would return in an hour and a half to collect them. I had to pick up a prescription for the flight surgeon and make a visit to the pay office before we returned to the parachute shop. Col Nole went to pick up the mail for The Ranch which was directed to a post office box number at March. When we returned to the parachute shop, the sergeant told me he had called his colonel and explained what had transpired when we left the chutes. His colonel instructed him to "give them anything they want." With all the chutes packed and ready, we returned to the flight line where our aircraft was refueled and ready. We flew over the same black spots I had seen when I first came to The Ranch. Col Nole called the Groom Lake/Watertown tower with his authorized call signal for entry into the restricted airspace.

I was at The Ranch for 120 days and during that time, a number of Air Force pilots checked out in the aircraft. Rumors were circulating that the aircraft and personnel were being moved from Albany, Georgia to Del Rio, Texas. Housing in Del Rio area was scarce and rentals were being claimed by phone. My wife had called from Albany and talked with Stillman Long, a real estate agent in Del Rio, who arranged for us to have a rented house when we arrived.

Eight to ten aircraft were being sent from The Ranch to Laughlin AFB. Pfeiffer left The Ranch and returned to Albany briefly before his relocation to Laughlin AFB. Between January and June 1957, James Childress and I had moved to Albany. We were the only people who had already had one permanent change of location that year which made for a real dilemma. The Secretary of the Air Force would have to approve a second move. Col Nole told us there could be no waiver for a second move within one year. What Col Nole was really trying to tell us without being direct about it was to get our pay records, and get back to Albany to cool our heels for about forty days.

One of the men we met at The Ranch was going to buy a car in Riverside to drive back to visit his girlfriend in Georgia. Childress and I rode with him and Childress was dropped in Mississippi.

When I returned to Albany, I told my wife the problem with the move to Del Rio. It was a difficult situation to say the least. I met with a captain of the new group at Albany, and he told me I no longer belonged to any unit at Turner. With some time on my hands, my wife and I went to visit relatives in St. Petersburg, Florida.

When I returned to Albany, I went to meet with the owner of a moving company. I asked if the company had moved Turner people to Del Rio recently; the owner smiled and said he had made a million dollars on those moves. I explained my situation and told him I needed to be moved to Del Rio. I realized I was talking to the right person, and I was finally going to get a break. This man said the magic words, "Let's talk." The owner told me to get a copy of the shipping list when I moved from MacDill to Albany. He offered to move me from Albany to Del Rio; I was to sign the shipping documents and leave a copy of my new orders. He would enter the dates and send the orders to the Air Force office to get paid. The moving company owner said he had done this a number of times. He would send my household goods to Del Rio and then direct his truck to San Antonio to pick up an east coast bound load. The day after I talked with the owner of the moving company, his crew came to pick up my family's household things and we headed west on Highway 90. When we arrived in Del Rio, we checked out the house my wife had rented by phone, but we arrived before our household goods. I went to the 4028th Supply Office at the base and requested the loan of a couple of mattresses for my family to sleep on until our things arrived.

The next day I went to the 4028th SRS and reported in to Col Nole. He was quite surprised to see me. "What the hell you doing here, Nelson?" he asked. I wasn't supposed to be there for another 15 days. He asked if my family had arrived and I told him we already had rented a house in town. The colonel told me to take off a few more days and the wing would get orders covering me. By the time I returned to the base, my orders were ready, and I promptly sent copies to the mover in Georgia who had been so generous with me. I then reported for duty in the Physiological Ssupport Division (PSD).

TDY with the 408th SRW

In the dead of winter 1958, I went TDY to Eielson AFB, Fairbanks, Alaska on a nuclear debris collection mission, more commonly known in the wing as air sampling. The most significant thing I recall about that tour was it was so incredibly cold; I was happy to return to Texas when it was finished.

When I returned to Laughlin, Col Elsworth Powell, Director of Materiel, had been checked out in the U-2 in 1958. I had been trained in PSD to work with the partial pressure suits for the pilots. One day Col Powell called and asked for me: I was to be at the flight line in thirty minutes. An aircraft had flamed out and was waiting at the Naval Air Station in Corpus Christi, Texas, approximately 150 miles from Laughlin.

The colonel told me to get ready for an overnight trip. I learned early on with the 4080th that TDYs sometimes came on short notice, and I always had a small bag ready. The C-54 Skymaster we were taking to Corpus Christi had been recently repainted, and the paint was not even dry. Col Powell ordered the tape peeled off, and we were immediately airborne en route to Corpus Christi.

The Navy boys had helped our pilot out of the U-2 and pushed it into their hangar to wait for our recovery team from Laughlin. Without pogos to keep the wings level, they were resourceful and put a barrel under each wing. The first thing our maintenance techs did was install the pogos under each wing. Col Powell told the team the aircraft would be ready tomorrow morning. We spent the night in the Navy quarters, and the next morning the crew chief ran up the engine for testing. The same pilot was going to fly low to Laughlin making the pressure suit unnecessary. The Navy guys had not seen anything like a U-2, and our pilot put on a show for them by making a spectacular takeoff that almost stood the aircraft on its tail. The Naval Air Station is probably still talking about that takeoff. Laughlin called Col Powell to report the U-2 had arrived there. When we returned to Laughlin in the C-54, the paint shop was ready with the paint to start all over.

Crow Flight

In early 1959, I went TDY to Plattsburg AFB, in Plattsburg, New York on a mission called Operation Crow Flight for another sampling operation. Some of our crews went to Ramey AFB, Puerto Rico for nuclear debris collection in the southern hemisphere. Major Joe Jackson was our detachment commander at Plattsburg. We had two flights scheduled in one day, one for a 7:00 am takeoff. I went to preflight the personal equipment the night before and discovered an oxygen regulator malfunctioned. There were no spares. I was there all night in the altitude chamber testing it, but the regulator would not function properly. The next morning the pilot came in, and ate his steak and eggs breakfast in preparation for the flight. Major Jackson came in, and I had to tell him to "put him down," the pilot could not fly the mission. Jackson then called Laughlin to report a cancellation; reason, safety of flight. Later that day the regulator part was brought from Buffalo, New York and the flight was rescheduled for the next day.

Promotions became frozen, and I could see no change or improvement in the near future. I requested to be reassigned off the U-2 program to no avail. I made a trip to The Pentagon and met with some people I knew there. The result was a reassignment in July 1960 to Torrejon AFB, Madrid, Spain, where my family and I spent three years. We lived in town in a lovely house, and traveled throughout Europe, a great experience for all of us. When it was time for reassignment, I applied for MacDill AFB, but was assigned to Nellis AFB, Las Vegas, Nevada for three years. As NCOIC, I was responsible for five personal equipment shops at Nellis where the base trained pilots at Fighter Weapons School. I was up for promotion to Senior Master Sergeant E-8 with 22 years 6 months service and had been assigned a line number for the order of selection. However, in early 1968 my wife became very ill. With her illness continuing to be a concern for the family, I decided in 1968 to retire from a career that I had enjoyed. We returned to St. Petersburg, Florida where we had family.

After I retired from the Air Force, my wife was diagnosed with a cerebral hemorrhage, and I knew we had to have some good insurance benefits. I was hired at Sears, and worked there for 22 years. My wife passed away in 1978, and in 1990 I retired from my second career.

Gerald E. (Jerry) McIlmoyle
Venice, Florida

The Pressure Suit
The David Clark Company in Worcester, Massachusetts, made the first partial pressure suits for us. This entire process was done "in the black" with the CIA directing every aspect of the trip. The company also made full pressure suits for astronauts, helmets, earphones, mikes and other devices used by our bomber and fighter aircraft crews.

I went there in late 1956 or early 1957 with instructions not to bring military ID card or dog tags. We were told to bring only civilian clothes and no GI issue underwear. I went to David Clark Company to be fitted for two partial pressure suits. In my mind's eye, I can still see the humongous room with row upon row of sewing machines operated by women sewing bras and corsets, the original products of the company. In the middle of the room was an oldtime wooden stairway leading to a basement where the corridor ended at a green door. Behind the green door were a few people sewing what looked to me like flight suits. At the back of the room was a black door leading to the next room. Inside this room were only a few people and I was instructed to remove all clothes except undershorts. I was told to climb on the two-foot high elevated round platform and stand at a brace.

A stoop-shouldered, wizened old man entered the room. With a tape measure dangling around his neck, he wore a white shirt with sleeves held away from his hands by black armbands. This skillful man proceeded to measure every inch of my body, and I mean every inch. He even used a cup that he could adjust to determine the volume of my "you know what apparatus"! Then he said, "Okay, we are through. Come back in the morning. A car will come again for you. We will then determine any adjustments that must be made."

The next day I returned to the company. Again I was instructed to strip down, don a set of inside out "long johns" and then put on the pressure suit. The company people hooked it all up, showed me how it should be worn and proclaimed no adjustments were needed.

They gave me two bags containing two partial pressure suits and handed me a folder of airline tickets. The company rep told me, "The first ticket takes you to New York and you will stay at a designated hotel for two days. Go see all the sights, a ball game at Yankee Stadium, Statue of Liberty, Empire State Building and Grant's Tomb just like you are a tourist."

I did the tourist routine. On the third day I presented the tickets at the airline counter and flew all over the country, changing planes and airlines. Casper, Wyoming was experiencing a blizzard and I almost got stranded there, but continued my journey and finally arrived back in Great Falls, Montana where I had begun. This was a memorable trip for sure.

Joseph (Joe) Ruseckas

(Deceased February 2009)
Wife: Marcia (deceased May 2008)
Joe submitted the following prior to his death.

My own flight career began during WWII from February 5, 1942 to February 24, 1946. I served in the Air Force Reserves until my honorable discharge with the rank of Major.

Following my retirement, I was employed by Civil Aeronautics as a flight check pilot and had the opportunity to meet David G. Clark when I flew with him for his own check flight. That meeting was the beginning of a new career for me. Mr. Clark offered me a job as a pattern maker with his company. The current pattern maker was leaving the company on maternity leave and a position was available.

I was then employed by the David Clark Company. Inc. in Worcester, Massachusetts. The company had a Government contract and it designed, furnished and supported the pressure suits the U-2 pilots and astronauts wore for high altitude flights. The company was awarded the NASA contract for all Gemini flights. I was not assigned to the 4080th SRW but was "adopted" into the organization because of the close association with many of its personnel. Pilots came to the Worcester facility of David Clark Company to be measured and fitted with the custom-made suits. I accompanied them to Wright Patterson AFB for chamber flight qualification. It was very special for me being personally involved in the pressure suit project from design to implementation.

I had the opportunity to work with the Air Force and Navy to design and make full pressure suits for X15 pilots. Chuck Yeager was the first to be fitted and I was responsible for his measurements and fitting. The Navy was set to make an altitude record in 1953 in a Douglas 553. I went along on the flight in the bomb bay and recorded the altitude of 83,000 feet.

The Air Force got into the X15 project with Scott Crossfield. He did a test in a Clark suit that I measured and fitted for him. The U-2 program came along and pilots required a partial pressure suit. Every U-2 pilot came to the David Clark Company in Massachusetts. I accompanied the early pilots to Wright Patterson AFB to see that the suit passed testing before the pilots were assigned to the program.

Mr. Clark started out with a knitting company in the 1930's and later left to start his own company that made a two-way stretch fiber used in girdles. He became acquainted with a Navy flight surgeon stationed on the aircraft carrier, *Franklin Delano Roosevelt.* As early as 1946, the Air Force contacted the Clark Company about developing early model pressure suits.

Mr. Clark's flight surgeon acquaintance again contacted him and requested the company's help to provide ear protection for flight line personnel. Mr. Clark asked me to design the ear muffs and sent the early model to Pratt & Whitney for test. The end result was so successful a half dozen were made and sent to the carrier. A call came back almost immediately to make more. The Clark Company earmuffs have distinctive green domes with the letters "DC" and are presently used by many flight personnel. We later put headsets and microphones in the earmuffs and we

Joe and Marcia Ruseckas.

were the first to produce the headsets for football teams. It all started with the call to Mr. Clark from the flight surgeon aboard the carrier *Roosevelt*.

At the time I worked to support the U-2 project, my wife, Marcia, understood that I could not tell her where I was going or what I was doing due to the security classification. Like military wives, Marcia accepted my career choice and she ran the household and cared for our daughter, Connie, in my absence.

Marcia has suffered some major health problems in recent years that have left her incapacitated, but she was in those days, as she is now, my "Co-pilot". My "Co-pilot" was unable to attend the 2005 reunion with me, but my daughter, Connie, accompanied me and shared in the many memories we all recalled those many years ago. It was also a pleasure to meet some new friends as well.

Thomas J. (Woody) Woodall

Morgantown, West Virginia
Wife: Betty

It Started in Texas

I entered the Air Force in August 1961 from my home in Morgantown, West Virginia at age eighteen. Although I had traveled to Pennsylvania, Ohio, Maryland, Virginia and Washington, DC, I had never been to Texas. Basic training was at Lackland AFB, San Antonio, Texas during the hottest part of the summer. When I had completed basic, I was selected to remain at Lackland and attend six weeks of Medical Helpers School. Then I was assigned to attend Physiological Training Specialist School for another six weeks at Brooks AFB, Texas; actually it was just across town from Lackland. After graduation at

Brooks, I must have been ready for a real assignment; I received orders to report to the 4080th SRW at Laughlin AFB, Del Rio, Texas, only 150 miles west of San Antonio. I was destined to spend a great deal of my Air Force career in Texas.

Airman Richard Nielson became my guide at my new duty station in the Physiological Support Division (PSD). He also worked in PSD and spent two days showing me around the shop. When I arrived at PSD, I reported to Major Aubrey Mahaffey, Chief of PSD and MSgt James Kimball, NCOIC. Richard took me to the new duty section and introduced me to all the guys. My supervisor was TSgt David Watson who shortly thereafter became my training instructor and mentor throughout my Air Force career. Two other airmen, Jay Barnett and Donald Mathews, were also in on-the-job training (OJT), but they were about three months ahead of me. When I asked how soon I could start my OJT, Sgt Watson asked if I would be willing to stay after hours for him to catch me up with the other two airmen in the classroom. I agreed and within a month I was up with the other airmen. All three of us took our five level test at the same time, and we all passed. The five level was part of the skill level test we were required to pass to qualify for promotion. While we were in basic training, we were Level 1 Unskilled, Level 3 Training OJT, Level 5 Skilled, Level 7 Supervisor, Level 9 Superintendent.

In addition to Major Mahaffey, Sgt Kimball and Sgt Watson, the other NCOs in the unit were Clem Francis, Ralph Cline, Toby Bernstein, Clifton Perkins, Regis Fredette, Jesse Gamble, Walter Hand, Samo King, Larry Land, Billie Lloyd, Edward Sears, Eugene Sekinger, Kenneth Stevens and Joe Terrell.

In addition to Richard Nielson, Jay Barnett and Donald Mathews, the airmen in the unit were Edgar Darden, Bobbie McAffee, Tommy Miles, Elbert Parris, Sebert Quick,

Airman Thomas Woodall, PSD specialist, after hooking up the pilot. The next step would be for another PSD specialist to double check the hook up then the Mobile Officer would go through his checklist. The pilot in this picture is Jack Carr. August 1964

Kenneth Walker, Roger Wilson, Paul Arnold, Karl Kilpatrick, James May, Robert Wilson, and Gary Brady.

Assigned later were NCOs Walter Russell, Robert Spearman, Donald Linker, Raymond Gray, Mathew Dionisi, James Register, Bobby Hanks, Richard Peterson, Jack Zimmerman, Gilbert Franco, Paul Perkins and Roger Lau.

Airmen assigned later were Burton Kimball, Wendell Shinault, Dave Dwiggins, Wayne Mackinnon, Robert Cunninghan, Ronald Liford, William Miller, Larry Reynolds, Johnnie Rarbush, Robert Zasada, Carmen Montoya, Larry Ellis, Roger Griffin, Donald Roberson and Graham Malone.

As a PSD specialist, I was required to inspect and maintain high altitude partial pressure suits, helmets and gloves worn by the U-2 pilots. Specialists assisted crew members donning and doffing the special purpose clothing. When the pilot was ready to board his aircraft, the specialist integrated the partial pressure suit and seat kit and connected all the hoses to the appropriate connectors in the aircraft. I was also cross trained to perform the duties of a Personal Equipment (PE) Specialist. The PE specialist inspected parachutes, survival equipment, seat kit, non-high altitude helmets, oxygen mask and instructed the pilots on the use of the equipment.

I had been in the unit about two weeks, but my flight line badge had not yet caught up with me. Security with the 4080th SRW was extremely strict throughout the base, most especially on the flight line around the airplanes. In addition to identification of the

Thomas Woodall, Jim Eichnor, David Dwiggins and William Miller. The picture was taken at a nightclub at Ciudad Acuña. Eichnor was with the Medical Group. Woodall, Dwiggins and Miller worked at PSD. Sometime in 1962.

wearer, the badge indicated the areas that were approved for access. Air Police security could detain anyone without authorized clearance to an area.

An example of the tight security was demonstrated one day when Airman Barnett and I were sent to the Oxygen Shop a few hangars from our shop to pick up some seat kits that had been inspected by Mike Santo, the Tech Rep for Firewell. The regulator, manufactured by Firewell, was in the survival seat kit that was part of the pilot's life support system. I was later trained to perform these inspections. On this particular day, neither of us had our flight line badges. Our instructions were to have a NCO go with us to vouch for us if we were stopped by the Air Police. None of the NCOs wanted to go with us so Jay and I got into the Metro Van and proceeded on our own. Jay drove and said he would go inside to get the kits while I stayed in the van. Five minutes later a truck with four Air Police raced up to the side door of the hanger and rushed inside. It only took a few minutes for the Air Police to come out with Airman Barnett. Poor Barnett. He had his arms up, hands behind his head and they put him spread-eagle on the ground. Before I could decide what to do, one of the Air Police came to the van and told me Barnett wanted me to go back to PSD and bring Sgt Kimball to vouch for him. As I was starting the van, the same Air Policeman turned back to me and yelled, "Wait a minute! Where is your flight line badge? I replied, "I don't have one either." It took only seconds for him to jerk me out of the van and put me spread eagle next to Barnett. Sgt Kimball came a half hour later and pretended not to know us, but then he explained to the Air Police what had happened and he got us out of the mess. A couple other NCOs had their butts chewed out over that one for not ensuring we had badges.

Airman Thomas Woodall and Airman Carmon Montoya at Williams AFB, AZ, waiting on pilots undergoing Altitude Chamber training. Sometime in 1964.

Shortly after I started my training, a U-2 had to abort a mission with a maintenance problem and land at Barksdale AFB, Louisiana. Sgt Sekinger was on the recovery team from our shop and I was selected to go along as a trainee. A C-123 flew the recovery team to Barksdale; it was only a short time before the U-2 problem was repaired and it was launched back to Laughlin. We then loaded up the C-123 and prepared to depart. The C-123, being a very noisy airplane, required everyone to wear ear protection. About fifteen minutes into the flight, Sgt Sekinger brought me a parachute and told me to put it on. Because of the aircraft noise, I really could not hear what he said, but I understood to put the parachute on. This counted as my third airplane flight; the first was from West Virginia to Lackland for basic training and the second was the flight to Barksdale. After we landed at Barksdale, I learned we had lost an engine. Considering the C-123 only had two engines, I realized the seriousness of the situation. Sgt Sekinger was pleased that I was calm during the emergency; he never did find out that I had no clue what was going on until after we landed.

We were at the barracks one day during an extremely hot day the summer of 1962. The barracks had air conditioning, but the equipment was struggling to keep up. Then strangely, a cold front blew through in the afternoon, and the temperature dropped about 50 degrees Fahrenheit in just minutes. Sgt Gamble had a Citroën automobile parked in front of the barracks with the windows up. With the rapid temperature drop and the heat inside the car, the rear window shattered. My room was at the front of the barracks facing the parking lot and I actually heard the windows explode.

On October 1, 1962 I was selected to go on my first long-term temporary duty (TDY) assignment. It was to OL-5 at Eielson AFB, Fairbanks, Alaska. Jessie Gamble joined me on the TDY and Jay Barnett was already there. October at Laughlin AFB was a pleasant 75 degrees when we departed. I recall landing in Alaska, exiting the C-124 and being so cold that I could not talk until we were inside the building and warmed up. We worked seven days a week, fourteen hours a day. I do not remember the time difference between daylight and darkness, but it seemed like it was dark most of the time. We were at Eielson when the Cuban Missile Crisis started.

Many of the 4080th veterans know about the Soviet Union overflight made by Chuck Maultsby. We launched the aircraft and waited and waited and waited. Word finally came five hours after he was due to land that Maultsby had landed in Alaska just across from the Soviet Union over 500 miles from where he had launched. Jessie Gamble went with the recovery team and we were told all flights were cancelled until further notice. We did not fly again for five days. We were all happy that Chuck Maultsby made it back safely, but we were saddened to learn Rudy Anderson was shot down over Cuba a couple days later.

It was extremely cold at Eielson on December 28 when we rotated back to Laughlin. Someone said it was minus 60 degrees Fahrenheit; I'm not sure it was that cold, but we all wore our Zone 5 gear: parka, gloves and boots. The C-124 Globemaster we boarded had not been warmed up before we arrived. With all the gear I wore, I actually went to sleep bundled up and I did not wake up until we landed in El Paso, Texas where it was a balmy 78 degrees.

It was only a short hop then to Laughlin. The TDY was a success and it added to my training for a job that I enjoyed.

When a flight surgeon was not in attendance during a TDY, one of our duties in PSD was to give the pilots a mini physical exam before they dressed in their partial pressure suit. The exam consisted of checking blood pressure, temperature and pulse. I was working alone for an early morning launch. Jessie arrived before the launch because two of us were required to be on duty. That morning the pilot's blood pressure was 160/102, extremely high by anybody's calculation. I checked his blood pressure again with the same reading. Here I was, an airman third class, on my first TDY, alone and scared to death. Many things ran through my mind that morning while taking the blood pressure reading. We normally did not perform these mini physical exams. I had been raised and trained to always do the right thing so I reported it to the Mobile Officer on duty. The mission was scrubbed. I later learned the pilot had a history of blood pressure problems. That information would have been helpful had I received it sooner.

The barracks at Laughlin had a laundry room with washers and dryers to use free of charge. Since we were always short of funds, it was a great way to save money. One of my friends who shall remain nameless was doing his white underwear. At the last minute he decided to throw in a ***red*** civilian shirt. Of course, the result was his white underwear was now a pretty shade of pink. He picked up the nickname "Pinkie" until someone told him to wash his underwear in Clorox bleach to remove most of the pink color.

On January 25, 1963 I was selected to go with a recovery team to Fairchild AFB, Spokane, Washington. One of our airplanes had landed there with a maintenance problem. This time I was the only one from my shop selected to go. I didn't know how many airmen one- stripers had ever been selected to represent the shop for this type mission, but I was thrilled the brass had that faith in me. I had a friend from tech school who was stationed at Fairchild. When I learned it would be the next morning before the airplane was fixed, I called him. We met at the base cafeteria and had a nice visit. My excitement about being selected for this mission did not end when we returned to Laughlin. I learned I had been promoted to Airman Second Class; I could add another stripe to my sleeve.

Each shop within the 4080th SRW was identified by different colored caps. We were allowed to wear baseball caps with our logo stitched in white. Operational Maintenance Squadron (OMS) wore green caps, Field Maintenance (FM) wore red, Armament-Electronics (A-E) wore black and Physiological Support Division (PSD) wore dark blue. Not only did it make us feel special, but on the flight line it was easy to identify who worked in which shop. In those days baseball hats were sold with straight bills. We spent time wetting the bills and putting rubber bands on them to get that exact curve so we did not look like dorks. A few years after I left the Air Force, my family and I attended an air show at Andrews AFB, Washington, DC and viewed a U-2 on display. The first thing I noticed was an airman wearing her dark blue PSD cap standing next to the display.

In March 1963 I was selected to go TDY to OL 18 at Panama Canal Zone. Jessie Gamble was the NCO who went with me. Since he and I had been to Alaska together, we had become friends off duty as well. Jessie liked to clean the section and I liked to dress, hook up the pilot and do all the inspections on our equipment. We made a deal. He would keep the section spotless and assist me when I needed help. The arrangement worked out well, but we kept it between us because he was actually the one in charge. We were blessed with crew members who also liked it.

Robert Wilke and Don Webster were two of the pilots with us. Major Wilke set up a Jungle Survival School for the crew members, and Jessie and I were invited to attend. We did everything the pilots did, including being hooked up to a parachute harness in the water with a Mae West flotation vest under our arms. We were pulled backwards through the water 100 feet behind a motorboat. We were instructed to wait until we were pulled under before releasing the parachute harness and deploying the Mae West vest. Another exercise was for each of us to be hooked up to a parachute harness and put on a platform in a tree. We were instructed to step off the platform, stop the swinging motion then release the harness and drop four feet to the ground. Then we continued on into the jungle for more training. I have a vivid memory of eating an iguana, and I'm glad to say that was the last one I ever ate.

Major Wilke and Captain Webster loosely organized us into a basketball league while we were in Panama. Webster played on the team and Major Wilke was the coach. I had played basketball in high school so I was recruited on the team. Other squadrons from the base participated in the league as well as units from the nearby Army base. We took third place. Not too shabby since we had never even practiced together.

Don Webster scheduled a tour of the Balboa Beer Brewery for our group, and a bus picked us up at the detachment. The Balboa staff took us on a tour of the plant and then to their visitor center. We were offered samples of all the different kinds of beer they made in addition to a variety of cheese and crackers. The most interesting person at Balboa was a gentleman who was the "Beer Taster." Our group threw a lot of questions at him, such as: How can I get a job like you have? How many beers do you get to taste every day? We all had a great time and it was a nice break in the routine.

I had the pleasure of working with Captain/Dr. Emory J. Sobiesk, a Flight Surgeon in Panama. His desk was in our duty section so Jessie and I became well acquainted with him. At the time the Air Force had a policy that stated a supervisor was required to complete a performance report for a subordinate under his supervision for 90 days or more. For that reason, our TDYs were usually no more than 89 days. We were delayed in Panama past the eighty ninth day and Dr. Soviesk was asked to do a performance report for me. It was a great evaluation and I'm sure it helped my promotion to Airman First Class.

When I returned to Laughlin in June 1963, I had orders directing me to report to Davis Monthan AFB, Tucson, Arizona on July 3. I learned from Dr. Sobiesk he was also going to Davis Monthan and would be driving there. He invited Bert Kimball and me to ride with him.

Since the entire wing was being relocated to Davis Monthan, we helped pack our shop. I helped Regis Fredette move bins in the supply room that had not been moved in years. Behind one of the bins was a parachute block, a piece of balsa wood cut to fit at the rear of the ejection seat behind the seat kit. The purpose of the block was to allow the parachute to rest on it and take the weight off the pilot's shoulders during flight. Each pilot had one carved to their preferred size with their last name on it. The one I found had the name Powers on it. Sgt Fredette quickly grabbed it out of my hands and said he would take care of it. I never saw that block again.

I took a 30-day leave in September 1963 and planned to use the military hop system to get home to West Virginia without spending a lot of money for commercial airlines. I signed in at base operations in the tower at Davis Monthan, and after only an hour, I was told a T-39 was leaving for Wright Patterson AFB, Dayton, Ohio. They had one empty seat. However, there was a general officer onboard and I would have to ask permission to ride. I asked and was approved. An officer signed in after me and tried to bump me off the flight, but he was denied. It was a first-come first-served operation and I was there first. A few hours later we landed in Dayton and I took a bus the remainder of the way home.

When I was ready to return to Davis Monthan, I went to Andrews AFB, Washington, DC, where my oldest brother was a Senior Master Sergeant and the NCOIC of Personnel. He arranged for me to get on a C-54 going to Kelly AFB in San Antonio, Texas. There were no other flights bound for Tucson and I had to take a bus the remainder of the way to Davis Monthan.

On November 20, 1963 we received word that Joe Hyde's U-2 went down in the Gulf of Mexico. It was in the news until November 23 when President Kennedy was shot. Captain Hyde was one of our pilots flying TDY out of Barksdale AFB. All of us working in support of these brave men took it personally when something happened to "our" pilots. Almost a year later on September 18, 1964, Robert Primrose crashed due to a gust of wind. The same feeling of tragic loss gripped us.

In December 1963 I was selected for a TDY to OL 19 at Barksdale AFB, Louisiana that extended through March 1964. This was the detachment that flew missions over Cuba. Joe Terrell was the NCO from PSD and Bill Miller was the junior airman from our shop. Flights were launched daily and pilots flew every third day.

Captain David Ray was one of our crewmembers in the detachment, a very nice fellow. He had brought his family with him and they had rented a house off base. When he had an early morning flight, he drove his car and gave me the keys. He had asked me to take the car to his wife at 8:00 so she could have it during the day; she then drove me back to the base and picked him up when he returned.

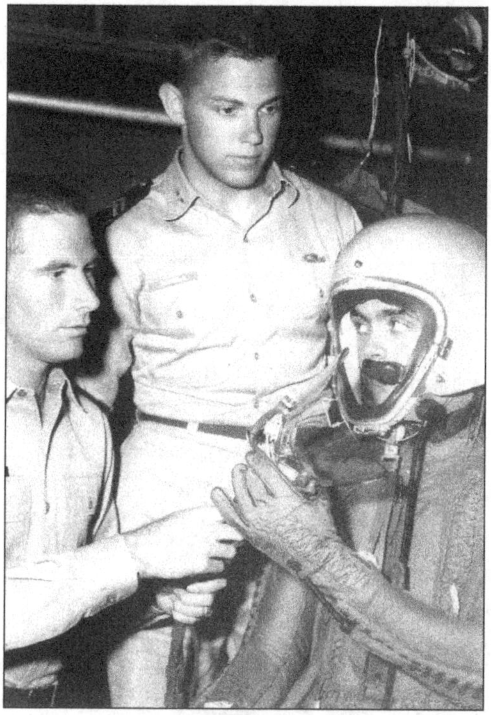

Partial pressure suit demonstration. Gary Dickinson, USAFA ' 64, John Patton, USAFA '63, Airman Thomas Woodall, PSD (in suit), June 1962.

Most pilots carried a knife strapped around their ankles. Captain Ray had a handmade knife purchased from R.H. Ruana Knives in Bonner, Montana. It was a large Bowie-style knife and I always had admired it. He asked if I would like to purchase the knife and I told him I was not sure I could afford it. The knife was too heavy to be strapped to his ankle. Captain Ray asked me to purchase a Buck knife at the PX and he would trade me even for the Ruana knife. The Buck knife cost $12; it was a bargain for the handmade Ruana knife. Years later I gave the knife to my oldest son and told him the story of how I had received it.

During this time we worked seven days a week and many hours during the day. The U-2 was scheduled to take off, fly the mission, land, and the film was immediately offloaded. A T-39 waited for the film and flew it directly to Andrews AFB where it was then sent daily to the interpretation facility. There were three men in our shop; two were required for launch and one for recovery. Joe and Bill had taken some time off, but I had worked 21 straight days with no time off. Joe knew I had family in the Washington, DC area, and he asked me about taking some time off. He talked with Captain Ray about approving a three-day pass for me and getting me on one of the T-39 flights. Captain Ray talked with Lt Col Joe King, the detachment commander, and received approval. I had three brothers and one sister who lived near Washington, DC; it didn't take long to

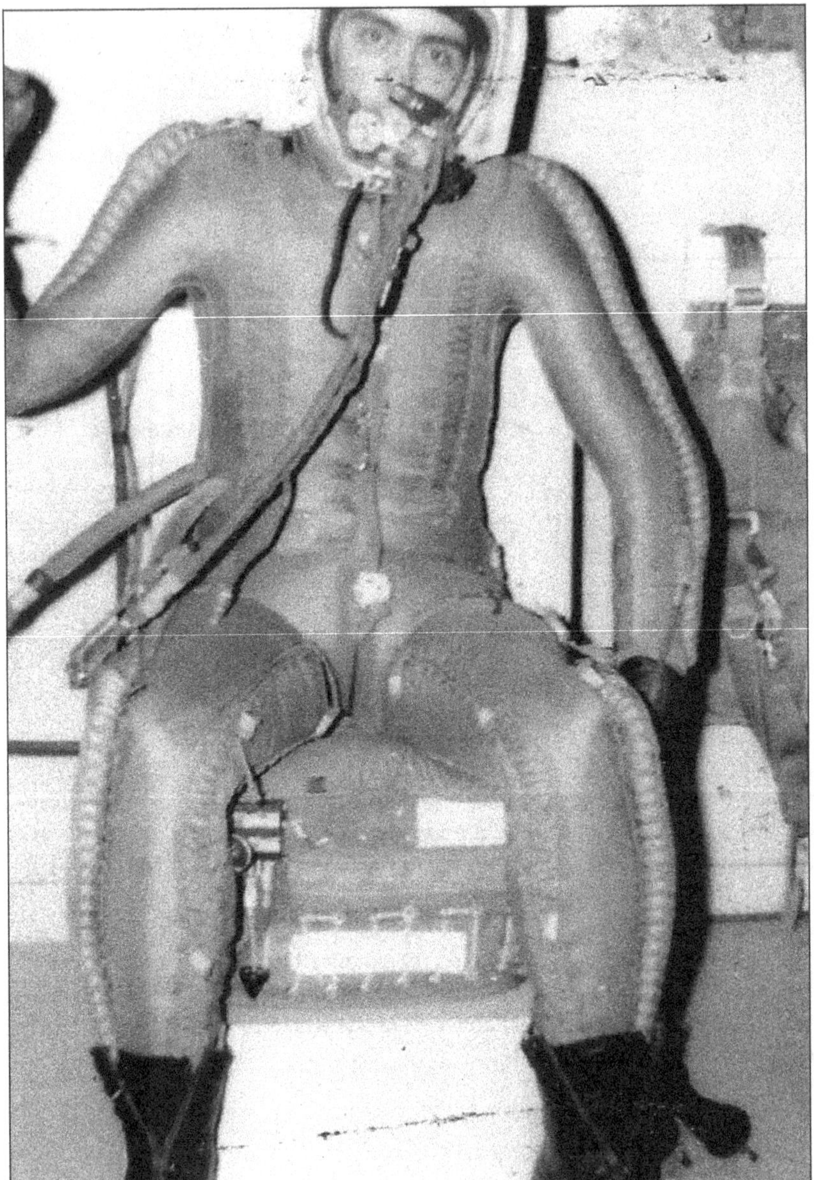

Airman Thomas Woodall, PSD, in partial pressure suit. Note that the left hand is pushing the "push to test" button that inflates the suit. This was done after dressing the pilot in the PSD shop and also after hooking up the pilot in the aircraft. The test was for proper inflation, to check for leaks around the face shield and to make sure the seal did not leak around the pilot's neck. The seat kit had survival rations, an inflatable life raft and a life support system in it. The life support consisted of a regulator that was set to inflate the suit in case of a rapid decompression. It also had a small oxygen bottle in it to supply oxygen to the pilot in the event of a bail out. October 1962. (Note - a pilot would not perform this test. A PSD specialist would push the button. Woodall is only doing it in this picture for demonstration).

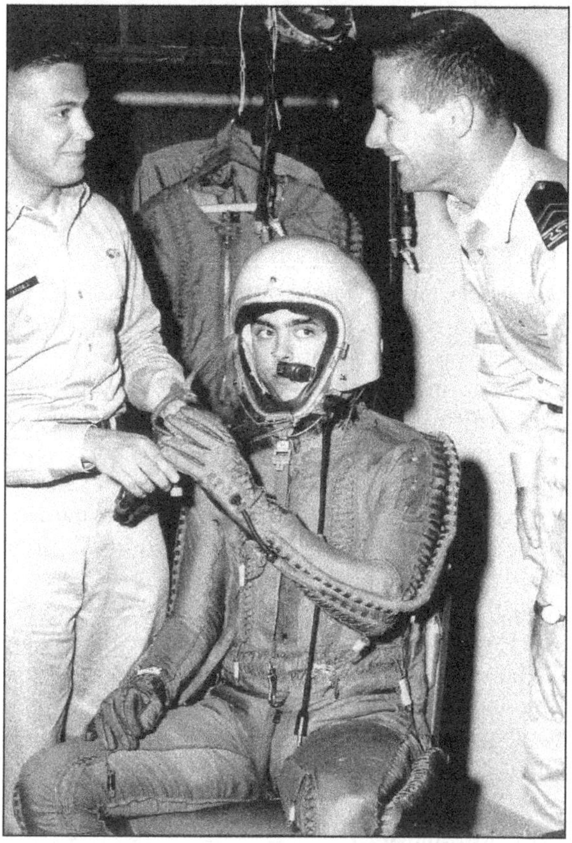

Partial pressure suit demonstration. Gary Dickinson, USAFA '64, John Patton, USAFA '63, Airman Thomas Woodall, PSD (in suit), June 1962.

call them and make arrangements to meet me. My parents came from West Virginia and we enjoyed a mini family reunion.

On my last day, my brother who was assigned to Andrews took me to the base to catch my return flight. When I checked in, I was told I was not listed on the manifest. It was impossible for me to get on the return flight. My brother drove me to the commercial airport where I bought a ticket to Shreveport, Louisiana. I was one day late getting back, but it was an excused absence because Captain Ray had forgotten to list me on the return manifest. He offered to pay for my ticket, but I was so appreciative of being allowed to go visit my family, I declined the offer.

Security around the U-2 aircraft operation was always extremely high. One of the airmen in my unit got into serious trouble for talking about our mission to the wrong person. It was a situation where the airman was just trying to impress a couple of young ladies, but was overheard by someone who turned him in as a security risk. Rumor was that he told the girls what time the airplanes took off so they could watch from a nearby road. The airman was reduced in rank and reassigned to another job. I saw him a year later and he had regained his lost stripe. He was sad about being taken out of the U-2 program. The testimony of Detachment Commander, Lt Col Forest "Whip" Wilson saved him from a jail sentence. The airman said he was extremely grateful that Col Wilson saved him from a ruined career. The airman, only nineteen, was a good person; he had made a serious error in judgment.

We rotated back to Davis Monthan in March 1964. Tucson was a nice area and we did a bit of sightseeing around the area. We also hunted deer, dove, duck, quail and turkey, and gave the married guys any game we bagged. Money was short for everyone, and especially for one of the fellows with a family.

On June 6, 1964 I went on my last TDY to the most coveted destination: OL 11 at RAAF Laverton, Melbourne, Australia. A C-130 Hercules flew us and the equipment to Australia with stops at Hawaii and Fiji. I don't recall how many hours the flight lasted, but it seemed like forever.

Airman Edgar Darden joined me on that TDY. Nicknamed "Dude", Airman Darden was the senior airman and a pleasure to work with. We only flew on Tuesdays and Thursdays so we had a lot of time off.

There was an English Rover four-door sedan that passed from one detachment to another during each TDY. Another airman and I bought the car and split the cost of $120. Since he and I did not hang out together, we made a deal to share the car every other day. The steering wheel on the right side took some getting used to. I always said that just because I was left handed did not mean I liked to drive on the left side of the road. We had to put in a new clutch while we were there, but we did the work ourselves and saved some money. When we left Australia, we sold the car to two new airmen for $60 each. What a lucky deal that was.

I met and dated a young lady soon after I arrived there. She was in the Women Royal Australia Air Force (WRAAF) stationed at Laverton. She had bed check at 10:00 p.m. Sunday through Thursday. Only once did I return her late to her barracks. It was my last night there and the car became stuck in the sand on the beach, but I managed to dig us out. We spent a lot of time in Melbourne on weekends. It was a very nice city and the people were friendly. It was hard to leave when my tour was up. That was a memorable TDY because I turned 21 while I was there.

A group of us went to a night club for dinner and a show. The show featured a female impersonator. None of our group knew except me because my lady friend had told me. From our seats, the impersonator looked like a beautiful movie star. One of our airmen seemed to be smitten with the performer and I have to admit I encouraged him. At the end of the show, the wig came off and the top of the gown came down showing everyone the performer was a man. Needless to say, our airman was truly embarrassed.

We returned to Davis Monthan in early September 1964. I was outside on yard detail and I heard a "thump." I looked to the runway and saw smoke where the aircraft would be on final approach. A short time later I learned one of our pilots, Major Primrose, has crashed.

While I was in Australia, one of the Republic of China Air Force pilots bailed out of one of our aircraft near Tucson in August 1964. Then on December 19, 1964 the very same pilot bailed out again near Tucson. He was brought back to the hospital on the base. I was directed to go to the hospital and stand guard outside his room. My instructions were not to let anyone in other than medical staff and 4080th SRW personnel. When I arrived at the room, the door was open and the pilot was face down on the bed with his butt uncovered while a medical technician removed cactus needles. An Air Policeman arrived shortly after to relieve me.

While at Davis Monthan I frequently worked the afternoon shift starting at 2:00 p.m. Monday and ending when the last airplane landed about midnight. The shift was actually very slow; once the airplanes were launched there was not much to do until they returned. The remainder of the week we worked from noon until about 8:00 p.m. It was a long shift each Monday when most of the night flights were scheduled. PSD had a dining area for the pilots to eat their pre-flight meal and we knew the cook. He was free to leave once the aircraft had launched. We asked him to leave a large pot of coffee with milk and sugar for us. Soon after that PSD had a lot of visitors from OMS and FM who stopped by for coffee and chat. That is when I became a lifelong coffee drinker.

While waiting with the OMS and FM guys visiting PSD on Monday evenings, we played some card games, the favorite being Hearts. One crew chief, "Catfish" Davis, liked to play practical jokes. His favorite was to tie the shoe laces together on anyone who dozed off while waiting for the aircraft to return. He was one of the frequent visitors to PSD for cards and coffee. One Monday evening he had not yet arrived, but three of us were playing cards. A chair was left for him at the table and I put a thumb tack on it. It was out of character for me to do something like that. Davis did not show that evening and in the heat of the card game, we forgot about the tack. Captain Ray was the mobile officer that night. He came in, grabbed a cup of coffee and sat in the chair that had been reserved for Davis before anyone could say anything. Captain Ray did not see any humor in the prank and demanded to know who had done it. I confessed and explained what it was about. Thank goodness he was very understanding, but he asked that we not do anything like that again. A couple days later he walked through our duty section and rubbed his behind as he passed through. I was embarrassed.

PSD techs had a lot of friends on the flight line, especially in the heat of the summer at Laughlin and Davis Monthan. The tarmac would reach well over 100 degrees. The PSD vans used to transport the pilots to their aircraft had huge air conditioners. In addition to a single seat for the driver, the van had bins for equipment and a Lazy Boy chair for the pilot. We took the van out on the flight line an hour before the aircraft returned and recovery procedures began. It did not take long for the OMS and FM guys to realize our van was running and the air conditioner was on. They drifted over for a break from where they were working on the flight line.

While I was in PSD, I gave numerous demonstrations of the partial pressure suit. I was always the one who dressed in the suit. Periodically the Air Force would send a full pressure suit to replace the partial pressure suits, but they never worked out. I dressed in the latest model to test it out in the aircraft. The cockpit was so small that not one of the full pressure suits would fit during the time I was there. If I could manage to squeeze into the cockpit, I could not move to do anything. I was six feet tall, about 180 pounds and I was told that was why I was chosen.

Before I made a firm decision about re-enlisting, I was nominated for Airman of the Month in January 1965. Five other airmen from different shops were also nominated. After the interview process, another airman was selected. I understood he got all the votes on the selection panel; I can say I was nominated once for Airman of the Month.

I took my discharge on August 7, 1965 with mixed feelings. The guys from the shop threw a party for me with cake and a lot of goodies that I truly appreciated. At that time I was not sure what I was going to do with the rest of my life. I had no idea how hard it was going to be to leave a job I loved and people who were so congenial to work with. I am very proud of my service with the 4080th SRW.

Two weeks after I returned home, I applied for a dispatcher job with a large tank truck company. I was hired and began work there on August 25, 1965. I worked my way through the ranks there and up into management. After 44 years in the industry, I retired in October 2009. After a few months off, I'm thinking of starting another adventure. I wonder if the 9th Recon Wing is hiring.

Dragon Lady Doctors

"The art of medicine consists in amusing the patient while nature cures the disease."
Voltaire

Robert W. Paret

Knoxville, Tennessee

In 1952 I flew 100 missions in Korea in the F-84A, C and G. When I became a physician, I transferred to the Medical Corps of the Air Force and became a Flight Surgeon. I regained my pilot rating and became dual qualified shortly before I left active duty and joined the Texas National Guard. Through the ANG I was appointed as Assistant to the USAF Surgeon General for ANG Affairs with the rank of Major General USAF MC.

I was one of the Flight Surgeons who supported the 4080th SRW through the Physiological Support Division. There were at least two and sometimes three Flight Surgeons assigned to the Wing. First names that come to mind are Bruno, Doug, Bob Self, one other whose name is lost to memory, and myself. One Flight Surgeon was required to remain at Laughlin AFB to support the remaining pilot cadre when temporary duty units were in action.

Before every flight, the pilots began their preflight at PSD. The first item on the preflight was a physical exam consisting of the usual vital signs. Through questions and observation, the Flight Surgeon would determine if any additional exams were necessary to approve the pilot for flight. If there was any problem identified in the exam, the pilot

Robert W. Paret MD.

Bob Paret preparing for a flight.

would be grounded and a replacement scheduled. Following the exam and clearance to fly, the pilot went to the dining area for his high protein meal. After dining, he was given some relaxation time before getting into the partial pressure suit with the help of the PSD technicians. Oxygen pre-breathing followed. The technicians then connected the pilot to a mobile oxygen tank and he was transported to his assigned aircraft in an air-conditioned van. The pilot was helped into the cockpit by the same technicians who quickly connected his suit to the aircraft oxygen system.

Most TDYs required a Flight Surgeon to accompany the detachment if high altitude physiological support was not available at the remote location. When time was critical, a PSD technician took vital signs freeing the Flight Surgeon to proceed with the physical exams. I went on TDYs to Howard AFB, Panama, East Sale, Australia, Alaska, Fiji Islands and Hawaii. Some of the other Flight Surgeons supported the Cuban Missile Crisis from MacDill AFB, Florida.

Dragon Lady Caregivers

"Ask not what your country can do for you; ask what you can do for your country."
John Fitzgerald Kennedy

Maintenance

Once there was a very pretty young thing nicknamed "Dragon Lady." She was extremely lithe and graceful, yet gorgeous and ugly at the same time. Her personality could go from the fairest lady in the world to the biggest screaming banshee one could imagine. The guys who gave her this strange name were themselves called "Dragons." Some liked to take her up, up and away to glory and beyond. Some had the enviable job of being with her every day. Dragon Lady was also mysterious and tried her best to hang around all those handsome Dragons. Ah, what a lady! And, at over 50 years, the Dragon Lady is aging gracefully and hanging on to her loveliness; she is still one heck of a girl. The Dragons, most of whom have not aged nearly as gracefully, still love her deeply.

Glenn Chapman, TSgt. (Ret.) USAF
Author, *Me and U-2, My Affair With Dragon Lady*

The Dragon Lady at rest in the hangar, pogos in place. Photo courtesy of Lockheed Martin Co.

U-2 maintenance operations. Photo courtesy of Lockheed Martin Co.

It took a team of well-trained men and specialized equipment to support the U-2 program. Although the job duties varied greatly, no one took their work lightly. The 4080th SRW consisted of only 900 people comprised of pilots and navigators, in addition to the operations, maintenance and support staffs. The Wing Commander was directly responsible for the entire cadre of personnel. He reported to the Strategic Air Command Headquarters. In 1962 Air Training Command (ATC) assumed control of the base, and support units then rolled to the new command. However, units directly involved with the U-2 support (food service, motor pool, finance, personnel, civil engineering, etc.) had a TOP SECRET area called "Warehouse B". Direct duty of operations and maintenance squadrons were the primary units of the 4080th SRW. The 4080th also had its own Security Police and Medical Units separate from the ATC support unit.

In addition to the 4080th Wing Headquarters, these support units were Operational Maintenance Squadron (OMS), Field Maintenance Squadron (FMS) and Armament and Electronics Squadron (AEMS or also known as A&E) which performed direct maintenance on the U-2 aircraft. Assigned to each of these maintenance squadrons were civilian Technical Representatives (Tech Reps). They were employees of and supported contracts for such vendors as Lockheed Aircraft Company, Pratt and Whitney, Hycon, Perkin-Elmer, and TRW. They were not specifically "hands on" maintenance workers; they were the "answer men" when problems arose in the equipment of the company they represented.

Organizational Maintenance Squadron

OMS was responsible for all Airplane General (APG) maintenance ensuring the aircraft was always fully flight ready prior to being scheduled by Operations. With exception for a few administrative, supply and support staffs, OMS was made up entirely of specialists known as Crew Chiefs. Two Crew Chiefs, a primary and assistant, were assigned to each aircraft and ensured that their designated aircraft was fully flight ready.

Field Maintenance Squadron

Jet Engine Build Up (JEBU) was comprised of specialists who worked on the J-57 and J-75 engines of the U-2. This was not a flight line function, but was performed in the shop. Engine changes were the primary work performed by JEBU which could be the result of periodic maintenance required and certain inspections. Changing an engine was a difficult job. It required precision teamwork to complete the job correctly and safely.

Sheet Metal: Sheet metal specialists spent most of their time working on the aircraft itself. Repairing damage or replacing pieces lost in flight were things the specialists dealt with daily. Sheet metal specialists worked with very precise tolerances. They took great pride in their skills and were indispensable to the program.

Machinist Shop: Almost 100 percent of the machinists' time was spent on the aircraft or the ground support equipment. It was a common occurrence for specialists to strip a screw head while attempting to replace a panel on the fuselage. A machinist would be dispatched to remove the screw so the specialist could finish the work order.

Hydraulics Shop: The hydraulics specialists actually had the dirtiest job. Everything they touched used hydraulic fluid that leaked on them regardless of the precautions they took to prevent it. There was a Murphy's Law at the Hydraulics Shop that stated, "The hydraulic fitting that was leaking was always the most difficult to see, access and repair."

Pneumatic (O2) Shop: The responsibility of the Pneumatics Shop was to repair anything to do with air supply system difficulties. The biggest responsibility of that shop was pressurization of the cockpit. If the cockpit lost pressurization, the pilot's partial pressure suit would instantly inflate to provide 14 pounds per square inch artificial pressure.

Instruments Shop: Technicians of this shop maintained all instrumentation in the aircraft, including the Optical Sextant, which was the primary navigation reference for night missions.

Egress Shop: Better known as the "ejection seat" that hurled the pilot from the aircraft in an inflight emergency, the Egress Technician's primary area of expertise was the maintenance and operation of the ejection system.

Armament and Electronics Squadron (A&E)

Radio Shop: The Radio Shop, better known as Comm, maintained all radios in the U-2.

Radar Shop: Like Radio, Radar had only a few units that were their responsibility. The primary unit in the early days was the ARN-6 Radio Compass Unit. It was a small unit set in area. It used conventional AM radio stations as a navigational aid.

Auto Pilot Shop: When the U-2 came to the 4080th, there were no auto pilot specialists in the Air Force. In 1958 the Air Force authorized a new Air Force Specialty Code (AFSC) called Automatic Pilot. The auto pilot system was considered more electrical than electronic so the personnel were assigned to FMS and later became part of A&E.

SFERICS: This was the cover name for the electronic countermeasure equipment carried in the U-2. In reference books it was described as "the study of lightning." However, with the 4080th SRW, it was the gathering of electronic intelligence or ELINT. The main SFERICS platform that went into the equipment bay was System 4, a more passive ELINT system. System 9 and System 12 were also used but carried a higher level of security classification.

Nephography: See Section "What is Nepho?"

Ivory Tower: Ivory Tower was the name of a weather platform that was carried in the U-2 equipment bay. It appeared quite primitive to the naked eye. It was nothing more than a piece of three-quarter inch plywood cut to fit inside the Q-Bay with a variety of weather equipment on the platform.

James E. Ballard
Ashland, Alabama

TDY to England

On January 14, 1959 I went TDY to RAF Brize Norton, England with our RB-57D-2. The officers that accompanied our detachment were Edward Abrams, Joseph Roure and Capt Wilkerson. We only flew our birds at night while we were there. January in England was cold, foggy and mostly wet. One evening we were towing one of the birds

Top row, left to right: Unknown, Capt Marsh, Capt Blum, last two on right Unknown; kneeling, left to right: Unknown, James Ballard, Jim Wemple, Sgt Harris.

back to the hangar, three of us on the tug and one other maintenance tech in the cockpit riding the brakes. There were no taxi lights on the aircraft. A security vehicle with lights out was parked at the edge of the taxiway in the grass. The taxiways at Brize Norton did seem a bit smaller than ours back home. The long wings on the RB-57D-2 collided with the security vehicle, an almost predictable result given the situation. The security guys were upset about their vehicle being damaged, but we were more concerned about our aircraft. The wing was damaged, and I knew the aircraft was scheduled to fly the next day.

Only one thing to do, fix the aircraft. We put the aircraft in the hangar and notified our commander. He wasn't angry; he simply wanted it fixed as soon as possible. It took a little time to locate the sheet metal tech; he was at the club hoisting an adult beverage. He returned to the hangar and started to work. It took several hours to complete, but the wing was fully repaired. The aircraft was ready for the scheduled mission the next day.

Hugh W. Bell

Memphis, Tennessee
Wife: Effie, deceased August 12, 2009.

My Early Days

My military career began when I bid goodbye to my family in Jeffersonville, Georgia and enlisted in the Army Air Corp on April 10, 1944 bound for basic training at Keesler Field, Biloxi, Mississippi. For a young eighteen-year-old, it seemed like a long way from home. Following gunnery school at Fort Myers, Florida, I was assigned to the lst Photo Recon Squadron at Smokey Hill Air Base, Salina, Kansas, as a tail gunner on a B-29 crew for eighteen months in World War II. I was promoted at nineteen-years old to Staff Sergeant and joined my crew en route to Okinawa; we arrived the second day after World War II ended. I returned to the US on emergency leave, and at that time many of the troops were returning as well.

I volunteered to attend jet aircraft mechanic school for ten weeks in 1947 at Chanute Field, Illinois, and I returned to Chanute in 1948 to attend jet engine school. My career goal had been to be an aircraft mechanic. To that end, I volunteered to get all the technical training available to me to support my stripes. While I was stationed at Clark Field in the Philippines, I volunteered for a ten-week training course on aircraft electrical systems at Yokota Army Air Base, Japan. Throughout this period of my Air Force career, I was a crew chief, responsible for everything related to a specific aircraft.

Our F-80 aircraft came dismantled to the Philippines by ship and were delivered by barge to Sangley Point Naval Base. I was in charge of the detail that reassembled the aircraft for the flight to Clark Air Base. Once the planes were put together, our enlisted team taxied them down the runway to "burn the brakes" in. The brakes had to be hot enough to rid them of any grease that would prevent a good hold when applied. (Of course, now only a rated pilot can taxi an aircraft, but times were different then.) Following that project I was promoted to Tech Sergeant in 1950

After an assignment in Japan as a C-47 crew chief, I was reassigned stateside to MacDill AFB, Florida. I was fortunate to be selected to attend the Boeing Company factory training school for the B-47 at Wichita, Kansas and subsequently was transferred to Hunter AFB, Georgia. With the training completed, I was assigned to Turner AFB, Albany, Georgia when the 508th Strategic Fighter Wing (SFW) became operational.

I helped start up the 508th SFW in 1952 as the first line chief of the 468th Strategic Fighter Squadron (SFS) with 25 F-84 aircraft at Turner AFB. TSgt Grimes and TSgt Malone were two of my flight chiefs at the time. Chuck Stratton was a young lieutenant fresh out of flying school and he later went to Laughlin AFB too. As line chief I was responsible for everything related to the aircraft to ensure it was ready for a scheduled flight. After I was promoted to Master Sergeant at age 26, I moved to Maintenance Control where I was assigned when the group relocated to the 4080th SRW at Laughlin AFB, Del Rio, Texas, in 1957. At that time, Master Sergeant was the top of the structure for enlisted rank. When the Super Grades, Senior Master Sergeant E-8 and Chief Master Sergeant E-9, came out in 1959, I requested reassignment back to the flight line. It was there I was promoted to both E-8 and E-9, respectively, and became the ranking Non-Commissioned Officer in the aircraft maintenance system. I was responsible for the 4080th OMS U-2 phase inspection section for two years. While I was in OMS, I was promoted to E-9, Chief Master Sergeant, and supervised over 40 men. With my E-9 promotion, I was reassigned back to Maintenance Control and relocated with the 4080th SRW when it moved to Davis Monthan AFB, Tucson, Arizona. I'm proud that we never had an unsatisfactory inspection by Quality Control while I was there.

One day at Laughlin OMS one of my dock chiefs had finished the inspection on a U-2 and was lowering the aircraft to remove the dolly that supported it. Much to his surprise, a ladder that he had not removed from the underside of the U-2 punched a hole in the wing. Since the wing is the fuel tank, it was quite an ordeal to repair the damage. First the engine had to be removed, then the upper part of the wing with a gazillion screws had to come off. It ended up being about a week's worth of work. When our colonel learned about the damage, his very understanding response was, "The wind blew the ladder over just as the chief was lowering the aircraft. He could not stop the process fast enough to prevent damage to the U-2." The lucky chief escaped without punishment.

From the Beginning

I was with the 4080th SRW from the beginning for seven years as an aircraft maintenance supervisor on the flight line in OMS and Maintenance Control. Laughlin AFB, Del Rio, Texas, was home to me and my family, and we enjoyed the congenial relationship with the local citizens. Several of my TDYs were as line chief with Project HASP, the atmosphere sampling flights. Twice a week, our wing flew missions to the North Pole and the South Pole sampling the upper atmosphere for radioactive material following the nuclear tests after World War II.

My planes flew from Ramey AFB, Puerto Rico. On one of those missions, we lost contact with our pilot. Fearing the worst, Local Air Sea Rescue planes were launched to search for the U-2 and pilot. The mobile officer continued to call out, but there was no response from the pilot. Finally, in desperation he said, "If you read me, hit the tone button twice." In return we heard a loud and clear "beep beep." We were all excited and grateful knowing "Our Guy" was safe. The wire in his helmet had broken and he could hear everything transmitted to him, but he could not send outgoing messages.

Too Close for Comfort

On a TDY at Hickam AFB, Hawaii, I went out to recover the pogos after a U-2 took off. As we picked up the first of the two pogos, I looked up to see a big C-124 Globemaster on final approach to land. The U-2s do not require much runway for take off. Thankfully our bird was already out of sight when the C-124 approached. We were grateful our old Jeep did not fail as we picked up the last of the pogos and shot off the side of the runway just as the C-124 zipped by with a blast of airstream. Way too close for comfort.

I enjoyed a great career in the US Air Force and still claim friends I have known since those early days. I retired at age 38 in 1964 with twenty years military service. My second career was with the US Postal Service where I worked for 27 years before retiring in 1992.

Donald E. (Donnie) Brown

Westwood, Massachusetts
Wife: Ann

Vietnam

It took a night of heavy mortaring in 1964 at Bien Hoa Air Base by the Viet Cong (VC), when twenty B-57 planes were destroyed, for the upper echelon to decide to issue us weapons for our own protection. A short time later, I was playing cards one evening with some of the food service personnel when the VC opened fire on us again. We grabbed our weapons and ran immediately to our assigned emergency bunker location. One food service fellow followed the rest of us, but he realized he didn't have his weapon. He ran back to the hooch (tent) and retrieved his gun. When he arrived at our bunker for the second time, he didn't have any ammunition for his gun. As scared as we all were, we had to laugh at the situation. Back he went to his hooch again. By the time he had returned with his bullets, the shelling had stopped. After that incident, our weapons went where we went. That was a long and scary night.

Alaska

In November 1961 when we were deployed to Eielson AFB, Fairbanks, Alaska, a mission was scheduled following detailed flight planning. Weather was always a major factor in the dead of winter in Alaska. Flight operations planners had determined the aircraft would not have sufficient fuel to return to our base so they planned to land at Elmendorf AFB, at Anchorage to refuel. After the launch, we prepared to fly out to recover the U-2 in a KC-97 refueler. All of our equipment was loaded, and we boarded the aircraft. Before takeoff, we were all fitted for parachutes, but our tech rep had a hard time getting fitted over his parka and many layers of clothing. The aircraft took off smoothly. An hour into the flight, the number one engine simply stopped, but the pilot restarted it within minutes. A short time later, number four engine went out, but it was restarted successfully. By now we were all quite nervous. While I was up front talking to the crew, smoke engulfed the cockpit. We were scared thinking we were going to have to "hit the silk" (parachute out). Our well-padded tech rep panicked and tried to get into his chute. It was humorous to watch; he put the chute on, took it off, put his parka on and started for the door. The only things visible were his flailing arms and it took him only fifteen seconds to get to this point. The source of the smoke was soon discovered to be an oily rag on the heater and the smoke diminished. We had a good laugh at the expense of the tech rep. After all that, the plane was directed to return to home base. What a long and crazy day.

Harold A. (Brownie) Brownback

Oklahoma City, Oklahoma
Wife: Mandy

I was a Staff Sergeant at Forbes AFB, Kansas when I was assigned to the Black Knight Project in October 1950. En route to Lockbourne AFB, Ohio, I detoured for jet engine training to Chanute AFB, Illinois. I was assigned to the 26th Strategic Reconnaissance Wing at Lockbourn until April 1956 when I was reassigned to Turner AFB, Georgia. At Turner I was ordered to the 811th Air Bomber Group and later reassigned to the 508th PD Maintenance Squadron, SAC. In May 1956 I went to the 4080th Strategic Reconnaissance Wing and transferred with the Wing to Laughlin AFB in May 1957.

We became a close-knit unit at Laughlin and everyone worked well together in support of the U-2 aircraft. I was an engine technician in field maintenance, and supervised a crew in engine change and test run of the aircraft.

Considering the difficulty finding housing, we were extremely happy in Del Rio. The local citizens were friendly and we became acquainted with quite a few people there. Our daughter, Judy Colleen, was born in the downtown hospital in August 1957.

Harold Brownback, 1956.

Harold and Mandy Brownback, 2005.

In July 1958 I was transferred to England. Although our assignment with the 4080th SRW was rather short, we left with a lot of fond memories. We made a number of friends there and we continue to keep in touch with them today.

Swinton Burroughs

Indialantic, Florida
Wife: Betty

Reconnaissance

It had its beginnings for me in 1954 when I was assigned to an RB-47 wing at Lockbourne AFB, Ohio. No more P-51s, P-47s, F-82s, F-80s – just big cameras in big aircraft. In 1956 I was informed that I was being assigned to the Black Knight program. Black Knight? What was that? Where was that? What was the mission?

Enough with the questions. Here are your orders. Get a flight to Baltimore. There, call this phone number and "they" will provide transportation to the Glenn L. Martin aircraft plant. "They" also gave me a briefing on a new aircraft "they" were building, a high-altitude craft. It was derived from the British Canberra which itself was no slouch on reaching higher altitudes. The first test flight was a couple weeks away.

During the daily training sessions on what was inside this craft (what made it go, how to maintain it) the other trainees and I were given tours of the plant to see how it was being put together. We were astonished to see workers smoking in the cockpit and around the assembly areas. Martin's view was that those guys would sneak a smoke every so often and the cigarette butts would end up in critical parts of the plane. By allowing them to smoke, ash trays were kept handy and the employees would police up the area at the end of their shifts. On one tour I asked to see their Engineering Department. Years earlier I thought I might become an aero engineer. They showed me an area with about 500 engineers all appearing to be chained to their worktables. I spoke with one of them whose sole job was to do all the calculations for the design of the small nose landing gear doors of another aircraft Martin was doing. He marveled that I could "tolerate" being in the Air Force and being told what to do all the time. "All in one's perspective," I told myself.

With the training completed my group at Lockbourne was transferred to the 4080th Strategic Reconnaissance Wing at Turner AFB, Albany, Georgia. Once there we became the 4025th Strategic Reconnaissance Squadron (SRS) complete with pilots, maintenance team, Squadron Commander Colonel Mulloney, and finally, some black and white RB-57Ds.

Early training flights out of Turner had the usual glitches. One was a recurring problem for Bill Shuman whose radio communications gear developed a glitch each flight at altitude. Maintenance responded each time with "ground check-OK." Colonel Mulloney said that wouldn't cut it and Maintenance responded that maybe Bill didn't know how to operate the radio. An infuriated Colonel Mulloney told Maintenance to NEVER say one of his pilots didn't know how to operate his equipment.

Some time later Tech Reps reported that Martin found the problem—aluminum wiring that had apparently cracked at some time during installation; upon reaching cold temperatures at high altitude, the wiring shrank causing a gap in the wire. Upon

Swinton Burroughs at the 2002 4080th SRW Reunion wearing a plaid blazer that each of the group acquired during 1957 TDY to Japan to distinguish themselves from locals at Yokota AB.

returning to low altitude, the wire expanded and closed the gap, thus the "ground check – OK."

In August 1956 a TDY for six RB-57s was cobbled together for a classified operation at Yokota Air Base, Japan, with Colonel Mulloney as Detachment Commander. Maintenance people stopped at Hickam AFB, Hawaii to service and prepare the birds for the next leg to Yokota. Only one aircraft had a problem that had us all shaking our heads. Keith Lindsay reported an opposite reaction to what he expected on the horizontal stabilizer trim. How could this malfunction have escaped the notice of other pilots on other flights? If the trim was hooked up in reverse, had it been that way since it left Martin in Baltimore? There was no record of maintenance ever done on the system. Regardless of all possibilities, we reversed the wiring and on the leg to Yokota, Keith reported all was well.

At Yokota the skunk-like appearance of the RB-57s attracted some attention, but guards around our parking area kept out the curious, except for one. A Lieutenant Colonel thought because he was in the same Air Force, he was entitled to know what these birds were all about. Early one evening he ignored the guard's order to vacate the area. A shot fired over his head quickly made a believer of him, but the next morning he stirred up a hornet's nest with the Inspector General's office, the Base Commander and the Base Provost Marshal. He was asserting his right to look closely at the RB-57s. Colonel Mulloney and Colonel Johnson, from SAC Headquarters, brought this whole episode to quick closure. Rumor had it the curious Lieutenant Colonel was promptly transferred to another base.

Somewhere along the way news reports said the Chinese had issued the 256th (or some such number) "serious warning" to the US regarding overflights. We heard this occurred frequently.

On one night flight Bob Chalmers returned to the Yokota area and was reporting difficulty in maintaining proper balance between his left and right wings. A sump pump automatically pumped fuel between the left and right wings whenever fuel consumption was greater in one wing than the other; but the pilot could control this situation. In Chalmers' case, nothing worked so he elected to land immediately. The Martin Tech Rep, Michael Vince, went with me and the ground crew to the now parked plane. We could hardly believe what we saw. The largest honeycomb panel on the bottom leading edge of the left wing had split away from the forward edge of the wing and was curled backwards, leaving the fuel cell looking like Niagara Falls. The jet fuel was cascading to the ramp below. It kept the fire trucks busy washing down the ramp, and the next day we moved the plane to a hangar. After a lot of conference calls, Martin decided to send a replacement panel, another tech rep, drawings and special tools, and design for trusses to support the wing while replacing the panel. In effect, we did depot work under field conditions.

What caused the panel to separate was a reason for alarm on all the RB-57s. It seemed an air leak into the honeycomb allowed the comb to exhale when the plane went to altitude, then to suck in air and moisture when descending. The moisture built up with each flight until so much had accumulated in the comb that it then froze at low temperatures while at high altitudes. With each freezing, the expanding ice caused skin and comb to separate. Inspections of wing panels became routine to try to detect any separation.

In the Spring of 1957 replacements arrived and we headed home. Back at Albany we learned that the Wing was moving to Laughlin AFB, Del Rio, Texas. A C-123 carried a group of us to Del Rio to check on housing. There had been a seven-year drought in Southwest Texas and the area looked bleak. There was one live bush at the entrance to the Officers' Club. It had flourished due to the Club rule to empty whatever remained in a drinking glass, ice and drink, on that bush.

A month later I drove my family to Del Rio and, amazingly, the drought had broken. All kinds of cactus and sage were blooming. When the rains first came, the water couldn't even penetrate the "caliche" soil. Rain had accumulated into a tidal wave that eventually reached US Highway 90 just in front of the main entrance to the base. On each side of the entrance road was a shallow swale that paralleled Highway 90. Local reports were that a car with three women passed the entrance road just as the tidal wave rolled across the highway and in moments the car was washed into the swale. Two of the women drowned.

Once the RB-57s were on base the U-2 began arriving from Lockheed Skunk Works with their pilots and ground crew. We used the hangar at the south end of the ramp for the RB-57s. It was only a matter of time before a rivalry developed between the U-2 folks and the RB-57 folks.

One day Bo Reeves, a RB-57 driver, asked me to ready an aircraft for him with "splash fuel;" he wanted the plane as light as possible. That day we observed a U-2 that took off and headed for the heavens like a homesick angel. "Pretty good," we thought. "Now, Bo, take that 57 skyward." Bo was on his brakes winding up his engines when Colonel Wyman, our Squadron Commander, unobserved by me walked up and slapped me on the shoulder. He said, "Burroughs, how much fuel did you put in that plane?" I told him and he responded, "You fool. Don't you know that won't cover the sump pumps in a climb out?" He raced for his staff car to chase down Bo just as he released the brakes.

In about 500 feet the bird was airborne then nose up. As Bo later told us, at 13,000 feet directly above his takeoff point, he decided he better level off while he still had fuel feeding the engines. We declared the 57 the unofficial winner, but Bo and I were declared losers for the day by Colonel Wyman.

Colonel Beauchamp replaced Colonel Wyman as Squadron Commander. His office on the second floor of the squadron operations building faced the big hangar doors. One day Colonel Beauchamp called the Operations Officer and me into his office with a complaint. The 35-gallon garbage containers clustered on the ramp were used to collect and separate various pieces of metal. The Colonel didn't like their appearance and he wanted those cans painted. Sergeant Murphy in my unit had wanted to transfer to the U-2 squadron, but because he was an outstanding Crew Chief, I turned down his request. I called him in and offered to approve his transfer if he could pretty up those cans that belonged to Maintenance. The next morning when I arrived at the hangar, I was horrified to see the cans. They were an indescribable color, something resembling baby vomit. It didn't take long before I had a call to report to Colonel Beauchamp. I was sure my career was on the downhill slide. The Operations Officer was also there and we reported to the Colonel. To my utter amazement, the Colonel said how pleased he was with the appearance of the cans and he directed the Operations Officer to do the same with his garbage containers. After this brief meeting, I found Sergeant Murphy and asked him what paint he had used on the cans. His answer: "All the left over paint in all the cans in the paint locker, blended together to give that 'beautiful' tone." It worked and he got his transfer to the 4028th SRS.

One day two of our most experienced pilots were doing touch and go landings in B-57Cs, landing at the south end of the runway, then rolling on again for a takeoff. There was a rise near the south end of the runway, putting it out of sight to those of us watching from near the hangar. On one approach one 57 touched down out of our sight. Then we heard the power poured to the engines but no plane appeared over the rise in the runway. The persistent sound of power but no visible plane was an ominous sign. I grabbed a vehicle and raced to the south end of the runway. Lo! A perfect "wheels up" landing!

A much chagrined crew, Keith Sims and Al Simpson, admitted the belly landing was so smooth they didn't realize at first they were wheels up. The timing of this incident was poor to say the least. The nearly two hours it took to clear the runway added to General McConnell's already infuriated state of mind. His plane circled overhead waiting to land for his first visit to the 4080th SRW since taking command of 2nd Air

Force at Barksdale. The incident, combined with several earlier U-2 accidents, resulted in Colonel Zemke's dismissal as Wing Commander. He was replaced by Brigadier General Austin Russell.

In September 1958 Colonel Swofford, Major Stu Spragins, Captain Yates and I went to Taiwan to affect the turnover of two RB-57s to the Republic of China Air Force (ROCAF). Each day we held classes with a translator to teach the Chinese maintenance troops how to look after the aircraft. All the Chinese officers spoke English, but none of the enlisted men did. Spragins worked with the Chinese pilots who had received training in the RB-57s back in Texas. Colonel Gabreski, a WWII ace, arrived with a squadron of F-104s. Members of his squadron had some pretty unkind things to say about our "big winged gliders." One day while Colonel Swafford was occupied somewhere else, we prevailed on Stu to make a max takeoff to show what our bird could really do. The F-104 drivers stood open-mouthed in astonishment. From then on, there were no more smart-ass remarks from them about our birds.

The Chinese pilots hosted a dinner for the four of us US officers and revealed their great sense of humor. Each food dish was brought to the table after a round of toasts to each other. Then one of the Chinese pilots would raise his glass and give a toast to the new dish. The Chinese were particularly jubilant because they had shot down four MiGs with their F-84s that very day. When the next dish arrived, one of the Chinese called for a toast to the new serving, MiG21. I asked what that meant and my host responded, "Dead duck." And duck it was, a tasty dish indeed.

Interestingly, the Chinese had a couple of large gun emplacements near the end of the runway. To ensure no Communist Chinese maneuvered their way on base trying to steal an F-84, the ROCAF installed a system of lights from the tower: green light meant the plane was cleared to go, red light meant shoot the plane down immediately.

We had replacements coming for each member of our detachment. Colonel Swofford had arranged for a building to use as a barracks that was located near Taoyuan Air Base, about 25 miles out of Taipei. When the new guys arrived, I had a GI bus take them to the hotel. The hotel was already full, mostly with GI's and their girlfriends. I had to distribute the poor innocent fellows fresh from Texas into a couple of rather unsavory hotels. The next morning they regaled me with lively stories; they said it was the first time they had ever been billeted on per diem in a "cat house!"

Back at Laughlin, I watched as a RB-57 piloted by Bob Schueler came in for a landing. While still rolling in front of Base Operations, the right wing slowly drooped and fell to the ramp. I think this incident precipitated the demise of the Black Knight program. In due time the RB-57s were assigned to other organizations such as the weather service. When the last of them left Laughlin, the flight line maintenance operation was consolidated into one squadron with a branch for the U-2s and a branch for base flight aircraft. Forrest "Whip" Wilson became the Squadron Commander.

While he was commander, Forrest promoted a landscaping improvement project for the desolate, barren "caliche" soil that surrounded the hangar. Our coffee fund bought oleanders and other plants plus grass seed. The result was such an improvement that it inspired like efforts around other buildings, notably the 4028th Operations building. Pilots contributed to help improve the appearance of the grass. That improvement inspired the production of an anonymous treatise spelling out the procedures to follow in removing weeds from the grass. For example, grasp weed tool, hold at 40 degree angle to ground, insert at root of weed, remove weed, etc. The commanding officer of the 4028th was not amused.

What was the price of maintenance? I had a call about midnight from a Crew Chief who informed me they had damaged a U-2 tail wheel strut while moving it. If they had to go through supply to get parts, they feared the repercussions. However, there was an alternative. Field Maintenance had a welder and a sheet metal specialist who said they could fix it quietly if I approved, and if I sweetened the deal with a case of beer. I made a trip to the San Felipe area of Del Rio and found a bar where a case of Mexican beer could be bought for about $3.50. The beer stayed in my car until the repair job was done. Sometime around 3:00 AM the job was finished and the beer was duly delivered. That was the last we heard about the incident.

In mid-September 1960 when the Del Rio area received a storm warning, five U-2s were airborne. They were directed to Laredo AFB and I was instructed to get a team together to go to Laredo to prep them for the return flight the next day. We drove through the night to reach Laredo with several flight line mechanics and a couple of medical personnel. Because Laredo did not have pogos to support the U-2 wings, Operations there dispatched a bunch of Second Lieutenants in flight training to support the wings and push the aircraft all the way to the parking ramp. At the parking area, they used 55 gallon drums under each wing tip skid, then used 50 pound sacks of fertilizer to hold the wings down in the event of high winds. They were unaware, though, the damage the sacks of fertilizer could do to the aluminum surface of the wings.

We brought pogos with us from Laughlin and they were installed as soon as we arrived. It turned out that the base had planned an Open House the next day for local folks in the Laredo area. Having the U-2s come in unexpectedly made their day. They got the word out to local residents by radio and flyers. Saturday morning was a beautiful sunny day and visitors thronged the flight lines. The pilots and I decided to give them a good show. The Personal Equipment crew did everything with a flourish. I borrowed a flight line van for our "acting" Line Chief to go through all the motions of preflight with each Crew Chief who then saluted the pilot. I went from plane to plane, trying to look important. Each takeoff was a max effort event for benefit of the visitors. We were rewarded with a lot of "ohs" and "aahs."

On another weather encounter Bill Shuman was flying near the base and reported that some strong winds were headed our way. For some reason his report was not acted upon, and those of us along the flight line watched as harsh winds buffeted the parked U-2s which were not tied down. A couple of them were pushed around and banged into each other resulting in some skin damage. After that dire incident, all U-2s not requiring work in the open had to be hangared. This imposed a heavy burden on Maintenance. They shuffled aircraft to fit in the hangar and removed those scheduled for flight each day.

An additional task was levied on me to check with the Weather people every evening to assure that the flight line was in shape for whatever winds or rain may be forecast. I usually did it by phone, but one evening I walked to Base Operations where the Weather people prepared their forecasts. Complex charts hung on the walls, teletype machines clacked away and maps covered the desks. I asked the "head honcho" what he had for the forecast. He studied the wall charts and gave me a "Hmm." He walked to one of the teletype machines, looked at it while it typed and then gave me a double "Hmm." He consulted with one of the other guys there and shuffled some papers around on a desk. Finally, he walked over to a door that opened to the rear of the building, stepped out, looked up to a perfectly clear sky, then said, "Major, I don't think you have anything to worry about tonight."

One day Sergeant Fred Covert and I went to check equipment inside a small hangar whose doors opened to the flight line. The doors were only opened about 10 feet and, as we discussed a problem, a tug used to tow aircraft went chugging past the opening. To our absolute amazement, no one was driving it! We both raced for the door opening to catch the wayward tug before it rolled toward an aircraft. Troops were running from several directions to catch the tug. Fortunately, one guy jumped aboard and brought it to a halt just yards away from an aircraft parked on the ramp. I recall that someone got a good chewing about properly setting the brakes on the tug.

Taiwanese Air Force pilots were trained in the U-2s at Laughlin. One of these pilots was on a night mission over New Mexico when he had a flameout. Futile efforts to restart cost him considerable altitude so he referred to his flight manual to locate a suitable landing strip. He chose a strip that had minimum facilities, and in the darkness of the rugged New Mexico desert, he made a silent landing. There was only one light on in a single building. With one wing tip on the ground, he managed to get himself disconnected and exit the plane. He headed toward the light but he was still in his pressure suit and bubble helmet. As he approached the building, he could see a man seated at a desk pouring over paperwork. The Taiwanese pilot entered the door and the building occupant looked up in disbelief. "My God," he said, "If the Chinese have taken this place, they've surely taken the whole West Coast!"

SAC had a management system applied to every squadron which awarded points based on the squadron mission. Every month points were totaled and the Wing Commander got all the Squadron Commanders together to review the standings. The squadron with the fewest points had the "honor" of tethering a goat in front of its headquarters for the coming month. One month the Hospital Unit was awarded the "honor" and the goat was transferred to the hospital commander. For a couple of weeks, we all noticed the goat grazing whenever we passed the hospital and then soon forgot about it. About the third week into the month, the hospital folks put on a feast around the Officers' Club pool featuring "cabrito," barbequed goat. It took a while for it to sink in; we had all eaten the goat.

In January 1962, Colonel Paul Rix and I were sent to Guam to assess facilities for handling three U-2s at Andersen AFB. Paul established needs for the Operations part of the planned detachment and I sought facilities for the required ground equipment. One facility designated for our use was a T-hangar originally built to accommodate one large aircraft except its tail would extend through a cutout area in the doors. It could house three of our U-2s. I asked the civil engineers what wind velocity it would withstand. They spent a day going through their old "as built" drawings to finally give me a response—135 knots. This went into my final report back at Laughlin. Several months later, we had a three-plane detachment at Andersen and a powerful typhoon headed for the island. Forecasters erred on the projected winds until it was too late to evacuate the U-2s. The typhoon hit with winds in excess of 140 knots. One of the large hangar doors fell inward and damaged two U-2s.

In September 1962 concern arose over the Soviets shipping some weapons into Cuba. One dark night I called my Maintenance crew to get three U-2s prepared immediately for a takeoff. I alerted the Line Chief and crews for those aircraft. It started to rain and all of us at the flight line were soon soaked. We received a directive to tow the planes out to the end of the runway where they would be positioned for takeoff. The Physiological Support Division guys got the pilots to the planes about the time the rain became a "gully washer." With all the electrical cables exposed to rain, I feared someone would be electrocuted; but the hookups and startups went well. After the first plane was off, a search was mounted for the pogos that were left in deep puddles of rainwater on the runway. We wasted a lot of time searching for the pogos. We decided to remove the remaining pogos on the waiting aircraft; ground crew held the wings and raced along with the plane until the wings maintained lift on their own. This procedure worked well and within a short time all three aircraft were airborne and became the first U-2s involved in the Cuban crisis.

The SAC Inspector General team made its first full-blown inspection visit with a group who was not fully aware of our mode of operation. Because of the frequency of TDY's, usually comprised of three U-2s and support crew, I maintained a board with all ground crew members' names, aircraft numbers, and personal data such as whether the wife was pregnant or sick. This added bit of information enabled me to select crews that were available and ready to go on a moment's notice. The board resembled a typical organization chart but that's where the similarity ended. The Lieutenant Colonel member of the SAC team assigned to Maintenance found some things he didn't like, but he reserved most of his wrath for the TDY chart.

The Lieutenant Colonel and I walked out into the hangar still arguing about my need for the TDY board. He was insisting that our flight schedule should be firmed up so many days in advance so that everyone knew well ahead what was coming up. He quoted regulation SAC 66-12.

One of the U-2s was parked in the hangar and we circled it while he decided he would go to Maintenance Control and straighten out this scheduling matter. While he belabored the issue, a Flight Chief came up and asked us to clear the area; the aircraft we circled had to be prepared for a special mission. "No, it was not scheduled for a flight," I told the Inspector, "But when SAC Headquarters said it must go, then it would." With that said, he just threw up his hands and walked out of the hangar. That's the last we saw of him.

James E. (Soup) Campbell

Mifflinburg, Pennsylvania
Wife: Linda

From 1958 to 1973 I supported the U-2 program with the 4080th SRW at Laughlin AFB and then with the 100th SRW at Davis Monthan AFB. I served as Crew Chief and later a Line Chief. I had an opportunity to see a lot of activity with the Wing and I worked with a lot of good men.

It was an unwritten rule that whenever a pilot blew a tire on the aircraft, he owed the Crew Chief a case of beer. We were in Alaska in July 1962 when Major Rudolph Anderson blew a tire on his assigned aircraft. Sure enough, he paid up promptly and I shared with the rest of the crew.

In 1963 at Davis Monthan, one of the Taiwanese students crashed a U-2 and bailed out safely. He later was assigned another flight on the day before Thanksgiving and subsequently reported to the Tower, "Flameout, bailout." Before the Tower had a chance to tell him to glide the U-2 in, he had already bailed out. I spent Thanksgiving Day picking up pieces of the aircraft over a huge area of the Arizona desert.

In February 1964 I was at Davis Monthan and I passed the Maintenance shack as I left work about 4:30 p.m. I was asked if I wanted to go on a ten-day TDY and I was instructed to get the other guys on the crew to be back at 6:30 p.m. I rushed to the mess hall to get the rest of the crew and we reported back to the flight line on time.

We loaded the aircraft until midnight and the KC-135 tanker that transported the 30 or so support crew took off at daylight. We arrived in the Philippine Islands at midnight their time with U-2 missions scheduled to take off early the next morning. We had only been there three days when the Philippine government demanded that we get out. We were once again loading and fueling the aircraft for a rapid departure.

A captain from the alert hanger chewed on us for taking their fuel truck. While he chewed on me, I continued to fuel up the U-2. He demanded my name, rank and serial number; I responded courteously and professionally. Of course, I knew I wouldn't be around long enough for him to do anything beyond his chewing. One hour later we were airborne with no plans to return to the Philippine Islands. In the haste to depart, two or three of our crew members were left behind in the Philippines, but they were recovered on a later flight. Once airborne, we were given orders to go to Guam.

The KC-135 with all our equipment and gear then went to Guam. I rode in the boom operator's area and observed the flight over the ocean. Prior to landing on Guam, the pilot had to dump thousands of gallons of fuel out over the ocean in order to get to landing weight. We stayed there three weeks. One evening at midnight we got the word to load up and we departed the next morning, destination unknown to us. Colonel DesPortes, the 4080th SRW commander, was along on the flight and he made a big deal of opening the envelope that contained our orders. He announced we were going to Vietnam. Most of us had never heard of the country. By the time we arrived at Bien Hoa Air Base, Vietnam, I had been up for a full 24 hours without sleep.

I vividly remember the day we landed at Bien Hoa Air Base, Vietnam on March 5, 1964, my 29th birthday. I had always heard about the "outback" and I thought this was it. The support team normally landed ahead of the U-2s and would be issued a truck for Mobile Control; however, this "Follow Me" truck driver refused to give us his vehicle. So we explained to him what he would have to do. Because of the U-2's bicycle gear configuration, the pilot holds a level position until the aircraft comes to a stop and one wing gently falls to the runway. We told the driver that the crew then goes to the high wing first to pull it down and insert the pogos. The first U-2 came in and the pilot dragged the wing the normal distance. Before we knew what he was doing, the "Follow Me" truck driver jumped out of the truck and raced toward the aircraft and grabbed under the skid to keep the wing up. Poor fellow, he absolutely fried his hand and to make

James 'Soup' Campbell with 'his' U-2, static display at LAFB, 1990.

matters much worse, there was tar embedded in the wound. I really felt sorry for the fellow but he just didn't listen to us.

We got the bird parked and we were soon in for another surprise. Here came a bunch of Vietnamese GI's holding hands! Now that was sure different for us to see. We learned it was a custom of their culture. Then they tried to climb all over the aircraft, but we quickly stopped that.

After getting the planes bedded down, we got on the bus to go up to the Compound. On the way, we passed a little building which must have been a civilian house; a young woman, probably a teenager, came out, squatted down and peed right there with not the slightest bit of modesty as our bus passed in clear view. Being young and slightly immature, all the guys rushed to that side of the bus; I thought for sure that bus was going to turn over.

We finally got to the Compound and we were told to walk around the hut until we found an empty bed. I found one, but not in the same hut with the other guys from the 4080th. The next day we scouted around until we found an empty hut, put some beds in and proclaimed it ours. In the hut next to ours were some Vietnamese Army guys. They were sleeping two or three in a single bed; now that really was a bit too crowded. There was nothing in our hut to use for storage so a couple of us went in search of a locker. We walked through the rows of huts and came upon the transient officers' hut. There was evidence of only three or four occupants. We found the locker we were looking for and away we went. For a long time, we were the envy of our hut with that locker.

We lived in huts, 12 men to a hut, with a Vietnamese maid assigned to each hut. For a box of Tide, a can of shoe polish and $5 a month, the maid kept the hut clean, did the laundry for all the residents, made beds and shined shoes. She would take the shoes to a long table outside the hut and gather around it with maids from other huts. They would start shining shoes and chattering away while they worked. It was a mystery how the maid could get the right shoes and clean laundry back to the right bed.

There was no place to get safe drinking water except at the mess hall. Our maid filled up liquor bottles with drinking water and brought an extra block of ice she managed to scrounge for us. During that first trip to Vietnam in 1964 the food was good, but in 1966, I returned on separate rations (paid for my own food) and the quality was not as good. There was no place to buy snacks except the BX, and there was always a long line when snacks were in stock and they sold out in a short time.

A swimming pool was under construction by Vietnamese workers when we arrived at Bien Hoa. To say their construction methods were primitive was an understatement. Instead of digging the hole with heavy equipment, there were a number of people out there using a hoe and short handle shovel to put dirt in a five gallon bucket. The bucket was then carried off by another worker, dumped and returned for another load of dirt. One day I saw that they had a small cement mixer on the edge of the hole and watched as it toppled over the edge into the hole. There was a lot of chattering and hand motions as they tried to figure out what to do next. The completed pool was finished a couple months after we arrived. I seriously doubt it would have passed any US construction inspections.

I was at Bien Hoa over 100 days before I had a day off. We reported for work at 3:30 a.m. and finished the day when the aircraft was finally bedded down by about 6:00 or

8:00 p.m. Even with all those inconveniences, that was by far the best TDY that I ever had and I did quite a few.

I remember writing letters to Linda, then my fiancé, from Vietnam. I would write a big "O" every few words; the "O" marked each time I heard gunfire or mortar shelling explosions. I didn't count the O's until I finished the letter and I saw that every two to four words were followed by a big O. I finally explained to Linda at the end of the letter about the O's.

The U-2 could not land in a crosswind. If an aircraft could not land at Laughlin, their alternate destination was Altus, Oklahoma. We then would gather a crew from Laughlin and fly to Altus in a C-123 to recover the U-2 and get it ready to turn around and fly back to Laughlin. On one particular flight to Altus, we had flown from Laughlin in the very early hours of the day and we finally launched the U-2 for its return flight. It was mid-morning and we had not even stopped long enough to have a snack, much less breakfast. We asked the bus driver that was taking us to the C-123 to make a stop at the convenience store for us to buy some drinks and snacks. A bunch of the guys came back to the bus with 6-packs of beer. Once we took off in the C-123, the ground crew gathered in a circle in the back of the plane and started having "breakfast." There was then the problem of eliminating the evidence before we arrived back at Laughlin. Fortunately, there was a small hole in the door that allowed someone to reach through to the outside. The opening was just big enough to toss those cans through; we left a trail of cans raining across Texas. The Navigator came running back to tell us to scatter because we had too much weight in the tail of the aircraft.

James 'Soup' Campbell (left) on Thanksgiving Day, 1961, Laughlin AFB.

I remember one particular U-2 incident while I was TDY at Barksdale AFB that had a rather humorous exchange with a local resident, although the pilot who lived through it might have a different opinion.

It was in 1967. U-2 #708 flew to 45,000 feet altitude when it experienced an explosion. The pilot ejected safely and free floated from 45,000 to 10,000. During that free fall, he got into a spin, but managed to pull his chute at 10,000 feet. He landed in a rural area around Pineville, Louisiana, and disconnected himself from his chute. He began walking down a nearby road still dressed in his pressure suit. A car drove toward him but sped on when the driver got a good look at the pilot in his other-worldly looking gear. The pilot finally came to a mobile home and knocked on the door. A young woman opened the door, looked at her visitor and immediately slammed and locked the door. He yelled through the door, explained who he was and asked her to call Barksdale AFB. After a few minutes, the young woman returned and spoke to him through the door. She said, "Barksdale said they wouldn't accept the charges!" The pilot pleaded again, "Ma'am, if you will just call, I'll give you the money back for the call."

Once we were notified of the accident, I was requested to accompany a Major from our unit to go to the crash site. Barksdale was responsible for the accident investigation, but most of the investigators had never seen a U-2 and weren't too sure what to do. I knew before we arrived at the site that my job was to get to the aircraft and remove the TOP SECRET communication box. There were a lot of people just standing around waiting for instructions. I went directly to the aircraft, removed the outside panel and took the communication box. I headed back in the direction I came from. On the road I saw a pickup truck and I asked the driver for a ride to the nearby store where I met up with the Major again. I showed him the box and he said, "Let's go. We got what we came for."

In the early days, the U-2 was involved in air sampling over Guam, Alaska, Panama, Hawaii, Australia and England to test for radiation. The device used to capture the air for testing consisted of basketball-size balls installed in the Q Bay. The balls were metal wrapped in wire and pressurized with outside air. Following each sampling flight, the balls were shipped to a lab for testing. The ball racks used during those flights from the 1950's to 1968 had gone back into storage until we learned that France was going to set off some test bombs, so the US started air sampling again. Out came the ball racks, but we needed the special cords to tie down the racks. Lockheed put in a rush order to make the special 6-foot long extension cords needed. Then there was a lot of test hopping when one aircraft crashed in 1968. One of the colonels told me to get the cables off the crashed aircraft, so off I went again with tools to remove the cables. I knew the rules about removing evidence from a crash site, but I had a ranking officer directing me to do it. When the chopper came back to get us, I was stopped by a different colonel who said I could not take those cables. I then reported to the first colonel about the location of the cables and he said he would take care of it.

When I was single, I volunteered to go TDY and enjoyed the traveling. After I married, I knew there was an Air Force policy that would not send a man TDY if his wife was pregnant. I was called about a TDY back to Barksdale but reported that my wife, Linda, was pregnant with our first child. Sgt. Ross took my place on that TDY. Then I was told about a TDY to Argentina for air sampling and I did go on that one because I knew I would be back before our son was born. So, I got the balls and cables ready for another mission in Argentina.

We flew night missions from a civilian airport in Mendoza, Argentina. All the crew wore civilian clothes and nobody there knew we were military. The ground crew had left the hangar after the aircraft took off; we knew it would be seven or eight hours before it returned. Being the Crew Chief, I was required to stay until the aircraft returned. I ran the night shift and I was there with a couple other guys when the phone rang. When I answered, there was a burst of Spanish and the words, "May Day, May Day". I couldn't understand anything except the words "May Day" so I quickly got in touch with our commander who contacted airport officials. We learned that a pilot had reported a loss of electrical power; however, he survived.

Line Chief Wayne Smith and I were sent to California for training when the U-2 engine was upgraded from the Pratt and Whitney J57 engine to the J75 model. The upgrade increased the thrust from 10,500 to 17,500 pounds. We went to Lockheed to learn about the proposed modifications. However, our attendance at that training had the stipulation that once we returned to the Wing, we would volunteer for Vietnam. So once again, off I went to Vietnam.

There was a huge infestation of rats on the base and I learned that plague was still a very active disease in Vietnam. We had received inoculations for the plague prior to departure from the US. The disease, we were told, was spread by fleas carried on the rats and the fleas needed a warm body to thrive. So if the rat died, the fleas went in search of another host, which could be a human. Rats were not poisoned because the theory was that if the fleas then left the rats, we would be at risk.

In the huts, rats walked on the overhead beams like they owned the place, and I guess maybe they did. I had nailed a box to the wall with a few things I wanted to protect from the vermin, such as writing paper and cigarettes. One day I saw something go into the box and I quickly slapped a writing tablet against it. The rat poked its head out of the box and made a hasty retreat right over Wayne as he slept in the next bunk. Wayne never woke up and the rat kept going.

I created a rattrap from a C-130 water separator; it was cone-shaped with the pointed end cut out. I wired it to a 10-inch board and placed a beer can in the homemade trap. The rat climbed inside the can and could not retreat. The Soup Trap reduced the rat population in our area by at least half.

L. Mendel Rivers was a powerful member of the US House of Representatives from South Carolina and Chairman of the House Armed Services Committee in the 1960's. His nephew was a member of our outfit when we went to Argentina. We were told there was a very dangerous bug in the country called "Achuga." If we were bitten, the bug could cause heart damage years later. One day Rivers' nephew came in with a nasty-looking bug in a bottle and asked if this was the bug that was so dangerous. He reported that he was bitten by that same bug. No one really knew what the Achuga looked like. Rivers' nephew got the brushoff by a lot of people. Finally, he invoked the name of L.

Mendel Rivers and he was immediately sent downtown for medical treatment. As it turned out, the bug he found was not the dreaded Achuga, but Rivers' nephew still got quick response to his question.

Joseph (Joe) Chapman

Joe is the son of Glenn R. Chapman (see "It Took a Dedicated Team")
Tucson, Arizona

Dad's Epilogue Thing

The U-2 Dragon Lady program was, and still is, one of the most prestigious units in the Air Force. In 1994, after seven years of bouncing around in A-10 units as a "crewdawg," I had the privilege of being assigned to the U-2 Periodic Inspection Dock in the 9th Maintenance Squadron at Beale AFB, California. For some guys, this would have been just another assignment to an aircraft maintenance outfit. For me, it was more than that.

About three decades earlier, my dad had been a member of the pioneering unit I was bound for. So I had a little bit of the living history of the unit that began with the 4080th Strategic Reconnaissance Wing (Light) in 1957, later morphed into the 100th Strategic Wing and eventually evolved into today's 9th Recon Wing. Pretty cool. So that's where my story begins.

Anyone who has been involved in Air Force maintenance knows that our Technical Orders (TO) change frequently. Most of the changes come about when maintainers develop faster or easier methods to perform a given task. Throughout the relatively short history of the USAF, one common denominator has always been present—the desire to get the job done in the fastest time possible with the least amount of work. This phenomenon is known in aircraft maintenance circles as the "shortcut," and is the root cause of a large number of the dreaded TO changes.

Every maintainer I have ever known has asked the burning question: "Who the hell decided to put the ____ behind the ____? What were they thinking? Damn engineers!" However, there are two sides to everything. While I've heard the "damn engineers" comment on procedures numerous times, usually between a few expletives, I've also heard some rather surprising comments. For example, "Who was the brilliant individual who came up with this idea? Now there is some ingenuity."

Invariably when a maintainer performs a task day in and day out, in addition to just plain getting good at the job, he'll usually come up with subtle deviations that make the job easier. Less time on the job equates to more time at the club, or anywhere that isn't in the shop. Some of the methods and procedures will eventually find their way into a TO or locally designed checklist, while others are handed down through time from one maintainer to another. So, here are a couple of my favorite examples of how the maintainers of yesterday have influenced those of us who have come along since, and some who have yet to meet the elderly but graceful machine known as the Dragon Lady.

Things aren't always as they seem, but sometimes they are!

Since the U-2 was originally the brainchild of her designer, Clarence "Kelly" Johnson, it seems only right that my examples begin with him. In the mid-fifties the CIA and the USAF needed a new intelligence-gathering platform. The wish list went out and the contractors began vying for the opportunity to be the winner of the latest lucrative government contract. Lockheed Aircraft Company's "Skunk Works" unit was awarded the contract, and the rest is history, or is it? In the interest of keeping costs down, Kelly had the foresight of using an already existing airframe for the basis of his design. Looking at a U-2 from various angles, the many similarities between the "Deuce" and the F-104 Starfighter would be obvious. The similarity arises because that is exactly how the CL-282 first began. It is better known to us today as the U-2A.

Some of the similarities are blatant, while others are more obscure. One of the obvious examples is the canopy of the early production U-2 mirrors the one installed on the F-104. In fact, the identification tag on the part itself is identical for both aircraft.

Because my Dad was a 4080th SRW Dragon, I found myself talking to him on the telephone about the Deuce on a regular basis. He'd ask me questions like, "Hey, do they still have ____ in the engine bay over by the ___?" Armed with my newly acquired knowledge from Dad, I'd set out to find out if "____ was still in the engine bay over by the ___." Sometimes I'd learn that the part wasn't installed anymore. However, more often than not, I'd learn that not only was it still used, but it was still in its original location.

One of the times Mom and Dad came to Beale to visit my family, I took Dad for a tour of the dock I worked in. Needless to say, when I introduced him to my co-workers as a 4080th Dragon, the questions flowed. After hearing the myriad answers, a few co-workers seemed to walk a little taller because it wasn't just the boss telling them about the importance of their jobs. Dad was a living history book, at least that was my observation. Moral of this story is: Any former Dragons who have the patience to listen to our questions or to tell a few good war stories, we always appreciated. With a former Dragon dropping in to the shop, we could get "the rest of the story."

Heads or tails? This one's a coin toss!

From the time I was knee high to a grasshopper, I liked to think of my Dad as the most important guy in the world. In grade school, we would say something like, "My Dad can do (enter any silly challenge) better than yours." Later in middle school, it sounds something like, "My Dad can kick your dad's ass!" That's why this story has so much meaning to me; it's how he saved the day.

During my Dad's time on the U-2 from July 1958 to April 1966, he was a Specialist. Yep, that's right; Dad's a "Grinner" and I'm a "Knuckle Dragger." For a little explanation of some maintainer lingo, a "Grinner" is a Specialist who works in the recon system arena. During the launch of an aircraft, the Grinners stand over to the side with big grins on their faces. When one of their systems has an "uh-oh", the Crew Chief usually turns to the Grinners who promptly fix the problem.

"Knuckle Dragger" is one of the nicer nicknames for a Crew Chief. There are others that are waaay more common, but I really can't mention them here. Most Specialists think that Crew Chiefs are lacking in the smarts department, otherwise they would be Specialists. However, those of us who are a little off the deep end would still be Crew Chiefs.

All this has made some very interesting conversations between us. Any Crew Chief or Specialist will tell you that the two cannot peacefully co-exist. Personally, I think the concept is obsolete because in all my time in the Air Force I've had pretty good relations with the Specialists. We're all on the same team and that's it. Maybe being raised by a

Specialist had something to do with my outlook, but I think Grinners and Draggers can get along just fine, most of the time.

Dad was a camera guy, and before he gets the chance to correct me, he was specifically a "Nephographics Technician." His job was to keep the optical intelligence gathering systems and the pilot's NEPHO System control equipment in top-notch working order. One of the tasks all the NEPHO guys dreaded was the alignment of the drift sight and hand control. The drift sight was essentially an upside down periscope the pilot used, for example, to track drifting patterns of the aircraft.

Control of the drift sight was maintained through an instrument like the exterior mirror control on newer automobiles. The hand control had to be calibrated or aligned for precision accuracy. This was a task that the NEPHO guys would rather not have to do because it meant working in a very tight area, and according to the manufacturer's instructions, the aircraft had to be on a fuselage cart. That was a lot of work and a lot of time spent contorting the human body of the unlucky NEPHO guy was who selected to perform the task.

There was one NEPHO guy, however, the other guys must have thought was absolutely insane because he actually enjoyed twisting his body into every imaginable position, or more likely just enjoyed the challenge. Or, maybe it was because he had a "shortcut" that made the job a little bit easier. After a few years working on the system, Dad did in fact devise a method of aligning the hand control that made the job easier. Trouble was, there was no tech data to support his method. The 4080th SRW Commander, Brigadier General John DesPortes, learned about Dad's "unapproved method," so he proposed a showdown between the manufacturer's tech rep and my Dad.

Dad was allowed to take the hand control out of alignment and the Tech Rep performed the procedure according to the manufacturer's guidelines. When he came out of the cockpit, General DesPortes climbed in and inspected it. Using a stopwatch to time both the Tech Rep and Dad, he told Dad to do it his way. The General took a look at Dad's handiwork and found everything to be exactly as it was supposed to be. General DesPortes demanded to know, "Chap, how on earth did you finish the task so rapidly?" I wish I could have been there to witness all this when Dad reached into his pocket and pulled out the tool issued by the US Mint. That's right, a simple United States twenty-five cent coin was the device used for the precision alignment of the drift sight. He proceeded to lay the quarter on the ground beneath the drift sight, clambered up into the cockpit and pointed out to the General how he did it.

General DesPortes climbed back in the cockpit and announced what Dad already knew. The hand control was exactly as it should be. He also asked the Tech Rep why one of his blue suiters (the uniform the NEPHO guys wore) had a much better grasp on the unit than an employee of the manufacturer. The tech rep immediately instructed Dad to have a checklist written outlining his "shortcut" as soon as possible so it could be implemented as an authorized procedure.

The story doesn't end there though. Years later while I was deployed with the Deuce, I lived in a hootch (hut) next door to the deployed photo guy, Keith Haas. Maybe it was fate that Keith and I were to meet, maybe it was just that our hootches were next door and we liked to play guitars together when we were off duty. Either way, Keith and I became instant friends with a lot of time on our hands to shoot the breeze. When I told him about Dad being a NEPHO guy, he expressed interest in meeting him. After we returned to Beale, Mom and Dad came for a visit. We invited Keith to come play guitars and meet Dad. We didn't do much pickin' and grinnin'; quite the contrary. I sat on the couch listening to the two photo troops swap stories for the rest of the evening. It was interesting listening to them compare their likes and dislikes about the job. An observer could believe that these two could be related, and they actually are two birds of the same feather.

Before he left, Keith invited Dad to tour his shop and meet some of the other Photo Dragons. Of course, Dad quickly accepted the invitation. I'll spare everyone the flattery and the "I remember when..." of most of the tour, and I'll fast forward to the final few minutes. Keith took Dad and me into a back room of the shop and Dad's eyes welled up. There on the bench in front of him was the newest drift sight and hand control. As if almost 30 years hadn't passed, Dad proclaimed, "I could still work on this. I probably couldn't keep up with you new guys, but I could still do it with my eyes closed."

Keith then reached into a small toolbox, known as a mini-kit, and pulled out a small round slug about the size of a quarter. Attached to the slug was a red and white "Remove Before Flight" streamer and the slug was etched with the words, "Hand Control Alignment Tool." If Dad's eyes weren't totally welled up by now, they were close when Keith proudly said, "Mr. Chapman, we always wondered where this came from. Now we know."

Hey, Joe, can ya give me a hand over here?

The U-2's mission is what we in the Air Force call "Real World." That's one of the reasons I've always said that the U-2 is the most important aircraft in the inventory. I like to tell the fighter guys, "Without the Deuce, the F-16s, A-10s and F-22s would just be a gun flying around with nothing to shoot at." Anyone who knows me understands what my preference is: Recces win hands down.

Because of the critical mission of the U-2, every second spent on the ground is precious. But it doesn't end after the aircraft breaks ground. The U-2 uses a set of outrigger gears called "pogos." The pogos keep the aircraft balanced with wings level during towing, taxiing or just sitting on the ground.

While pogos are supposed to stay installed on the ground, there is only one reason that they would stay in for an entire flight and that would be when a pilot is learning to fly the U-2. I personally have never seen a pilot use the pogos for this reason, but I've heard that it has been done. When the pogos are used in this sense, they act as a set of training wheels. However, this doesn't take long and just like a kid who is learning to ride a bicycle, as soon as the pilot has gained confidence that he can keep the aircraft level, the pogos will only be used for ground handling.

The last thing a U-2 ground crew does before the bird launches is to pull the pogo pins so they will fall out as soon as the wings begin to lift. This takes a couple of seconds, but when a mission is critical, seconds can seem like hours. Sometimes a pogo will fail to fall out of the wing causing a "hung pogo" and can cost not only precious time but a hazard to the pilot. In that scenario, the pilot might have to land the plane or fly to a designated area to shake the pogos loose.

During the 1962 Cuban Missile Crisis, missions were more important than ever. The ground crew looked for any way to save time without sacrificing safety. A young Assistant Crew Chief named Joe Kent had the solution. Everybody probably thought he had lost his mind, but nobody had any better ideas. The boss approved and said "Let's give 'er a try." The way these ideas work is when someone comes up with a great idea, they also get to be the first person, or guinea pig, to try it out. At the next morning launch, Joe was set to demonstrate how it would work.

After performing the preflight checks and getting the forms documented, Joe gave the signal for "give me air" and the powerful engine came to life. Hydro pressure came up and they pulled the gear pins. The Grinners did their preflight checks and the pilot taxied to the end of the runway. The pilot lined his Dragon Lady up for takeoff roll and Joe's show was about to begin.

Joe grabbed the wingtip and held it steady while the pogo crew scrambled to pull the pogo pins, and this time they pulled out the pogos completely. The pogo crew gave Joe the signal, which he relayed to the pilot, that all was okay. The pilot responded by stomping on the brakes and increasing the throttle. The powerful jet engine slowly revved up to takeoff speed and with a nod, Joe got ready to sprint.

The pilot released the brakes and within seconds the aircraft was picking up speed. Joe took a few more steps and the wing began to fly. He let go of the wing, bent to a crouch and gave a hearty thumbs up. Joe Kent had just performed the first hand launch of a U-2.

To this day, when time is essential and the mission is critical, the very same hand launch procedure is used to shave seconds off the takeoff and ensure safety of the crew, and of course, the aircraft. Everybody knows, including the pilots, that the airplane belongs to the Crew Chief. Joe Kent, a Crew Chief's Crew Chief, was the imaginative individual who came up with this idea. Thanks, Joe.

There's gotta be a quicker way to bleed this AMAD (Airframe Mounted Accessory Drive)

I'd like to close this epilogue by revealing how the guys listed above, and God knows how many more that I simply haven't met yet, have influenced my generation of U-2 maintainers. As I've shown with the examples above, when the pioneer guys started working on the U-2, they had to find their own "tricks of the trade" to make the job go smoother and to save valuable time during a critical launch. But the legacy doesn't have to end with them. They can be proud to know that their ingenuity has fueled a whole generations of U-2 maintainers.

One such story comes to mind while I was working in the Periodic Inspection Dock at Beale when Lockheed began the "sex change" of the R model U-2. Among the modifications was a major change in the engine. After 40 years of using a turbo jet engine, Dragon Lady was about to receive a turbo fan power plant. This story is about the Airframe Mounted Accessory Drive or AMAD.

Whenever the oil lines came off the AMAD or when the oil cooler came out, air would get into the system and would need to be filled and bled. I remember all too well the many nights we spent trying to get the air out of the oil system using the method outlined in the tech manual. Remember, I said earlier most good ideas stem from a desire to get the job done quicker and easier. Most of us resolved to the idea when we were briefed at shift change that we had an AMAD bleed, we were gonna be there all night.

One fellow, Craig Felty, wasn't resolved to that fate. He studied the blueprints and the tech manual, then observed how the system worked as we performed the task. It wasn't long before he got a machinist involved and built a simple hand crank. Little did we know that Craig's brainchild was going to change the way we bled an AMAD forever. Once the boss found out about Craig's tool, he insisted it become a legitimate process. Craig submitted his idea along with a sample tool and it was approved. In 2003 as a Blackcat in the 5th RS in Osan, Korea, I observed that Craig's tool was still being used.

The legend lives on!

I can't speak for every member in the current U-2 program, but I think they'd probably agree with me. I am very proud to have had the opportunity to serve in a unit with the prestige, honor and mission that was started over 50 years ago. I consider myself fortunate to have my name on the rolls of a unit that includes, Major General Pat Halloran, USAF (Ret.), the Crew Chief's Crew Chief Joe Kent, and especially my Dad, the Driftsight Dragon, Glenn Chapman.

To all the old Dragons who paved the way for those of us who came later, and for those yet to come, thanks for setting the benchmarks that we've come to follow. Hopefully, along the way, we've set a few of our own.

George Debinski

(Deceased May 14, 2000)

The following was submitted by George's widow, Terry.

> George came to Laughlin AFB from Georgia in 1957 and was assigned to the Sheet Metal Shop in Field Maintenance. His supervisor was Sergeant Ted Guthrie and Sergeant Marcos Villarreal was his First Sergeant.
>
> I grew up in Del Rio, but I knew that the town was oblivious about the activities at the base. George said that occasionally when he went to a bar in Acuña, the Mexican town across the border from Del Rio, there were local guys there who always asked what he did at the base. He always made up something to tell them that was far from the truth, and it satisfied the curious fellows for a while.
>
> We married on October 29, 1960 and George's First Sergeant promised him that he would not be sent TDY for at least a year. We bought a trailer and lived at the base trailer park. When I taught school at the local Catholic elementary school, I rode the bus with the base children bound for the local public school. Some of the base children were at my school.
>
> George went to Alaska once and to Australia twice. He told me where he was going but never what the unit would be doing there.
>
> We left Del Rio when the Wing moved to Davis Monthan AFB, Arizona, and we were at Tucson about 18 months. Many of the families who lived in the Laughlin trailer park ended up in the The Desert Breeze Trailer Park in Tucson. I remember Guthrie, Monge, Lockhart, Gabriel, Doria, Deliberto, Gomez, Ancira; there were so many others but time has faded my memory.
>
> George was reassigned to Okinawa and our daughter, Elizabeth Ann, was born August 24, 1966 at Camp Kue Army Hospital. Our son, Roger Eugene, was born

George Debinski, 1964.

on October 18, 1968 at Cannon AFB, New Mexico, where George was reassigned once again.

George and I enjoyed his tours of duty with the Air Force, but our time with the 4080th SRW at Laughlin and later at Davis Monthan was very special to us.

Russell (Ed) Eddington

California City, California
Wife: Sherry

The Early Days

I enlisted in the US Army Air Force on August 4, 1947 from my home in New Orleans, Louisiana bound for the 9th Infantry Division, Ft Dix, New Jersey. The US Air Force was established in 1947 as an independent organization and separated from the US Army. After I completed basic training, I was assigned to MacDill AFB, Tampa, Florida in 1948 where I joined the 838th Engineers Aviation Battalion as a heavy equipment operator. In 1950 I was transferred to the Air Force as part of the 307th and 305th Bomb Wings at MacDill. I served in Korea for six months as a heavy equipment and reciprocating engine mechanic on B-29 and B-50 aircraft until 1957 when I cross trained as a jet engine mechanic. With ten years' service and a grade of staff sergeant, I arrived at Laughlin AFB, Del Rio, Texas, in 1958 assigned to the Field Maintenance Squadron, Jet Engine Shop of the 4080th Strategic Reconnaissance Wing.

Russell Eddington, 1955.

In 1948 President Truman enacted Executive Order No. 9981 which directed equality of treatment and opportunity in all US Armed Forces. In time the order led to the end of racial segregation in the military forces. Most importantly, it was the first step toward racial integration in the US.

However, in 1958 when I arrived at Laughlin AFB, Del Rio, Texas, to join the 4080th as a jet engine mechanic, I was only one of seven black airmen in the shop. We were very much in the minority, and I felt animosity from some of my fellow airmen. I was confident in my abilities, and I knew I could perform with the best of them. I did not want to give anyone cause to doubt my abilities. Unfortunately, I was not considered for some TDYs because of racial issues in the host country. Off base in Del Rio, we were not welcome in some restaurants and theaters where many of our fellow airmen went.

My first TDY was in the spring of 1960 to Ramey AFB, Aquadilla, Puerto Rico, to support the U-2 aircraft for 90 days. At Ramey we prepared the aircraft for high altitude radiation detection sampling of the southern hemisphere. We experienced numerous problems with the engines in Puerto Rico related to the heat and humidity of the area that prevented the engine from being trimmed properly. Trimming the engines was critical to ensure they did not flame out at high altitudes. When the aircraft was properly trimmed, the pilot was able to restart the engine in flight and continue the mission. Calvin Sheets and I were the jet engine shop techs and ensured that it was ready to fly. It was a very exciting TDY, not only because of all the challenges, but also because we resolved the problems.

During my TDY in Puerto Rico, I learned that U-2 pilot Gary Powers had been shot down over the Soviet Union. We always worked under heavy security, but everyone was even more aware of the need for vigilance.

Alaska

When I returned to Laughlin AFB in the winter of 1961, I was sent TDY to Operating Location 5 (OL5) at Eielson AFB, Fairbanks, Alaska. Winter in Alaska is a memorable occasion. This time John Ladd and I were the two techs responsible for the engine equipment and for resolving all the problems. Our main objective was to keep the aircraft operational for the high altitude air sampling project over the northern hemisphere and the arctic. Without proper working engines, no one was able to fly and complete the assigned missions. John and I encountered several incidents that required us to work long hours with little sleep, but we believed in what we were doing and maintained our "can do" attitude.

Guam

In 1962 I went TDY to Andersen AFB, Guam. While I was there, Typhoon Karen blew through. One hangar door was blown off its hinges and three of our aircraft were destroyed. As bad as that was, we were fortunate there was no loss of life or injuries. However, we lost all our clothing, tools and other equipment due to the wind and rain from the storm. Some of the missions from Guam were for high altitude air sampling and photo reconnaissance.

Cuban Missile Crisis

When I returned to Laughlin from Guam, in October 1962 tensions between the Soviet Union and the US were coming to a boiling point. I supported this mission from Barksdale AFB, Louisiana and Laughlin AFB. Sadly, during this time we lost one of our pilots, Rudolph Anderson, and one of our aircraft. During the crisis, our wing flew and photographed more than 95 percent of the island of Cuba in search of the Soviet missiles delivered there. It was one of our pilots, Steve Heyser, who photographed the location of the Soviet missiles. Our wing was awarded the Presidential Unit Citation by President John F. Kennedy on his visit to Laughlin in 1962 for our outstanding accomplishment in Cuba. I was proud to be part of the effort on behalf of our country.

Australia

In March 1963 the 4080th SRW relocated from Laughlin AFB to Davis Monthan AFB, Tucson, Arizona, and formed the new 100th Strategic Reconnaissance Wing. I was selected to be part of the advanced group to move to Davis Monthan en route to OL11 at RAAF Laverton, Melbourne, Australia. We had only been at Davis Monthan a few days before we departed for Australia. Our mission in Australia was also high altitude air sampling in the southern hemisphere. Due to the extreme cold weather "down under" in March and April, I was diagnosed with pneumonia and was admitted to the RAAF station hospital for a few days; the treatment was outstanding. After a few antibiotics and a bit of rest, I was back at my job, eager to get on with our mission.

I returned to Davis Monthan in the fall of 1963. I recall I was on the flight line trimming aircraft when we received the tragic message that President Kennedy had been assassinated in Texas. What a sad day that was.

The Philippines and Vietnam

In February 1964 I was sent TDY to OL20 at Clark Air Base, Angeles City, Philippines. After completing only two missions, we were ordered by President Marcos to leave his country because he did not want the U-2s there. We hurriedly packed and departed en route to Guam where we stayed three weeks. When we left Guam, we had no idea what our destination was until we were airborne. Because we hurriedly departed in a KC-135 with equipment and personnel from the Philippines, we had not had an opportunity to completely tie down our fly away kits and other equipment. Most of the personnel onboard were required to hold down and secure equipment during takeoff. It was not until we were airborne that we were advised we were on our way to South Vietnam. We were once again the advanced party and we would be there to recover our aircraft when they arrived. Our mission was to photograph every inch of North and South Vietnam.

Field Maintenance Squadron and Operational Maintenance were separate units, but we worked together to meet a common goal. I was the Field Maintenance NCOIC and as such, I supervised personnel from the engine shop, hydraulics, sheet metal, pneumatic, instrumentation, electrical shop and aircraft ground equipment. We supported the organization in an outstanding manner and most of all we maintained our "can do" attitude, but like many, we were unsung heroes without much recognition for our efforts. However, I am proud of my accomplishments and the knowledge that I performed to the best of my ability.

Russell and Sherry Eddington.

During the first launch day in Vietnam, I was riding the left wing of the U-2 on our way to the launch pad. On the taxiway, I was startled to see a man dressed in black pop up out of the brush near the perimeter, probably Viet Cong. He held his gun and grinned at me as we passed by. That certainly scared me because we had no weapons, and no way of defending ourselves. Fortunately, we made it back safely and from that day on, we carried weapons out to the launch pad for early morning flights.

In 1966 I left Davis Monthan as a Tech Sergeant, Chief of the Jet Engine Shop, and a permanent change of station to Mactan Air Base, on Mactan Island, the Philippines. While at Mactan, I went TDY to Vietnam twice for 90 day TDYs. In 1968 I was reassigned to Edwards AFB and remained there until my retirement in 1971. I served in the military for a total of 24 years.

After retiring from the Air Force, I worked at National Aeronautics and Space Administration (NASA) as Senior Quality and Safety Engineer on the Space Shuttle Recovery Team until 1987. At that time my first wife, Rita, became terminally ill. I retired from my second career and cared for her until her death in June 1988. I returned to work for Lockheed Martin on the Space Shuttle Recovery Team in the same capacity I worked with NASA.

In 1991 I met my current wife, Sherry, and we were married in June 1993. I decided I had spent enough time in the workplace and retired again in 1997. Shortly after, I served as the Chairman of the Deacon Board at our church. I was elected to serve as Commander of the American Legion Post 476 where I have been a charter member for 40 years.

In 1998 I was asked to run for a seat on the city council of our community. I campaigned and won the seat where I served for four years; subsequently, I was appointed by my constituents to serve as Vice Mayor.

I have been blessed with 78 years of life and may God continue to bless me with many more.

Carlton L. (Lyn) Fite
Odessa, Texas

I was assigned to the Aerospace Ground Equipment (AGE) at Laughlin AFB, Del Rio, Texas. The unit provided ground support equipment for the T-33 and T-37. In 1963 SAC and ATC (Air Training Command) ground support shops were located in the same building at Laughlin on the northwest side of the runway. The missions of the two organizations were different, but at times each unit helped the other.

My most memorable experiences were when the CIA U-2s (we called them the Black Bandits) came in for a landing. They landed and taxied straight into one of the 4080th hangars. The hangar door closed immediately and the pilot shut down the engine. When those same aircraft departed, the U-2 engine was started inside the hangar, then the hangar door opened and it taxied out to the runway for immediate takeoff. The U-2 went almost straight up and out of sight. The 4080th U-2s were gray in color with USAF markings. The Black Bandits were solid flat black with no markings.

Lyn Fite and his 1951 Cushman motor scooter.

AGE shop in 1962, where Lyn worked.

At that time I recall Laughlin had two parallel runways. The AGE shop was responsible for servicing the regular Control Tower. We also serviced the generator on a portable Control Tower that was located about midway between the runways. The portable was used during the day when the student pilot flying was the heaviest. It was set on a built-up, earthen pad and had an open area under the building. One evening another airman and I approached the portable tower. From our pickup, the headlights revealed a person standing on the opposite side, only the lower legs visible.

Laughlin AFB was outside Del Rio, Texas on the Mexican border. From time to time illegal aliens gained access to the United States by night via the dark areas of Laughlin's runways. Having seen the legs on the backside of the Tower, and being young and not very bright, I jumped out of the pickup, came around the side of the Tower and crouched down. I was ready to leap upon this illegal alien. Much to my surprise, as I came around the corner in my crouched position, I was eye to eye with the biggest, badest German Shepherd dog I have ever seen. Holding his leash was a very large 4080th Air Policeman with a great big smile. He said, "Good evening, may we help you?" My great adventure and plan to capture an illegal alien came to a sudden halt.

Frank T. Hayes

Port Washington, New York
Wife: Josephine

The Early Tech Rep Business

I was a Philco technical representative (tech rep) to the 4080th SRW during the first eighteen months at Laughlin. Prior to the 4080th Strategic Reconnaissance Wing (SRW), I had been with the 506th Strategic Fighter Wing (SFW) at Tinker AFB, Oklahoma for two years. In January 1957, the 506th Wing Commander, Colonel Richard O. Hunziker told me there was a special project soon to be operational, and he recommended me for the assignment. The commander of the new operation was a good friend of his. A short time later, I received orders to visit the 508th SFW at Turner AFB, Albany, Georgia. I was briefed on the single-seat RB-57D-0. The first two-seat RB-57D-2 had arrived. After a month of evaluation and getting acquainted, I was told to report to Wing Commander, Colonel Gerald (Jerry) Johnson. I had been in the reception area for an hour when Captain Pat Halloran from the 506th came out. We were surprised to see each other. I never saw Colonel Johnson, but his executive officer told me to return to Tinker and prepare to report to Laughlin AFB, Del Rio, Texas in April 1957.

Arriving at Laughlin, I found the designation of the new wing was the 4080th Strategic Reconnaissance Wing (SRW) and the Wing Commander was Colonel Hub Zemke. I signed in with the Training Officer in Charge (OIC), Captain Ed Bailey and NCOIC Tech Sgt Don Baxley at the Armament & Electronics (A&E) Squadron and went to work on training requirements for the RB-57Ds of the 4025th Strategic Reconnaissance Squadron (SRS). A few weeks later on June 11, 1957, we were going to lunch when four strange looking aircraft showed up in the landing pattern, our first glimpse of the Top Secret Lockheed U-2, the Dragon Lady as it was nicknamed, which were assigned to the 4028th SRS. The high-risk business of strategic reconnaissance now had an aircraft designed from the ground up for the mission. It was like a hot rod fighter crossed with a glider wing and landing gear, a totally new concept tailored for long duration missions at altitudes where no other aircraft had flown. With the unique capability came added complexities for life support and flight characteristics new to fighter pilots, some of which were subtle and could be unforgiving. Terms like SFERICS, NEPHO, pressure suits, face plate heaters and quick disconnects were new. Achieving an initial operational capability in the harsh and unforgiving atmosphere of 75,000 feet came at great expense and much pioneering by the 4080th pilots. The physiological aspects of flying with pressure suits, the long endurance missions of ten hours or more and the unique flying qualities of the U-2 demanded perfection from the pilots and technicians with no room for error. Our 4080th pilots and technicians were the best in SAC who provided start-up operations with the discipline and guardianship of a flight test environment. Becoming operational was a massive undertaking.

The 4080th SRW was an unusual unit with unusual leadership from a unique background well suited for the challenge. The transition of the strategic recon mission from the RB-47E that flew at 40,000 feet to the extreme altitude of 75,000 feet and safety from high-flying MiG 17s had rendered their predecessor, the RB-47Es, obsolete for overflights. With a single pilot, the Dragon Lady would perform the mission of the three-man RB-47E.

The origin of the 4080th SRW traced back to Lockbourne AFB, Ohio where the Black Knight 4025th SRS had been formed in June 1955. In mid 1956, under the command of Lt Col Daniel C. Mulloney, the 4025th acquired photo recon RB-57D-0s at the Martin factory in Baltimore, Maryland and relocated to Turner AFB. It became the first squadron of the newly formed 4080th SRW. In September the 4025th SRS deployed to Yokota AB, Japan, accompanied by Wing Commander Colonel Jerry Johnson. Sgt Frank Lutrell was in Yokota and said, "When the first aircraft left the

Frank Hayes' Thunderbird.

Josephine and Frank Hayes.

runway on the first classified sortie, they heard on the Armed Forces Network radio that the Russian Ambassador in Washington had complained the US Air Force had penetrated their territory." They could not do anything about it, but their intelligence was superb. When the pilot of that mission returned, he wanted a rear-view mirror and each aircraft was then fitted with a rear-view mirror.

Some of the RB-57D-0s had also deployed to the Marshall Islands in the Pacific for atmosphere sampling tests over the Eniwetok Proving Grounds. The copper of the radio sense antenna in the canopy of those aircraft had oxidized. In May 1957 the deployed RB-57D-0s returned as the 4080th SRW was settling into Laughlin. Lt. Col. Daniel C. Mulloney, a superb commander of the 4025th SRS, was lost in a crash at Andrews AFB, Maryland in mid-1957. Major William J. Gregory, also a remarkable commander, then became commanding officer of the Black Knights. Many of the crews and technicians came from the 508th and 31st, both outstanding SAC wings.

The leadership of the 4080th traced back to the 56th Fighter Group of World War II fame. Zemke's Wolf Pack, as the unit was known, had 1006 victories and 40 aces to its credit. A combat pilot who brought down five or more enemy aircraft, confirmed on gunnery film, was officially credited as an Ace. Pilots included Jerry Johnson, Bob Johnson, Dave Schilling and Francis S. Gabreski, under the command of Hub Zemke, a full colonel at only age 25. Both Zemke and Jerry Johnson were Triple Aces. The 508th was activated in the summer of 1952 at Turner AFB as a Strategic Fighter Wing with Colonel Cy Wilson as wing commander and Colonel Jerry Johnson as deputy commander.

My Own Mission

On my contract, instead of working on equipment made by Philco, I provided technical support for general electronic systems. It included classroom instruction, on-the-job training and investigation of problems affecting maintenance, reliability and safety. My monthly reports were sent through channels to Headquarters 2nd Air Force at Barksdale, AFB, detailing progress on training and problems investigated. This included recommended changes, interim work-around procedures and locally designed test aids. The work was accomplished in the form of training projects, tailored to help young technicians learn to write discrepancy reports and recommend solutions. Copies in their personnel records helped at promotion time, a practice that pleased the first sergeant.

The growing tech rep business attracted attention of *Reader's Digest* magazine which featured a very negative article. It reported that civilian advisors were being paid more than two-star generals, a disservice to both the Air Force and the tech reps. Although everyone had known of a bad example, the 4080th tech reps were appreciated and the article was soon forgotten. However, Headquarters SAC took exception to the *Reader's Digest* article and a few weeks later SAC's *Maintenance Digest* featured an article on tech reps titled, "A Boy's Best Friend."

In the engineering world, tech reps were at the bottom rung of the ladder and Philco ranked at the very bottom of the ladder. At the top of the totem pole were the prime contractors who had greatest responsibility. While the pay was meager, the real-world experience would someday prove valuable. About half of the tech rep pay was in the form of expenses and those new in the business could barely afford a decent car. The bulk of the contract money went to pay for administration, benefits, field supervision and a home office support staff. Some of the other tech reps were Charlie Hinton, Jim Chalk and Pete Petchel from Martin, Joe McIntyre from Sperry, Jim Fraleigh from Federal Electric, John Holly and Dwyer from General Precision Labs, Frank Ramsay from Hoffman, Jim Bell, Larry Brooks, Dick Gilbert from Lear, Joe Ruseckas from David Clark, two tech reps from Ramo Woolridge, one from Perkin Elmer, Duane Rauch from RCA, one from Firewell and two from Ford to support the U-2 engine. Transistors were a new feature and electronic units were being compacted and shoehorned into aircraft, making system cooling critical. The electronics industry was young, but the support personnel were from the Korean War generation. Technical material was scarce in libraries and book stores. We had a good team of tech reps working in a desolate location to guarantee success of a project critical to national security; we shared a huge responsibility, and we worked together toward a common goal.

Life at Del Rio

About half of the tech reps were bachelors and five of us rented a big white house on the west side of Del Rio. Some of the married tech reps found apartments at Fort Clark in Brackettville, 30 miles east of Laughlin. The nearest television station was 165 miles away in San Antonio and reception was poor. We were always designing better antennas. Del Rio had one of the nation's first cablevisions, but it was only a little better than direct reception.

Air conditioners in the local homes were rare and a good swamp-cooler was a luxury. For restaurants we had McFarland's, excellent for Tex Mex cuisine and chicken fried steak. The Civilian Club specialized in great barbecued *cabrito* or goat meat, and the

Roswell Hotel featured daily specials. The best restaurant of all for Mexican food was Mrs. Crosby's across the Rio Grande in Villa Acuña. Fifty miles southeast of Del Rio was Eagle Pass. Across the Rio Grande from Eagle Pass was the city of Piedras Negras and the Moderno Restaurant, good for a tasty steak. I was one of the lucky ones and became the "adopted bachelor" of Major George Ahrens and his wife, Ricci, who I knew at the 506th.

Before Crow Flight deployments began, Pat Halloran and I made a few weekend trips back to Tinker to visit our old friends. Taking shortcuts on the secondary roads, Pat's navigational expertise was impressive. He remembered every fence corner and landmark and never missed a turn. Those Tinker visits were special. When heading back to Del Rio on Sunday, a group of our friends assembled at the Officers Club to see us off, including Colonel Dick Hunziker. We were fortunate when we rode in Pat's Buick, we had air conditioning. However, in my Thunderbird, we only had ram air. One Sunday morning we heard the temperature in Wichita Falls, which was on our route, was 106 degrees. On that trip we were in the Thunderbird, and we had to be resourceful to survive the heat. We bought two bags of ice, cut holes so ram air blew through the ice bags. It was so successful we drove through Wichita Falls with the windows up and savored the cool air.

Pat joined the Laughlin Aero Club, and one weekend he flew us to Austin in a TriPacer for a football game. That introduction to flying sparked my own interest to become a pilot. I can say I was introduced to flying by the very best. Lear tech reps Larry Brooks and Jim Bell were pilots, and I flew with them a few times.

Del Rio and Val Verde County, the area surrounding Laughlin AFB, were in an economic crisis when we arrived there. Poor relations between the previous operation

Frank T. Hayes, 2007.

at Laughlin and the City of Del Rio prompted the USAF to close the base. In April 1957, the former pilot training wing had relocated flight operations out of Laughlin. The few remaining Air Training Command personnel present were awaiting final transfer orders. Some local businesses had been closed and boarded up as a result of the lack of customers. A delegation of Del Rio civic leaders had gone to Washington with promises to implement an Air Force friendly "welcome mat" and they succeeded in getting the base removed from the closure list. Unlike the lush green of today, most of Val Verde County was like a desert. A seven-year drought had taken its toll and area ranchers suffered losses that killed the weed crop their cattle fed upon. Everything was brown and dry; ranchers leased land in Mexico and many herds of cattle were shipped to Florida. During one severe dry spell, we went three months without rain. Del Rio was nicknamed the Mohair Capital of the World and the goats seemed to be the only thing that withstood the hardships well.

An epidemic of the Asiatic Flu swept through the area and closed Del Rio schools for three months in early 1958. Through the exercise of caution, staying home, etc., the younger and healthier base personnel managed to avert a flu epidemic at the base.

U-2 Operations

The U-2 was being pushed into service; for maintenance, we used Lockheed blueprints and any other available documentation. Those were supplemented with standard operating procedures we wrote as we went along. Analysis sections tracked the serial numbers of every black box, actuator and aircraft for failure trends.

SAC had developed an excellent system of checks and balances for tracking statistics on safety, reliability, man-hour expenditures, flight hours and training. A filing system was designed to permit inspection for deficiencies by any inspector from any SAC unit. Multiple failures on a particular serial number or a sudden increase in a component failure rate prompted an investigation and initiation of corrective action such as design or procedure change or additional training. SAC placed major emphasis on classroom and on-the-job training. Working on an aircraft or in a shop was considered on-the-job training. The remainder of a technician's duty time was in the classroom or on a training project. The SAC work environment encouraged its personnel to assume all the responsibility they were capable of to minimize downtime and help the unit achieve 100 percent performance. Every small section of the entire unit had a major stake in the wing achieving or exceeding 100 percent of the scheduled goals each month. Pride and the competitive nature of the leaders right down to the shop level technicians, inspired everyone with motivation and incentives unique to those of SAC fighter units.

Everyone learned to work through the organization to get things done and to advance based on the merit system. We were a team and everyone shared in the unit's success. It was the SAC culture.

To maximize altitude, every ounce of excess weight was eliminated from the design of the U-2 and RB-57D structures and equipment. To gain a few feet of altitude on the RB-57D-2, Sperry omitted the tilt motor of the ground map radar antenna and set the tilt as a fixed angle optimum for the mission altitude. New honeycomb panels were used in the lightweight structure of the RB-57D wing. Rain water intruding into the cells of the honeycomb wing panels froze at high altitude, resulting in delamination and

4080th SRW Tech Rep Frank T. Hayes.

grounding of the RB-57Ds. Ironically, Jimmy Rogers' new hit song "Honeycomb" was introduced that week.

In October 1957 the Soviets launched their Sputnik satellite. In the race to orbit a satellite, our first Vanguard missiles had exploded on the launch pad at Cape Canaveral. These events further validated the urgency of the U-2 program.

New personnel had come from units where they had excelled in their specialties. I have never worked with so many conscientious and talented people who were experts in their fields. Security was always on a "need to know" basis and it was everyone's duty to be cognizant on a daily basis. When a plane was out of commission, we worked around the clock until it was repaired. Working with a young two-striper on a U-2 on the far side of the pitch-black flight line at 2:00 a.m. tested our sense of security and made us appreciate those guarding the perimeters of the base.

Constantly on guard for security breaches, we modified our conversation habits and vocabulary to avoid saying anything that could accidentally evoke curiosity or an unwanted question. If we spotted an electrical harness that could potentially chafe and needed an added clamp, we did something about it. After alerting the Lockheed tech reps, I went to an A&E supervisor to help initiate corrective action through official channels. For my part in squadron safety briefings, I coordinated with Captain Pat Halloran. My part was usually a short briefing on problems under investigation and work-around procedures needed for interim use. When I found something affecting safety of flight or flight procedures, I went to see Pat. If Pat was away, I saw Roger Cooper who I also knew from the 506th. It was a time to get feedback on operational problems and emphasize steps to improve reliability. To minimize electronic system operating hours, we stressed the importance of turning power switches off. For example, one day a U-2 in the hanger for maintenance poured thick black smoke from around the seal of the pressurized equipment bay hatch. A much greater disaster seemed imminent.

The U-2 was pulled out of the hanger into a swarm of fire trucks and the hatch carefully removed, only to reveal a totally charred ARC-34 UHF radio.

For RB-57Ds of the 4025th squadron, I coordinated with Captain Tony Martinez. Except for the six two-seat D-2s and one single-seat D-1, the remaining RB-57s were single-seat photo recon D-0s, with standard Com/Nav, IFF and some with an ASN-6 and APN-81 Doppler radar. The six new RB-57D-2s had APN-107 ground map radar, APN-69 beacon and a complex ELINT system with solid-state recorder and an Electronic Warfare Officer (EWO) in the back seat. Operational problems had been narrowed down to twelve needed modifications and installed on Project ReDo aircraft Serial No. 965. Tony was the project officer. Captain Marsh and EWO Captain Blum also flew the test flights. After twelve test fights, the installed changes were validated for a formal retrofit. The D-2s later deployed to Germany in 1959 and the 4025th was deactivated in 1960. On the D-2, for the EWO's seat ejection sequence, the initiator yanked his ECM displays forward to clear the path for his legs, then his seat ejected. Fortunately, EWO ejection never became necessary.

With long duration missions and growing complexity, SAC pioneered the science of human factors and development of powerful habit patterns that were impervious to distraction during an emergency. Scientists studied the physiological aspects of long missions, worked on ways to help combat fatigue and stay alert during the final phase of long duration missions. When a pilot is almost home after a long flight with everything going well, it is that time to expect the unexpected. This necessity of strong habit patterns was driven home in every squadron briefing and SAC periodical. Every step of every procedure was performed in the exact same sequence every time. A tool was never laid down in an aircraft.

When a new pilot was checked out on takeoff and landing, the U-2 instructor rode "runway chase" in a supercharged 1957 Ford Station Wagon that could accelerate from zero to sixty in about eight to ten seconds. One of my first projects on the U-2 was the installation of UHF command radios in these two station wagons. A short time later we received two Cessna U-3As, the military version of the Cessna 310 aircraft that also had UHF radios installed for flying "airborne chase" of new pilots in the landing pattern. The ARC-34s were supposed to operate on 24-volt battery power, but most required more than 24 volts and the belt driven generator had to be functioning. The generator belt slippage caused loss of UHF communication in rainy conditions. A standard operation procedure was written to authorize extra tight adjustment of the generator belt. U-2 pilots nicknamed the Cessna 310 the "Blue Canoe." Single engine fighter pilots hesitated to log the twin engine time in the Cessna.

One of the first changes we made on the U-2 was the addition of a relay to actuate the IFF Emergency Mode when the canopy was jettisoned. One Friday evening, the Engineering Officer handed me a three-page brochure on the KWM-1 Single Side Band radio made by Collins Radio Company. He asked, "Is there any way you could have a training course ready to teach on this by Monday morning?" I said, "Yes," and spent the weekend unraveling the secrets of single side band suppression and the benefit of concentrating all of the transmitted power into a single side band. A few days later we received an installation kit from Lockheed and went to work on the installation. The antenna was strung from aft of the upper equipment bay hatch to the upper vertical fin. It was an amazing system and for daytime ground checks, technicians called SAC people in Torrejon AB, Spain. At night they could communicate with stations around the world. Periodic reports via the KWM-1 permitted monitoring of a U-2 flight during the long eight to ten hour missions. When accident investigators found evidence of fire on the pilots' oxygen hose, we devised an urgent action modification to add external wiring that bypassed headset and faceplate heater wires imbedded in the oxygen hose. I worked with Sgt Lewis Nelson of the Life Support Section on installing that urgent modification on each aircraft before the next flight.

The RB-57D had major problems; it flew at lower altitudes than the U-2. Even many SAMs and MiGs flew at higher altitudes. After a series of startup problems, the loss of three U-2s, two T-33s, and a B-57C, a command change was deemed necessary. On November 12, 1957 Brig. Gen. Austin J. Russell became the wing commander of the 4080th SRW. He brought with him a SAC troubleshooting team who scoured critical functions looking for flaws, anything that needed to be fixed, anybody that needed to be fired, including tech reps. The member of the team closest to me was Major Irving A. Shulkin, who took over as A&E commander.

Major Shulkin gave a thumbs-up report on me, but Colonel John Harvey wanted to talk to me personally, eyeball to eyeball. He wanted to know about my background, education and details how I became a tech rep without a college degree. I gave him honest answers, restated the pledge I had given other commanders I had worked for, and he was pleased. That's how thoroughly General Russell's team examined the 4080th SRW. At their previous wing, this team had implemented changes needed to scramble B-47 bombers in twelve minutes. The team had an exceptional track record.

Other factors affecting the 4080th operations were the shortage of jet fuel that limited flying hours. After a conflict between military and commercial air traffic in the Western Region, the Federal Aviation Administration (FAA) took over military air traffic control and required FAA flight plans for all military pilots.

General Russell soon made the decision to reduce operations for 90 days and concentrate on training. I was tasked with preparing a remedial training program for all disciplines in the A&E Squadron, about 650 technicians. We developed a multiple choice 105 question test that was equally fair to specialists of all A&E systems. To discourage guessing, one point was marked off for an answer left blank and two were marked off for a wrong answer. Every onboard technician took the test and newly arriving A&E personnel were not allowed to sign in until they took the test. It was a shocking experience. The best technicians in the Air Force began to worry about promotions or loss of a stripe, but it underscored the urgency of the matter. Everyone had to dig out their text books, and as their tech rep, it was my opportunity to contribute to their success.

Our most productive technicians scored in the 65 to 80 point range. Two scored 102, and a master sergeant in Field Training Detachment aced it with 105. At this time Air Training Command decided to conduct an experiment at the 4080th. Instead of beginning radar systems, five Basic Electronic Fundamentals Course graduates came directly to the 4080th for hands on aircraft experience before continuing at Keesler AFB, Mississippi. This was an amazing success. The young technicians were thoroughly motivated, eager to learn in the classroom and on the job. They constantly challenged each other on theory and came to me for answers; they were a joy to work with.

By the time testing was completed, we had amassed an enormous amount of data. I sorted the data into categories for each discipline, and prepared a thirteen-page report with bar graph and pie chart displays. The report contained narratives to summarize the overall test results, the range of scores for the most productive technicians and the range of scores where we could best invest the remedial training. Major Shulkin submitted the report to Wing Training Office where other training progress reports were combined and forwarded in a single package to Headquarters SAC and ultimately to Headquarters USAF. The 4080th received the Air Force Outstanding Unit Award for training and became the pride of 2nd Air Force.

I prepared an accelerated course outline on basic electronics fundamentals that included a review of the theory and mathematical formulas. We began with a math review. I knew we had the best technicians in the Air Force who excelled in their work, and I wanted to help them continue that pace. My heart went out to those uptight about learning and passing tests. I insisted it was not complicated and devised aids to simplify instruction and back up my assertion. For home assignments, each student brought in ten questions; they were obligated to help each other with explanations. We created a learning atmosphere where students could think freely without being stressed. Frequent quizzes and tests helped the students become more at ease. For those frightened of trigonometry, I assigned them an exercise to make up their own sine cosine tables. It brought out the best in all of us, student and tech rep. We were all young and what we lacked in experience was compensated for by determination and long hours. I wore geeky horn rimmed glasses and a necktie; at age 25 I was like an old man to the technicians I taught.

For quality of maintenance leading up to this point, I've never worked with more competent and conscientious technicians with so much pride in their work and security awareness. The refresher of fundamentals for lower scoring students made all more studious and the overall competence was better prepared for the forthcoming deployment of multiple detachments. We had classes of twelve students; after completing three classes, it was a thorough refresher that served all of us for many years.

Similar training projects were underway throughout the wing and after 90 days, our fortunes began to improve. Another valuable asset came to the 4080th, Lt. Col. Ernest L. Worley who took over as commander of A&E in February 1958. He was well liked and most worthy of that unique electronic squadron. Lt. Col. Shulkin had been promoted and moved up to become Director of Materiel. MSgt Frank P. Luttrell, one of my favorite A&E supervisors, moved up to manage Wing Quality Control. He was a hard worker, cheerful and a natural leader. This was the first time a wing level function came under the control of managers from A&E. Frank said, "With graphs showing the performance of all major components, it was soon possible to anticipate the occurrence of failures, and performance immediately improved for all systems. When 2nd Air Force inspectors came, they were amazed at what was being done." PSD NCOIC SMSgt Calvin Holly transferred to Wing Quality Control. In the summer of 1958 oxygen problems resulted in the loss of three U-2s and two pilots. The team worked 72 hours without sleep to examine all possible causes.

After the first year of the 4080th in residence at Laughlin, the people of Del Rio included the base residents in civic events. We had formed a small Sports Car Club that was invited to participate in the county fair and the parade on Mexican-American Day.

Scott Smith from the 506th had a Jaguar XK-140 and I had a Thunderbird. We drove our sports cars in the parade all through Del Rio and Villa Acuña.

In May 1958 Laughlin held an Open House for dependents and residents of Del Rio. Takeoff demonstration of a U-2 and RB-57D-0 regaled spectators with their launch and near vertical climb out of sight. To commemorate the event, the Laughlin Recon, the base newspaper, featured a full-width photo of a U-2 on the front page, the first such news release.

The Next Chapter

With mixed emotions, in late October 1958 I signed out of the 4080th and left Philco for a better-paying job at Republic Aviation on the new F-105 Thunderchief for which my work at Laughlin had prepared me. The F-105 was touted as the first fighter that would go through its service life and never see combat. It was the world's most powerful single-seat aircraft and could carry a bomb at supersonic speed, a record held until the advent of the F-22. The F-105 was a grand challenge, but we paid dearly for the lack of the SAC culture. My only other project that ever compared with the U-2 was development of the F-105F Wild Weasel, which like the U-2, attracted the best talent in areas such as design, program management, flight testing, and technicians. The Wild Weasels had SAC EWOs who used their electronic savvy to defeat the SAM radars. My heart and soul went back to my time in SAC. At the SAC 2000 celebration in Omaha, I had the opportunity to thank Lt. Gen. Jerry Johnson for putting my name on his tech rep list all those many years ago.

On April 30, 1960 I was at Nellis AFB, Nevada with F-105s of the 4th TFW from Seymour Johnson AFB, North Carolina. At lunch time I spotted Pat Halloran's yellow 1955 Buick convertible with its Del Rio license plates. I put a note on his windshield and that evening we met for dinner at the Thunderbird Hotel. A little after midnight we walked out of the hotel and spotted the dreaded news headline all of us hoped never to see, "U-2 Shot Down Over the USSR." For someone involved with the program, nothing could prepare you for this shocking news. It was comforting to have been with Pat when we learned this news.

The 4080th evolved into a very efficient, well organized, close-bonded unit, and at no time have so few consistently contributed so much to our national security. We shared a unique bond of trust with countless "silent heroes," who without fanfare performed outstanding feats. Security prevented deserved recognition for many, just the priceless reward of respect and admiration of their small fraternity.

We left Del Rio with cravings for barbecued *cabrito* and Tex Mex cuisine never again quite satisfied elsewhere. We carried with us wonderful memories of the warm-hearted people of Val Verde County, the shopkeepers of Villa Acuña and Mrs. Crosby's Restaurant. We even developed an ear for that unique "key of G" music from across the Rio Grande. Sixteen years later, I returned to Villa Acuña for dinner at Mrs. Crosby's and I was surprised to be remembered by Mrs. Crosby's daughter and some of the shopkeepers. I was pleased to find on my return visit that Val Verde County had turned green.

Richard Kemp
Canton, Georgia

My four short years in the 4080th SRW were some of the best years of my life. I joined the Wing in the Spring of 1961. My first exciting experience with the U-2 was an engine installation that damned near took my head off. To install the J-57, it was first hung on a track that was bolted to the top of the inside of the fuselage and the roller/hanger bolted to the top of the engine. It was rolled in and out on an engine stand. The clearance between the engine and fuselage was so tight that as it was rolled in, the mechanics had to push the engine from side to side to clear other components. I was tasked to do that job on my very first engine installation. As the engine started to roll inside, I bent over to crawl under the engine. Something in the roller broke and the engine fell about six inches into the fuselage, missing me by inches. Six inches doesn't sound like much but that engine weighed about three tons. Needless to say, it scared the crap out of this then-18-year-old airman.

In early 1962 several other mechanics and I were dispatched by C-123, the noisiest airplane inside ever to fly. We went to Biggs AFB in El Paso, Texas, and recovered a U-2. The aircraft had suffered a flameout en route to Lockheed Skunk Works in California for overhaul and update. Only members of the 4080th SRW were allowed to work on the U-2s. That made it necessary to send us to Biggs to repair and launch the aircraft on to California. After the repairs were made and preparations were made to launch, someone up the chain decided to pull the pogos and hand launch due to the rough taxiways and runways. A man was stationed on each wingtip to balance the airplane while it taxied and started the takeoff roll. With a very small amount of lift, the pilot could control the balance with the ailerons. It was quite a show for those who have never witnessed this feat. We had large crowds of spectators from the base to observe this maneuver. I remember the Base Commander was a very tall, thin full bird colonel and his response after having seen the hand launch was: "Now by God, boys, I've been in the Air Force for a long time and I have seen airplanes take off every way you can think of, but that's the first time I've ever seen two guys throw one up."

Later that year I was sent TDY to Eielson AFB, Alaska. Since the beginning of time, there have been certain individuals in every military unit who know every secret. In this case it was the base bus drivers at Eielson. At that time, most of the U-2s were bare metal with the insignias painted on. While we were there, our airplanes were being rotated back to the factory and the replacements were arriving with the new all over gray paint scheme. Not long after the arrival of the newly painted U-2s, a bus driver inquired of his 4080th passengers, "How do those things take off silver and come back gray?"

At that time, too, the number of missions we were flying increased. As a result, we were given additional aircraft and more personnel were sent from Laughlin. One such engine mechanic was Phil Champion; forgive me, Phil, if you read this. At that time of the year

Richard Kemp.

Richard Pratt (left) and Richard Kemp (right). The two were close friends in West Virginia.

Richard Kemp with his private plane in 2006.

in Alaska, the sun came up about 4:00 AM and it did not get dark until about 11:00 PM. The transport of choice was the C-124 Globemaster. I swear that thing flew backwards most of the time. Phil's flight arrived around 4:00 PM that day and they were all tired from the long flight. We got them some chow and finally settled in their quarters around 5:30 p.m. Phil had a reputation for always being a little late for work. I explained to him that the Line Chief was very strict and would not tolerate any tardiness. I told him to be sure to get to the flight line by the 8:30 AM for roll call the next day. By 6:30 PM Phil was fast asleep. Two and a half hours later at 9:00 PM a couple of us rushed into Phil's room yelling that the Line Chief was mad as hell and he wanted Phil down on the flight line-NOW. He dragged himself out of bed, looked out the window and saw bright sunlight. He dressed and flew down the hall. Someone asked him where he was going at 10:00 at night. Phil said if he hadn't been so tired after just two hours' sleep, he would have killed me then and there.

Not much was known about us because of the mission we were given and the veil of secrecy we worked under. The members of the 4080th SRW were not getting much recognition. We never felt neglected because we did our jobs with pride and for love of country. God Bless America and Dragons everywhere.

Arthur L. (Art) Kveck
Euless, Texas

The Flight from Turkey
We finished our mission at Incirlik Air Base, Adana, Turkey with a B-57D in March 1960. There were two aircraft assigned to carry our personnel and equipment; one, call sign Oil One Two, flew our advanced echelon team. I was assigned to the second aircraft, call sign Oil Two Nine. When we left Turkey for our next detachment at RAF Brize Norton, England, we were transported on a C-119 Flying Boxcar. The flight plan was scheduled with a refueling stop at Athens.

The first premonition I had this was not going to be a routine flight came when we boarded the aircraft. There were enough parachutes for all of us, but the red service tags attached to each one meant the parachute had been condemned. Stapled to the red tags were yellow tags proclaiming the parachutes were serviceable items with the inscription "For One Time Use." "Okay," I thought, "How many times would we actually be expected to use them?" Being compliant airmen, we adjusted the straps for our own fit and stowed them in an accessible area. That accomplished, I settled in for the trip. Unlike a civilian passenger plane, the C-119's seats were constructed of nylon webbing material and installed along the sides of the interior. Each seat had a seat belt and shoulder harness.

The flight departed Turkey and flew to Athens where we refueled and pressed on. Our route was more or less straight down the Mediterranean Sea. Without warning the flight crew began experiencing difficulty controlling the number one engine's propeller. They were able to control it by using the nitrogen pressure that was designed to "feather" the propeller if it became necessary. After using all available nitrogen, the propeller went into a flat pitch and was no longer controllable; it was just like a huge speed brake.

The flight crew instructed us to put on the parachutes, you know, the ones with the red and yellow tags, and get ready to bailout because the plane was going down. When

Left to right: Tony Martinez, Wallace Thompson, unknown, the chap who bailed out with his bag, Art Kveck, Greenstein, the Jew who went to the altar in the Catholic church, and a chap who spoke fluent French and was able to communicate with the Italians.

the command was given, the bailout procedure was followed. The procedure, initiated by the flight crew, was an overhead alarm signal and a command by loudspeaker announcing an emergency in progress. We donned the parachutes, checked straps and buckled for tight fit to prevent injury when the canopy opened.

The designated jump master lined us up at the open door, and at the pilot's command sent the first guy in line out head first to clear the structure of the aircraft. Most of us went out the left rear door. I was the last one in line for this door, and Airman Hope stood in front of me frozen in the doorway. We didn't have time to waste so I kicked him out, and quickly jumped. I looked up at my canopy, grateful to see it spread out above me. The aircraft had descended at such a rapid rate, much faster than the parachutes, that when I turned, I saw below me the top of the airplane I had just left. I swung once in the chute. When I swung again, my feet hit a fence and I sat down in a farmer's pigpen, with the pigs. The aircraft was so low when we bailed out that the total time under the chute was less than a minute.

One of the other guys on the plane bailed out the door on the right side and took his suitcase with him. When he dropped to the ground, all he had left of the bag was the handle he was holding. The flight crew tried to land the plane on the beach, but it skidded and went into the sea.

We had landed near Catanzaro, Italy and the only person in the town who spoke English was a fellow who returned to his native land from Rome, New York, not the other Rome in Italy. He owned the local wine shop. How fortunate that was for all of us! It just seemed like a natural place to meet, and all of us, including the flight crew,

Art Kveck's C-119 in the Italian surf.

gathered there. Because it seemed we had escaped "The Big One," most of us went next door to the Catholic Church to give thanks for a safe landing. Joining me at the altar was a fellow I knew was Jewish. I thought that was rather funny, and so did he after a few glasses of wine. There was a US Navy Long Range Radio Navigation Station near there, and they were notified of our predicament. A truck came for us and took us to their station; they provided us with clean clothes and something to eat. They were really great guys, even if they were Navy.

Three men were hospitalized at Catanzaro with injuries; six others were transported to the US Naval Hospital at Naples. The remainder of the men escaped injury. One chute became entangled in an electric power line, but the airman escaped injury. However, the power line snapped and plunged the nearby town into darkness.

The next day we boarded the truck again bound for an airstrip where a Navy plane flew us to Naples. When we arrived, Tony Martinez, our detachment commander, was there to meet us. He looked like a hero who had come to rescue us. There we were with only our dirty fatigues, no money, no passports, nothing except donated Navy skivvies, tee shirts and socks. Tony managed to get us some money so we could buy some necessities at the Navy Ship Store until we arrived at RAF Brize Norton.

Tony made arrangements for a C-130 Hercules to take us from Naples to England where we were able to buy more clothes and personal articles that had been lost in the bailout and crash of the C-119.

This was an adventure I wouldn't trade for anything, but I certainly would not care to repeat it. As you can see, the pilots are not the only ones who get to bail out of airplanes; we enlisted folks can do it, too. And, successfully, I might add.

I retired after a 26-year career as a Chief Master Sergeant. After I left the 4080th SRW, I became a flight engineer and flew cargo airplanes, C-124, C-121, C-141 and the C-5.

Following my retirement from the Air Force, I went to work for United Air Lines as a pilot and pilot instructor. I wouldn't take a million dollars for my Air Force career, but I wouldn't give a nickel for any more.

Comments by Anthony Martinez

I was assigned to C-119 call sign Oil One Two and took off from Incirlik on Saturday, March 5, at 10:45 a.m. local time en route to RAF Brize Norton via Athens and Naples. The first leg was uneventful and we arrived at Athens at 3:05 p.m. for refueling and took off at 4:35 p.m. local time headed for Naples. C-119 Oil Two Nine landed about fifteen minutes behind us.

One hour and forty-five minutes out of Athens, Oil Two Nine notified my flight crew they were experiencing difficulty with a runaway propeller. One more transmission relayed they were losing altitude, then radio contact was lost.

My flight crew received messages through the Naval Air Station that indicated C-119 Oil Two Nine had crashed or ditched. While my C-119 was on final approach to Naples, the pilot was directed to return to the crash site, approximately an hour away. However, the weather began to deteriorate and our plane returned to Naples. We landed at 8:20 p.m.

Art Kveck's C-119 after he bailed out.

CATERPILLAR CLUB
Certificate of Membership
A/1C. A.L. KVECK
is a member of the CATERPILLAR CLUB having saved his life by parachute
SECRETARY
IRVIN Air Chute Life Preserver of the Air
DATE OF JUMP 3-5-60

Immediately after I landed, I collected all information I could gather regarding the accident and relayed it to Sixteenth Air Force, TUSLOG Detachment Fifty, Seventh Air Division, Second Air Force, Strategic Air Command Headquarters and the 4080th Strategic Reconnaissance Wing. The reports I received indicated everyone on board had either parachuted safely or successfully crash landed. One of the reports said four people had been injured and required hospitalization.

The following day, Sunday, March 6, a Navy R-3D landed in Naples with six of the crash survivors who were checked and cleared at the Navy Hospital. They had been determined to be in the best physical condition after the crash. They were taken by truck from the crash site and flown from Taranto. The fourth man allegedly hospitalized, SSgt Walls, had accompanied Capt Mattarocchia to the dispensary in Catanzaro and was soon released. Actual hospital cases were Capt Mattarocchia for back injuries, TSgt Watson for a fractured ankle, and A2C Hope for bruises and contusions. The remaining six members of our team were being taken care of at the US Coast Guard Station near the scene of the accident.

I had been in telephone contact with Sixteenth Air Force Command Post. Sixteenth directed me to divert C-119 Oil One Two and other members of the advanced echelon team, with MSgt Harrison in charge, to Torrejon Air Base, Spain. I remained at Naples to provide coordination between the crash-site activities and Torrejon, Incirlik, Laughlin and Barksdale.

One of the immediate problems resulting from the accident was the salvage of classified documents and equipment onboard the wrecked airplane. Salvage or documentation of destruction of the classified items was arranged through the Accident Investigation Team that was already at work at the crash site. It was critical to preclude compromise of either our past assignment or the project planned in the UK.

On Sunday afternoon, the C-130 with others of the advanced echelon team arrived at Naples. Major Abadin, troop commander, spent only a short time on the ground. He

Arthur Kveck.

was to be the first line officer to arrive at RAF Brize Norton. He would have responsibility for establishing contact with Seventh Air Division of the USAF, the lead unit on this portion of the TDY. The Seventh Air Division, located at High Wycombe Air Base near London, had operational control of all SAC units in the UK. The second advanced echelon team was unable to do much in the way of tactical planning because Dr. Young was the only officer present. Major Crowe and Capt Wood were to join us at RAF Brize Norton, but they had not yet arrived in England.

On Monday, March 7, I received information the tactical aircraft had left Adana at 6:00 GMT, and were to stage through Torrejon. At 9:30 a.m. local time, I established contact with Capt Barlow through the US Coast Guard radio facility at Naples; he advised me of the plans for evacuation of the salvaged cargo and remaining uninjured personnel. Colonel Wallace, from Operations at 322nd Air Division at Evereaux Air Base, France, was officer in charge of the Accident Investigation Team. He reported that all our personnel, except the three injured men, would soon be in Naples. They would be able to continue the trip to RAF Brize Norton in a few days.

Later that day, I made arrangements for the six airmen at Naples, to go to the Air Force Clothing Store at Pangoli, for a minimum supply of apparel. Throughout this event, my experience with the Navy personnel at Naples could only be characterized as extremely cooperative. They took care of our enlisted men and kept me in contact with Headquarters Sixteenth Air Force.

The publicity angle of the accident was a particular concern to me. I was reluctant to release any information on the crash due to the classified nature of the overall operation. On Sunday, I received clearance from the Public Information Officer at 16th Air Force to release at least the names and hometowns of the six airmen presently in Naples.

On Tuesday morning, March 8, I received a message that the Accident Investigation Team had determined the wrecked C-119 was "damaged beyond economical salvage or cannibalization," and would be disposed of by giving it to the Italian Air Force. The

Italians also operated the C-119 and they could have used some spare parts for their own aircraft from the remains.

On Tuesday afternoon I received a message from the disaster scene that advised all survivors, including flight crewmembers, had been sent to Taranto at 7:00 a.m. local time by surface transportation. The three injured airmen remained in the hospital. From Taranto a C-130 flew them to Naples where they remained overnight.

On Wednesday morning, March 9, I joined the group and we took off at 11:20 a.m. local time and continued our flight to RAF Brize Norton. We arrived at our destination at 2:10 a.m. GMT. All members of the 4080th SRW's Operating Location 1B, minus our three injured airmen left behind in Italy, were finally together again.

Harry R. Magill

Moreno Valley, California
Wife: Dixie

"The Great Turkey Raid"

During the Cuban Missile Crisis, most of us guys were restricted to the base, even the married fellows. We stayed in the 4080th A&E dorm located directly across from the Chow Hall where we ate all our meals. I had a front-row seat for what became known as "The Great Turkey Raid."

I'm not sure of the thought pattern of the airman who initiated the raid. He managed to get into the kitchen of the Chow Hall. He confiscated a whole cooked turkey and delivered it across the street to the dorm. There he invited all the residents to join him in the feast. We did have a lot of turkey and enjoyed the great feast.

Sometime later the Base Police arrived and asked if anyone knew how the turkey seemed to "fly" from the Chow Hall to the dorm day room. Most of the guys were mum, but the turkey liberator confessed that he had delivered the turkey to the dorm. The humorless Base Police took custody of the remains of the bird and returned it to the Chow Hall. This marked the turkey liberator as the hero of the downtrodden airman, and to this day he is still one of the Squadron's heroes; just ask anyone who was there that day. Maybe Rooster Robinson can better explain that caper.

Samuel R. McDowell, Jr.

(Deceased April 28, 2007)

Sam provided the following prior to his death.

> In mid-1959 I was sent TDY to Taoyan Air Base, Taiwan for three months as an engine technician to the Republic of China Air Force (ROCAF) for the RB-57D. Sgt. Shelhorne, an autopilot technician, worked with me at Taoyan. We helped the ROCAF maintenance guys with a problem they experienced with one of the aircraft engines. RB-57D #5643 was losing power as it gained altitude. It was over-compensating and reducing too much fuel. I suggested they replace the fuel control; but to my surprise, the problem persisted. The maintenance guys asked what they should do next and I repeated my first suggestion – to change the fuel control. They said they had already changed one fuel control. They were dubious about my firm stand on replacing the fuel control again, but they ordered another

one and installed it. To their surprise and my absolute delight the problem was corrected.

We discovered that the first replacement fuel control had the same deficiency unit. I was told that after that episode, they wanted to change the fuel control for every problem. Sadly, that plane was shot down on October 7, 1959 by a PLA SA-2 missile killing the pilot, Capt Ying-Chin Wang.

We worked with Line Chief Chung who spoke English very well as did other members of the maintenance team. The Chinese treated us well; I enjoyed my only maintenance TDY. Concerning any cultural or scientific pursuits I engaged in there, I respectfully take the Fifth.

At Laughlin AFB I was in charge of the Jet Engine Shop and did not have the opportunity to go TDY. Adolph Janosky and Harold Brownback were with me in the Jet Engine Shop. I was in Quality Control for a long time and maintained updated blueprints on the U-2. The engineers referred to these change orders when they experienced an unusual problem.

I had another change of career fields to the PMEL shop. I was only a TSgt. at the time and I was put in charge of the shop over fellows with higher rank as sometimes happens in the Air Force. Nobody complained, least of all me. I just continued to do my job. Guys in my shop were frequently in and out on TDY. Sometimes I had to be creative in order to keep the guys busy. Once I assigned each man to take a tech order and develop a test for everybody else. George Devers was assigned "exiting B-57C precautions." He nearly stumped everyone with his question. I don't recall his question, but the correct answer was: Be sure the seat belt pin is in place.

I worked in several different career fields and I can say I never had a bad assignment. There was something about each one that I enjoyed. I retired April 1, 1971. My career had a lot of events that occurred on April 1. One event was that I was assigned to Laughlin AFB on April 1, 1957. After retirement I moved to Indiana and then to Kentucky where I now reside and own a printing business that produces family histories.

I still reminisce about my tour with the 4080th SRW. It was a high point of my career and I made some great friends in that unit.

Marion E. Neal

Charleston, South Carolina
Wife: Doris

TDY to Alaska

I bid my family goodbye and departed Laughlin AFB, Texas on October 1, 1962 on a 90 day TDY to Alaska. A great place to be in spring or summer, Alaska in the dead of winter was not on my agenda of places to visit. However, as a career man, I packed and went where I was ordered to go, this time to Eielson AFB, Fairbanks, Alaska. Our mission was nuclear air sampling over the Arctic Circle to determine radiation levels. While we were in Alaska, the Cuban Missile Crisis was in full swing from Laughlin and later at Barksdale AFB, Louisiana.

I was an E-8 Senior Master Sergeant Line Chief in charge of everything related to the U-2, and it was my responsibility to ensure the plane was operational for a scheduled mission. The Operating Location (OL) Commander was Colonel Forest Wilson. Colonel Wilson's first air sampling mission over the Arctic was one I remember to this day. Somewhere over the frozen tundra, the generator went out on his U-2, and he came back on a wing and a prayer. He literally had to guess his direction back to Eielson because his instruments were out. It turned out that he was a very astute guesser. He was over the Aleutian Islands with his windshield fogged up, without navigation equipment or instrumentation. North American Defense Command (NORAD) identified his aircraft on their radar and scrambled two fighter aircraft to intercept him. With one fighter on each of his wings, Wilson wagged his wings hoping they would understand he was friendly. The fighters escorted him to Elmendorf AFB, at Anchorage where he landed.

I took a maintenance crew from Eielson to Elmendorf and changed the generator in Wilson's aircraft. We checked out the aircraft and performed other maintenance to ensure he would be good to go for the return flight to Eielson.

Colonel Wilson and I went to have coffee and got him squared away through the command channels at the base. The wing commander at Elmendorf showed up, met with us and then sent us off to Eielson. This was at a time when we endured a great deal of scrutiny from the White House.

Chuck Maultsby's Arctic flight

Routine sampling flights were still in progress at Eielson; however, with the 50 degrees below zero Fahrenheit temperatures, we had to be selective about dates when we flew. It was so cold, tires were freezing to the concrete. We had heated hangers where we could performed our maintenance routines in relative comfort for the aircraft, and our technicians. On October 26, 1962 Churck Maultsby took off and flew a sampling mission around the Arctic. On his return to base, he became disoriented, ran short of fuel and got lost. Two F-102s from Galena AFB, a forward operating base under the 5072d Air Base Group at Elmendorf AFB, were scrambled to intercept Maultsby. He landed at Kotzebue, a radar station 33 miles north of the Arctic Circle on Alaska's western coast.

I organized a special preparation for the flight to Kotzebue to refuel Maultsby's plane. Our OL Commander, Colonel Wilson led the recovery team. One of the Physiological Support Division (PSD) people was with me. We loaded fuel into 55-gallon barrels and took two C-47s Gooney Birds full of materials and fuel. By the time we arrived, Maultsby's batteries were dead with not even enough power to crank the engine. Kotzebue, was an Army base, and the personnel were unfamiliar with Air Force operations. The unit commander and an NCO were very helpful; they probably didn't have many drop-in visitors at Kotzebue. They helped us determine how to put batteries together and get enough voltage to crank up the U-2. The first thing we had to do was put fuel in it. The JP-4 fuel we used had become contaminated and unusable. We spent the night straining the fuel through a chamois cloth to have enough fuel for Colonel Wilson to make it back to Eielson. At daybreak, I went to see Wilson and he asked me if I was ready to try it. I told him I was definitely ready to go.

The runway was covered with twelve inches of snow, and where it had been plowed, eight feet of snow was piled on either side of the runway. We took a Jeep out to survey the runway and Wilson looked at it and declared, "We'll get this son of a bitch out of here."

We had brought an Auxiliary Power Unit (APU) with us which we used it to start the aircraft. We put Wilson in the aircraft, hooked him up and he took off. The runway was so narrow the wingtips of the U-2 struck both sides of the snow banks. Then I had the C-47s reloaded and we took off for Eielson too.

Roger ('Big O') Owens

(Deceased June 25, 2002)

The following memories were submitted by Roger's widow, Patricia.

> Roger was with the 4080th Civil Engineering Squadron from 1959 to 1961. His group was responsible for maintaining the runways at Laughlin AFB. He told me about the many snakes they had to deal with when they were working on the runways there. The Del Rio area seemed a haven for snakes.
>
> The enlisted guys' pay wasn't very good in those days. However, we wives were resourceful with what we had. A few days before payday when money was very short, several families would get together and share whatever we had in the refrigerator or pantry. We had a big community meal. It wasn't a gourmet feast, but it was just a wonderful time of sharing with our friends.
>
> To this day Roger's TDY bag is still packed as it was when he last used it. He missed his family on those TDYs, but we understood his job came first.
>
> Roger retired after 25 years in the Air Force. For the next eight years he worked as a rural mail carrier around De Leon, Texas.

Roger ('Big O') Owens.

Art and Martha Reichert.

Roger and I had three children – Roger Jr., Richard, and Peggy. Peggy was born at Laughlin hospital. We have two grandchildren, Allyson and Albert. Albert is carrying on the military tradition; he is in the Army.

Arthur A. (Art) Reichert
(Deceased July 26, 1991)

The following memories were submitted by Art's widow, Martha.

Art was stationed at Barksdale AFB, Louisiana from September 1952 to April 1956. It was during this period that we met and married.

In April 1956 Art was transferred to Turner AFB, Georgia where he began his association with the Black Knights, later known as the "U-2 Project". We relocated to Laughlin AFB in 1957 along with about 500 Air Force families. The nearby small town of Del Rio had many unpaved streets at the time. There was no base housing and the local people were closing in carports and garages and renting them to us. Art and I managed to find a tiny house that consisted of a bedroom, bath, kitchen and living room. It had been purchased from the base as surplus property, and we were grateful to have it. Our landlord and landlady were wonderful people; their name was Hill and they owned the Hill Lumber Company.

Soon after our arrival, it began to rain. It was a welcome relief from the town's dry, dusty climate. Having never lived west of my native Louisiana, I finally got acclimated to the area after about a year and a half. The next exciting event was the construction of base housing where we were privileged to live in brand new quarters. Our only child, son Tommy, was born at Laughlin AFB Hospital in May of 1960.

Everything was changing rapidly for the families. Our husbands' work was classified TOP SECRET which meant they could not discuss anything at home. On a regular basis the Base Commander would call for the wives to meet in the base theater. He would explain to us that we shouldn't get upset if our husbands couldn't tell us what they were doing. He thanked us for our support and told us how important we were to the success of this project. Of course, that really made us feel special. It was not unusual to get a telephone call from our husbands saying, "We're on alert and I don't know when I'll be home."

Art was in the 4080th Armament & Electronics. He worked on the cameras for the U-2. Art and I had a close bond with the fellows he worked with as well as their wives and families.

In June 1963, Art and I relocated to Davis Monthan AFB when the 4080th SRW was transferred there. I felt that we had the best of everything; we had Air Force friends and through my work a number of civilian friends. We considered it a pleasant "mix."

Art was transferred to Offutt AFB, Omaha, Nebraska in January 1968 and it was the end of our involvement with the U-2 project. It was also our most difficult assignment. When Art was sent to Thailand for a year, our son and I returned to my hometown in Louisiana to be near family. Art spent the last 14 months of his AF career at England AFB where he retired in 1971.

Sadly, Art was in a fatal motor vehicle accident on July 26, 1991. Prior to his death, Art and I often talked of the time we spent with the U-2 project and the many wonderful people we met.

Glenn Simmons

Lancaster, Pennsylvania

Wife: Marianne

I supported the U-2 program for four years and it was certainly an interesting time in my life. My assignments were in Administration and Operations of the 4025th SRS and propulsion, ground power and orderly room for the 4080th. I kept the jet engine records that were recognized as the best in 2nd Air Force according to the Inspector General auditors.

My memories of those days include Airman Shelby, Airman Fariar, Chief Warrant Officer Underwood and all the jet engine mechanics.

One of my most memorable experiences was when we received a radiation sample that had to be wrapped in a lead sheet and sent to Isotopes in Nevada. President Eisenhower's visit to the area to dedicate the Amistad Dam was a highlight of my tour there. John Wayne's visit while making the movie *The Alamo* was another memorable event of that time.

Marianne's memories:

I was 17 years old when Glenn and I married. When I had saved enough money, I went to Del Rio to be with Glenn and we found an apartment on Fourth Street. Our first child was born December 25, 1959. If it wasn't for the Air Force, I would not have

Glenn, Marianne and Diana Simmons, 1960.

been serenaded in Mexico, an event I remember to this day. I also enjoyed living in the town of Del Rio and meeting so many friendly people, both in town and on the base.

Richard W. Staats

(Deceased October 16, 2001)

Memories submitted by Richard's widow, Reiko.

Richard and I met during his tour of duty in Japan in 1952 and were married 48 years when he passed away in 2001.

Richard was assigned to the U-2 maintenance unit first at Turner AFB, Georgia and at Laughlin AFB, Texas. His last station was at Davis-Monthan AFB, Arizona. He supported the U-2 program for a total of 11 years.

Our two children and I were accustomed to Richard's frequent absences. One year the Christmas tree remained up until April when Richard returned and the family celebrated together. During the Cuban Missile Crisis, Richard had 30 minutes to pack and leave on TDY to a destination I had not been told. When President Kennedy announced on television of the tension building in Cuba, I thought then that Richard had gone to Florida. On that particular TDY he was gone more than a month.

Richard had another mysterious foreign destination that I remembered. He was directed to pack a civilian suit, white shirt, tie and dress shoes. Money was

Dick Staats.

Reiko and Dick Staats.

always in short supply and Richard did not have a suit. Richard's Commander told him that funds would be arranged for him to have a suit. I thought their destination might be a Communist country but I was not sure.

Richard served in Vietnam for one year and returned in 1973 to Albuquerque, New Mexico. He later went to Virginia and retired in Pennsylvania where I currently live.

Memories of Cyndi Staats

I don't really remember much about Del Rio because I was just a baby when my parents were there. However, my mother and father have told many stories of the time they were stationed at Laughlin AFB. My parents' eyes would brighten as they retold tales of how the close-knit community supported each other. I recall that my parents were close with a rancher in Del Rio named Mr. Cox who helped them from time to time. My father told stories of deer hunting on the Cox ranch. To this day, my mother stays in touch with other families she met during that time. Although they are scattered across the country, they write as though they just transferred from their last assignment.

William J. Turpin
Oceanside, California

I was known by friends and co-workers as "Turp." From 1956 to 1968 I was part of the 4080th SRW and the 100th SRW at Turner AFB, Laughlin AFB and Davis Monthan AFB. My assignment was with the Field Maintenance Squadron structural repair shop, better known as the Sheet Metal Shop. Our motto became, "You bend, we mend." Our shop made high-pressure hydraulic lines, control cables, fiberglass repairs and all manner of sheet metal repairs. We did some minor and other extensive repairs on the U-2s. I was also with the B-57 program and supported the drones.

A number of names come to my mind of friends and co-workers who shared those times. I had some fun times and hard work with Donald Swann, Lowell Foster, Emanuel Peevy, and "Soup" Campbell.

My most memorable experience was a TDY to Australia. I met many wonderful people there and made a lot of good friends. I missed them when I had to leave; seeing real kangaroos and koalas were a special treat.

The Air Force gave me a great education seeing different parts of the world and experiencing new things. However, with the good times came the bad times of being separated from my family and loved ones for extended periods and missing out on family events.

I especially enjoyed the camaraderie of the Air Force, and I now keep in touch by email with some of the guys.

Turp's wife of many years, June, who was with him during his Air Force career passed away in February 2003. He has since married Judy, a long-time family friend.

Gordon E. (Joe) Warner

Carrollton, Texas
Wife: Jane

The Beginning

I am an Iowa farm boy born and raised not far from Radar O'Riley's hometown of Ottumwa (you know, from the television series *M*A*S*H*). We lived in the last house on the last road so if we saw a dust cloud, it was either the postman or someone was lost. We had no running water or electricity, and I attended school in a one-room schoolhouse until the eighth grade. The day I turned seventeen, I asked my dad if I could join the Air Force, and he said, "Why not?" Now keep in mind, the farthest I had ever traveled was to the Missouri state line to buy fireworks and to the Iowa State Fair in Des Moines. You can only imagine the culture shock I experienced on my first airplane ride to Oakland, California for eleven weeks of basic training with folks from all over the country.

After basic training, it was on to Aircraft Mechanics Technical School at Amarillo AFB, Amarillo, Texas where I was told I would be working on the F-89 Interceptor. Upon completion of technical school, I received reassignment orders for Turner AFB, Albany, Georgia. The saga begins.

In February 1956 after a short visit with my folks in Iowa, I traveled to Albany and presented my orders to the guard at the main gate. He quickly told me I was in the wrong place because there was no organization by that name on the base. I was totally flabbergasted. In time everything got sorted out, and I found my way to the open bay barracks that was to be my new home.

I did not know there was a master plan for forming a new wing. I learned later the plan was to take the top graduates from technical school, mix in some three to six year Korean-war veterans, and top it off with some of the meanest "brown shoe" sergeants that ever held a wrench. The term "brown shoe" was applied to those men who were

OL20 Maintenance Group in front of Joe Warner's U-2 #703 - 'Soup' Campbell fifth from left back, arms crossed; Donnie Brown, third from left, middle row; Joe Warner, sixth from left, middle row; Bob Ingram, fifth from right, back row.

members of the Army Air Force and were issued brown shoes or boots. When the Air Force came into its own in 1947, everyone was issued black boots.

So there we were, an eclectic mixture of humanity thrust together to form one of the most unique squadrons of all time. The only problem was we had no airplanes. With no planes to work on boredom set in very quickly. One of the sergeants' favorite past times was to gather us young guys after roll call and have us sweep the hangar floor while they drank coffee in the break room. After we finished sweeping, they came out, looked at the floor, kicked over the trash cans and we would start all over again. Some days this went on until noon. What they failed to tell us was that they were observing attitudes and determining who would be the future crew chiefs.

Eventually some of us were assigned to an inspection dock working on the B-57 aircraft and some just disappeared for a few weeks. In 1957 the 4080th Strategic Reconnaissance Wing moved to Laughlin AFB, Del Rio, Texas and we began receiving the U-2s from Lockheed.

Everyone has their favorite story about the U-2, and I am sure you have heard most of them. What struck me most about the aircraft was that there were no instruction manuals for the aircraft. Now keep in mind that I had just finished mechanic training where the instructors had pounded daily that we never ever do anything without "the book." Here I was working on an aircraft that was supported by Lockheed with the original blueprint drawings but no maintenance manuals. All the maintenance was accomplished by asking another maintenance tech or one of the Lockheed tech reps,

Joe Warner, 1959.

who would then consult the drawings. When we went TDY to an operating location, ten five-drawer filing cabinets with the aircraft drawings were critical equipment to be loaded on the transport aircraft. Of course, using those drawings was another story. Finding a needle in a haystack would have been an easier task than finding the specific drawing that was needed. That was where our own Little Black Book with common part numbers (not girlfriends' phone numbers) became a "must have at all times" for each crew chief.

I worked my way up the ladder to crew chief and went on several deployments. The principle aircraft I was assigned to was #703. At that time it was designated as an E model which meant it had aerial refueling capability.

My first TDY was in the summer of 1958. It was Joint Task Force 7 at Eniwetok Atoll. This was an exciting time for me to witness first-hand the atomic tests. We were 35 miles from ground zero for most of the shots, and I could feel the heat from the blast even at that distance. The Atomic Energy Commission had a B-52 that usually took off at 3:30 a.m. Since the island was in the form of a dog leg with our living quarters on the short part of the leg, it seemed as though the plane was coming right through our tent. The high point of the trip was a shot referred to as OAK. Our instructions were to roll up the tent sides and put everything on top of our bunks. When the shot went off, it was announced that the wave action would start in fourteen minutes. The time came and went with no wave action. Then suddenly the lagoon dried up right in front of my eyes.

The bottom of the lagoon could be seen for at least 100 yards. Just as suddenly the action reversed, and the bottom half of the island was covered with the waves of the sea.

Our wing operated primarily as a TDY organization. When we were at home station, it was training, training and more training. Everyone pretty much hated it. For a long time the normal rotation was three months TDY, and seven to nine months back at home. In later years the rotation plan changed resulting in more frequent TDYs due to a shortage of qualified personnel.

I would be remiss if I did not mention the wives of our organization. They were the glue, the force behind the guys, any and all superlatives would work here. I was in Alaska on a TDY from Laughlin AFB and returned to Davis Monthan AFB, Tucson, Arizona. My wife, Jane, took care of closing up the house in Del Rio, packed and arranged shipping of everything, rented a home in Tucson and had it all set up when I returned. One tough lady!

Then there was the TDY that continues to be a topic of conversation, the infamous trip to Clark AFB, Philippines and on to Bien Hoa Air Base, Saigon, South Vietnam. This trip had been in the works for some time, and we had several premature starts. We only had three U-2 aircraft with inflight refueling capabilities, and they were needed for this deployment. James (Soup) Campbell was crew chief on #707, Donnie Brown was crew chief on #680 and I was crew chief on #703. These three aircraft were equipped with

Joe's U-2 #66703 in flight. Photo courtesy of Lockheed Martin Co.

J-57 engines because they had inflight refueling capabilities. Later they were designated as the F model when they were reconfigured with the J-75 engine.

When we were alerted for an immediate departure, I made a habit of taking an empty suitcase to the assembly point. There had been frequent dry runs and premature starts when we were released immediately after checking in. As luck would have it, one of these turned out to be the real thing and off we went. The boots I had on were pretty well worn, and by the time we arrived in Vietnam, I had to put paper in the soles. One day a C-130 dropped in and I gave the loadmaster $20 to bring me a new pair of boots on his next trip. I never again saw the loadmaster with my boots or my $20.

When we arrived at Clark AFB, Philippines, we had been flying for what seemed an eternity, and we were all bone tired. The word we received was to have at least two of the aircraft ready to fly as soon as possible for a mission the next day. This aircraft has an extremely sensitive center gravity and the weight and balance have to be figured on every mission. There is a lot of math involved; at home base, it was done by someone with a big calculator. Our line chief gathered Soup, Donnie and me together and said we had to do the weight and balance by hand. We looked at each other, and Soup spoke first, "I don't think I can do it." Donnie chimed in quickly and said, "Me neither." The line chief looked at me and said, "I guess that leaves you, Warner." I was still there eight hours later when they came back to do the preflight, but we got the job done.

All the crew chiefs felt very protective of "our aircraft." To this day, Soup, Donnie and I know the whereabouts of "our" U-2s. Soup's #707 is on static display at Laughlin AFB. Donnie's #680 has the distinction of hanging suspended overhead in the Smithsonian Air & Space Museum in Washington, DC. My own U-2 #703, well, it holds a special place in my heart.

I had approximately eighteen years with the squadron and many, many enjoyable times. I do not have any bad memories. When I retired in 1976, I was the night liaison for Colonel Eddie Dunagan, Deputy Commander of Maintenance for the wing. As the night liaison, I was in charge in his absence. There were a few exciting nights, but most of the time the duty was a bit boring because nothing of any significance occurred at night.

Albert (Dan) White, Jr.

Cat Spring, Texas
Wife: Linda

Panama

In March 1962 I was sent to Panama on a six-month TDY. The operating location (OL-18) was headquartered at Howard AFB which was located inside the perimeter of the Army base, Fort Kobbe. Major Melbraaten, the detachment commander, asked if I could fix a malfunctioning ship-to-shore radio on a friend's fishing boat and I agreed to give it a try. I was familiar with a lot of radio equipment through my job. I was required

Alaska May 1961

Panama OL-18 May 1962

Panama OL-18 August1962

to maintain the radio systems on the U-2 which included repair or replacement of the boxes.

When I saw the radio on the boat, I discovered it was badly corroded and required some time to clean up and restore it, but I was finally successful. After installing the repaired radio in the boat, Major Melbraaten and his friend invited me to join them on a trip through the Panama Canal at the Miraflores Locks. What a treat. The canal, built in 1914, connected the Atlantic and Pacific Oceans via a 48 mile ship channel with locks. All sizes of ships passed through the canal to save an estimated fifteen days by sailing around the southern tip of South America.

We were in a small fishing boat sharing space in the lock with an enormous cargo ship that had paid an exorbitant fee to pass through from one ocean to the other. The most striking memory I have of that event was looking up at the huge ship going through the locks with us. One small error and we could have been crushed like a bug against the side of the lock and not discovered for some time.

England

A month after returning to Laughlin AFB from Panama, in early October 1962 I went into my shop, the 4080th Armament & Electronics (A&E), for the day shift. Before I could even start work, Sgt Richardson, the radio shop supervisor, told me to return to the barracks and pack a bag. He said a plane was waiting for me on the flight line. I was going TDY to RAF Upper Heyford, England, OL-7, and I would replace the radioman there. I rushed off to the barracks, quickly packed and returned to the flight line where a U-3A waited. A captain and first lieutenant had finished the preflight, and we were ready for takeoff. I discovered I was the only passenger for a trip to Forbes AFB, Kansas to meet a KC-135 tanker. When I arrived, I learned I would be the only passenger on that

Dan and Linda White.

flight too. The flight crew told me to take any seat in back and get ready for a long flight. When I left Laughlin, it was still warm even in October, and I had dressed in short sleeve fatigues with field jacket. My compartment in the KC-135 was anything but first class. It was extremely cold in my area, but the crew was toasty warm on the flight deck.

Upper Heyford was an active RAF base, but we operated apart from their operation and we had only casual contact with anyone. Our detachment commander was Arthur Leatherwood. The Operations Officer was Pat Halloran and assigned pilots were Tony Bevacqua, Bob Pine and Dave Ray.

Shortly after arriving in England, I learned the base was on alert, but I wasn't sure of the reason. While I listened to BBC Radio one evening, I learned the US had blockaded Cuba because of the presence of missiles from the Soviet Union. It was a time of great concern. Many of the enlisted men and I spent evenings close to the radio to learn if we were going to war with the Soviet Union. All turned out well for us in the ground crew. However, we did lose a couple of our pilots, Rudy Anderson and Joe Hyde, who gave their all. We remember them for their duty and sacrifice.

I enjoyed my time at Laughlin AFB with the A&E radio group. Some of the team were Sergeants "Rich" Richardson, "Bat" Masterson, Cliff Fortner, and Airmen Lee Brazer, Don "Cooch" Coucherio, Sam Bell, Bob Montella, Frank Sweeley, Clint Allred, and Bill Withrow, my roommate.

To Launch a Recon Around the World

"Aviation in itself is not inherently dangerous. But to an even greater degree than the sea, it is terribly unforgiving of carelessness, incapacity or neglect."
Anonymous

Cuban Missile Crisis

October 1962 is a date that is vivid in the collective memories of many Americans, but most especially the men of the 4080th Strategic Reconnaissance Wing. They were charged with flying over the island of Cuba to photograph the presence of Soviet missile sites. The clarity of the photography taken from their U-2 aircraft made it easy for President Kennedy to determine how to proceed to protect our country.

The Joint Chiefs of Staff (JCS) planned and directed the execution of all Cuban overflights. No flights took off before the JCS briefed the President and he authorized each mission. The SAC Recon Center at Offutt AFB, Nebraska transmitted the approved orders through the chain of command to the wing command center.

At the Wing level pilots were designated for the scheduled flights. Support functions, such as Maintenance, Photography and Operations were alerted of the forthcoming events. Physiological Support was notified which pilot was scheduled to fly and the technicians had his gear ready when he reported. The pilots tasked for these missions were:

Major Rudolph Anderson
Major Buddy Brown
Major Steve Heyser
Captain George Bull
Captain Ed Emerling
Captain Roger Herman
Captain Charles Kern
Captain Gerald McIlmoyle
Captain James Qualls
Captain Robert Primrose
Captain Daniel Schmarr.

The camera maintenance personnel had special pride in their work. These missions were what they had trained for and they were ready. It was a favorite saying of the unit, "If the camera doesn't work, there was only a training flight that occurred." The following people were there to support the NEPHO operation at McCoy AFB:

F. M. Shipley	Glenn Chapman
Bob Ingram	Joseph (Rooster) Robinson
Jim Manis	John Bell
Jerry Fogel	Ricky Mickle
Bobbie Black	Jim Combs (Hycon Tech Rep)

Ray Callahan Tom McClung (Perkin Elmer Tech Rep)
Frank Gault Jim Lobig
John Washburn B. C. Fowler
John Farris

When the pilot returned from his flight, the photography specialists quickly offloaded the film and sent it in a waiting aircraft to Washington, DC for processing.

Buddy L. Brown

Knoxville, Tennessee

Cuban Missile Crisis October 1962

My mission photographing and locating Soviet missiles on the island of Cuba began October 1962. Prior to the Strategic Air Command (SAC) being assigned the Cuban mission, the CIA had been monitoring the weapons' movement with their own U-2Cs. As a result of the increasing tension between the United States and the Soviet Union, President Kennedy wanted to avoid embarrassment of a clandestine CIA plane being lost over Cuba. The President decided USAF pilots would fly the reconnaissance program. The wheels were put in motion.

There were 11 pilots initially involved in the "Missiles of October" crisis. This is my personal account of my first Cuban mission and the events leading to it. I don't remember how I was notified, but Jerry McIlmoyle and I were flown out to Edwards AFB (North Base) to sit in and listen to the dialog between the SAC brass and the Agency (CIA) brass regarding who should take over and fly the Cuban mission, the CIA or USAF. The meeting was in the evening at the North Base Operations building. Jerry and I were seated at the back of the small auditorium listening to the heated dialog between the two agencies' big chiefs. I thought we were both there to get checked out in the Agency's "C" model if SAC was to be assigned the responsibility for this mission. Rudy Anderson and Steve Heyser had already been qualified in the "C" model. The dialog became heated; in fact, Jerry and I were asked to leave before the discussions continued. I don't know what happened for the remainder of the meeting, but the next day I was flown back to Laughlin AFB along with our contingency of Laughlin brass. We arrived late in the evening. The next morning, I went down to the 4028th operations and briefed the boss and mission planners on what I had heard and observed at the meeting at North Base. I was surprised to learn that particular contingency had been planned months earlier and was "on the shelf". There were many secure calls made and our operations and maintenance activity increased dramatically. The end result was that the 4080th SRW had replaced the Agency and had been assigned the reconnaissance program over Cuba.

I was selected, along with several other pilots, to fly the initial recon missions. We all reported to Operations in the early afternoon, and received a quick overview and mission update. We were directed to go home and immediately start our required eight hours of crew rest. We were to report back to Operations at 0100 the next morning. I went home, took a sleeping pill and hit the sack. The next morning, I reported to Operations along with the other primary pilots. We started our final briefings. I looked around and it seemed everyone from our Wing was in the briefing room.

After the briefings, we went to PSD (Physiological Support Division) for our pre-mission meal, modified physical, and mission update. The PSD guys helped us get into

Cuban Missile Crisis pilots and the commanding officers. Back row, left to right: General Thomas Powers, CINCSAC, Captain Edwin Emerling, Major Buddy L. Brown, Major Steve Heyser, Captain James Qualls, Captain Roger Herman, Colonel John DesPortes. Front row, left to right: Captain George Bull, Captain Charles Kern, Captain Gerald McIlmoyle, Captain Robert Primrose, Captain Daniel Schmarr.

our pressure suits. It was raining when we started dressing. During our pre-breathing period, I could tell it was one of those Texas thunderstorms. The rain came down with greater intensity and the winds, lightning and thunder all had increased. The weather was looking bad outside. I thought we would never be cleared to take off in weather like this. The crosswinds were quartering tail wind and were way out of limits. The increased thunderstorms were pounding the area. Much to my surprise, SAC executed the mission. I was transported in our PSD vehicle to my aircraft. The rain was so severe, I could hardly see more than a couple of feet in front of the van. The strong winds were shifting the vehicle as we drove out to the aircraft.

The bird I was to fly had slipper tanks installed which contained electronic intelligence collection equipment. It had been spotted on the apron just off Runway 13 (130 degrees). "Great," I thought, "The winds were blowing from approximately 280 degrees with a quartering tail crosswind, and now were way out of U-2 limits of 25 knots." I got out of the PSD van and walked about 20 feet to the ladder to get into the cockpit. The cockpit looked like it had filled up with water. Not so; it was just raining so hard it seemed that wet. I hoped all that water wouldn't short out any of my electronics.

The Mobile Officer was soaking wet, I was soaking wet and everything around us was soaking wet. The Mobile Officer told me to complete my cockpit check solo so he could close the canopy. I completed my cockpit check and signaled Mobile that I was ready to start my engine. I looked out the left side of the canopy watching the wind blow sheets of rain across the runway. The whole scenario was unbelievable, and the Mobile Officer was going to launch me into that? Say your prayers, Buddy Boy.

This was a radio-silent mission, so only light signals were used to start, taxi and clear for takeoff. I led my bird and followed the light wand for the 50 or so feet I had to taxi to the active runway. Sitting in the cockpit, I felt the strong wind buffet my aircraft. The rain was still incredible after all this time. I got a green light, gave the bird full power, released brakes and started my takeoff roll. All during the takeoff roll the aircraft was buffeting. "I hope my pogos drop freely," I thought to myself. As soon as I lifted off and established my climb, I set my controls to the Gust position, slowed to turbulent air penetration speed, and turned every light in the cockpit to "High."

The lightning lit up the sky like daylight, and all the while I was being bounced around. This roller coaster ride lasted until about 50,000 feet when I finally broke out into a clear night sky. What a relief. I hoped everyone made it okay. I continued the climb to altitude, changed from Gust to Fair position, locked in the autopilot and settled in to start my celestial shots. I think there were about six of us that took off that night, and all would return to Laughlin AFB after completing our Cuban missions. I was designated to recover at McCoy AFB, Florida. I crossed the Gulf and after a few hours, I picked up my initial coast in point in the western part of Cuba around Pinar Del Rio.

About 15 minutes before entry, I powered up my B configuration camera, set the mode and checked all the aircraft systems. I crossed over into the Cuban land mass; all my camera equipment was on and operating normally. All my targets were in the western part of Cuba. The weather in Cuba that day was cooperating and my areas were clear. Tracking and staying on course were easy; I used the drift sight. There were many checkpoints to verify my position. After flying my programmed recon track, it was time to head back to McCoy AFB. I exited Cuba and headed north to Florida. Everything was still "radio silent." Before I started the descent into McCoy AFB, I was authorized to make my first radio call and requested landing instructions.

The weather at McCoy was great. I entered traffic from the downwind side, turned base onto final and made a full stop landing. My pogos were inserted, and Mobile cleared me to taxi and led me to my parking spot. As I was taxiing in, I observed a lot of activity at the ramp. Several vehicles converged on my bird as I completed my engine shutdown. The ladder was rolled up to the cockpit and the Operations Officer on the ladder turned out to be Major General Compton, the SAC Director of Operations. What a surprise that was! He welcomed me back and we exchanged a few words while my "B" configuration camera was being downloaded. I had completed my first Cuban mission.

Several more U-2s arrived at McCoy within the next couple of days. The initial cadre of U-2 pilots there with me included Rudy Anderson, Steve Heyser, Jim Qualls, George Bull, Charlie Kern, Jerry McIlmoyle, Pinkie Primrose, Danny Schmarr, Roger Herman, and Ed Emerling. Up to this point I had not been checked out in the Agency's "C" model; however, a few days later, Jim Barnes, a CIA pilot and friend from other bases, flew in a "C" model and gave me my checkout.

To this day, I don't know how we took off from Laughlin on that historic night with no hung pogos and no aborts. Without a doubt, our Guardian Angel was on duty watching over the 4080th Wing that night.

On what would be forever known as "Black Saturday," October 27, 1962, I was assigned as the primary pilot for my target area in and around western Cuba. The secondary target area pilot was Rudy Anderson. If my target area was forecasted to be weathered in and the secondary target area was open, the secondary pilot would fly. As it turned out, my area was clobbered so Rudy flew his target area. He was shot down that day by a SAM and became the only pilot to be lost during the Cuban Missile Crisis. I remember that day. Some of us were out on the golf course because we could only fly every other day. From the golf course, we could see any U-2 entering the traffic pattern for a full stop landing. I was talking to "Chopper" Kern as we approached the green that was a high point on the course. I looked at Chopper and said, "I don't know what happened, but Rudy should have been back by now."

Later that day we were all summoned to report to Operations. We were briefed on the loss of our fellow pilot, Rudy and his U-2. It was sad to lose one of our own. We had all flown our scheduled missions knowing that it could have been our last. But those thoughts never entered my mind; I had a job to do and I did it.

Richard Henry
Venice, Florida

There were 13 days of the most dramatic world events of my lifetime and I had a front-row seat. Even as President Kennedy and Premier Khrushchev frantically looked for ways to pull their countries back from the edge of disaster, they found it difficult to control their own military machines, let alone the rapid pace of outside events. Kennedy ordered saturation reconnaissance of Cuba to keep track of the Soviet missiles located there.

Every single U-2 pilot who was not on duty in Alaska or stationed elsewhere overseas was called into service. My squadron flew as many as six missions a day over Cuba. We observed launch pads recognizable by their peculiar slash marks; also observed were fueling and checkout vehicles, communication lines and prefabricated storage bunkers. The USAF was so intent on carrying out Kennedy's orders that it ignored normal safety precautions. In the predawn hours of October 17, 1962, four U-2s took off from Laughlin AFB at Del Rio, Texas at 10-minute intervals in a blinding thunderstorm that would normally have grounded such a flimsy aircraft. The wingtip of the U-2 piloted by Major James Qualls barely missed the runway because of strong crosswinds. Qualls recalled, "We were just about mapping the entire island." Colonel DesPortes, Commander of the 4080th SRW joked that he didn't have many pilots or aircraft left to fly over Cuba.

At McCoy AFB, Florida, tensions were simmering between the Air Force "blue suiters" and the CIA support personnel who were responsible for servicing the U-2s and taking charge of the intelligence materials, such as the photographic film. The Agency people were still smarting from what they perceived as a power play by the Air Force in persuading Kennedy to deprive them of the mission over Cuba. "They were very resentful and made no bones about hiding it," said Anthony Martinez, Operations Officer for the AF U-2 squadron.

According to U-2 pilot Gerald McIlmoyle, CIA personnel "looked for fault in everything we did". Jerry recalled that a CIA officer reported him to Washington for allegedly displaying signs of nervousness by urinating beside his U-2 shortly before takeoff. McIlmoyle had a good defense: he wanted to spare himself the laborious task of relieving himself aboard the aircraft when he was trying to focus on taking pictures of Soviet missile sites.

On October 25, McIlmoyle returned from an overflight of Cuba with an alarming story about being targeted by an SA-2 missile site near the town of Banes on the northeast coast of Cuba. The CIA's U-2s had a device for detecting when they were being observed by enemy radar. When a radar system painted the plane, a yellow light appeared in the cockpit. When a missile locked onto the plane, the light turned red.

The yellow light had already appeared by the time McIlmoyle made a scheduled turn over Banes. As he gently banked his aircraft, he saw two contrails zip up from beneath him and explode in the sky above. They looked like SA-2s. There was still no red light in his cockpit. McIlmoyle figured that either his detection system was not working properly or the operators of the SA-2 had fired the missiles blind, without engaging the guidance mechanism, in order to deprive him of the usual warning.

Higher-ups were skeptical of McIlmoyle's story. A three-star AF general who reviewed the electronic intelligence told him bluntly, "You weren't fired at." McIlmoyle, a Captain who later rose to the rank of Brigadier General in charge of the President's nuclear codes, believes to this day he was targeted.

If Rudy Anderson was concerned about McIlmoyle's report, he kept his worries to himself. According to colleagues, Anderson was determined to fly more missions than anyone else, which meant somehow leaping in front of Richard Heyser who was ahead in the rotation. Operations Officer Martinez recalled, "Rudy was in high gear all the time. He was very competitive, patriotic and very, very dedicated. He was an absolute perfectionist."

According to Heyser, Anderson came to him at one point to ask if he could take a mission that Heyser had been scheduled to fly. Since Heyser had already racked up a large number of special missions, he was less concerned than Anderson about cramming in as much flying time as possible. Heyser remembered telling Anderson to check with Lt. Col. Martinez who was responsible for drawing up the roster. Heyser said, "If it's okay with him, it's okay with me. As a result, Martinez scratched my name out and put his name on the roster."

Exactly when this incident took place is unclear. Heyser says it happened on October 26, the day before Anderson's fatal flight. But flight records show that Anderson had already caught up with Heyser in number of missions by that point, which suggests that the incident may have taken place earlier.

McIlmoyle also recalled Anderson going to Martinez on the evening of October 26, expressing an eagerness to fly, and asked to be put on standby the following day. Martinez could not recall this particular episode, although he said it is "plausible," given Anderson's sometimes "intense" personality.

The following morning, at least three other missions were scrubbed at the last minute, making Anderson the next pilot in rotation. Capt. Roger Herman had the job of clearing Anderson for takeoff. He followed him up the ladder to the aircraft and ran through a checklist of 30 or 40 items. He made sure that Anderson's oxygen supply was connected properly. Maps and TOP SECRET target folder were neatly stacked by the side of the ejection seat. A final preparation, called "press to test," supplied a surge of oxygen that briefly inflated Anderson's partial pressure suit and filled the cockpit. When he was certain everything was in order, Herman slapped Anderson on the shoulder. "Okay, Rudy," Herman said, "Here we go, have a good trip, see you when you get back." Anderson gave a thumbs-up sign as Herman closed the canopy.

Minutes later, Anderson's U-2 roared down the runway and headed toward Cuba. "Target number 33 destroyed. Target number 33 destroyed."

Joe Glenn Hyde, Jr

Deceased November 20, 1963

The following story appeared in *Southwest Texas LIVE*, October 17, 2006. It was written by Joe Glenn Hyde III and the article is submitted here with his permission.

The Sky Still Burns in Your Memory

On November 20, 1963, from Barksdale AFB, near Shreveport, Louisiana, a USAF U-2C took off on a reconnaissance sortie just after 6:00 AM to take photographs of the Island of Cuba.

One year and one month after the end of the Cuban Missile Crisis, Strategic Air Command (SAC) U-2s from the famed 4080th Strategic Reconnaissance Wing were tasked with continued overflights of Cuba to ensure that the Soviet Union would not redeploy its offensive, medium-range nuclear missiles only 90 miles from Florida. Barksdale AFB was the temporary duty location for the U-2s performing these missions.

The pilot wasn't new to the Cuba mission. He had been flying U-2 missions for over three years. Nor were sorties over Cuba just routine. At the end of the Cuban Missile Crisis, the Soviet Union had removed their nuclear missiles trained on the US homeland. However, the Soviets left Cuban President Fidel Castro with a gift of brand new SA-2 surface-to-air missiles like the one that shot down another U-2 pilot, Francis Gary "Frank" Powers, over Moscow in 1960. Castro was also given a squadron of state-of-the-art MiG 21 fighter aircraft that were clumsy at high altitude, but still considered a formidable threat.

During a previous deployment of support for the Cuban mission that year, this U-2 pilot was awarded the Distinguished Flying Cross (DFC) for out-maneuvering a MiG 21 that attempted to meet it head-on. In all, during his short tour as a U-2 pilot, in addition to earning the prestigious DFC, he was about to pin on his fifth Oak Leaf Cluster to an Air Medal, meaning it was his sixth Air Medal. Even by today's standards, with frequent deployments to war zones of Iraq and Afghanistan, earning six Air Medals within three years is the exception, not the rule. The pilot had an "aw shucks" attitude about the medals. He said that everyone in his unit got them just for doing their job.

By 11:00 AM, the pilot completed the zigzag flight plan over hostile territory taking classified pictures of the areas assigned his mission. He was approaching Key West, with the coast of Florida looming larger in the mid-morning sun. Earlier in the mission, in a required radio position report back to SAC command post, the pilot indicated that his autopilot had failed.

Flying the U-2 was hard enough with the aid of an autopilot. Flying the U-2 without an autopilot was dangerous, especially at high altitude where the air is extremely thin. The airspeed indicator allowed for only three knots (about 5mph) of deviation. If flown too slow, the U-2 stalled and lost altitude quickly. If flown too fast, the U-2 entered a regime called "mach tuck" where the aircraft will exceed the speed of sound and probably break apart. This regime was known among the U-2 pilots as the "coffin corner."

The U-2C flown that November day was a former "Agency" bird, a term used to describe U-2 airframes that were once inventoried by the Central Intelligence Agency (CIA), but transferred to SAC when the USAF assumed more of the high altitude reconnaissance missions in the early 1960s. The U-2C rather than the U-2A was the preferred airframe to use for the dangerous Cuban overflights. It had a more powerful engine and a better suite of threat detection instrumentation that informed the pilot when he was under attack by enemy surface-to-air missiles or other aircraft.

Agency birds, because of their origin in the clandestine world, were modified on occasion to improve mission effectiveness, sometimes at the expense of safety. In this case, the U-2C flying that day had previously had its "stall strips" removed to improve range and maneuverability. Stall strips were installed on the wings of most U-2s then to create a more noticeable stall warning by creating more turbulence over the wings that would warn the pilot of an impending stall. Without the strips, inadvertent stalls were more likely.

With no stall strips, no functioning autopilot, and an airspeed tolerance of only three knots, even a small deviation in temperature or turbulence can quickly put the U-2C in an out-of control situation. With those conditions present that morning 40 miles south of Key West, ground radar following the mission watched in horror as the U-2C plunged almost vertically and disappeared from radar. Within eight minutes, search and rescue aircraft spotted an oil slick at the location the plane disappeared from radar. Ten days of extensive search continued, and the wreckage was salvaged beneath 100 feet of water in the Gulf of Mexico. Hope remained alive for a long time because the survival gear was found, and it appeared that the pilot had departed the aircraft. Maybe, just maybe, the pilot would be found floating, alive, in the water somewhere. With each ticking hour, then days, hope diminished until the search had to be terminated. The body of the pilot was never found.

The pilot of that U-2C was my father, Captain Joe Glenn Hyde, Jr. He was only 33 years old when he died.

My father earned his pilot license at the age of 15. For three years at his high school in Georgia, he was an all-state tackle and in college, a star guard for the University of Georgia Bulldogs in 1948 and 1949. After a nose injury threatened to prevent his dream of a career as an Air Force pilot, he became a capable assistance coach for the Bulldogs in his junior and senior years in college. He accepted an ROTC commission and eventually earned his pilot wings at Greenville AFB, Mississippi.

His first assignment was as an instructor pilot at Greenville AFB. In modern terms, he was what is now called a "First Assignment Instructor Pilot," or FAIP. It was during this tour that he met my mother, Marianne. After his FAIP assignment, he was sent to Korea to fly the F-86. A year later he was assigned to Laughlin AFB as a T-33 IP.

It was a dreadful assignment. No fighter pilot would choose to return to a trainer airplane after a tour flying the F-86. But Dad had a wonderful personality, demeanor and competence for being an IP. His USAF flying records indicate that with volumes of letters of recommendation from senior officers hailing his instructing abilities. SAC needed a strong cadre of IPs at Laughlin to maintain flying skills of the pilots in the recently assigned and secretive U-2 program. The U-2 mission did not afford the pilot much opportunity to practice instrument approaches or landings so the T-33, or T-Bird, was used as a companion trainer.

One story related to me about my father was of a check ride he endured in the T-33 upon arrival at Laughlin. On short final to Laughlin's Runway 13 for final landing, the evaluator pilot deliberately shut off the fuel switches causing the engine to flame out just before touchdown. My father landed safely and allowed the aircraft to coast to a stop. After both pilots exited the aircraft, the evaluator smiled and admitted that he had deliberately shut off the fuel in order to evaluate how my father would handle the situation. Not amused by this illegal and dangerous act, my Dad, who had arms of steel forged from years of football, cold-cocked the evaluator pilot right then and there.

The pilots of the classified U-2 program were some of the most highly regarded pilots in the USAF. "If I am going to be in this business, I want to be on the first team," he told my Mother. After a year of knocking on doors at Laughlin, he was accepted into the U-2 program in 1960. Now he was on the "first team." By flying the U-2, he felt completely fulfilled with his new assignment in Del Rio.

The U-2 community has always seemed like part of my family. During the 4080th SRW reunion in Del Rio in 1993, I learned the details of Dad's accident from some of the pilots who participated in the safety investigation. Although no one knew for sure, the theory was that Dad's U-2 stalled and entered a flat spin. The theory was that he attempted multiple spin recovery maneuvers as the aircraft plunged from 70,000 feet altitude. At 10,000 feet, and according to procedures at that time, he attempted to eject. However, the sink rate and centrifugal G-forces of the spin during the long fall exceeded the operational capabilities of the ejection seat. They doubted his parachute ever deployed.

Some 24 years later in 1987, I learned all about spins in the T-37B as a student pilot at Vance AFB in Oklahoma. On training sorties, students were trained to deliberately place the aircraft into a spin and apply spin recovery techniques. The words for the spin recovery, in shortened phrases still ring in my head to this day-- "Idle, neutral, aft, left spin, left needle, right rudder, BOOM! Stick abruptly full forward after one turn. After spinning stops, recover from dive." The enhanced spin training in place today is probably a result of multiple mishaps involving spins during my Dad's day in the cockpit. In current procedure manuals for all aircraft I have flown in the USAF, there is the warning—should aircraft control be lost at any altitude, an ejection above 15,000 feet offers the best chance of survival. They added 5,000 just for Dad.

I elected to stay in the Air Force and served primarily as an instructor pilot in the T-38 at Laughlin and as a B-52H instructor pilot at Barksdale. I retired from the 96th Flying Training Squadron (Reserves) in August 2006, ending 20 years of service with an assignment as a reserve T-38C instructor pilot at Laughlin, flying the same skies that Dad had enjoyed for a majority of his own flying career.

In the Memorial Student Center at my alma mater, Texas A&M University, there is a Bible verse inscribed in stone that reads, "Greater love hath no man than this, that a man lay down his life for his friends. John 15:13." That is the identical verse read at the memorial service for my Father held on December 7, 1963 in his hometown of La Grange, Georgia.

The most moving tribute to my father was read by his commander, Colonel John DesPortes. It reads as follows:

JOE GLENN HYDE, JR., Captain, United States Air Force
As an officer – Dedicated, dependable, one of the finest.
As a combat crew of the Strategic Air Command – Competent, reliable, eager.
As an individual – Gentleman, great physical and moral stature.
As a citizen – A great representative of his state, his alma mater, and his country.
As a man – Honest, confident, proud of his heritage, a pillar of strength.
As a friend – Loyal, inspirational, sincere.
As an American – Who could rank higher than Joe Glenn Hyde, Jr. who gave his life for all in the cause of freedom?

Young Americans elect to fly for the US Air Force for a variety of reasons today, but it still remains true that service and dedication to our country are foremost on the minds of many of the sharp, young men and women I instructed at Laughlin AFB over the years. In today's political climate of two concurrent "hot wars" in two different countries, the stakes are higher for them than they were for me, yet many continue to volunteer for service.

Every time a new pilot graduates from Laughlin AFB, they are fulfilling the legacy of those who blazed the path before them. The line of preserved airplanes on static display that greets visitors at the entrance of Laughlin AFB should remind all of us of those heroes. Each plane carries its own story and the story of the heroes who flew them into history.

The U-2 community has a poem that is read as a tribute to comrades who died while flying that dangerous aircraft. The poem is as follows:

They were born of the Sun,
They flew for a short while towards the Sun,
And left the sky burning in their memory.

The skies above Laughlin AFB burn in the memory of Joe Glenn Hyde, Jr. and all who have slipped through the clear, blue sky above the Southwestern Texas sagebrush while serving this country on the "first team," as aviators who were summoned to defend this wonderful land and the freedoms we cherish. I hope we never forget that.

I'm sure my Dad would have it that way, too.

Ward G. Graham

(Deceased May 8, 2004)

The following was submitted by Ward prior to his death.

Terrifying Days After the Crisis

In the Spring of 1964, I was one of several U-2 pilots assigned to fly recon missions over Cuba from Barksdale AFB, Louisiana. Our squadron had been maintaining surveillance of Cuba since October 1962. The "authorities" had determined there was no longer a need to continue these flights. Most of the pilots and airplanes were returned to Davis Monthan AFB, Arizona for reassignment to other missions.

Don Webster, a tech rep, and I were the last pilots left at OL-19 with our commander, Lt. Col. Joe King. One evening in April, Don, the navigator and I were in Colonel King's quarters celebrating the demise of OL-19. We were in the midst of heavily imbibing what Rush Limbaugh calls "adult beverages" when Colonel King's phone rang. It seemed to us that when Colonel King answered, he snapped to attention. What we heard on his side of the conversation were statements like, "Two pilots and airplanes, sir. How soon to launch? Well, sir, both pilots have been drinking, so it would be about 11:00 tomorrow, 12 hours from bottle to throttle, you know, sir. What's that? Waive the regulation? Yes sir, then we can be there by 20 degrees sun angle tomorrow."

Joe flipped a coin and Webster lost the toss. He went to bed to sleep for a few hours. The navigator and I received and planned a route for him to fly over Cuba. Later, we rolled Webster out of bed, got him some breakfast and plenty of hot coffee. The sun peeked over the horizon, and a half-inebriated Don Webster staggered off into the murky dawn. He probably wondered why he was flying to Cuba when the mission had supposedly been shut down.

Don was airborne and making his check-in calls. We listened to the radio and learned that Fidel Castro, Cuba's dictator, had made a bold statement that he would shoot down the next U-2 that violated his airspace. We were all shocked. We knew that with his 24 SA-2 surface-to-air missile sites he could easily bring down a U-2. In 1962 his SAMs had killed one of our squadron mates, Major Rudolph Anderson. We were on pins and needles until Don called his "coast out" message. He had not been fired upon.

While Don was airborne, a classified message came into OL-19 Operations laying on a mission for the next day. Tomorrow would be my turn. The next morning, I made my way south over Sarasota VOR to Key West. I was very apprehensive. I had flown a few missions over Cuba in the past, but it was with the understanding that Castro's dogs were on a short leash and would not track or fire upon us. That day the 90 miles from Key West VOR to the coast of Cuba seemed like an eternity. The island shape began to loom on the horizon. To this pilot it had the appearance of Darth Vader.

Castro continued to echo his threat and Don and I alternated days flying over Cuba. We each flew two or three missions a week for two weeks. Why didn't Castro fire on us? Some months later word reached us that then-President Johnson had called Castro's bluff with something like this: "You may have my U-2, but it will cost you your island!" With the stakes that high, Castro backed down. No aide in the White House elected to pass that message to the two pilots who assumed they were facing death on every mission.

It was during these two weeks that God got my attention and I began asking questions of myself like, "Is there a God? Is He knowable? What would happen to me if I died?" I even tried to get into the Barksdale Chapel one night to find answers to these perplexing questions, thinking that if I "showed up," God, if He existed, would reveal His program to me.

About two months later I was in Panama on another U-2 detachment and God answered my questions through another U-2 pilot, Major Clair McCombs. Backed with biblical references, McCombs showed me how I could know God personally through Jesus Christ, have my sins forgiven and be given the guarantee of eternal life. I would gladly fly those Cuban missions for such an outcome!

Charles W. Kern

San Antonio, Texas
Wife: Nancy

Dragon Lady Comes of Age

From the time it entered service with the USAF, the U-2 was assigned mostly routine missions including air sampling and domestic photography. During the month of October 1962 an abrupt change in the missions brought the Dragon Lady to the attention of the world.

Steve Heyser, Rudolph Anderson and Jerry McIlmoyle quietly left the squadron for several days and traveled to Edwards AFB, California to check out in the CIA's U-2s. Steve and Rudy flew the first missions over Cuba in "borrowed" CIA U-2s. Jerry flew his first mission from Laughlin AFB. The "take" (photography) from these early October flights wrote the pilots' names in the history books. The US had confirmation of the presence of Soviet Medium Range Ballistic Missiles (MRBM) on the island of Cuba, only 90 miles from Florida.

I first joined this action on October 16, 1962. Steve and Rudy were already on location, and the rest of us pilots were getting ready to deploy. We were still at Laughlin AFB when the FRAGORD, slang for Supplemental Operations Order, arrived and the mission planning area went into lock down mode with heavy security. U-2 launch times were set for 4:00 AM to 5:00 AM in order to reach the photographic targets over Cuba at the best angle of the sun for the film exposure. Five aircraft were scheduled for the task, and I was assigned as Mobile Control Officer.

The morning I preflighted each aircraft during pilot hookup and checkout, a series of Texas-sized thunderstorms passed over the Laughlin area. Maintenance had brought out the houdah, an umbrella-like apparatus used to shield the pilot from sun and rain, but it could not begin to keep out the torrential rain that cascaded on the tarmac. We were soon thoroughly soaked. That must have been an omen of the events that were to come.

After the pilot came onboard (I don't recall which one), I checked his oxygen and pressure connections and meticulously ran the aircraft checklist using our challenge-response method. I completed all my tasks so we could close the canopy and get the pilot out of the rain. He lowered the canopy lid, and after checking intakes clear, I gave the pilot the start signal, index finger pointing up and rotating. We operated in complete radio silence. With the power unit and air starter running, the pilot signaled inward with thumb to ground crew. Whoosh! The air blasted into the turbine starter and within seconds, the low whine of the engine signaled its starting stages.

An unrelenting rain, such as I had never seen, lashed and pounded us. Was this how Noah felt? I turned the headlights of the mobile vehicle directly on the aircraft to aid the ground crew in pulling pins and chocks. I signaled thumbs up to the pilot, clearing him to taxi. The pilot taxied the few feet to the runway and the maintenance crew pulled the pogos to ensure none hung up on takeoff.

I sat in my chase vehicle and watched the dark, helmeted shape in the cockpit turn in my direction. Unable to determine the pilot's thoughts at the moment, I knew for sure he was focused on flying a successful mission. My vehicle was off his right wing with the dome light on. The wind and rain continued their driving intensity.

Ten seconds to brake release and the pilot increased the engine speed. In seven more seconds, the pilot rammed the throttle full forward and disappeared instantly in a cloud of spray, steam, vapor and darkness. I knew he had made it off safely when the engine roar, heavily muffled by the continuing downpour, faded evenly and quickly.

After the aircraft launched, I returned to the Physiological Support Division (PSD), home of the team assigned the job of shoehorning the pilots into the pressure suits. Other launch officers like me were deep in thought and envied those who had been selected to fly the first missions. None of us had any idea of the unique situation developing in the Caribbean and that we, too, would be packing within hours to join the team at OL-X, the classified designation for McCoy AFB, Florida. Our orders came that night. We loaded ground crews, operations officers, mission planning navigators, the Mobile Control station wagon and all the remaining pilots on the giant C-124 Globemaster and launched for McCoy. Considering the momentous events unfolding, it appeared we were all lost in our own thoughts, maybe even prayers.

The day had finally arrived for the U-2 to show what it, and those flying and supporting the aircraft, could do for the Air Force and for our country. After years of training and flying routine missions, the Shady Lady, a term of endearment for the bird, was on her way to the adventures for which she had been designed. She would have a permanent place in aviation and diplomatic history. What a thrilling time to be part of her metamorphosis.

After arrival at McCoy AFB, the team was immediately involved in mission planning and flying. There were certainly enough missions to go around with eleven pilots and ten aircraft. Though I don't recall exactly what we did during our non-flying hours, I'm almost certain it probably included "hoisting a few" at the overcrowded Officers Club. Rudy Anderson was a very serious guy and didn't participate in much of the partying like many of the rest of us. He was the standby pilot and Mobile Control Officer the next day when two other pilots and I were scheduled to fly photographic collection missions over Cuba. Up to this point, there had not been much apprehension about these missions. That attitude changed swiftly and brutally.

Early in the morning of October 27, 1962, four of us followed the normal preflight routine: briefing, physical exam, breakfast of steak and eggs. We suited up with the help of the PSD techs. While pre-breathing 100 percent oxygen for one hour prior to takeoff, we studied the target folder, and once more reviewed the Green Card. The Green Card displayed the navigation log on one side with oxygen consumption predictions and fuel consumption log on the reverse side.

Thirty minutes before takeoff, the PSD team squeezed us into the pressure suits. The outer garment protected the pressure suit laces from catching on the various switches, knobs and handles in the cockpit. I then strapped on my shoulder holster with my long-time companion, the .357 Magnum. For years I carried this same gun on my missions.

I took a deep breath and held it so no ambient air could enter my lungs, and I changed the walk-around oxygen bottle for a full one. The air-conditioned van carried the pilots to the already preflighted U-2.

We were met at the aircraft ladder by a calm, softly smiling Rudy Anderson, the Mobile Control Officer. I climbed up the ladder and into the "office," as the cockpit was known. The PSD guys were doing their thing, snapping and connecting everything. A PSD tech switched me to the aircraft oxygen system. I held my breath while he performed the QD (quick disconnect) and safety clipped it. I checked with a firm pull on the connection to ensure it was latched. I fastened the lap belt and shoulder harness over the pressure suit and oxygen hoses. We certainly didn't want those hoses or anything else in the way during a seat separation and ejection. The PSD tech performed a "press to test" and a surge of oxygen inflated all the pressure suit capstans and breathing bladders. Suddenly it was very crowded in that small cockpit. The final check of the face seal determined it was properly seated and securely fastened. The PSD tech patted my helmet indicating "all okay" and then he turned it over to Rudy. Rudy connected his headset and mike with a click and switched us to "hot mike" so we could talk while running the checklist. I heard the sharply amplified sounds of my own breathing through the headset.

Rudy was Chief of U-2 Flight Standardization, and since I was an FNG (fairly new guy), I didn't joke around. I had to concentrate on the immediate task of preparing for engine start and launch. We went through the entire checklist, and then through the last chance recheck of crucial oxygen system and every connection. Rudy untied the string on the TOP SECRET folder and laid out in the proper places the maps, Green Card, pencils, dividers and plotter. One final scan of the cockpit and Rudy gave another pat on the helmet, then clicked off the hot mike. He backed off, and the maintenance tech rolled the ladder away. I waited for clearance to start. I waited and waited and waited.

After an excruciatingly long period, I finally got the signal. The signal was not to start but to get out of the cockpit and stay on oxygen. Somebody "up the line" was trying to decide whether we launched or not. PSD rolled the ladder back, brought a walk-around oxygen bottle and unhooked me from the aircraft system. I left the cockpit and climbed down the ladder to the ramp. A short time later back at PSD I was told the White House had scrubbed the mission. We were directed to leave one airplane and one pilot ready to go if clearance was received.

In a situation like that our unwritten rule was that the Mobile Control Officer was always the spare pilot and would normally be the next to fly. When the mission was scrubbed, I would not fly if there was a reschedule. With that mission cancelled, Rudy automatically became the next pilot. Some of us mildly protested, but Rudy prevailed. He reminded us of the unwritten rule and jokingly, that he was also the senior guy.

After changing out of the pressure suit and back into a normal flying suit, I went back to the visiting family quarters where we were housed. It was only a short time later that Rudy and the next Mobile Control Officer, Ed Emerling, received the call to return to the flight line for what was to be Rudy's final mission.

For lack of something better to do, a few of us headed for the on-base golf course. My golf game was lousy, and I wasn't enjoying it at all. But it did beat sitting around waiting for tomorrow. When I arrived back at the house a couple hours later, I learned Rudy was missing. Ed Emerling, as the Mobile Officer, went back to his position at the flight line just in case Rudy might return. Perhaps, we thought and hoped, the aircraft had radio failure or some other problem. Ed waited until the time that fuel would have been exhausted, then gave up and came back to the house. What followed was a somber evening, if not sober, watching television news.

We didn't fly for a couple of days, and we in the detachment didn't have any idea about our forthcoming participation in the momentous events played out on daylong television news. We received word the Commander in Chief of Strategic Air Command, General Thomas Powers, was flying into McCoy to talk with us pilots. Wow! Must be something really big for "The Man" to come down.

We speculated that Washington would order surgical air strikes to at least take out the SAM site that bagged Rudy. Maybe we would activate protective ECM (Electronic Countermeasures) to jam the other sites so they couldn't pick us up on their radars. Wrong on both counts. We would continue overflights but without ECM. Our leaders were not about to compromise the ECM equipment that would have to protect our strategic strike force bombers in case we went to nuclear war. That appeared more likely with each passing moment.

We flew exposed and vulnerable as hell. The next day we went in force, five aircraft flying parallel courses about twenty miles apart, staggered with five-minute separation. Our flight plan carried us directly to Cuba from the east tip to the west, bending fifteen to twenty degrees to follow the curvature of the island. This time we did take off and launch in radio silence. I was third in the order and therefore, in the middle flight track. Things went well, and to my left Guantanamo Bay slipped quietly by. The weather was great, and I felt good regardless of my uncertainties about the intentions of the enemy below. We felt sure President Kennedy had sent word to Fidel Castro to lay off the U-2s, but we were not at all confident about the compliance with the directive.

Suddenly, over the radio in clear audio came an alarmed voice: "Green Arrow! Green Arrow! Green Arrow! I repeat, Green Arrow! Green Arrow!" I said aloud, "Damn! That sonofabitch is after another one of us." That was the recall signal from the RC-121 monitoring our flights. I racked the airplane into an evasive hard left turn, heading for the nearest shoreline which was actually the south shoreline of Cuba, about 20 miles west of Guantanamo Bay. The airplane shuddered, and I eased up a bit and turned 90 degrees. For a few seconds I turned to the right then back to the left toward open water. Five or six very long minutes passed and I was out of range of the SAMs. Turning off the cameras, I flew east until clear of Cuba and headed for McCoy.

The mission was terminated for that day by the recall. From that point on, the missions ceased being a really fun thing to do. Although this particular mission ended in a recall, there were many others that went textbook.

Our equipment improved, and we became more knowledgeable about the intentions of the enemy. The shrieking of warning systems and the red signal, known as Oscar Sierra, alerted the pilot that a SAM was in the guidance mode. Following the launch, it was then locked on to the aircraft. We referred to the OS signal as the "OH SH*T" light on the right canopy rail. If that signal lit up, we were in deep you-know-what. Now, there's black humor at its best! That signal was definitely not something anyone wanted to hear at 70,000 feet.

The sweat brought about by trepidation of this nature is uniquely different from normal sweat caused by exertion or uncomfortable heat. Trepidation sweat has a singular pungent quality of its own, a particular scent that is unmistakable. It has been many years since my last combat mission over North Vietnam, but the leather pressure suit gloves I wore over Cuba and Vietnam have retained that distinctive scent to this day. Yes, I still have those gloves … somewhere.

U-2 Aircraft and Pilot Vanish

It seemed like all my personal episodes with the Lady in Black began with a phone call, someone on the other end of the instrument muttering a few sentences that ended with "Get down to the squadron ASAP." The phone calls always seemed to come within a couple of days after my return from a two or three month TDY to an odd-ball place halfway around the world where some nut was trying to take away his neighbor's cookies. The bottom line: It was not in the best interest of the US for that happen. The call then went out for the U-2s to go have a look. Other drivers were out reconning the places I had recently returned from; I was now eligible to leave again after a brief stay at home.

Standing left to right: Major/Navigator, Lt/Maintenance, Col William Hayes, Lt Col Wheaton, Hospital commander, Major Mahaffey, Lockheed Tech Rep Mike Cupito, Major/Maintenance, Airman/PSD. Kneeling left to right: Major Charlie Kern, Major Leo Stewart, Major/Navigator, Capt/Maintenance, MSgt John Hillman, Crew Chief.

Can't say I didn't ask for it though; I loved the job and I loved the aircraft. That's how my day started on July 28, 1966.

Upon arrival at the squadron, I was told a U-2 and its pilot had gone missing on a Cuban overflight mission. I had heard nothing about a missing U-2 so I was completely in the dark regarding the dilemma of Capt Robert "DD" Hickman and his aircraft. That would soon change; I was appointed to the Accident Investigation Board and briefed on all aspects of the situation. The Commander of the SR-71 wing at Beale AFB, California, Col Bill Hayes, was en route to Davis Monthan AFB to serve as the Board President. However, the initial overview would commence without him in order for Maintenance personnel to begin their records inquiries for the history of the aircraft as quickly as possible.

The initial briefing to the Board was very sketchy as we had little to go on at this early stage. Lt Col Tony Martinez, Commander of the 4028th SRS, briefed a dozen people including the wing safety officer, operations officer, pilots and maintenance officer, several of whom would become Accident Investigation Board members.

Col Martinez began the briefing with the scant facts known at this time:

- Capt Hickman had departed Barksdale AFB, Louisiana, location of the wing's Detachment OL-19, on Tuesday, July 28, 1966 at 0400 on a Cuban overflight mission to verify the island's adherence to the accords reached by the US, Soviet Union and Cuba following the Cuban Missile Crisis of October 1962.
- Capt Hickman's flight appeared to progress normally, including practice intercepts by F-104s from Homestead AFB, Florida. A turn by the U-2 to a planned southerly heading had put it on course to Key West, Florida. Hickman had checked in by radio with the F-104 flight and commented that he would "see them next week."
- He then turned to the penetration heading from which point, twelve minutes later, he would "coast in," meaning he would enter airspace directly over the Cuban coastline. At this specific point, the flight plan called for a turn back to the east. The turn was never made, and the aircraft continued on its last heading for nearly 3,000 miles, until it crashed near the top of a 14,000 foot mountain, 150 miles southeast of La Paz, Bolivia. Something had gone terribly wrong in that twelve-minute period between Key West and the planned easterly turn at the Cuban coastline.
- During its journey southward, the aircraft had overflown a US air base in Panama, and had been intercepted, somewhat, by a high altitude B-57 seeking a visual on the obviously stricken U-2 pilot. However, the B-57 could only close to about 10,000 feet below and was unable to report anything useful for our purposes.

As the initial briefing continued, more information came in during the day. A school teacher, whose classroom was on the ground track of the U-2, reported seeing the aircraft in an estimated 45 to 60 degree dive, trailing "smoke" and making a screaming noise. Her class was outside the school on recess, so the teacher was able to witness the last few seconds of the doomed flight. Almost immediately, a wing broke off and the aircraft did a half roll just before it disintegrated as it struck the mountainside in a steep dive at an estimated 400 knots.

The teacher reported the crash up the chain, first to her local police officials who then reported it to the Bolivian military authorities who then reported it to the American Embassy. Somehow the aircraft was identified as a US plane. Through US channels, the report filtered down to us.

The first indication to US authorities that there was trouble with Hickman's aircraft was when it failed to make the easterly turn at Cuban "coast in." US radars had tracked it on its southbound course and handed it off to Air Traffic Control, then to Panama Control for the attempted B-57 intercept.

At that point, all the US could do was to advise those countries in South America in the flight path that the ill-fated U-2 was headed south and would finally run out of fuel and crash. The *where* was only an educated guess, and not a very good one. The *when* would be approximately ten hours from takeoff, making it about 1700 local time on South America's west coast, 1400 in Bolivia.

After the initial briefing, we headed home to pack a week's worth of clothes, civvies and working uniform, and reported back to the squadron. We loaded our team of Accident Investigation Board members, baggage and necessary equipment, on "Old Shakey," a C-124 Globemaster that flew us as far as Panama. There we transferred the team and gear to a C-130 Hercules capable of operating at 13,000 foot elevation of the runway serving La Paz, Bolivia. The C-130 flight was also noisy and long, but the loadmaster was used to it and was prepared with a good supply of ear plug protectors for his passengers.

In La Paz, we were met by a group Bolivian soldiers with vehicles and drivers necessary for the grueling trip to the crash site. The arrival at La Paz was a shock to most of us; we had not given much thought to stepping out into the thin air over 2.5 miles above sea level. As soon as the airplane had depressurized, we immediately felt the discomfort. We grabbed our bags and started down the ramp. By the time we were on the ground, everyone gasped for breath. Lesson One: Take it slow and easy up here. We were also met at the aircraft by the legendary Col Ed Fox, USAF Air Attache at the US Embassy, Bolivia. For the past several years Col Fox had been a personal friend and confidante to presidents of several South American countries, including Bolivia, as well as chiefs of state and high ranking military officers. No surprise, he had already been to the crash site to ensure there were no classified elements laying around the area. Not to be concerned with that, there was nothing left of the airplane larger than small fragments with the exception of the wing that had broken off at the root in flight seconds before impact and fluttered to the ground. It had been carried away by natives and was likely now serving proudly as a roof for someone's hut.

We left Col Fox, but would make a courtesy visit and informal briefing when our team gathered at his home prior to departing for the US. We headed for the hotel exhausted from simply moving around in the extreme altitude. Dinner and rest were the orders of the evening. We had set up a meeting the next day to strategize our next move. The following day would be "Action Day" and a very long one as well.

We prepared to drive and hike our way to the site. We were up at 0300, had a quick breakfast and were on the road by 0400 in three carryalls driven by Bolivian soldiers. The carryall in another life had been similar to a Chevy Suburban with three bench seats and cargo space at the rear. A rugged vehicle that could traverse almost any terrain, it was the only thing that could get us to the site. A couple of the Bolivian soldiers spoke English, but I was the only board member who had even a limited grasp of Spanish. Communication did not get too complicated between the groups, and hand signals were understood. Our first stop was a small, non-descript building that housed the radio station at the airport. As Board President, Col Hayes had to notify USAF officials we had arrived in Bolivia.

While he was inside the radio station, I scrounged for something I could use to make a couple of walking sticks, one for Col Hayes and one for me. The best I could come up with was two boards, about one by four inches that I somehow pried off an old, discarded pallet. At this altitude there were no trees, and few other sources of wood. Nada. Zip.

Col Hayes' message was sent, and we departed immediately for the crash site. Three hours into our journey, we came to a river which I learned was crossed by ferry boat. Ordinarily, the trip to the crash site would have been about six or seven hours drive; however, this day the ferry operator had decided to go to the village, or somewhere away from the boat. After waiting over an hour, the soldiers became impatient, to say nothing for the rest of us. One of them fired a full machine gun magazine over the ferry operator's house. As one might imagine, the response was immediate. The ferry operator came pedaling his bicycle furiously, with many apologies.

The ferries were a story unto themselves. They were river-powered downstream and mule-powered upstream. The operator and his helper loaded two ferry boats to accommodate our three carryalls and team members, then untied them as the current took the boats downriver. Meanwhile, the ferry boat driver steered to one side and his helper used a pole to help push the boat to the opposite side.

When the boat reached the target-side dock, the helper tossed a rope with a loop over a piling, and the stern was likewise secured. After the boat was unloaded, a mule pulled it back upstream, this time to a release point on the opposite side of the river. If all the pylons, including the emergency ones, were missed by the loop-thrower (probably unlikely with all their experience), the ferry would end up in a large lake a couple hundred miles south.

It was only another 150 miles of rugged road to the site; the remainder of the drive to the end of the road was uneventful. The best description I could give about the road was that it was a dirt path strewn with rocks and boulders. Most everyone slept except the driver and me, he drove and I whittled away on the two walking sticks. *Damn, but that pallet wood was hard!* Guess it had to be to hold up under the abuse and reuse pallets were subjected to. A couple more hours and we would be there; then the going was really tough. It was all on foot for the remainder of the journey.

I finished the walking sticks just as we arrived at a "village," actually a small collection of mud huts. I was told the teacher, who gave the eye-witness account of the last few seconds of the doomed U-2's flight, lived here. What a God-forsaken place! There was nothing, absolutely nothing, but dirt and rocks of all sizes.

There were thirteen of us, plus the six Bolivian soldiers at this point. The soldiers led the way, and we began the long, difficult trek following. The trail was impossible to describe: rocks *everywhere*, up and down we went, around boulders as large as houses blocking the trail. It was hard to find decent footing with the rocks, shale, and loose dirt.

Feet wanted to slide downhill with every step. The walking stick was a great help, and I was glad I had seen its potential in the pallet at the airport radio station. This pace went on for a couple more hours; meanwhile, we were just trying to breathe. Mike Cupito, our Lockheed Tech Rep, turned blue and had trouble breathing, so we left him with one of the soldiers to keep an eye on him. Finally after a bit more hiking, we arrived at the crash site.

It took us four hours to get to the crash site, the return trip only three. The hike to the site took so long our time there was limited to two hours. We set up search patterns for different groups and began our task. The Holy Grail for us was the Oxygen Quick Disconnect (QD); it had been the culprit in several previous fatal crashes. If/when it was found, we were gone.

We searched the bits and pieces for a couple hours, and found nothing larger than a coffee cup. I watched the sun and calculated when we needed to leave to avoid being out on the badlands trail returning to the vehicles. In my broken Spanish, I conveyed that information to the leader of the Bolivian soldiers, and we agreed we did not have much longer. I called the guys together and told them we would be leaving in twenty minutes. To this point we had found nothing but small scrap pieces of debris. Then a bright shiny object caught my attention. I had to admit, my heart pumped like crazy and the adrenaline flowed strong. I reached down and pulled the small metallic object out of the dirt. It could have been anything; it was only about two by three inches and could easily have been overlooked in the search area the size of three football fields. This was it! Our Holy Grail had been found. I let out a "whoop" and told everybody we were going home now. Right now! I carried the found treasure in my hand most of the way back to the vehicles. It was not heavy—the two milled aluminum pieces mated together were slightly thicker than a cigarette pack.

Going back down the trail seemed much easier now that a key piece of evidence was in our hands – our spirits were lifted by the find of the QD. We slipped and slid a lot on the return hike. We met Mike where we left him; he was glad to see us and was happier to be leaving the area. The reverse route was the same including the ferry boat ride. Everyone was exhausted and slept on the long drive back to the hotel. The next day we rested and shopped for souvenirs for the families. Our official mission was successfully accomplished.

One thing remained; we had to attend Col Fox's informal dinner at his residence. As our US Defense and Air Attache official in Bolivia, it was customary to meet with him when our mission was completed and to give him a departure briefing. Since we had been told it was a casual event, we wore civvie slacks and sport shirts. The dinner was excellent, and we had an opportunity to meet his lovely, gracious wife. We said our farewells at the end of the evening and prepared to leave next day for home base on the C-130. We had an opportunity to recover from the altitude once we were onboard the pressurized aircraft. Our return flight would be via Lima, Peru where we spent the night and rid ourselves of the oxygen-deprivation headaches we had experienced for nearly a week. The following day's flight took us home to Davis Monthan AFB in Tucson, Arizona, where we began putting all the pieces together.

Back at home base, Col Hayes assembled all Accident Investigation Board members in a conference room for a brainstorming session. We had no evidence except the QD and not even a hint of the cause of the crash. The idea was for board members to suggest just about anything that came to mind as a possible factor or contributing factor. The central theme that kept coming up concerned the oxygen, and rightfully so, considering it had contributed to a few fatal crashes in the early years, although none in recent times. We looked at all sorts of bizarre situations, such as the pilot:

- Choked while having a drink of water, orange juice or while eating.
- Removed the pressure suit face plate to clear his throat of some object, or to eat and could not re-secure it.
- Had a heart attack.
- Was shot down by a SA-2 missile.
- Was shot by an F-104.
- Experienced some sort of failure of the oxygen system; i.e., accidental disconnect of the QD.
- Experienced oxygen system freeze or leak.
- Experienced pressure suit leakage or failure.
- Rendered incapable, unconscious or dead by some unknown physical/physiological event that precluded him from any sort of remedial action or prevented notification of his in-flight difficulties to authorities on the ground.

In addition to the situations we considered, we knew Capt Hickman was deemed to be in excellent health and physical condition, and only recently passed his airline flight physical. He had planned to leave the Air Force to join a major airline as a pilot.

The choices we were left with were not very good ones for sure. We were unsuccessful in recovering the faceplate leaving unanswered theories regarding its removal, reinstallation and relocking while at maximum operating altitude with normal cabin pressure at 29,000 feet.

The Accident Investigation Board was gaveled closed with mixed results.

Conclusions:

1. The cause, as determined by the Board, was that the pilot, Capt Robert Hickman, experienced a catastrophic physiological event of unknown etiology that rendered him incapable of any action to ameliorate his situation, and that he had probably died in flight.
2. The aircraft seemingly was performing well, having continued on course, on speed until fuel exhaustion and engine flameout. Even after the flameout, the aircraft, under control of the autopilot, continued to perform flawlessly. The autopilot was directly on course throughout the flight. Indicated airspeed had increased to an estimated 400 knots, far above the aircraft structural limit of 260 knots at which time a wing broke away from the fuselage. By this time, the aircraft was probably less than one thousand feet above impact point. Both the aircraft battery and inverter, powering the autopilot, were working nominally to the very end.

The Big Break

The Board's work was completed in three or four days, and it was time for all members to return to our primary occupations. We bade farewell to Board President, Col Hayes, each of us thinking most highly of him and secretly wishing our future commanders would be as fine a leader as he was. I saw him a few years later, and he told me the walking stick I whittled for him held a place of honor above his fireplace at his home.

The squadron wives gave Capt Hickman's widow comfort and moral support and helped her with packing and child care. I went to the Hickman's on-base quarters where they were all gathered because I wanted to ask her about her husband's health when she last saw him.

When Hickman was sent TDY to Barksdale AFB at Shreveport, Louisiana, for a two-month tour at the OL-19 detachment, the couple decided Mrs. Hickman would go to her parents' home in Baton Rouge, only a couple hours away, for the duration of the TDY. Since no missions were scheduled Friday through Sunday that week, he had gone to be with the family in Baton Rouge. He returned to Barksdale early Sunday afternoon to begin crew rest for a 0400 takeoff on Monday. According to testimony and aircraft records, the mission was aborted a half hour after takeoff due to equipment bay pressurization failure. (The cameras would not work in an unpressurized environment). The mission was rescheduled for the same time on Tuesday, the following day.

Capt Hickman had told his roommate at Barksdale that he had a terrible headache all weekend, confirmed by Mrs. Hickman, and couldn't shake it. He said he was going to take *two* sleeping pills so he could get some rest. None of this was ever disclosed to the Flight Surgeon, although Capt Hickman had preflight physical exams before both Monday's and Tuesday's flights.

This was a huge revelation, but didn't really change anything. It was decided by pay grades far above mine to let the findings of the Board stand as written. After all, Capt Hickman *was* stricken by an unknown, catastrophic, physiological event that totally incapacitated or killed him outright.

Afterword

At the Davis Monthan Officers Club on Friday evening, we sorted it all out over a few happy hour beverages. He had a brain aneurism that had blown out and finished him. That's the story of the Hickman accident to the best of my recollection some 55 years later.

Gerald E. (Jerry) McIlmoyle

Venice, Florida

My Participation in the Cuban Missile Crisis

The Cuban Missile Crisis began for Rudy Anderson, Steve Heyser, Buddy Brown and me on October 11, 1962. Our Wing Commander, Colonel John DesPortes, came to each of our homes at Laughlin AFB. When he made a house call, we knew something was going on and it was extremely urgent. The Colonel told us to pack our bags. We were headed to Edwards AFB, California. The plan was for us to take over the CIA's three U-2s.

Major General K.K. Compton, Strategic Air Command Director of Operations, was on the aircraft that transported us to Edwards. En route to Edwards he informed us that President Kennedy had directed the CIA U-2s be turned over to the Air Force. The USAF was to conduct photographic reconnaissance over Cuba. General Compton also told us that the President was still unhappy with the CIA's failure of the Bay of Pigs Operation the year before and he wanted the military to take over the Cuban mission.

CIA pilots instructed us in the differences between the Air Force and CIA U-2s. The next day CIA pilots Barry Baker and James Barnes conducted the ground school at Edwards AFB North Base. Both Barnes and Baker had been in my squadron at Great Falls, Montana before joining the CIA. They were obviously unhappy about being directed to give up their planes to us.

One major difference of the CIA U-2 and the AF version was the J-75 engine which enabled the CIA pilots to fly about 2,000 feet higher than the AF with their J-57 engine. Their birds also had a strobe display about the size of tennis ball on top of the instrument panel. The strobe display indicated direction and distance of any Cuban radar in operation. Lethal range of the SA-2 surface to air missile was 25 miles from the launch site.

The CIA planes also had an aural signal in the headset that would sound a warning when a surface to air missile went into its final radio guidance mode. It was a fluttery sound, called a fan song after the metallic sound of a paper hand fan used by women in the non-air conditioned church of my youth. The sound was soft but menacing. If the signal was heard, the pilot was to initiate a 30-degree bank turn and do an "S" maneuver back to the flight path and by then out of range of the missile launch site. The SA-2 could not turn with the U-2 at altitudes of 70,000 to 75,000 feet, the altitude we maintained en route to Cuba. To fly at that altitude, we flew short fuel and film loads. Each pound of fuel equals one foot in altitude. If we carried 300 or fewer gallons of fuel we could increase altitude by 2,000 feet. Another nice feature of the CIA U-2s was the thrust diffuser to spread and shield the jet engine exhaust from infrared homing sensors and prevent a heat-seeking device to guide a missile into the aircraft.

On October 14, Steve Heyser took off from Edwards and flew the first overflight of Cuba. He landed at McCoy AFB, Florida. Steve's film was immediately flown to Washington, DC for processing. President Kennedy was briefed on the photographic evidence of Soviet Medium Range Nuclear missiles installed in Cuba. The remaining two CIA U-2s were ferried to McCoy by the CIA pilots. Rudy deployed to McCoy and Buddy and I returned to Laughlin from where we flew our first overflights of Cuba. Buddy and I recovered at McCoy. By October 17, 1962, we had 11 U-2 pilots and 10 U-2 aircraft at McCoy. During those first days, we flew about five overflights of Cuba each day.

On October 25, the Soviets made their first attempt to shoot down my U-2 with two SA-2 missiles launched near Banes, Cuba. I received no signal from any of the warning systems. I wasn't even aware that I had been fired at until I saw the missile contrails in my rear view mirror. It was a gorgeous clear day with dark blue sky above and a blue-green sea below—those contrails were quite a contrast. I was in my turn north. I looked back over my left wing, and I saw the missile condensation trails went all the way back to the ground pointing to the Banes SA-2 site. I continued my turn to set up the cameras to record the contrails and burst clouds from the missile. I turned back to the right so the left wing was raised and the cameras began to record. For the next couple minutes, I continued taking pictures of the whole scene.

Two days later, our Operations Officer, Tony Martinez, held a pilots' meeting to discuss the SAM and MiG-21 threats and our tactics to evade them. It was real to us alright. We all knew the Soviet threat we faced and we realized we probably would not receive any warning of intercept attempts. Tony also stated the need to have a pilot standing by each day in case we were directed to fly more overflights than were scheduled. The increase in overflights had occurred several times previously. Rudy volunteered for the standby alert pilot duty for the next day. From then on we were directed to rotate the duty through our cadre.

We had three overflights scheduled for October 27 with Rudy as standby alert pilot. The three flights had taken off earlier in order to be over the target with the sun at the best angle for good photography. It was a bright clear day and the sky was a beautiful dark blue. Steve Heyser and I had not been scheduled to fly so we went out to play golf. Golf was our recreation as we could not fly for two days before another flight.

At about 11:00 a.m., Steve and I heard the unique sound of a U-2 taking off. We turned to see the aircraft climbing out at a steep angle. The plane was silhouetted against the blue sky, and we watched until it was out of sight. We both knew that it was Rudy going on a special mission and we silently prayed he would be safe.

Rudy's mission covered the area near Banes, Cuba, a known location of the almost finished Medium Range Ballistic Missile (MRBM) launch complex with a defending SAM site. The US radar site at Guantanamo Bay, Cuba reported they lost their track of Rudy at a time and location when he should have been on his photographic run over the target.

We never knew exactly what happened but I believe that Rudy had no system warning of the intercept. He was known to fly with intense concentration and dedication; I believe he was totally focused on flying the most stable platform in order to gather the best possible photographic intelligence.

On that date, October 27, 1962, after Rudy's shootdown, the Soviets capitulated and agreed to remove their nuclear tipped MRBMs from Cuba and cease construction of their associated launch sites. The crisis was over.

Perspective of Colonel Anthony Martinez

On the evening of October 13, 1962, Major General K.K. Compton and Brigadier General Robert Smith, SAC Deputy Chief of Staff Intelligence, arrived at Laughlin AFB in General Powers' own VC-97. The purpose of their arrival was to transport Colonel DesPortes and those of us on the recovery team (Operations, Maintenance and Physiological Support) for Steve's arrival the next day at McCoy. Upon arrival at McCoy, we took over the CIA's operation of all pilot facilities except the Communications Room. It was obvious that we were not welcome there, but we were there to do our job and we managed to do that.

We learned later that Mr. Cunningham, the CIA Operations Supervisor, had been sending communications to his boss. His messages were full of negative information indicating the Air Force people were not doing the job properly. He reported that we were forgetting to remove the covers from the camera windows, our pilots were sweaty and showed fear as they were being suited up. All allegations were completely false. It was definitely a sporty few days there.

Alaska, North Pole and Vietnam Flights

"Flight might not be all plain sailing, but the fun of it is worth the price."
Amelia Earhart

Robert C. Birkett
Tucson, Arizona
Wife: Betty

Landing in a Thunderstorm with Seven Gallons Of Fuel

I wrote a memo the day after the event, December 9, 1966, and placed it in the Pilot's Information File (PIF) where it remained until after the Vietnam War. When I read the memo forty years later, I realized it was "1960s pilot talk." For anyone, including pilots, reading the memo today, more questions than answers would be apparent. Some background information and explanation would be required to understand and appreciate the U-2 and what happened all those years ago. While thinking back about that night, I recalled serving on two Air Force accident investigation boards. After my Air Force retirement, I also investigated three fatal civilian industrial accidents. A major factor in all the accidents was Murphy's Law, "Anything that can go wrong will go wrong." Most accidents and incidents are the result of many small and unrelated things going wrong or coming together about the same time, rather than a single catastrophic error or failure of equipment or system. Did Murphy's Law apply to my incident? I can now see some of the events that came together that night.

- U-2 navigation equipment versus South Vietnam's aids to navigation.
- Delayed maintenance.
- Many large thunderstorms.
- Severe lightning effecting radio and radar reliability.

Background Information

A short explanation about air navigation in Vietnam versus U-2 navigation equipment: Lockheed's U-2 designer, Kelly Johnson, and the Central Intelligence Agency (CIA) installed navigation equipment compatible with "world-wide covert" U-2 operations. This meant World War II technology. A "radio compass" receiver pointed toward military and commercial broadcast stations, radio ranges and beacons and a very high frequency (VOR) omni directional radio used by most developing countries.

The early U-2s navigated over large cloud-covered areas and oceans using the same procedures Columbus used when he discovered the New World in 1492 – Dead Reckoning (DR) and celestial observations using a sextant mounted on top of the nose. Precision navigation required for photo mapping was accomplished by aiming a "spy glass" referred to as a viewfinder or drift sight ahead and below the aircraft to maintain the desired course. It was mounted under the nose. The viewfinder allowed the pilot to observe horizon to horizon 360 degrees under the Dragon Lady. GPS had not yet been developed. In Vietnam, the US military had installed the latest "state of the art" Tactical Air Navigation System (TACAN). All military aircraft were equipped with a TACAN providing both direction and distance to the transmitter. However, it was not possible to install the TACAN in the U-2 because there was no space available in the cockpit. The transmitters were located next to the runway on most airfields. In South Vietnam there was only one weak VOR located at the old French airport in Saigon; the US called it Tan Son Nhut Air Base. In addition, three Ground Control Intercept (GCI) radar sites covered Southeast Asia. They had an effective range of 250 miles. A Ground Control Approach (GCA) radar was located at Bien Hoa Air Base. The GCA radar controller "talked" the pilot down to the end of the runway by giving heading and altitude instructions. During poor visibility weather conditions, GCA was the only way a U-2 pilot could make a precision instrument approach to the runway at Bien Hoa.

A pilot designated as the U-2 mobile officer was a backup to the primary pilot. On all operational missions both the primary pilot and the mobile officer prepared to fly the mission. Both went on the twelve hours crew rest, ate a pre-mission meal and had a preflight physical with a Flight Surgeon. However, if the primary pilot failed his physical, the mobile officer had a physical and became the mission pilot; the roles reversed and the primary pilot then became the mobile officer. Following the physical was the mission briefing with actual and forecast weather conditions, latest intelligence, including code and recall words. The mobile officer delivered the mission kit to the aircraft, performed the preflight, and set up the cockpit to the start engine checklist.

The Physiological Support Division (PSD) technicians assisted the mission pilot dressing in the partial pressure suit. The cockpit of the early U-2 models was not large enough to accommodate the full pressure suit worn by astronauts. The U-2 pilot was

Capt Bob Birkett at Bien Hoa AB, 1966.

fully pressurized from the neck up and physically constrained from the neck down by a skin-tight suit similar to a corset. The transition between the two suits was accomplished by a rubber bladder the pilot pulled down around his neck and tucked back under, it then resembling a turtleneck sweater.

Positive oxygen pressure against the tight bladder combined with body moisture formed the seal for the tiny pressure chamber for the pilot's head. The full body partial pressure suit was required because blood boils at 63,000 feet altitude, and we were subject to pressurization failures, such as flameouts, canopy seal problems, etc. above 70,000 feet.

To prevent "the bends" the pilot breathed 100% oxygen a minimum of 30 minutes before takeoff to remove the nitrogen from his system in case of loss of cabin pressurization. Normal cabin pressure was 29,000 to 29,500 when cruising above 70,000 feet. Thirty minutes prior to takeoff a PSD technician drove the pilot in an air conditioned van to the aircraft. A canopy on wheels called a houdah covered the cockpit; in warm weather a large air conditioning duct blew cold air directly on the pilot. The PSD technicians adjusted the pilot's parachute, attached a survival kit to the parachute, buckled him into the ejection seat, connected the radio cables and transferred him from portable oxygen to the aircraft system. Ten minutes prior to takeoff the mobile officer checked the pilot and his oxygen lines, closed and locked the canopy. The pilot started the engine.

The mobile officer's job was then to supervise the maintenance crew who followed the U-2 on to the runway to recover the pogos (outrigger wheels) that fell off during takeoff. The mobile officer monitored the pilot's flight on UHF radio in the mobile truck or in the operations office. Once the aircraft was out of UHF range, the Strategic Air Command (SAC) with worldwide HF radio coverage could relay information to/

Capt Bob Birkett at Bien Hoa AB, 1966.

U-2 Quonset supply hut following the rocket attach, Bien Hoa AB, Vietnam.

from the pilot. One of the HF antennas was mounted on the side of the crew trailer. The pilot could send an "A-OK" code word at key navigational points or other signal as appropriate. The operating location (OL) commander or SAC Headquarters could recall the pilot by broadcasting the recall code word on the HF net. The mobile officer monitored weather conditions and base status to ensure no surprises awaited the pilot after being airborne for ten or more hours.

If there were any potential problems with the recovery phase, the mobile officer consulted with his operations officer and/or OL commander and offered a recommended solution for the pilot prior to his entry for landing. For example, the pilot could be advised to divert to an alternate base, to land on a crosswind runway or to hold at altitude until a storm had passed. Fuel consumption at altitude was about 100 gallons per hour and about double that amount at low altitude. At the completion of a mission, the aircraft had only about 200 gallons of fuel remaining.

Landing the Dragon Lady was the most critical and most difficult task to master during training. Of the original 55 U-2 aircraft, nearly half of them crashed during a new pilot's first flight. The early U-2 models with the J-57 engine going from idle to full power took as long as 17 seconds. It felt like a lifetime waiting for the thrust to kick in and save your butt. The pilot did not have instant power for a "go around" and try again.

On final approach, the mobile officer called the distance above the runway to the pilot. As the pilot approached touchdown speed, he could not see the runway ahead of him, but had to rely on his peripheral vision and mobile's radio calls to adjust for height above the runway until the aircraft stalled. If the nose wheel touched down first, the gear strut would compress and then expand, pitching the nose up causing a slight skip or a porpoise, a condition to be avoided. A porpoise could result in a crash driving the main gear up into the fuel tank and forward engine compartment, a potential disaster for sure.

When the new and larger U-2R models were built in the late 1960s, these critical landing problems were minimized by design changes and a two-seat trainer was built. The partial pressure suit was replaced with a full pressure astronaut suit and the sextant was replaced with a TACAN.

When safely on the ground, one wing would drag on the runway. The maintenance crew in a vehicle behind the mobile officer manually lifted the lowered wing and reinstalled the pogos to allow the pilot to taxi to the ramp.

The Storms

On December 8, 1966 I flew a mission above 70,000 feet altitude north of the Demilitarized Zone (DMZ) that took me over Laos and North Vietnam, just south of the Chinese border. The weather had been clear in the "area of interest," but as I passed the DMZ headed south, I passed over scattered thunderstorms. I was soon over solid cirrus clouds with the tops of some storms reaching 65,000 feet. The radio compass needle pointed in the general direction of Bien Hoa, but was erratic as it pointed toward the numerous lightning flashes. The radio compass carried a delayed maintenance write up which meant no parts were available to resolve the problem. When I called the mobile officer, Ted Rose answered. He and the U-2 Ops Officer, Charlie Kern, were en route to the weather station to check the radar. "Stay at altitude. A big storm is over the base," he directed. Ten minutes later Ted told me to start descent immediately. One storm was passing over and another was predicted to move in the area within twenty minutes. He said the northwest area looked best, but there were thunderstorms in all quadrants.

Capt Bob Birkett at Bien Hoa AB, 1966.

At this time the radio compass needle swung indicating I was over the station, and I turned northwest to start a rapid descent. In retrospect, I believe I had passed over a severe thunderstorm fifty miles north of Bien Hoa. The lightning may have caused the radio compass needle to swing, leading me to believe I was at that time over Bien Hoa. The sun was now just setting at altitude and as soon as I started down into the clouds, it became dark except for the lightning flashes. I had called GCI for "flight following," a request for them to monitor my progress. GCI advised their radar antenna had just taken a hit and was out of commission. My last observed position was northwest of Bien Hoa, and I was told to contact Saigon Approach Control. I advised Saigon Approach Control I was passing 50,000 feet and would start a left turn at 40,000 feet. Their radar was out and they told me to contact Bien Hoa GCA when I got lower. Bien Hoa GCA was loaded with aircraft landing between thunderstorms, and I was busy trying to avoid the storms in the dark. I was down about 10,000 feet trying to descend below broken clouds so I could pick up the lights of Bien Hoa and Saigon.

GCA was not as busy now, and they asked me to squawk the emergency code and make several identification turns. To my disappointment, they advised me that their radar had been hit by lightning and was out. Ted reported the second storm had hit, and it was too late for me to land. The mobile radio faded out as I descended lower. With the GCA not picking me up on their radar, I realized I could be a lot farther away from Bien Hoa than I thought. I was down to 4,000 feet and unable to avoid the storms any longer. I retracted the gear and speed brakes, slowed to best speed for turbulent weather conditions and started a slight climb in the storms. The radio compass was useless for navigation, and with GCA out, I turned thirty degrees to the right toward Tan Son Nhut VOR. As if I didn't have enough to worry about, the "low level" fuel warning light came on indicating I was down to forty gallons, about twelve minutes to flameout.

It was now dark with heavy turbulence and lightning. I didn't need to look at the wings to know the effect of the turbulence; I could feel the wings flexing. I had been hand flying from start of descent, sheer pilot muscle manipulated the flight control surfaces. The autopilot was designed for maintaining high altitude, straight and level flight, for optimum camera results. It was designed to disengage in turbulent conditions because the flight controls were not power assisted.

My plan was to advise the mobile officer when I passed over the VOR and the direction I was headed. I was planning my bailout between storms. It would at least give Search and Rescue a general idea where to look for me. As I came out the side of the storm, I passed over the VOR and the low clouds to my right were illuminated by the lights of Saigon. It was a most welcome sight. I called Tan Son Nhut tower and declared an emergency. I was the only aircraft still up so I had their full attention. I spiraled down, circling the VOR through the clouds and made visual contact with the runway at 3,000 feet in a medium rain shower.

The stall strips would not extend on my first attempt because of ice on the leading edge of the wings. I landed into a thunderstorm that moved down the runway towards me; I was able to clear the runway on a "high speed turn off." I shut the engine down with seven gallons on the fuel counter, only three minutes of flight time. The big storm then hit and pelted the area for thirty minutes. During this time I flew the wings and held the brakes while the rain and wind buffeted the aircraft.

Soon all the storms in the area dissipated. Ice that accumulated on the wings fell off when the wing flexed in the turbulence. Some of the ice had damaged the leading edge of the horizontal stabilizer.

When I arrived back at our compound later that night, I stuck my head in the commander's trailer to tell him I was back safely. I said, "Sir, it got pretty exciting up there tonight."

He replied, "Exciting up there? You should have been down here."

As the pilot, I had ultimate responsibility for my aircraft. About an hour had elapsed from the start of my descent above 70,000 feet to landing at Tan Son Nhut Air Base. What had it felt like being in those storms with the LOW fuel warning light on, no ground radar assistance and turbulence all around during descent? In a couple of words, busy and focused. Many turns were 45 to 60 degree bank angles, approaching 90 degrees a few times. In the moderate to severe turbulence, a couple of steep banks were not intentional. As conditions deteriorated, I had but one goal: Find a runway and land. If I had flamed out before landing, I would have had only once choice. Eject.

The next day I talked with one of the weather forecasters; he told me he had been at Bien Hoa for a year. He had never seen so many thunderstorms pop up at one time. I knew it was bad, but maybe it was better I didn't know just how bad it was. A portable VOR was installed at Bien Hoa Air Base shortly after this incident.

The Rocket Attack – Bien Hoa Air Base, Republic of Vietnam, May 12, 1967

The following is an excerpt from my diary of that day:

> RVN—Mortar attack at 0100 (1:00 a.m.) this morning. 7 pieces of shrapnel came through my end of the trailer. I had left the room seconds before it hit. Approx. 160 inbound rounds of mortar, rockets and recoilless. 6 people were killed, approx 50 injured, a Quonset hut burned, 6 airplanes destroyed.

Our compound was a special security area assigned to the U-2 and DC-130 TDY units of the 100th SRW from Davis Monthan AFB, Tucson, Arizona. It was surrounded by an eight-foot high barbed-wire fence and a 24-hour sentry. Within the compound were two air-conditioned trailers. One trailer housed the two U-2 pilots and the operations officer, and the second one was for the operating location (OL) commander and the DC-130/drone operations officer. Two open-air barracks called hutches were residence for the DC-130 and helicopter crews, flight planners, intelligence officer, flight surgeon and tech reps. Rounding out the compound was a Quonset hut for operations and two sandbag bunkers.

The DC-130 launched the reconnaissance drones, and the helicopters recovered them inflight as they parachuted down over the Gulf of Tonkin after flying over the Hanoi area. The OL commander, a bird colonel, and his operations officer spent 95 percent of their time coordinating and managing the complex DC-130/drone/helicopter operation while the single engine U-2 operated relatively problem free.

The first inbound woke me, and I immediately dressed in my flying suit and boots. I was ready to go out the trailer door headed for the bunker when the next rocket hit forty yards away damaging our compound. A visiting Headquarters SAC colonel had just arrived and was assigned to our trailer where he slept on the couch. After sixteen hours of jetlag, he did not even wake up for the first incoming rocket. From the door, I shouted at him to get to the bunker immediately. As I turned to go out the door, the next rocket hit, jolting our trailer.

The bunkers were dark and very crowded. One of the DC-130 crew took a small piece of shrapnel in his upper right thigh as he ran to the bunker. The incoming mortars and rockets gradually became less frequent and less intense. From inside the dark bunker, we heard emergency vehicles and shouting around our compound. There was no means of communication to or from our bunker. About thirty minutes after the last mortar, Charlie Kern and I left the bunker before the "all clear" signal to see if we could help. An Air Police barracks a couple of blocks away had taken a direct hit. We assisted a couple of the troops with minor wounds. It was only a short time before the emergency response team had the situation under control.

The two of us surveyed the damage and reported to the OL commander in the other bunker. Although he was glad to receive the information, he was unhappy his U-2 operations officer and a U-2 pilot left the bunker before the "all clear." When the "all clear" signal was sounded, we returned to our trailer. Outside our trailer adjacent to the door was a four-inch galvanized iron pipe with an HF antenna mounted on top. A piece of shrapnel had gone through the pipe at shoulder height and left a 1 1/2 inch hole. If I had not stopped to wake the visiting colonel, I could have been next to the pipe when it was hit. In my room, several small pieces of shrapnel had lost most of their energy penetrating the end wall.

I have photos of the destruction inflicted on the base that night. An A-1E prop aircraft was totally destroyed in a concrete bunker and the U-2 supply Quonset hut burned. Closer to home, pieces of shot shrapnel landed inside my trailer on my pillow

Barracks at Bien Hoa AB, May 12 1967.

and sheet where I had been sleeping moments before the mayhem. Outside the rockets left a hole in the street four-feet deep by six to eight feet across.

Bien Hoa Air Base housed thousands and had only a few air conditioned trailers. About half of the troops lived in open-air hutches and half in tents. I felt a little guilty living in such comfort in a "war zone" while others of much higher rank, such as colonels and generals, slept in the open-air hutches. However, the decision regarding sleeping quarters for the U-2 pilots was made at a much higher pay grade than mine, and who was I to argue with that? With Coors in the refrigerator, I soon got over any guilty feelings.

Russian Surface to Air Missiles

The Russian Surface to Air Missile (SAM) sites in North Vietnam were centered in and around the Hanoi/Haiphong metro area. Their range extended across the Chinese border to the northeast, to about 70 miles north/northwest and west of Hanoi and extending south/southeast to the Gulf of Tonkin. This allowed us to enter a dead-end corridor from the west along the Chinese border to gather photo and electronic intelligence then exit back west while remaining out of the SAMs lethal range. Our SAM radar warning system consisted of a small four-inch scope, a flashing red light called the OS (Oh S**t) light and an audio alert beeping signal. In addition, our electronic defensive system jammed MiG and SAM radars if they were a threat or were attempting to lock on to our aircraft. When a SAM site started tracking us, we received a beep and a strobe line on the scope appeared in the general direction of the site each time the rotating SAM search radar swiped our aircraft. Three o'clock on the scope meant the SAM site was directly off the right wing. When the SAM site "locked on" with their height-finding radar, a beeping tone sounded and a flashing red light with white "OS" in the center alerted us to the critical situation. It meant the missile had launched, and the SAM site was "data linking" guidance information to the missile. When MiG fighters were airborne, our GCI sites would broadcast their approximate heading, altitude and speed on guard channel every few minutes. Guard channel was monitored by all aircraft and was only used by aircraft needing emergency assistance.

My Route

Following my departure from Bien Hoa Air Base, the planned route for the mission was northeast 110 miles to Ban Mo Thout. I turned northwest, crossed the northeast corner of Thailand, and then headed north into Laos over Vientiane, the capital city. I continued north until just short of the Chinese border and turned east northeast. Three miles south of the Chinese border, I crossed the Red River and continued east northeast. I turned southeast just short of the Chinese border, then headed southwest across the Red River again, and south over Dien Bien Phu and the Plain of Jars, the site of earlier French defeats. My route took me then southeast along the North Vietnam/Laos border covering the Ho Chi Minh Trail, across the DMZ, south to Ban Mo Thout, and finally southwest to return to Bien Hoa.

The MiGs

On May 5, 1967, just before I turned east toward the Red River, I heard GCI on guard channel reporting MiG information. "Two MiGs climbing eastbound from Hanoi." A couple of minutes later, Guard Channel reported, "Still climbing, starting a right turn and accelerating."

I was busy checking my position through the view finder and updating my log. The next thing I heard was, "MiGs flying northwest up the Red River above 40,000 feet." This did not concern me because in the F-104 practice intercepts in the US, none were ever successful intercepting a U-2 at a 90-degree angle, the same angle the MiGs were flying in relation to my route.

To attempt an attack on a U-2 at over 70,000 feet altitude, a fighter had to be flying nearly Mach 2 at 45,000 to 50,000 feet. The fighter would have to be 25 miles directly behind and zoom up on the U-2 trading airspeed for altitude. In order to bring down a U-2 flying above 70,000 feet, the fighter would have to be ten to twelve miles directly behind just prior to reaching their max altitude of 58,000 to 60,000 feet and launch a heat-seeking missile before they started their own descent. The U-2 onboard warning system would alert the pilot who would then simply make a turn to foil the intercept. The pilot would also see the MiG contrails through the viewfinder. The MiGs could not see the U-2 as it was above the contrail level at approximately 58,000 to 63,000 feet in Southeast Asia. In short, fighters were not a realistic threat to the U-2. I was not overly concerned and I was not even sure the MiGs were attempting an intercept on me. Maybe the MiG pilots were en route to China for a little R&R (rest and relaxation).

Just as I crossed the Red River, the SAM warning system lit up indicating a radar lock-on. The warning system also indicated I was directly over the SAM site, and the next signal was the missile launch OS light. Immediately I disconnected the autopilot and started a right max rate turn. At maximum altitude we flew 3 to 4 knots below high speed buffet and 5 or 6 knots above low speed stall. In a bank or turn this difference decreased because of increased wing loading required to turn. Above a 12-degree bank

A destroyed A-1E Skyraider at Bien Hoa AB, May 12 1967.

a pilot would have been in a high speed buffet and a low speed stall. This situation was commonly known among pilots as the "Coffin Corner." In order to recover from the coffin corner, the pilot had to descend and/or decrease bank angle. With a missile launched toward me, decreasing angle of bank or leveling out was not an option. I lowered the nose and extended the speed brakes and landing gear. Pulling the throttle back even a small amount would have risked a flameout, not where I wanted to be with a missile on the way. I lost a couple thousand feet as I turned the buffeting/stalled U-2 westbound. Suddenly all the warning lights and tones were silent. I re-engaged the autopilot and scanned the area below and behind for the telltale sign of a missile, a vertical contrail and a "telephone pole", as the fighter pilots called a SAM missile. I saw none. I did see two arching contrails below and behind me at about 55,000 feet crossing from my left to right. GCI reported, "The MiGs have crossed into China and are no longer a threat." I transmitted my abort code and picked up my remaining route back to Bien Hoa. At debriefing the intelligence officer and navigator who planned the mission said there was no known SAM site located near the Chinese border. They were stunned when the recorders confirmed my report. The next day we drove to Tan Son Nhut Air Base where the camera film had been developed and evaluated overnight. After careful review, it was concluded there was no evidence of a SAM site in the area.

The intelligence analyst concluded the North Vietnamese/Russians had set a trap. They knew we would observe a SAM site under construction as we did in Cuba, and we would avoid the area prior to it becoming operational. They had apparently moved just a radar transmitter to the border area. The intelligence analyst speculated that if they had waited five minutes longer to turn on the transmitter, I would have been trapped. He asked what I would have done. I would not have flown back over what I had to assume was a new SAM site and violating the Chinese border for any reason was absolutely

Major Bob Birkett at Bien Hoa AB, May 12 1967.

Lt Col Bob Birkett, Akrotiri RAF base, Cyprus, 1976 - his last flight.

prohibited. I would have had to fly within the SAM warning rings on my map to attempt to escape the pocket I would have been trapped in. I would have had a few minutes to think about it while circling within the trap. I told them I would probably have made a run for it to the southeast and the Gulf of Tonkin, staying as close to the Chinese border as possible for the following reasons. Flying southwest I would have been within range of SAM missiles on both sides and if I did get hit, the last place I wanted to bail out was over North Vietnam near the Chinese border. By flying southeast, any SAMs would only be coming from my right. Turning into or toward any SAMs and with the onboard jammers, my chances would have been much better. Plus, I figured if I was hit and had to bailout, with a little luck the prevailing westerly winds would have carried me toward the Gulf of Tonkin and friendly US Naval rescue forces. But all that was speculation because I had avoided the trap.

Buddy L. Brown
Knoxville, Tennessee

My Busiest U-2 Mission

I say this was my busiest mission, but it would be more correct to say this was "one" of the busiest missions. There were a couple of northern missions out of Eielson AFB, Alaska using celestial grid navigation that also got my attention. The worst thing about flying north and using grid navigation was the need to out guess the gyro precession rate and in which direction. Would they precess in the direction forecasted for the next rating period? Also, remember, once over the extreme northern latitudes, every direction is south. The gyro should indicate the correct south longitude heading for the next flight route segment, not one headed south. This happened to Chuck Maultsby, but that is another story.

Jim Qualls would also remember our 100-plus days on Okinawa where we flew only System IV night missions into the northern reaches of the Sea of Japan. Landing the next morning, we would have red, blood-shot eyes. For any non-technical folks reading this, in the mid-1950s, the U-2s had no high tech navigation systems. Our primary navigation tool was simply the sextant.

Now a little explanation for those same non-technical folks, the System IV was a signals intelligence electronic detection system or SIGINT. It consisted of a large number of antennas to cover frequencies the Soviet Union used for command and control, missile tracking, aircraft control, radar frequencies, etc. Information collected was stored onboard the U-2 and later analyzed to determine how far the Soviets had advanced their electronic technology.

Okay, back to my original story. I forget the exact date Jerry McIlmoyle and I flew these particular missions, but I vividly remember it was winter. The purpose of the mission was to collect SIGINT into the Bering Sea in order to map the Soviet radar order of battle. The equipment bay of the U-2 was loaded with a specially designed System IV – a SIGINT package that expanded the frequency spectrum. I think the project code name was "Venice Lake II." I vividly remember the mission planning for it was rather complicated. It got complicated because it was a coordinated mission with a C-121 radar aircraft to monitor us and ensure that we did not deviate outside a very narrow corridor. The C-121 was originally a Lockheed Constellation converted to a Navy aircraft with Airborne Early Warning (AEW) capability. During our pre-mission briefings, several local SAC permanent staff personnel sat in and made useless suggestions that had nothing to do with these missions.

However, the C-121 would be monitoring our collection leg once we were in the target area in the Bering Sea off the Kamchatka Peninsula. In the briefing, it was determined that the C-121 would send coded messages consisting of a bunch of numbers. We had to write down the numbers and evaluate whether we were north or south of our track, left or right of course and how far in either direction. So at each celestial plot, in addition to taking three star fixes and plotting the position based on celestial information, we now had to write a bunch of numbers from the sextant and evaluate whether to throw out the celestial information and use the C-121 plot or vice versa. As if that wasn't enough to do, we had to copy all of the Fox Trot "do not answer" high frequency transmissions. A Fox Trot message was a coded SAC Headquarters communication to control a particular mission using a series of numbers transmitted at high frequency. Using a translation device in the cockpit, the numbers were converted into a coherent message. The Fox Trot message would give instructions to continue the mission, to abort the mission and land at a designated recovery base, to be alert for Soviet fighters being scrambled, etc. Response to Fox Trot message commands did not require an answer, just compliance. It also kept electronic transmissions to a minimum to avoid giving away the aircraft's position. The C-121 monitored our position via radar tracking to maintain the designated course, thus the comparison between our celestial and the C-121 plot.

I remember Jerry McIlmoyle and I sat in the briefing room and listened to the dialog between the C-121 jocks and the permanent SAC staff; we were shaking our heads. At one point, one of the SAC guys said, "I don't know how you're going to do all this stuff." Those were my thoughts exactly.

Well, the briefing was finally over and I was scheduled to fly the first mission; I think Jerry flew in the C-121 to monitor my mission as it progressed. Looking at my map boards, I had little pieces of paper stuck all over my route with the numbers the C-121 may or may not transmit while I was in the sensitive area.

My takeoff time was about 10:00 p.m. in the dead of winter in Alaska, so it was an all night mission. The U-2 had a specially designed System IV installed. Marshall Hughes was a civilian electronic whiz employed by Ramo Wooldridge, the company that built the System IV. Hughes had designed an array of new antennas to collect some special intelligence from the Kamchatka Peninsula. Kamchatka, located west of Alaska bordering the Bering Sea on the east and the Sea of Okhotsk on the west, was the location of most all of the Soviet ICBM experimental test facilities and several fighter bases. To operate the System IV wasn't too difficult; when flying north, turn the antenna switch to the left. When flying south, turn the switch to the right. Heck, even I can remember that one.

From the briefing, we headed for the BOQ to begin our crew rest period. The next evening after the pre-mission briefing which included a weather update and C-121 procedures, call signs, etc., I was fitted into my pressure suit and transported out to the bird. It had just been pulled out of the hangar and was ready for my arrival. The winter temperatures in Alaska remained at about minus 30 degrees to minus 50 degrees so the U-2 was kept inside the hangar until just before the pilot arrived. Once in the cockpit, I was hooked up, completed the cockpit check, replied to the challenge response, started engines and taxied out to the active runway. I received the "cleared for takeoff" signal, advanced the throttle and was on my way.

The mission was to fly from Eielson down the Aleutian chain to Shemya, then make a right turn in the northern direction into the Bering Sea and on into the corridor-collection area. The C-121 had taken off from Eielson hours before me in order to be in position to monitor my progress. I received one "Fox Trot" message from the C-121 that they were in position. The navigator/mission planner pre-computed all my fixes to be three-star fixes. It made for extra work but I was using the Rudd Star Finder (Computer RADAR AID, Type R-1) to plot my fixes so it cut down on time to plot and evaluate my position. (By the way, I still have that plotter.) We were told that "higher authority" directed us to stay within the corridor.

For the next three-plus hours, I was constantly writing down the C-121 transmitted numbers, evaluating their position information, taking three-star fixes and evaluating one or the other for my position. (Remember, this was in the dark of night and I was in a constrictive pressure suit.) Fortunately, the altitude winds were as forecasted and I had a stable platform for my celestial. As far as I knew, I copied all the Fox Trot messages designated for me. When the mission was completed, I returned to Shemya and back to Eielson AFB. When I started my descent for landing at Eielson, the weather was near minimums with heavy ice fog. I wasn't too concerned about flying a final approach at 80 knots, I couldn't get into too much trouble. I was cleared to start my approach and landing when GCA reported, "The field is now below minimums. Do you want to continue with your approach or proceed to your alternate?" I responded, "Continue approach." I told the GCA final, "It's just you and me now anyway." I was only going 80 knots, and by the time I got to the runway, it might be above minimums. I continued my approach and it seemed to take forever. I was really bushed, but I drank my last pint of orange juice just prior to my penetration so I could remain alert before I started my descent. Finally, the centerline strobes started filling my windscreen; the field was still zero-zero. As the strobes continued, GCA called out, "You're passing over the end of the runway." I then put my head back against the headrest using my peripheral vision to keep the runway lights even on my left and right sides of the canopy. I continued my descent until I touched down on the runway. After the first skip, I held the aircraft off until it settled into the runway. I couldn't see much past the nose of my bird, but the mobile folks walked in front of me with their wands guiding me to the taxiway and back to the hangar.

When the next mission was flown, Jerry was primary pilot and I flew in the C-121 as observer. I remember the C-121 was an interesting flight, but it lasted about 10-12 hours. I sat in the back and watched the radar screen as Jerry's mission progressed; I could relate to what he was going through and how he would return to Eielson with blood-shot eyes. I believe the intelligence community got what they were looking for with these missions, but I don't think the C-121 monitoring was really necessary.

Bill E. Bye

Prescott, Arizona
Wife: Janet

I was assigned to the 4080th SRW in October 1961. My first recollection was standing in the Navigation Planning Room asking Bob Yates, "Where do we go from here?" I was thinking about career progression. Bob replied, "You have arrived." Apparently I was the first officer assigned through normal channels. I recalled frequenting the flight line snack shop with Ed Schug; we both enjoyed miniature cigars.

My first TDY was to Eielson AFB, Alaska with John Wall and Buddy Brown. They were part owners of an older Chevrolet they named "Simone." They had purchased the vehicle for local transportation there and had invested many hours of tender loving care restoring it. I wonder whatever became of Simone? One of those memorable events at Eielson was planning Don Webster's flight to the North Pole.

While on TDY at Bien Hoa, South Vietnam, Meteorologist Freddie Haman forwarded the high altitude wind information to me on scraps of paper. My thoughts were, "Here we are using low tech communications for this high tech operation."

Those were some of my best days in the Air Force; I just didn't realize it at the time.

Edward B. Dixon

Vero Beach, Florida

My Tiksi Run

In 1960, pilots Dick Leavitt, Jim Bedford, John McElveen and I with our navigator Charlie Brown, were chosen for a special mission. Our U-2s were modified with a 15 nautical mile notch under the viewfinder handle. We each flew a practice mission along the Gulf Coast of Texas maintaining 15 nautical miles off the coast with the help of the viewfinder notch.

In February we TDY'd to Operating Location 5 at Eielson AFB near Fairbanks, Alaska. Joe Jackson was our Detachment Commander. There were also 30 very important support crew members who took part in the mission. The mission was to fly 15 nautical miles off the coast of USSR to Petropavlovsk on the south to Tiksi Air Base on the North Coast.

The missions were divided into about eight segments. Each end mission was 3,650 nautical miles, which was a stretch for sure. The U-2 Handbook said it could fly 4,000 nautical miles to air flameout. In the Arctic, the temperature at U-2 altitude is about 20 degrees warmer than over the US. The U-2 would level off about 2,000 feet lower and use more fuel. After each of us had flown a mission, we were promoted to Spot Major. We were in "high cotton" because Dick Leavitt was already a Spot Major.

In the Arctic, the ocean was frozen and covered with snow. We observed the ocean had a light gray tinge probably due to the salt content of the water. The terrain had only grass, no trees. Three rivers flowed north out of the USSR and they were fresh water, no gray tinge. Just where was the coast?

Dick Leavitt was chosen to fly the Tiksi mission. Unfortunately, he became disoriented and over flew Soviet territory; luckily he was not spotted by the Soviets. We ceased flying special missions off the coast of the USSR while the fellows in the corner office thought about it. We didn't seem to have cause for an international incident. Meanwhile, we flew nuclear debris collection missions over the Pacific Ocean looking for a reported Soviet nuclear bomb detonation residue at high altitudes. Then word came down that we were going to resume flying special missions and now it was my turn to try for Tiksi.

I knew #953 to be a great, reliable bird. It was well trimmed, would fly straight and had a fine autopilot and Mach sensor. I asked our commander, Joe Jackson, if I could use it and he readily agreed.

The weather was satisfactory so the mission was on. I took off at 0800 and coasted over Wainwright Beacon at 62,000 feet altitude. The weather was clear with unlimited visibility. My celestial lines of position were at an angle to my flight path. So, I had neither a speed line nor flight line information.

I recognized a landmark about an hour from Wainwright near Fairbanks, Alaska. The frozen ocean was criss-crossed with many vehicle trails. My aircraft shadow was visible in a circle halo of ice crystals below me to the right. I patted old #953 on the dash and told her that she was doing a great job.

On my fourth celestial shot I looked up and saw land. I was flying faster than planned; therefore, correcting to the left made me coast in too soon. I turned to the right, turned on my camera and headed for the 28-nautical mile channel between the Soviet mainland and the New Siberian Islands. I could see the Tiksi Bay ahead. The camera gently rocked the aircraft as it went through its repositioning cycle.

I flew west past the bay at Tiksi, turned 90 degrees left so it was on my right. I passed Tiksi Airfield, waited for two more cycles of the camera. With the autopilot off, I turned 180 degrees to the left, as steeply as I dared to get out of there. I exited through the channel between the islands and headed for home.

As I entered the Alaskan ADIZ (Air Defense Identification Zone), I called Wainwright and gave them my estimated time of arrival. I was ahead of schedule by about 20 minutes. They gave me a challenge and asked me to fly the maneuver code. The

Maneuver Code is in a numbered sealed envelope that each pilot picks up at Operations when the flight plan is filed. I reported that I was light on fuel and asked to read them the code. They concurred. Flying the code would have used up an additional 5 minutes of fuel. Since I had been airborne for seven hours, I'm glad they felt sympathetic.

As I neared Eielson, I began to let down and requested an approach time. Control gave me a 20-minute approach time delay. The low fuel level light came on and I had 40 gallons remaining. I put old #953 in gust control. It reduced wing loading by raising the flaps a few degrees and was a safeguard in turbulent air. I cancelled my Instrument Flight Rules clearance and spiraled down over the runway under visual and landed. On the runway as the crew installed the pogos, I had 22 gallons remaining of the 1,335 I had started with. Now that is what I call cutting it close! Old #953 got another pat on the dash.

Roger Herman
Fort Worth, Texas

Trouble Over the Arctic

One of the 4080th SRW's major U-2 projects of the early days was completed by 1960. Project Crow Flight, a High Altitude Sampling Program (HASP) for the Armed Forces Special Weapons Project (AFSWP), had done its job of providing the Agency with a background of radiation levels at altitudes from 40,000 feet to the U-2's maximum altitude. The two-year project of long north-south flights from Plattsburg AFB, New York, Ramey AFB, Puerto Rico and Ezeisa International Airport, Argentina had shown a decline in radiation during that period. Apparently, it was due to the voluntary test ban then in effect.

Our sampling program was reduced to two six-week projects each year from three locations. This reduced our TDYs considerably and the flights were shorter. One of the locations was Eielson AFB, just outside Fairbanks, Alaska. I was scheduled for the Fall deployment in 1961. It was projected to last from September to November, not a bad time to be in Alaska.

As often happens in the military, we listen for words like "Standby for change!" I returned home from a shopping trip with my wife on Saturday of Labor Day weekend at Laughlin AFB. I received a call from the Command Post directing me to "Pack up, we're moving out." The Russians had broken the Test Ban Agreement. Three of the pilots were flown to Palmdale Airport in California to pick up newly modified U-2s to fly to Eielson AFB. Our easy six-weeks deployment was now an indefinite deployment. The Russians were testing on Novaya Zemlya, an island in the Arctic Ocean just north of Siberia. AFSWP was going to have us sampling all over the area – north, west, south of Alaska and even long flights straight across Canada.

During this testing period, the Russians announced they would detonate a 100-megaton device. They did detonate a large device. It was estimated to be only in the 50-megaton range, but still a large explosion. The detonation occurred late at night, Alaska Time. I went to the weather station for a briefing the next morning, and the meteorologists indicated they had observed a slight rise in atmospheric pressure. It spread across the Arctic and had resulted in a rise in pressure at Eielson.

At the end of October, with days becoming shorter and colder, AFSWP found a favorite route that we flew almost daily. We proceeded northeast from Eielson to a point on the northwest Canadian coast, and then almost due north to the north coast of Banks Island. We descended to 40,000 feet and flew northeast to Ellesmere Island, a point approximately 250 miles north of Thule, Greenland. We reversed course and returned to Banks Island, still at 40,000 feet. For our return to Eielson, we climbed back to normal cruise altitude. I don't know why the "higher ups" picked islands to overfly since we were flying in pitch dark and couldn't see them anyway. This route went directly over the magnetic North Pole and, required Grid Navigation. We didn't follow the SAC procedure used by the bomber crews. We neared the magnetic pole and the aircraft went into a slight bank to hold heading due to rapid changes in variation. Rather than upset the gyro, we went to free run on the slaved gyrocompass and used that heading as our reference. It was surprising how little precession we experienced when we didn't mess with the gyro. The sun was now setting around 3:30 p.m.. Our takeoffs were planned around 7:00 a.m. so we could land in daylight and tail in on the ice-covered runways and taxiways. We relied on the sextant for navigation, so at the start we hoped for a good shot of a well-known body. The sun would make a very brief appearance in the southeast as we flew to the northeast. The navigators computed a celestial shot for us. Most notably, the sun was normally around a minus six degrees elevation for a few moments before disappearing again.

On my day of fun, I proceeded to the descent point. I leveled at 40,000 feet and encountered one of the J-57 engine's quirks. It was not unusual to encounter those quirks sometimes on maintenance test flights. We were required to level off for a short period at 40,000 feet to run a few checks, and continue the climb to max altitude. We added power for the continued climb as the engine would chug or compressor stall. It might take several tries to get it through that range. Since we were going to max power, once we got it through that range, we could continue flying with no further problems. In my experience flying over the Arctic, I wasn't going to max power. I needed an intermediate power setting for cruise at 40,000 feet. I could ease it through the stall range but the power at that point was too high for my cruise at 40,000 feet. Four or five times I tried to ease it back to my cruise power setting, and each time it would revert to chugging. I couldn't complete the assigned mission at a non-chug power setting, in pitch dark and with surface temperatures of minus 55 degrees. I didn't feel this was the time or place to fool with a balky engine.

The mission was aborted. I reversed course and started a climb back to normal cruise altitude. Although I couldn't complete the assigned mission, everything was now pretty well under control. I no longer had celestial for grid navigation; I merely had to fly a reverse course on my free-run gyro. Within 20 to 30 minutes, I should pick up a radio beacon on the north coast of Canada.

Now the fun started! Once established in the climb and back on course, I made a call to the SAC Command Post at Eielson asking them to advise our detachment of my situation. Everything was under control; I gave a rough estimated time of my arrival back at Eielson. If I had known what was about to happen, I would have claimed radio reception problems.

The 15th Air Force Command Post at March AFB, Riverside, California heard my call to Eielson. Since Eielson is under their command, 15th AF wanted to get into the act. Bombers must have a two- or three-page emergency checklist to report any unusual situation. The Command Post probably has to log all this information just as a CYA (Cover Your Ass) procedure. So 15th Air Force Command Post started asking me questions. For example: How many crewmembers were aboard and where were they located; how much fuel and where was it located; etc, etc? When 15th finished, the Command Post at Laughlin AFB back in Texas started calling. The 15th AF Command Post then told Laughlin to get off the radio because they (15th AF) had an emergency in progress. Laughlin, being part of 2nd AF and not familiar to 15th AF controllers, advised 15th AF that the aircraft in question belonged to 2nd AF and by golly, they would talk to it. Sometimes, people on the ground can be a bigger problem than the airborne problem.

I reported another successful conclusion to a fun day in the U-2. We finally packed up and went home prior to Thanksgiving. The Russians took a break for the Winter. The next year, as the Russians resumed testing, AFSWP decided to fly directly to the North Pole; there was nothing to navigate by on the surface. But that was another year and another crew.

U-2 Entry into Vietnam

The 4080th SRW became involved in Vietnam operations quite suddenly in February 1964. Much like our entry in the Cuban Missile Crisis, the "Powers That Be" decided it was time for the military to become involved in the reconnaissance of Southeast Asia (SEA). You could say that we stole this mission from the Agency (CIA) just as we had done with the Cuban operations a year and a half earlier.

This operation started for me as my involvement in the Cuban operation had begun in 1962 from Laughlin AFB. Now we were comfortably situated at Davis Monthan AFB, Tucson, Arizona. I was scheduled for a Monday night celestial training mission. I received my weather briefing and presented my clearance to the dispatcher at Base Operations. He informed me that my training mission had been cancelled and I was advised to return to the Squadron.

The Squadron people were somewhat evasive, but they told me to go home on crew rest. They told me I would be called when it was time for briefing, between 12:00 midnight and 1:00 a.m.. I was told to pack for an indefinite stay in a tropical climate.

The plan was to deploy three U-2s to Clark AB, Philippines and become operational in minimum time. The plan was for three aircraft to be ferried to Hickam AFB, Hawaii. The aircraft were to be refueled and regenerated and ferried on to Clark with inflight refueling over Wake Island. Flight time from Hawaii to Clark was approximately 13½ hours. Two KC-135s supported the group for logistics and IFR (Instrument Flight Rules). The first support aircraft departed Davis Monthan early. They were to be in Hawaii for the arrival of the U-2s. This allowed the pilots for the second leg to crew rest en route prior to their demanding air-refueling leg. Pilots aboard the first support aircraft were Steve Heyser and Jerry McIlmoyle; C. B. Stratton would fly the second leg. Jim Qualls, our Detachment Operations Officer, flew the first operational mission the morning after his arrival at Clark.

Early on the morning of Tuesday, February 14, 1964, I departed Davis-Monthan en route to Hawaii; Jim Rogers and Bob Spencer followed. We flew three U-2Es (J-57 powered, IFR capable). Before daylight I crossed the Southern California Coast; it was a very uneventful, if somewhat boring, flight to Hawaii. Shortly after sunup, as I was descending towards Hawaii and within radio range, I was contacted by the Hickam Command Post. They reported that the first support aircraft had encountered extreme headwinds and would be 50 minutes behind me. The normal light winds at our altitude allowed the three U-2Es to pass the KC-135 en route to Hickam. We spent quite some time circling the area and getting an early morning aerial tour of the Islands.

We finally landed, and everybody hit the ground running. All three aircraft were in good shape. The three of us pilots completed our debriefing, and we became Mobile Control Officers for the continuation leg. The first KC-135 spent minimum ground time before departing for Clark. Jim Qualls again left with the first support aircraft. It was time for the "Ball Buster" U-2 flights.

Our timing was critical for the second support aircraft because we had to do some of the refueling over Wake Island. The second KC-135 was readied and parked at the end of the runway, with engines running. I was Mobile Control Officer for C. B. Stratton in the last U-2 to depart. The minute Stratton was airborne, a jeep rushed me to the crew ladder of the KC-135. The aircraft began moving towards takeoff position before I was strapped in my seat.

I watched the inflight refueling of the U-2s over the KC-135 boom operator's shoulder. I didn't envy those three guys—the U-2 pilot, the KC-135 pilot and the boom operator. Wake Island was about one-third of the way to Clark. The U-2 pilots displayed immense stamina and deserved a lot of admiration for what they accomplished. They were awarded a well-deserved Distinguished Flying Cross (DFC) for their flight.

The second KC-135 had to stop at Andersen AFB, Guam to refuel before proceeding to Clark. The reason was two-fold—there was a delay in the refueling area; some of the KC-135's fuel tanks were used for the special fuel for the U-2s. A little trivia—we missed Ash Wednesday. We departed Tucson early on Shrove Tuesday, landed and departed Hawaii before noon on Tuesday. En route to Guam we crossed the International Date Line putting us into Ash Wednesday. We spent a few hours on the ground to refuel at Andersen late in the evening before departing for Clark where we arrived early on Thursday morning.

Most of us were up late after arrival at Clark. Those of us not recovering from an exhausting U-2 flight were present for the launch of our first operational mission over Vietnam flown by Jim Qualls. The target was a small inlet in the southern part of North Vietnam (NVM). We were searching for a NVM gunboat. This was a prelude to the infamous Gulf of Tonkin Incident. Jim encountered solid cloud cover over the entire area and was unable to do any filming. I flew the second mission on Friday, same target, same result. Jim Rogers flew the third mission. His target was the same, but he was directed to remain in the area. Rogers waited and waited for any breaks in cloud cover; still no luck.

Things started falling apart. Jim returned and just after lunch, a number of us decided to hit the golf course. It was a warm, bright sunny day, and we needed a way to kill some time. While on the golf course, a clubhouse employee caught up with our group and told Steve Heyser he had a phone call. Colonel DesPortes was en route to Guam and we were to go to Guam, too. The US Embassy said we didn't have diplomatic clearance to bring U-2s into the Philippines. For years the Agency had operated their U-2s from the US Naval Air Station just west of Clark. The Agency had a large presence in the Embassy and it sounded like retaliation for the Air Force taking over one of their missions. Whatever!

We had to move the airplanes immediately. We left Clark on February 18, 1964 and relocated to Andersen Air Base, Guam. Jim Rogers, Bob Spencer and I ferried the U-2s to Guam after a late departure from Clark. I wasn't feeling well after golfing so long. My pressure suit seal across the back of my neck and the helmet frame across my forehead were uncomfortable. That late at night, there were no radio stations broadcasting and the only one I could pick up was Voice of America. The broadcast was in a foreign language, but they did have music. Every 15 minutes they would play a few bars of *Columbia, The Gem of The Ocean*. The music and a celestial shot every 30 minutes were the only things to break the monotony. Flying against the clock, we arrived in Guam early on February 19. There we cooled our heels until March 4.

In wintertime Guam is an ideal vacation spot. However, we didn't execute a max effort deployment to sit around for days waiting to complete our mission. Boredom and frustration became strong emotions to us. During those two weeks, things became routine. On base there was a tight, nine-hole golf course that had been hacked out of the jungle. Golf was good recreation, but we broke the evening routine by going to the open air theater to watch thrillers like Errol Flynn in his swash-buckling movies. We had to remember to carry our raincoats because in the middle of the movies there always seemed to be a shower. That was normal tropical weather in Guam. After sunset the air rises over the warm landmass dragging in moist air from the ocean producing showers. The brief showers cool the landmass stopping the whole process for a short period. The good news was the movies were free!

On March 3, 1964, we received orders to bypass Clark and proceed directly to South Vietnam. Our detachment was located at the Vietnamese Air Force (VNAF) Base located at Bien Hoa, some 30 miles northeast of Saigon. The base had a beautiful, new 10,000-foot concrete runway, ramp and taxiway but no hangar space. The rest of the base was rather primitive. Bien Hoa was a widespread piece of real estate that housed not only VNAF operations but also a number of small stores, residences and a club.

Before our departure for Vietnam, every one of us was required to receive the necessary inoculations—plague, cholera, etc. Again our threesome, Jim Rogers, Bob Spencer and I, flew the U-2s into Bien Hoa AB on the morning of March 4. Because of our scheduled flights the next morning, we couldn't receive inoculations before leaving Guam. When we landed at Bien Hoa, the local USAF Flight Surgeon was waiting for us. As soon as we got our arms out of the sleeves of our flight suits, we were hit with the needle.

The USAF at Bien Hoa flew B-26s and the A-1Es, a multi-place ex-Navy attack aircraft. The B-26 had been grounded for some time due to a wing problem. This boded well for us because the only air-conditioned quarters were the B-26 pilots' alert trailers. They were located near the flight line which was quite a hike from the US cantonment area where the mess hall, operations, club, etc. were located. At first, we thought we had hot showers and flush toilets in the trailers, but it was not to be. We were told the water was potable, drinking water only. Back to the open-air showers.

The flight line operations were constricted and primitive. Remember, we were not yet at war and the US was there only in an advisory capacity. US military dependents still lived in Saigon. We had to share crowded flight line facilities with the USAF A-1s.

Their ramp and maintenance area consisted of a wide patch of asphalt with a lane along the edge reserved for a taxiway with a number of rows of A-1s parked perpendicular to the taxiway. A sort of nose dock building ran the length of the parking area behind the aircraft. It was more of a "lean-to" and just deep enough for the nose of an aircraft. The U-2s couldn't park in line with the A-1s. The A-1s had propellers and when they cranked up, their propellers shot off dust and rocks that would have damaged the fragile skin of the U-2s. We commandeered three of the nose dock spaces. The U-2s had to be pushed into the nose dock between the rows of A-1s. The rows of A-1s were not quite far enough apart for the U-2 wingspan. One U-2 wingtip would just miss the tails of the A-1s on the left while the other wingtip went under the nose of the A-1s on the right. The large, four-bladed prop on the A-1s had to be rotated as the U-2 wingtip parked under the nose. We did not bring our Mobile Control to Vietnam so another primitive aspect of our flight operations was the WWII weapons carrier truck. It was equipped with a UHF radio that we borrowed from the Vietnamese for our Mobile Control chase vehicle.

We got off to a good start after our arrival in Vietnam. The weather cooperated and on the third or fourth day, under perfect weather conditions, we launched two aircraft to photomap the entire country of South Vietnam and several missions over NVM and Laos.

Colonel DesPortes summoned me with a message indicating that I was to return home as soon as possible. I learned that Lockheed was ready to evaluate the second of two new autopilots built specifically for the U-2. These autopilots were installed in one of the Agency's U-2Cs. I had been selected for the first evaluation the previous December. I had just returned from Barksdale AFB and the Cuban operation where we flew U-2Cs borrowed from the Agency. Lockheed wanted the same three pilots who flew the original evaluation to fly the second for comparison purposes. I jumped on a T-39 that same evening that was transporting our exposed film from that day to the photo lab at Clark. I caught a military charter flight from Clark to Travis AFB, California where I was picked up by one of our Wing's C-123s for a late night arrival back at Davis-Monthan.

When I arrived at Edwards AFB North Base for the evaluation, I learned I was the only one of the original three pilots returning for the second evaluation. I came back from halfway around the world for this evaluation. The other agencies, the CIA and Systems Command, didn't think it was important enough to send their pilots.

I hadn't finished my original tour in Vietnam, so I returned for a 90-day tour in late July 1964. The detachment had been reduced to a two-aircraft operation. Two of us incoming pilots ferried two "A" models into Bien Hoa and the two remaining "E" models were ferried by rotating pilots back to Davis Monthan.

Things had changed a lot since I left the detachment in March. We now had a Ford station wagon as one of our regular Mobile Control units. General Thomas Powers, Commander-in-Chief of SAC, had sent some surplus property from the deactivated Bomber Wing at Biggs AFB, El Paso, Texas. The alert facility at Biggs included several air-conditioned, three-bedroom house trailers. They were flown to Bien Hoa on a C-130 and installed adjacent to the US cantonment area. The trailers were connected to the area electricity, water and sewer systems. Two of the trailers were used for crew quarters and one for Operations. The fourth slightly smaller trailer was designated for Physiological Support equipment and quarters for our detachment Flight Surgeon. Compared to what we had when I left, this was almost like a country club.

Flight line security was provided by the Vietnamese military prior to the Gulf of Tonkin Incident in August 1964. We armed our own personnel to provide security for our flight line operations. There had been a report that a Viet Cong infiltrator was on base for the express purpose of sabotaging the U-2s. As a result of that information, security procedures at Bien Hoa changed drastically.

A squadron of B-57s from Clark was deployed to Bien Hoa. The squadron required night weather formation penetration. One plane crashed in a mid-air collision. The next morning an F-100 squadron was deployed from Clark. The weather still required an instrument approach. After one of the F-100's broke out on final approach, he was shot down. The large, concrete ramp was now pretty well congested. I wrote to my wife that I felt the safest while flying; the approach to landing was the hairiest part of the flight.

With these recent events, SAC determined a three aircraft operation was in order. Bob Powell arrived a few days later with the third aircraft. During his debriefing, he said he felt sorry for one guy who transmitted several times that he was under missile attack. Later, Ed Perdue returned from his mission into the Hanoi-Haiphong area of North Vietnam. From Ed's debriefing, he heard about Bob's comments. Ed yelled, "You SOBs. That was me!" Ed had started a turn when missiles came at him, and he saw two "telephone poles" go by and detonate above him.

After my return to Davis Monthan in late October 1964, the Command Post asked me if I remembered the combination to the safe in Operations at Bien Hoa. When I was at Bien Hoa, Operations was manned 24 hours a day and there had been no need to ever lock the safe.

Consequently, the combination was never passed on. A while later the base came under mortar attack. Everybody hit the trenches and the safe was locked for what was probably the first time. The Navigator was the only casualty during that attack; a piece of shrapnel caught him in the derriere.

Michael (Mike) Horochivsky

Lompoc, California

Wife: Machi

I was a member of the 4080th SRW from May 1963 to November 1964 and was assigned to the Wing Laboratory Branch. In June 1963 I was assigned to the 2nd RTS Photo Lab at Barksdale AFB, Louisiana in support of precision processing of the photos taken over Cuba. In February 1964 I was assigned as Chief, Wing Laboratory Branch and went TDY to Tan Son Nhut Air Base, Saigon, Vietnam to support Operation "Dragon Lady."

As a symbol of our high *esprit de corps* at the Photographic Processing Center (PPC), all PPC members had obtained modified "Aussie slouch hats," also known as "Gung Ho hats," embellished with a red, white and blue ribbon, the 4080th SRW emblem patch, the Vietnam and Tan Son Nhut patches. After about two weeks in country, the PPC Commander, Lt. Col. Jacobs, called a meeting. I recalled his face was quite pale as he informed us that the Viet Cong had placed bounties on all members of the 4080th SRW, $10,000 for officers and $5,000 for enlisted personnel, dead or alive. That was a sobering thought, so we put away our "Gung Ho Hats" and anything that referred to our unit. Apparently, our mission had made quite an impact on Viet Cong operations.

The US Navy provided military buses as transportation for all military in the Saigon area. The buses had meshed steel bars over the windows as protection from periodic

Michael (Mike) Horochivsky.

shelling from the Viet Cong. The photographic personnel from the PPC were allowed to sleep in air-conditioned hotels in Saigon. It was necessary because of their long working hours and primarily to always be alert in their precision photo processing activities. It rained almost every day while I was there; when it was not raining, it was very hot and humid. The buses would pick up our personnel either at their hotel or at specific locations within Saigon. After work, buses returned our personnel to their hotels.

We had a long bridge to cross over a river whenever traveling between Saigon and Tan Son Nhut AB. Vietnamese National police dressed in white uniforms guarded the entrance of the bridge at each end, 24 hours a day. The GIs labeled these police as "White Mice" because they "always happened to be missing" if something was about to happen there. This would be primarily during the dark hours when most incidents occurred. There was a common expression at that time: "Vietnamese in the day time, Viet Cong at night." Several times at night the "White Mice" were missing; when the bus crossed the bridge, everybody was sweating, and it was not due to the weather.

About a week after my arrival at the PPC, I noticed 42 AR-15 rifles in one of the closets. It appeared as if nobody took care of them. The firing mechanisms in some of them were frozen. I asked the commander why these weapons were in the closet. He said they were for our protection. After informing the commander of the condition of the rifles, I was assigned to clean and maintain them. It took about two weeks for our lab personnel to clean the rifles in their "spare time." I then asked the base Security Police where the firing range was located and they told me on the northeast perimeter of the base. My immediate response was, "Wait a minute. Isn't that the same location where we hear the "boom boom" sounds of Viet Cong mortars firing every evening?" The reply from the Security Police was, "Yes, we secure it during the day and the Viet Cong operate there at night!" I went back to the PPC Commander and informed him that we would not fire the AR-15s at the firing range after all.

Occasionally, the Viet Cong used powerful plastic explosive bombs to destroy buildings in Saigon. I remember two such incidents. The first one occurred in May 1964 before I arrived at the PPC. The PPC operated out of the same building as the permanent party Reconnaissance Technical Laboratory. In fact, some photographic equipment was shared between both units. An American captain, a photo interpreter, was assigned to the permanent party laboratory. He worked along with a Vietnamese major who was an intelligence officer. All during the captain's one-year tour, the Vietnamese major offered to show the captain some of Saigon. The American captain was skeptical about going into Saigon at all, especially at night. Finally, a couple weeks before his scheduled return to the States, the major talked the captain into going into Saigon. Their destination was a small nightclub. That night the Viet Cong blew up the nightclub with a plastic explosive bomb. Four people were killed immediately and another 16 were wounded. The American captain was evacuated to the Philippines for surgery to remove a piece of shrapnel in his wrist. The Vietnamese major lost one of his legs and died a couple of days later.

The second incident involved the plastic explosive bombing of the third-story cafeteria in a seven-story hotel that housed American military and civilian personnel. Our PPC Commander, Lt. Col. Jacobs, had just finished eating lunch there and had exited the building when the entire third story was completely demolished by a plastic explosive bomb. It was about 1:00 p.m. with a light rain settling on the area. I was a couple of blocks away at a bus stop, waiting to catch the Navy bus to go to Tan Son

Gung Ho hat briefly worn by Michael Horochivsky in Vietnam.

Nhut. I heard a loud explosion somewhere off base. Lt. Col. Jacobs arrived at the bus stop and we sat together on the ride to the base. I noticed that Colonel Jacobs was extremely pale and shaking, and I asked him if he was sick. He then told me about the explosion and that he had just two weeks remaining before rotation to the States. His quarters were at Tan Son Nhut and he said he would never again go into Saigon. He was one very nervous individual during his last two weeks at the PPC.

Shortly before Lt. Col. Jacobs' departure, Lt. Col. Daniel R. Orlitzki arrived from the States to assume command of the PPC. I knew him when we were assigned to the 8th RTS at Westover AFB from 1959 to 1961. Because of our previous acquaintance, I was selected to meet him with a staff car upon his arrival at Base Operations. After he briefly met with Colonel Jacobs at the PPC, he decided to go to a hotel in Saigon. I urged that he consider remaining on base. There had been angry, political, mob demonstrations in Saigon for the past three days. All American personnel working at Tan Son Nhut were advised to stay on base until these demonstrations were over. Despite the warnings, Colonel Orlitzki insisted on going into Saigon. Both of us sat in the rear seat of the staff car and I placed an AR-15 rifle on the floor. The weather was hot and muggy and the car had no air conditioning so we opened the windows. After we crossed the bridge into Saigon, we were immediately surrounded by an angry mob. We quickly rolled up the windows and started to perspire profusely. I mentioned to all in the car not to look anyone in the eye, so we kind of looked down and occasionally peeked out the windows. I felt that it was likely the mob would break the windows and attack us. They shouted and shook our car. Four hours later, we finally arrived at Colonel Orlitzki's hotel, a trip that would normally take 30 minutes. I returned to the base by another route, but it still took three more hours. Lt. Col. Orlitzki came to work the next day with all his luggage; he had decided to stay on base until the demonstrations ceased five days later.

For anyone who has ever been in Southeast Asia or near the equator, the taste of "swamp" water is a unique experience. We were fortunate at the PPC. We had to manufacture distilled, pure water at the lab for precision photo processing. Soon the word was out and many people on base learned about our water. They would come at specified times with gallon containers and we would provide them with "the best water in Vietnam." I filled a gallon jug with this water every day and froze it at the lab. Then I took it back to my quarters and drank it as it thawed out. Every morning I drank two glasses of water mixed with orange Tang. After two months, I swore off Tang forever.

During my entire tour of duty at Tan Son Nhut, I only went into Saigon three times. The good hotels built by the French also served outstanding French cuisine. The one meal I remember was a filet mignon dinner. It started with a large shrimp cocktail followed by a filet mignon about five inches in diameter, three inches thick surrounded by bacon covered with a tasty mushroom sauce. The steak was served on a hot, sizzling metal plate embedded in a wooden plate with French fries, enough to serve four people and a fresh vegetable salad with French dressing. The dinner was accompanied with a large bottle of "Ba-Mi-Ba" beer (Vietnamese for 33). What did that delicious feast cost? It was a mere 95 cents!

I purposely did not include any stories about work at the photo lab. However, I would be remiss if I did not mention that all the photographic personnel did an outstanding job. On average, they worked 12 hours per day. There were days, however, when the team worked non-stop for 24 to 40 hours. It was a pleasure to work with such dedicated men.

Charles W. Kern
San Antonio, Texas

Operation Black Box

Background
Following the end of World War II, the Soviet Union and the Western Allies continued to regard each other with suspicion and distrust. The Berlin Blockade (June 1948 to May 1949) was the most significant international crisis that led the old enemies to a new dimension, the Cold War. Beginning in 1948 SAC B-52s were on "Alert" and/or flying "around the clock" missions with nuclear weapons aboard, their potential targets deep inside the Soviet homeland. There was well-founded concern about the survivability of a major portion of the SAC strike force when inevitably confronted by the formidable Soviet Surface-to-Air Missile (SAM) defense.

Enter the U-2
The "13" came into U-2 operations practically unannounced and unknown, at least to us drivers, but that was not unusual. We had a very basic briefing on its purpose, and how it was supposed to perform. It didn't take a genius to make it work; the equipment performed as programmed without the U-2 driver's interference. However, a major issue was the lack of printed Tech Data available for drivers and maintainers that led to significant future problems. But I'll explain that a little later.

Charlie Kern celebrating 1,000 hours in the U-2.

I was Commander of OL-19 from September to November 1966 at Barksdale AFB, Shreveport, Louisiana. Prior to my stint as commander, I had flown numerous missions over Cuba to ensure compliance with the agreement between the US, Soviet Union and Cuba. When the first "13" arrived, there was immediate controversy with the Line Folks (common term for maintenance personnel) over procedures, installation, removal and storage of the unit. Keep in mind, the highest level of security was required for the system wherever it was installed or stored. Even those of us on location had no idea of its huge significance on such a grand scale. In retrospect, that was probably a good thing. Everyone went about their business as usual – except for Maintenance.

Tech Data AWOL

The maintainers were not about to take responsibility for performing any maintenance on this very expensive gear without Tech Data, the documentation and instructions for service or repair of the equipment. Working on an aircraft without Tech Data went against everything drummed into the technicians by some hard-nose training instructor, including SAC's iron-clad insistence on following the written documentation to the letter.

Finding a solution to satisfy the maintenance dilemma would be a challenge. Our aircraft and pilots were being targeted by Cuban radar. Cockpit information showed that missiles were in guidance mode, indicating SAMs had been launched, when in fact, they may not have been. Oh, Sierra!

The Cuban Missile Crisis was many months behind us, but that didn't alleviate our concern for those being targeted and locked on by the Soviet SAM's fire control radar. When this occurred, a red light the size of a beer bottle cap lit up in the cockpit. Imprinted on the lens of the red light were the letters "OS." It didn't take long for that to be interpreted as meaning "Oh Sh*t." Along with the red OS light, a shrieking audible warning sounded in the headset. When a pilot was aware of these two warnings, it was really sweat time. If nothing else happened within a minute, such as a searing, bright flash of light, then everything was good.

Although the trigger wasn't pulled except on a couple of our missions which were near misses, one couldn't count on it *not* happening again if some enemy renegade on the ground hit the launch button. Truth of the matter was we simply had no way of knowing the intentions of the SAM site commander. It was critical to get the "13" operational. We felt we were flying on borrowed time.

After many messages and phone calls, SAC Headquarters sent the Tech Data to the OL. However, the issue was not resolved before my tour was up and I found myself in another brouhaha with the System 13 and its elusive Tech Data.

System 13 to SEA

After departing OL-19, I returned home to Davis Monthan AFB where the family reunion lasted only a week. One day in late November 1966 I received one of those ominous phone calls with orders to report to the Squadron Operations Office as soon as possible. We never discussed U-2 operational matters by phone due to strict security measures.

The Squadron Commander directed me to collect my gear and prepare to leave for OL-20, Bien Hoa Air Base, South Vietnam. I was replacing Leo Stewart who had

Rocket attack damage, Bien Hoa Air Base, South Vietnam, summer 1966.

Rocket attack damage, Bien Hoa Air Base, South Vietnam, summer 1966.

Chuck Maultsby, Bien Hoa Air Base, South Vietnam, summer 1966.

Chuck Maultsby and Charlie Kern, Bien Hoa Air Base, South Vietnam, summer 1966.

U-2 Maintenance Office after rocket attack, Bien Hoa Air Base, South Vietnam, Summer 1966.

Rocket attack damage, Bien Hoa Air Base, South Vietnam, summer 1966.

punched out of a U-2 in Vietnam. He survived his crash, but the aircraft was a loss. Stewart was the U-2 Operations Officer and had been summoned for an immediate "fireside chat" with the CINCSAC to explain the loss of the million dollar bird. I was ordered to get there immediately.

My Return to SEA

It was a long flight to Bien Hoa via Tan Son Nhut Air Base, South Vietnam on a Military Airlift Command DC-8. This was my third SEA TDY. I had plenty of time to think about Stewart's crash. Based on my fresh experience with the System 13, I wondered if the crashed bird had that equipment onboard. Had they received Tech Data for installing it? Had the batteries used for destruction of the "13" been connected? I wondered about a lot of stuff during that long trip, but I had no answers.

Upon arrival at Tan Son Nhut, my choices of transportation to Bien Hoa were an Army chopper, quick and reliable, or the long dusty bus ride. I caught the chopper to take me to Bien Hoa, the wartime home of our now single-aircraft detachment OL-20 we shared with a conglomerate of resident cats and dogs. The major tenant, the US Army Special Forces, which would play a paramount role in future events, was next door to our dusty, crowded patch of earth.

The Story Is Out

Feet on the ground, I went straightaway to the Sferics (spooky stuff) Shop and caught up with the NCOIC. I told him we had some things to discuss and cleared the shop of all but the two of us. I first asked him if the crashed bird had a System 13 onboard. It did. I

Rocket attack damage, Bien Hoa Air Base, South Vietnam, summer 1966.

U-2 Maintenance Office after rocket attack, Bien Hoa Air Base, South Vietnam, Summer 1966.

then asked if they had received all the necessary Tech Data for the "13." They had not. I asked if the destructor batteries had been connected. After a brief pause, he reached over to the desk with his foot and pulled out the bottom drawer with the toe of his boot. He pointed to the batteries and said they were the ones that should have been in the aircraft.

System 13 Goes Missing

Someone had made the critical decision to fly the mission with System 13 onboard, but without the destructor connected. Knowing what little I did about the potential consequences of the "13" falling into enemy hands sent a chill from head to toe. I was dumbfounded and shocked by this egregious lack of security.

The bright spot in all this—following the crash our pilots went with Special Forces troops and blew up the U-2 with satchel charges. All was okay now, right? Quite the contrary, all was not okay. The tail had broken off while the aircraft was in out-of-control flight, and was not with the wings and fuselage when they came to rest in the jungle. The System 13 was mounted on the tail, along with the crippled destruct system.

The tail of U-2 #690 was at least 50 miles north of Bien Hoa Air Base, maybe in the treetops of the jungle canopy or perhaps on the jungle floor. In either case, it was in enemy territory. With these scant facts in hand, I reported to the OL-20 Commander, Col Rafferty. He was deeply engrossed with the other half of OL-20's world—DC-130s, drone testing and employment—and he had little interest in this problem of the lost System 13. His response to me was, "Go and find it."

A-303 (MOBILE GUERRILLA FORCE) - OPERATION BLACK BOX 1

OPERATION BLACK BOX - DECEMBER 1966

DEPARTMENT OF THE AIR FORCE
100th Strategic Reconnaissance Wing OL-20 (SAC)
APO San Francisco, California 96227

Home

SUBJECT: Letter of Appreciation
TO: Colonel Francis J. Kelly
Commanding Officer, 5th Special Forces Group (ABN)
1st Special Forces APO 96227

1. On behalf of the 100th Strategic Reconnaissance Wing, Operating Location 20, Strategic Air Command, I would like to express my sincere appreciation to specific members of your command for the invaluable assistance rendered in the recovery of certain electronic equipment of a crashed organizational aircraft. Convey my deepest gratitude to the following members of your command for a job well done.

COMPANY A, 5th S.F.G. APO 96227

LT COL Thomas M. Huddleston, On scene coordinator (ABN)
SGM Richard D. Finn, On scene NCOIC (ABN)

A-303 (MOBILE GUERRILLA FORCE) - OPERATION BLACK BOX 2

281st Aviation Company, APO 96227

1LT Robert J. Reynolds, Helicopter Crew
CW02 Thomas E. McElhinney, Helicopter Crew
PFC Wilfred P. Paye, Helicopter Crew
SP/5 Charles R. Clark, Helicopter Crew

Detachment A-303, 5th S.F.G. APO 96227

CPT James G. Gritz, Ground Search Party
CPT Steven M. Yedinak, Ground Search Party
1LT Charles K. Chilton, Ground Search Party
MSG James C. Howard, Ground Search Party
SSG Dale R. England, Ground Search Party
SFG William A. Kindoll, Ground Search Party
SSG Dennis H. Montgomery, Ground Search Party
SFG George W. Ovsac, Ground Search Party
SSG Dennis H. Montgomery, Ground Search Party
SFC Patrick D. Wagner, Ground Search Party
SGT James C. Donahue, Ground Search Party
SSG Joseph J. Cawzey, Ground Search Party
SFC Lowell T. Glossup, Ground Search Party

This and following page: Citation awarded to members of 5th Special Forces Group for their actions in Operation Black Box. Courtesy of Stephen Sherman, RADIX Press, Houston, TX, www.specialforcesbooks.com.

Headquarters, 5th S.F.G., APO 96240

CPT Robert J. Weinfurter, Intelligence Coordinator

B-55, 5th S.F.G. APO 96227

MAJ Clarence M. Hooper, MACV Coordinator

19th TASS APO 96227

LT COL James E. Poore, ALO 5th INF DIV (ARVN)

MAJ Joe W. Carr, ALO "A" Company, 5th S.F.G.

CPT Charles L. Pocock, FAC Phuoc Long Sector

2. On 8 October 1966, an aircraft of the Strategic Air Command Operating Location 20 crashed approximately four miles SE of Song Be in Phuoc Long Province. It was subsequently discovered that certain electronic equipment of an extremely sensitive nature was lost during this crash and was very possibly in a position to be compromised. A compromise of this particular instrument would gravely affect US national security. Assistance was sought from the US Army, 5th Special Forces Group to provide an organized search of the area for the lost instrument.

3. The search was to take place in dense and practically impenetrable jungle, deep in Viet Cong held territory. The 5th Special Forces Group immediately responded to this seemingly impossible task. On the fourth day of the search, a patrol that was forced to search by crawling on hands and knees due to the dense jungle, radioed back that they had recovered what appeared to be the

missing instrument.

4. A helicopter was dispatched from the 281st Aviation Company to make a positive identification and possible jungle pickup. A Forward Air Controller directed the helicopter crew into the area and the pickup was affected by means of a 100 foot rope lowered from the helicopter into a bomb crater, the only semblance of a clearing in the area. It was determined at that time that it was definitely the missing instrument. The mission then returned to Bien Hoa and the instrument was determined to be uncompromised.

5. On behalf of the Strategic Air Command, I wish to express our deepest gratitude for the efforts of these determined soldiers and airmen that accomplished this seemingly impossible task. Be assured that the security of the free world has been greatly supported by the professional manner in which this job was accomplished.

s/Charles D. Rafferty
t/Charles D. Rafferty, Colonel, USASF
Commander, Operating Location 20

A True Copy:
J. I. Chavez
1LT, AGC
Assistant Adjutant

With open-ended orders like that, the search began. The first thing was to get a map with the course line having the crash site precisely depicted. From this spot, all calculations would emanate—air and ground speed, altitude, rate of descent, winds aloft. All had to be estimated to give us a vague idea of where the tail might be found and where to begin our search, unless we were lucky enough to spot it in the treetops from photos.

I scheduled a low altitude (10,000 feet) U-2 mission to give us adequate lateral photo coverage of the area with sufficient detail while keeping the aircraft out of range of ground fire. The crash site and aircraft remains had been pinpointed at 55 nautical miles on the 012 degree radial of the Bien Hoa TACAN. That was the only solid information available to us. It was a clue, although not a very good one because the aircraft had been traveling at an out-of-control speed between 300 and 500 knots. One other flimsy clue was the altitude of pilot ejection and separation from the aircraft. It was estimated to be "around" 50,000 feet altitude.

The film from this search mission was delivered to the large Photo Interpretation Center at Tan Son Nhut. I spent the next 48 hours there going through the pictures frame by frame, searching for the tail feathers of #690. All to no avail.

Reporting these results to the Col Rafferty, I was instructed to "forget the whole thing." I didn't. I couldn't.

Soon after I arrived at Bien Hoa, I had discussed the "13" situation with one of our U-2 Tech Reps, Travis Mason, who had previously been on detachments with the CIA U-2s. A short time later, I met with Mason and shared my slim findings with him. He

Montagnard Cambodian soldiers and Special Forces team assembling for the search for System 13.

Montagnard fighter who was a team member searching for System 13.

Special Forces team leader Captain James (Bo) Gritz.

was as shocked as I was about being told to "forget the whole thing." Events coasted along for a couple of days while I contemplated my next move.

As events unfolded, it became quite clear that I did not need to be concerned about what "Insignificant Me" was going to do about the situation. It was settled quickly and unexpectedly by the arrival of a "How-Goes-It Group" from Davis Monthan who were there to have a look at the drone program. The team consisted of Brig Gen Cole, the division commander, a squadron commander, and several other "horse holders." I was in the outer administrative office trying my best to be inconspicuous when the next thing I heard was a bellow from Gen Cole, "WHAT???!!!"

The general got SAC Headquarters on the phone, and it was most definitely a one-way conversation interspersed with many "Yes, Sirs." I figured this was no place for me and beat a hasty retreat. I had heard enough to realize the missing System 13 was the focus of all the attention. The OL commanding officer was getting ripped.

Enter the Special Forces

After the visitors had departed, I expected the worst. I was not disappointed. My new directions were to find the "13" no matter what it took. I immediately called the local Special Forces Commander, LtCol Thomas M. Huddleston, and asked for a meeting with him ASAP. He invited me to his office, and I beat a path to his dusty corner of the base. After relating the whole story to him, including the consequences if the enemy found the "13," he was inquisitive regarding its purpose which I alluded to only briefly. The Special Forces detachment took on the task and designated their mission, Operation Black Box.

Montagnard soldiers pulling the System 13 from the mud.

The System 13 with bayonet placed across it for reference.

System 13 being pulled onboard the helicopter. Charlie Kern is in the gunner's position.

Special Forces radio gear used by the team searching for the System 13.

Special Forces radio operator.

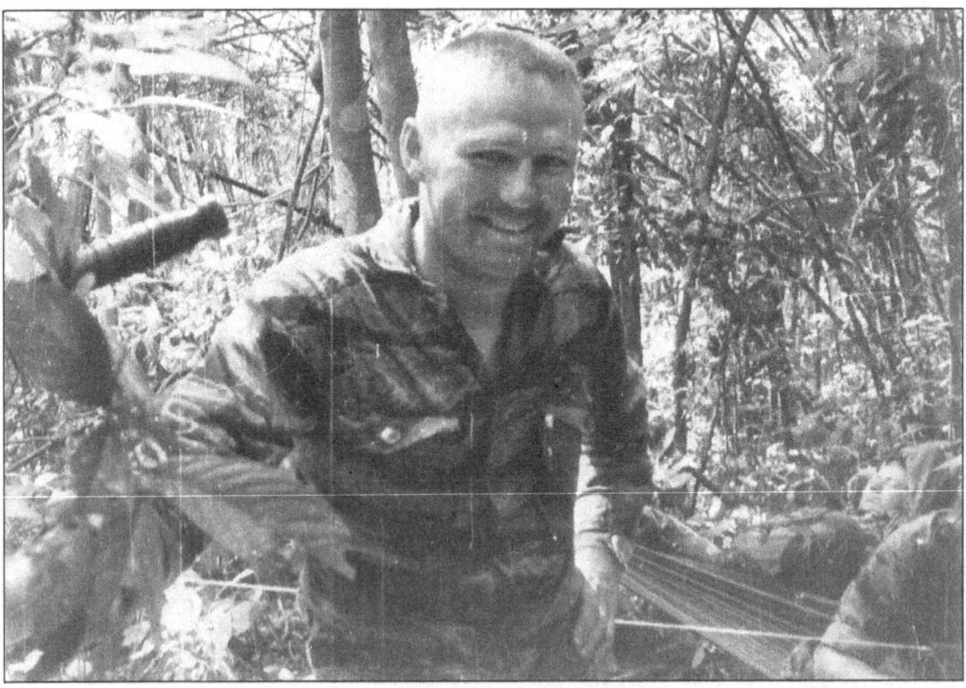

Special Forces sergeant who was a member of the team searching for the System 13.

Col Huddleston called his staff together, and we discussed what they needed from us. As it turned out, not much, just a map with all calculations on it. They asked for a summary of how we had determined "ground zero," where the tail had the best chance of coming to earth. The estimated flight data was melded with our knowledge of previous crashes caused by excessive speed, and the aircraft breakup pattern, as all had somewhat similar signatures. For example, the tail usually separates first, before the wings. After our meeting, they told me they would be in touch.

On Sunday night, the Special Forces search party departed from somewhere in northwest South Vietnam in two C-123s and with approximately 25 Montagnard mercenaries of the 3rd Mobile Strike Force. Col Huddleston checked in with me daily to provide an update after his team leader called from the field. The search party contacted Col Huddleston on the fourth day, a Thursday, and he called me immediately to request identifying information. It was noon when I received *the* call I had been waiting for. Col Huddleston said he thought they had found the prize. The search team wanted the "13's" serial number and any other specs that might be used to identify it. He wanted me to go with him on the chopper to bring it home. Of course, I went.

Ten minutes later Col Huddleston and Sergeant Major Richard D. Finn (a giant if I ever saw one; he was at least six feet nine inches), pilot and co-pilot picked me up in a Huey on the ramp at Bien Hoa. Before takeoff Sergeant Major Finn handed me a flak jacket which I started to don. He smiled broadly and said, "We usually sit on these." I quickly got the idea of what to protect! But there were several lying on the floor, so when we got to the Hot Area and everyone got busy, I surreptitiously slipped one on. Maybe Special Forces guys thought they were bullet proof, but I wasn't in their league.

Sergeant Major Finn and the pilot talked on the radio to the team on the ground, organizing the pickup point of the "13." I tried to stay out of the way while watching the expert retrieval of our prize. The problem was that there was no suitable landing place in the jungle. The pilot determined the only choice was to let down into a bomb crater to avoid the trees. The chopper actually had to hover over the crater a few yards from the troops on the ground. However, before the pickup was made, a reward was sent in. The Special Forces fellows had sized up the Montagnards and determined a couple dozen pairs of combat boots and a couple cases of Coca Cola would make a suitable reward. All the booty was attached to a cable and winched down to the waiting guys below.

The men on the ground attached the chopper's lift cable to the System 13 and Sergeant Major Finn started to winch the package up to the chopper. I had told the chopper pilot not to move the bird out of hovering position until the package was safely onboard. I was afraid something unscripted would happen, like the thing would come loose and fall back into the jungle. As soon as the box was tied to the cable, the dumbass pilot put the chopper in high gear and took off with the "13" swinging in the breeze on a 50-foot steel cable. Finn kept winching while I held my breath; I figured we only had one chance at this. He wore a harness that was tied to a ring in the floor. As soon as the package was near skid level, he climbed out on it, grasped the package and pulled it up with his foot to pause it there. Col Huddleston handled the lines, making sure they didn't get fouled.

We continued on for ten minutes with Finn hanging on to the "13" with one hand, holding on to the chopper with the other while standing on the skid. The chopper continued to a small clearing in the jungle used by the Forward Air Controllers and

Special Forces officers on the team.

Team members on the move.

Montagnard soldier.

other "special activities" as a landing strip. We landed and met an O-1 aircraft and pilot, where I transferred with the "13" for movement to Bien Hoa. I radioed to OL Operations, gave them an ETA and asked for the U-2 mobile control officer to meet me on the ramp in front of the control tower. We were exhilarated to have that baby back in our hands; at least I was. We delivered our lost "13" back to the Sferics Shop and took the rest of the day off. Well, there was one more task before taking a break.

I reported to the OL Commander, Col Rafferty, that the mission was successful. I don't remember if he said anything at all. He just looked at me, then turned away. But that was fine with me, everyone else was happy. I knew he had been burned badly, and in his mind, it was all because of me. He would never forgive or forget that I had caused him such indelible grief. Later events would bear that out.

After Action Report

The next day I called Col Huddleston to express our thanks for the great job he and his Special Forces troops had done in recovering our lost System 13. He had set up a meeting with participating parties. Capt James "Bo" G. Gritz, team leader of the ground troops, came to Bien Hoa from the field and was present in the meeting. He reported they located the equipment four miles south of Song Be, the capital of Phuoc Long Province, and sixty miles north-northeast of Saigon. Gritz told me the jungle was so dense the searchers were crawling on their bellies, parting the undergrowth with both hands. When one of the searchers pulled back the jungle growth, he spotted the box imbedded in the soft jungle floor, only partly visible above the mud. Locating and recovering this valuable defensive ECM equipment was so incredible, it defies belief. But the photos tell the story.

Contrary to other accounts on the recovery of the System 13, there was no raid on the Special Forces camp by the Viet Cong, nor was it taken to their camp, nor was there a firefight in which the "13" was liberated by ground forces.

The Air Force was grateful to have this valuable equipment returned, and later issued a Letter of Appreciation to the Special Forces detachment in recognition of their successful completion of Operation Black Box.

What respect and admiration I felt for these Special Forces soldiers, and what a spectacular task they had accomplished, truly a mission impossible. They started with only an educated guess to begin the mission. An "X" on the map marked the likely spot where the "13" landed. The ground team probed many square miles of dense jungle for a box two feet long by one foot square, half its length buried in the mud, their task had been sketchy at best. Even today it boggles the mind: The assembly and transport of a group of Montagnard soldiers almost a hundred miles to secret bases during the night; the highly effective search pattern employed; the incredible discovery of the crown jewel "13;" the delivery of the jewel to the chopper; and the organization to meet the O-1 at another clandestine base and transfer the prize to that aircraft for safe return to USAF custody.

What a helluva show! I will always be in awe of the US Army Special Forces' unequalled professionalism and effectiveness.

Epilogue

At the end of our various tours of duty in Vietnam, we all went to other assignments mostly within our own services. I never saw Col Huddleston again, or any of the other Special Forces troops. Col Rafferty died shortly thereafter on a handball court in Tucson of a heart attack while on active duty.

Cozier Kline

Pottsboro, Texas
Wife: Jan

Roger Cooper's Emergency Landing on a Frozen Lake in Canada

During my four years of flying the U-2, I never had anything happen that was unusual. However, I was flying on that winter day when Roger Cooper lost power over the middle of Canada. Roger called me over the radio the minute he flamed out. We had previously talked about such an occurrence. At that time we agreed we would enter into a circle flight to glide down so that in case of a failed air start we would have a pretty accurate position. I made a notation on my mission planning green card of the exact time he called me with the flameout.

After 35 minutes, when I thought he should have had his first chance for attempted air start, I began calling on the SSB radio to the SC-54 flying behind us. I was exactly one hour in flight behind Roger, so I decided to start a flight circle over our route exactly one hour after he called me.

Meanwhile, I finally got a response from Barksdale SAC Command Post on the SSB radio; no one else would answer. I asked Barksdale to call the Laughlin AFB Command Post and start a relay between us to see if they could contact the SC-54 rescue aircraft; Barksdale complied. I passed on the exact time of Roger's flameout and my best estimate of the coordinates of his position as Roger and I were flying the same routes. By proceeding ahead exactly one hour on my flight plan, I thought I could be of help to Roger.

I arrived at my estimate of Roger's position and started circling. By my calculations I would have about 15 minutes flying time left when I got back to Minot AFB. About 30 minutes after circling, I was able to talk to the SC-54 on SSB radio and told them when Roger flamed out. The SC-54 needed to go to full military power on their aircraft and get down to Roger's location. The SC-54 said they had received a radio call on SSB radio and were already "balls to the wall" headed to where they thought Roger would be. The SAC command posts were already on the ball at getting the Canadian people involved. It turned out the Canadians had a helicopter that supplied the information of who might be near Roger's projected location. The helicopter located and rescued Roger.

I was entering the landing pattern at Minot AFB when the Tower called and said there was a Colonel from SAC Headquarters who wanted to talk to me. I told the Tower to tell him I was too damn busy right then and I was flying on fumes. I told the Tower I would call him back after I had landed. The Colonel only wanted to ask me about everything we had in our survival pack, in the seat pack and a bunch of other stupid questions.

The final chapter to this story was that Ray Haupt flew to the frozen lake. He took Roger's U-2 off on a bulldozed short runway on the frozen lake, and flew 300 miles to the nearest Royal Canadian AFB. There further checks were made on Roger's U-2. Ray flew it back to Minot and we put Cooper's plane in the hangar. About 2:00 a.m. the next morning, we got a call at the BOQ that one of the U-2s had smoke coming out of it. We all rushed down and towed it out of the hangar for the fire trucks to extinguish the fire. There were some wire bundles that had chaffed bare and that may have been the source of Roger's problem.

Ray B. Lodin

Glendale, Arizona

Wife: Sandra

I spent seven years supporting the U-2 program. I would have continued to serve the Air Force but I was forced into retirement in December 1964.

During my time with the U-2 program, I was assigned to Mission Planning in Flight Operations. My job was to assist the pilots in planning their missions, such as determining time and distance to their destination. I enjoyed the interaction with the pilots: Jim Black, Ajack Moon, Buzz Curry, Buddy Brown, Pat Halloran, Jerry McIlmoyle, Mike Pierce, Joe Jackson, Ray Haupt, Roger Herman and many others.

While TDY in Australia, a lady friend took me down to the ocean to watch the small penguins return to their nesting spots. It was a fascinating experience. The beach was crowded with people watching them as we were. The penguins were so focused that

Ray Lodin, Bien Hoa Air Base, 1964.

they just walked among the people and headed for their nests. It was during the TDY to Australia that we learned President Kennedy had been killed. It was a sad ending to an otherwise pleasant TDY experience.

I enjoyed the TDYs and took advantage of new experiences. In addition to Australia, I was able to go to Puerto Rico, Alaska and Hawaii. In Saigon, Vietnam, I flew in, went to a French restaurant and witnessed the bullets across the river falling like fireworks.

During the Cuban crisis, I went to Florida to plan the pilots' missions and coordinate time over the target for the best photos. Weather conditions were a big consideration in planning these missions due to the angle of the sun.

Charles (Chuck) Maultsby

(Deceased August 14, 1998)

The following is an episode from a manuscript edited by Chuck's widow, Jeanne.

Accidental Overflight of the Soviet Union

The latter part of September 1962 I was notified that I had been tapped for my second tour in Alaska. I didn't look forward to going back that time of the year because, unlike summer months when it is daylight 24 hours a day, the winter months are bitter cold and dark almost the entire day. I would much rather have been flying missions out of our Operating Location in Australia. It is summer there during our winter months in the US.

Off I went on a KC-135 back to Eielson AFB, Fairbanks, Alaska. Lt. Col. Forrest "Whip" Wilson was the Detachment Commander. Captains Don Webster, "Wee" Willie Lawson and I were the U-2 "drivers" and the three navigators who did our flight planning were Captains Billie Bye, Bob Yates and First Lieutenant Fred Okimoto.

The missions being flown were the same High Altitude Sampling Program (HASP) missions I had flown during my previous tour, with one exception. Don Webster was the first U-2 pilot to fly to the North Pole and back. He covered a distance of 3,000 miles. It was celestial navigation all the way, using the stars for a fix. The only radio beacon used was located at Barter Island, located off the north coast of Alaska. From there, the Pole was nothing but ice caps and polar bears.

"Wee" Willie Lawson was the next U-2 driver to fly to the North Pole. My turn would come later. I sat in on all the flight planning and briefings to be prepared for my own flight. Unlike the other HASP flights, this one was to be accompanied by a Duck Butt flight as far as Barter Island where they would orbit and wait for the U-2s return. Duck Butt was a search and rescue team flying a Douglas DC-4. If we were forced to bail out between Barter Island and the North Pole, they would make every effort to locate us. We understood the chances of a successful Duck Butt rescue were slim.

The team said if a pilot bailed out over the North Pole, they could make one orbit before heading for the nearest landfall. It was no use having the para-rescuer suffer the same fate. I asked one of the jumpers what he would do if he had to bail out over the Pole. He said, "I wouldn't pull the ripcord." I was sorry I asked. With that in mind, I wasn't sure why the rescue guys tagged along after I heard that response. They couldn't land on those jagged ice caps. Even if they were lucky enough to find the pilot, by the time a ground party could reach him, he would either be frozen solid or decomposing in the belly of a polar bear.

"Wee" Willie didn't have to worry about either of the two prospects. His flight went according to plan and he returned with some of the most radioactive material collected to date. The Russians must have popped some mighty potent caps.

On October 25, 1962 Billie Bye, Fred Okimoto, Bob Yates and I planned my flight to the Pole for the following day. The same Duck Butt team sat in on the briefing that followed the flight planning, but I didn't ask them any questions. I already knew their answers and once was enough.

Since my takeoff was scheduled for midnight on October 26, I tried to get plenty of sleep during the day. It was next to impossible. Throughout the day, people were tromping in and out of the BOQ in their heavy snow boots. The harder I tried to sleep, the more awake I became. I finally gave up and went down to our Operations building and sacked out on a cot. No one would show up until three hours before my takeoff time.

I woke around 8:00 p.m. and went to the Officers' Mess for a breakfast of steak and eggs. Bob, Billie and Fred were there. They didn't get much sleep either.

The preflight preparations were completed. I took off on time and proceeded directly to Barter Island. Duck Butt gave me a call on a prebriefed frequency and said we both should arrive at the same time over Barter Island. They wished me luck and said they would keep a "light in the window" for me.

Over the Barter Island radio beacon, I set course for the Pole and prepared to take the first fix. Right on the button. Our navigators were masters of their craft. All went according to plan until I was about halfway between Barter Island and the Pole. Streaks of light started dancing through the sky making it difficult to take a fix on the star I was shooting. This was my first experience with the "Aurora Borealis" or Northern Lights. It couldn't have occurred at a worse time. The further north I went, the more intense the lights became. I held my heading and hoped the star I thought I saw was the right one.

The last few fixes before reaching the Pole, if in fact I did reach it, were highly suspect. I had no reason to believe I was off course, despite the suspect fixes. I decided to go ahead and do a 90-270 degree left turn that would put me over the Pole. It was: 90-270 degrees turn, then left turn for 90 degrees, then immediately reverse the turn for 270 degrees until heading back along the same track, only in the opposite direction. This new track should have headed me straight for Barter Island. I was out of radio range with Duck Butt. There was not anything they could do, but I would have felt comfortable hearing a friendly voice now and then.

I had never flown over a landmass that had not a single light from horizon to horizon. Of course, there were no lights on the ice caps, but didn't the Duck Butt crew say they would "leave a light in the window" for me? The first two fixes I took after leaving the Pole were wishful hoping and I realized something was terribly wrong. I began calling in the clear, hoping somebody out there might hear me and steer me in the right direction. I thought I was on the right track for Barter Island, but the ETA (Estimated Time of Arrival) was some time away.

It wasn't until I was out from under the Aurora Borealis force that I knew for sure I was off course, but which direction? I didn't bother to attempt to take any more fixes; I would just fly time and distance and hope for the best. I was approximately 300 to 400 miles north of Barter Island, or I thought I was, when the first radio contact with Duck Butt was accomplished. I even heard someone in our command post at Eielson calling over the single side band radio, but they couldn't receive my call. Surely I was in range of the radio beacon on Barter Island, but I couldn't pick it up. Had it shut down or what?

As the ETA for Barter Island wound down to 30 or 40 minutes, Duck Butt called and said they would start firing flares every five minutes. They started immediately. Duck Butt orbited over Barter Island and reported the radio beacon was operating okay. They received a transmission loud and clear. I didn't see any flare and asked them to fire another one. By this time I should have been over Barter Island and I should have been able to see the flare. They fired another flare. Again I saw nothing. It was all I could do to fight off a panic attack. I was either many miles east or west of Barter Island, but which?

The navigator aboard the Duck Butt called and asked me if I could identify a star. I told him I had the Belt of Orion constellation about 15 degrees left of the nose of the aircraft. Several minutes later the navigator called and told me to steer 10 degrees left. Immediately, I received another call from an unknown source, using my call sign, telling me to turn 30 degrees right. What the hell was going on? The navigator in Duck Butt didn't hear the latest call, so I was certain I was miles west of Barter Island. I received a call again from the unknown source with a definite Western-sounding voice telling me to turn right 35 degrees. I challenged him, using a code only a legitimate operator would know, but I received no response.

Duck Butt called and asked me if I could see a glow to the east on the horizon. I replied, "Negative." Transmissions from Duck Butt were getting weaker by the minute and the last one I heard was, "Turn left 15 degrees." The transmissions from the unknown source were loud and clear, but I ignored them. I selected the emergency channel broadcast and yelled "MAYDAY! MAYDAY! MAYDAY!" as loud as I could. I had about 30 minutes of fuel left, with no prospect of landing back at Eielson or anywhere else for that matter. The U-2 carries enough fuel for nine hours and forty minutes of flight and I had already been airborne nine hours and ten minutes.

Suddenly I picked up a radio station directly off the nose of the aircraft; it sounded like Russian music. It came in loud and clear. Now I knew where I was! The suppressed panic was now real and seized my lungs. I heard my own pulse pound in my ears. Through my panic, I knew for sure I wasn't going to be another Gary Powers and spend time in a Russian prison.

With what little fuel I had left, I decided to get as far away as possible from that radio station. I turned left until it was directly behind me and I kept calling "MAYDAY" until I became hoarse. "Why bother," I thought, "There's nothing anyone can do, so I may as well save my breath."

Twelve minutes of fuel left now. I made a call in the clear, to let anyone who might be listening, know that I was going off the air. A sense of despair overwhelmed me. I shut the engine down. Here I was just above 75,000 feet over God-knows-where, encased in a pressure suit which had inflated to keep my blood from boiling and all I could think of was, "This is a fine mess you got yourself into, Charlie."

When the suit inflated, I neglected to pull the lanyard to keep the helmet from rising. I had a hell of a time seeing the instrument panel until I finally got my helmet back into position. The helmet face shield and the windshield immediately fogged over.

I wanted to conserve the battery so I could make one call before I punched out. I thought for a moment the altimeter was stuck. At least 10 minutes went by before the aircraft started to descend. With my face close to the faceplate, I could lick the condensation off. Now all I had to do was keep the wings level, maintain a rate of descent for maximum range and hope my Guardian Angel wasn't taking a nap. The silence was deafening. I could only hear my own labored breathing.

Up to now Mother Nature hadn't extended an invitation to relieve my bladder, but wouldn't you know, she makes a call at the most inopportune time. I wasn't about to unzip the pressure suit and have my "winky" pinched off during ejection. Besides, I didn't think I could find my "winky" under all the winter gear I was wearing. I felt like a 40-pound robin. I wandered off the heading I had established. That it would not have mattered that much, but I still wanted to feel I was in control of an impossible situation.

Twenty minutes passed since flameout. Damned if I didn't see a faint glow on the horizon directly in front of me. I thought I'd hold this heading and rate of descent until I reached 20,000 feet. If I'm in an overcast condition, I'd better punch out. I didn't want to meet up with a mountain, if one was in my flight path. If there aren't any clouds, I would descend to 15,000 feet and take it from there. I descended through 25,000 feet. There wasn't any cloud cover and my pressure suit started deflating. I thanked God. Now I could look around because it was light enough to see the terrain, which was blanketed in snow.

There were no mountains in sight, but what I did see was breathtaking to me. There were two F-102s, one on each of my wings. They were both flying near stall speed and their angle of attack looked dangerously steep. I activated the battery switch and gave them a call on the emergency frequency. They welcomed me home and said they had been following me for the past 15 minutes. They also said I had just passed over a little airstrip about 20 miles back. I told the F-102 driver off my left wing that I was going to make a left turn, so he'd better move off. He said, "No sweat, come on."

When I turned into him, he stalled out and disappeared under my wing. He said, "While I'm down here, I'll look for that little airstrip." As I passed through 10,000 feet altitude, I decided to attempt an engine restart. I was still gliding at 160 knots indicated airspeed and didn't have quite the engine RPM for a restart but I tried anyway. Was I ever relieved to hear the J-57 engine come to life!

I descended below 5,000 feet. The F-102 drivers were getting nervous. They were used to setting up a flameout pattern with a high key of 10,000 feet, but they weren't flying a glider. I reached 1,000 feet flying over a truck. I could not detect any crosswind, which was one less thing to worry about. I started a left turn out to sea and the F-102 drivers came unglued. "Bail out! Bail out!" they screamed. I continued my turn on around to low key, lowered the flaps and decided I was getting too much thrust out of the idling J-57. I shut it down. Everything looked good so far. I was coming up on the truck now with more airspeed than I wanted.

As I passed over the truck at about 15 feet, I deployed the drag chute and kicked the rudder back and forth. That took care of the excessive airspeed. The U-2 still didn't seem to want to stop, even without an engine.

Call it luck or the help of that Guardian Angel, I think I made the best touchdown ever. I hardly felt a thing as both landing gears settled in one foot of snow. When the U-2 came to a complete stop, I just sat there staring straight ahead. I was physically and emotionally drained.

I don't remember how long I sat there, but a knock on the canopy startled me. I turned to face a bearded giant who was grinning from ear to ear. He reminded me of the television character, Grizzly Adams. I breathed a sigh of relief; he wore a parka that I recognized as US Government Issue.

Before I opened the canopy, I unbuckled the seat belt and shoulder harness, made sure all switches were off and stowed the maps that had been useless to me. I took off the faceplate and I sucked in a breath of real air. I opened the canopy and the bearded giant said, "Welcome to Kotzebue." I replied, "You don't know how glad I am to be here." It was bitter cold as I tried to climb out of the cockpit with all my heavy flight gear. My legs were numb and I didn't think they would support my weight. My new-found friend sensed the difficulty I was having, so he put his hands under my armpits and gently lifted me out of the cockpit and put me on the snow as if I was a rag doll. He wasn't even standing on a ladder or box!

There were several more personnel from the radar station that gathered around, plus a half dozen Eskimos who came from the shacks I saw while airborne. Grizzly gave me a hand taking off the helmet and had someone place it in the vehicle the rescuers drove. The two F-102s buzzed us rocking their wings, then headed east. I thought, "I have to thank them somehow for making this landing possible."

My bladder was about to burst so I excused myself and shuffled to the other side of the U-2. The Eskimos followed me, but when they saw what I was about to do, they politely turned their heads. More people showed up to look at the strange bird until there were about 20 or so gathered to see and hear the ruckus. I never before in my life had such a large audience to watch me tinkle.

The radar site commander let me use a secure phone in his office and brought me a mug of hot coffee to sip on. I finally got hold of "Whip" Wilson. He had been standing by the radio since I took off. I told him the aircraft was okay, no damage done, but the fuel tanks were dry. He said a C-47 was loading up now with drums of fuel and maintenance people. Whip said he would be along to fly the U-2 back to Eielson. I asked if anyone had notified Jeanne, my wife, that I was overdue and he said no one had. Good. At least she wouldn't know a thing until I told her. Whip let me know that my little excursion over Russia sure had the White House and SAC Headquarters shook up. I thought, "I'll bet."

It took several hours before the C-47 landed at Kotzebue. I had time to unwind and get acquainted with the radar site personnel. The site commander asked if I would like to see where I had been. He took me to a room with the largest plotting screen I had ever seen. There was a map about 15 feet square of the polar region including Alaska and Siberia overlaid with plexiglass. He flipped a switch and a battery of lights illuminated the entire screen. There was my entire flight from start to finish, indicated by little tick marks made with a yellow grease pencil. The tick marks traced a path from Eielson AFB direct to Barter Island, then to the North Pole. A 90 degree turn over the Pole was indicated, but instead of a 270 degree turn in the opposite direction, it looked like I turned 300 or 310 degrees before rolling out and heading for Siberia. At this point, I was beginning to understand my flight path. I followed the tick marks where the Duck Butt navigator told me to steer 10 degrees left and later 15 degrees left. The tick marks made a sharp left turn and headed for Kotzebue. I was about to slug the radar site commander and ask him, "Why in hell hadn't I been given a steer when all along you knew where I was," but my attention was directed to six little tick marks on either side of my flight path as I changed course to Kotzebue.

I asked the commander, "What are those little curly cues?" He replied, "Six MiGs were nipping up trying to shoot you down." Well, that got my attention and I thought, "Shit! I'm glad I didn't know it at the time. Phew!"

I stumbled over to a chair and took the weight off. I feared my legs were about to give out. He pulled up a chair alongside mine and said, "I know what you are thinking and I don't blame you. There is a good reason why we couldn't help you. I can't tell you, but maybe someone higher up will." I said, "Gee thanks. I hope the reason justifies throwing away an aircraft and crew."

I was still digesting all that I learned when the phone rang and someone in another room said it was for the U-2 pilot. The call was from one of the F-102 pilots stationed at Galena AFB who escorted me to Kotzebue. He said he was glad to see that I had made it down safely and apologized for yelling, "Bail out" when I turned out to sea at 1,000 feet. He had never seen a U-2 before and couldn't believe one could glide like that. I invited him to come visit us at Eielson and we would give him a "cook's tour."

The C-47 finally arrived from Eielson with Lieutenant Colonel "Whip" Wilson, several maintenance personnel and enough fuel to get the U-2 back to Eielson. When Wilson checked the aircraft forms, he noticed I neglected to fill out my takeoff and landing times. I remembered my takeoff time at midnight but couldn't remember when I landed. The radar site had me logged down at 10:25. That was 10 hours and 25 minutes of flight time. The U-2 had only nine hours and 40 minutes of fuel; that meant I had 45 minutes of glide time. There was that Guardian Angel again.

Wilson took off in the U-2, and I climbed aboard the C-47 with the maintenance crew for the long haul back to Eielson. "Wee" Willie met the C-47 and told me I had 30 minutes to pack all my gear because there was a KC-135 waiting to fly me to SAC Headquarters at Offutt AFB in Omaha, Nebraska. I was to brief my flight to the Commander in Chief of the Strategic Air Command, General Thomas Powers and his staff, especially the part over Russia. He also told me that Major Rudolph Anderson had been shot down over Cuba that day by a SA-2 surface-to-air missile. That was depressing news on top of everything else I had recently experienced. Everyone that knew Rudy would sorely miss him, myself included.

I don't remember how long the flight to Offutt AFB took, but it couldn't have taken long enough to suit me. I wasn't anxious to meet General Powers. I was the only passenger aboard the KC-135 and that made me extremely anxious about the briefing I was to give at SAC Headquarters. General Powers must have deemed it crucial to learn the circumstances surrounding my overflight of Russia. He must know all the details by now, but I supposed he wanted to hear it directly from me.

The KC-135 flight crew was curious to learn why they were flying me to SAC Headquarters, but they never came right out and asked. They had probably been briefed not to discuss the reason for this flight with anyone, especially me. They did provide that hot meal I was hoping for so long ago back in Eielson.

We landed at Offutt and a staff car took me to the SAC Headquarters building. A full colonel met me and escorted me to the underground Command Post. The room was a beehive of activity. People were actually running from place to place, as if their lives depended on it. Adjacent to the Command Post was a briefing room with a table that could seat at least 20 people. At the head of the table was an easel with an aeronautical chart on which my flight was plotted to the North Pole. A sheet of paper covered the portion of my flight after leaving the Pole. A colonel told me to take a seat and General Powers would be with us in a few minutes. General Powers entered the room and eight other generals followed. Those ranking generals looked as if they hadn't been out of their uniforms for days. Their eyes were bloodshot and some hadn't seen a razor in the past 24 or more hours. I stood at attention while they were all seated. General Powers sat directly across the table from me. He looked extremely tired, but he was clean-shaven and wore a fresh uniform.

As soon as everyone was seated, with all eyes riveted on me, General Powers said, "Captain Maultsby, how about briefing us on your flight yesterday." I stood at the easel while describing the type mission I had flown. I used the pointer to indicate the route I had flown from Eielson to the North Pole. I mentioned the difficulty I had taking fixes because of the Aurora Borealis.

Until I pointed to the North Pole, no one stopped me to ask questions. General Powers then asked, "Captain Maultsby, do you know where you went after leaving the Pole?" I said, "Yes, sir." The other generals squirmed in their seats as if they were sitting on tacks. General Powers said, "Show us, please." I took the pointer and lifted the paper that had covered my flight path after leaving the Pole. The other generals really became excited now, but General Powers only smiled. He asked, "How did you know?" I told him that I saw my flight path plotted at the radar site at Kotzebue. General Powers turned and looked to each of the other generals and asked, "Gentlemen, do you have any more questions?" They all nodded negatively. He turned back to me and said, "Too bad you weren't configured with a system to gather electromagnetic radiation. The Russians probably had every radar and ICBM site on maximum alert."

General Powers thanked me for the briefing, told me not to discuss my overflight with anyone and left the room. The other generals followed in order of rank, and the last to leave the room was a brigadier general. He stopped in front of me and said, "You are a lucky little devil. I've seen General Powers chew up and spit out pilots for a helluva lot less."

The colonel who escorted me into the Command Post asked me if I'd like to wait in his office; he said there was a U-3A flying up from Laughlin AFB to pick me up. It wasn't due for another hour or so. I thought now would be a good time to find out why I wasn't given a steer when every Tom, Dick and Harry had my flight path plotted. The colonel wouldn't tell me why, but he did say that my overflight came close to starting World War III. If it hadn't been for my "MAYDAY" calls, the Russians may have pulled the trigger. He told me that when President Kennedy was informed about my overflight, he simply said, "There's always some son of a bitch who doesn't get the word." Well, if I had gotten "the word", I wouldn't be sitting here now. Just one steer would have prevented all this commotion.

A phone call from Base Operations announced the arrival of a U-3A from Laughlin. I thanked the colonel for his hospitality and left the underground Command Post still wondering why I wasn't given a steer. It bugged me for years before I learned the reason.

Captain Ed Purdue was waiting for me in the flight planning room in Base Operations. He said everyone back at Laughlin had been sweating me out. Ed didn't think anyone had told Jeanne and I was thankful. He was anxious to hear all about my fiasco, but when I told him General Powers told me not to discuss the flight with anyone, he didn't pursue the issue.

Ed said that he flew through some pretty nasty weather on his way up and hoped it had cleared for the flight back. The weather station forecast wasn't optimistic. Just north of Enid, Oklahoma we ran into icing conditions and couldn't maintain altitude. We called Vance AFB near Enid, told them we were icing up and requested immediate landing instructions. To make matters worse, one engine was losing power which increased our rate of descent. We requested a straight in GCA (Ground Control Approach) and declared an emergency. When GCA picked us up, we were already below the glide path and still descending. I thought, "What a way to go and after all I'd been through in the past two days." GCA was screaming for us to level off; we were way below the glide path. I could see the ground now through light fog and was certain we wouldn't make it up to the runway. I swear Ed was trying to hold the airplane up by pulling up on the yoke. It worked because we touched down in the overrun 50 feet from the runway.

I arrived back at Laughlin and I recited the same briefing for my Wing Commander, General DesPortes. Not one word was spoken throughout the entire briefing, except for an occasional muttered, "Oh, shit," when I described the six MiGs after my fanny, no one asked a question until I finished. Everyone seemed more interested in the thoughts that went through my mind during the ordeal rather than the cause of the overflight. They all were glad not to have been in my place. General DesPortes thanked me and said, "Now get back to Jeanne and the boys and take the next two days off."

Jeanne met me at the door with a "cool one" and said, "After you change your clothes, I'm dying to know what all the commotion is about. Just tell me one thing with a quick "yes" or "no"; does it have anything to do with Rudy Anderson being shot down?" I replied that it did not, "However, if the boys come in, I'll have to wait to fill you in on my latest escapade."

Jeanne sat attentively, her huge eyes looking larger as I went through the events of the past three days. "Well, that's it. Now you know what all the commotion was about." She just shook her head and said, "I let you out of my sight and you try to start World War III!" Before she could say another word, Chuckie and Shawn came bursting through the door shouting, "What did you bring me?" I felt like saying, "I brought your Daddy's ass home in one piece."

SAC Headquarters sent a team of navigators down to Laughlin to get a look at the article known as the U-2. Some had never seen a U-2 much less the navigation aids it carried including a periscope sextant and coffee grinder. The team was led by a full colonel, who when introduced to me, said he remembered my name associated with another incident but couldn't put his finger on it. I was chosen to escort the team because they were aware of my overflight. I let them sit in the cockpit of the U-2 and explained what the instruments were and how they were used. I could tell they were disappointed in what they saw. They were expecting all sorts of sophisticated equipment. After they observed the flight planning for several days and results of the local flights, they all agreed that a U-2 pilot certainly earned his flight pay.

Many years later at Davis Monthan AFB, Tucson, Arizona I received a call from a major inquiring if I was the same Maultsby who landed a U-2 at Kotzebue back in 1962. I told him that I was, and I invited him to visit the squadron first chance he got. I didn't really expect him to accept.

Weeks went by before the major showed up at the door of my office. We spent about an hour recalling the events that took place in those infamous days, October 26 and 27, 1962. He wasn't the radar site commander at Kotzebue back then, but I certainly did remember meeting him. Just as a lark, I thought I'd ask him why I wasn't given a steer, since my flight path had been plotted from start to finish. He was surprised that no one ever told me although I had made several inquiries. He didn't go into detail how my positions were relayed to the radar site, but he did mention some satellite station off the coast of Siberia on an island that could relay the information without giving their position away. Apparently Uncle Sam regarded the satellite stations more important to our national defense than one lost U-2 aircraft and pilot.

That explanation never satisfied me. Kotzebue could have contacted Duck Butt and they could have given me a steer before I wandered out of radio range.

Addendum by Colonel (Ret.) Charles Kern

Anyone who has flown missions around the Iron Curtain is most certainly aware of the hazards. The Soviets transmitted false signals on radio and navigational aids under their control. They would try to get Allied aircraft to navigate on them, leading our pilots into Soviet or East German airspace. It was called "MEACONING." There were specific procedures in the En route Supplement for reporting such contacts. I had one reportable incident in four years of flying around Iron Curtain countries. It sounded like the real thing to me, except it was coming from a place I didn't think it should have been.

Addendum by Colonel (Ret.) Anthony Martinez

I have talked with Leon Schmutz, the F-102 pilot who was the wingman of Captain Dean Rands. It was Rands who intercepted and escorted Chuck Maultsby to Kotzebue on October 27, 1962. Schmutz said he and Rands were on alert at Galena with their Deuces (F-102s) and armed with only air-to-air missiles. They were scrambled to the west to intercept the U-2 that had been tracked over Soviet territory. The Deuces were controlled by "CAMPION," the Early Warning Radar site near Galena, Alaska. About 30 to 40 minutes after their takeoff, they were vectored to the U-2 target. The U-2 was intercepted at an altitude of 45,000 to 50,000 feet altitude. Rands, the flight leader, made radio contact with the U-2 pilot. They continued to escort him toward Alaska, but it was slow going. They had to do some turning to stay with him. All this time they were under control of CAMPION. Rands said he and Schmutz were not aware that MiGs were airborne and were attempting to intercept. He said he did not know exactly where they were when they intercepted Maultsby's U-2. But if you measure 40 minutes flying time at 400 to 500 knots west of Galena, it places you over or near the Siberian land mass. Kotzebue is on the north end of the Alaskan Baldwin Peninsula and there is nothing west of that but open water of the Chukchi Sea. Chuck was blessed by many fortunate events that happened that day leading up to his successful landing.

Gerald E. (Jerry) McIlmoyle

Venice, Florida

U-2 Entry into the Vietnam War

In 1963 the 4080th Strategic Reconnaissance Wing had moved from Laughlin AFB in Del Rio, Texas to Davis Monthan AFB in Tucson, Arizona. The tempo of U-2 operations had increased and it seemed like we were meeting ourselves coming and going. We were going on temporary duty assignments and flying the U-2 all over the world. I had returned from two months in Alaska and was looking forward to a long stint at home. It was February 1964 and the Tucson weather was fantastic and great for flying the U-2.

I had just returned home from the flight line when there was a knock at our door. There stood our Wing Commander, Colonel John DesPortes. Twice before I had answered a knock on the door and he had been standing there—smiling. The first word out of his mouth was "Maaj," that was his Alabama drawl for Major. I knew Colonel DesPortes' visit did not portend well. The first of his previous appearances signified the start of the Cuban Missile Crisis; the second was when he asked me to accompany him to break the news to the wife of a fellow U-2 pilot who had died in a crash in California. Colonel DesPortes instructed me to pack my bags and be at Base Operations for departure on a KC-135. He said Steve Heyser, Chuck Stratton and I were going to deadhead (fly and sleep) that night en route to Hickam AFB, Hawaii. Three other U-2 pilots were preparing to fly three U-2Rs, the mid-air refueling model, to Hickam. Steve, Chuck and I were all qualified in the U-2 mid-air refueling. In the morning we would fly those U-2s to Clark Air Base in the Philippines. DesPortes said we were to plan on an extended stay.

I was the last to arrive at Base Operations. I guess I took too much time saying goodbye to my wife, Patty, and our kids, Patrick and Ruthie. The entire navigation section was there gathering maps for our flights from Hickam. The navigation crew was even gathering all the maps they could find of North and South Vietnam.

I remembered that at the end of the Korean War President Eisenhower had emphatically stated publicly he would never involve the United States in a land war in Asia. At that point in time we had advisors stationed in South Vietnam but no independent military units. We got airborne out of Davis Monthan AFB, for Hickam AFB, Hawaii with our navigation, maintenance and PSD teams on board the KC-135.

Steve, Chuck and I were told to get as much sleep as we could because we had a long flight ahead of us. I took a Seconal and went right to sleep. We were each to fly a U-2 the next day from Hickam AFB, to Clark Air Base, Philippines with one mid-air refueling near Guam.

At Hickam Steve, Chuck and I were advised that the Strategic Air Command (SAC) Advanced Team (ADVON) had already set us up with office space and a place to sleep. The Navigation Team started planning our flights for the next day with takeoff schedule for 6:00 a.m.. Our maintenance crews did not get much sleep either; they recovered the U-2s being flown in from Tucson, servicing them with fuel, oil and oxygen. They fixed any maintenance problems identified on the U-2 flights to Hickam from Tucson. We were directed to start flying reconnaissance over North Vietnam (NVN) as soon as possible. The PSD guys worked all night getting our pressure suits ready to wear for the next morning's scheduled launch. The three of us were to fly over Wake Island and Guam and conduct our inflight refueling; we would continue on to Clark Air Base. A total of 15 hours was scheduled to elapse from the time we put on our pressure suits at Hickam until we removed them at Clark. Someone dragged us from bed and drove us to the flight line to go through our pre-flight ritual of getting a medical check and eating a steak and egg meal (high protein, low residue). We would also pre-breathe oxygen to eliminate 75 percent of the nitrogen from our bodies to prevent the bends. Fifteen minutes before each takeoff the PSD technicians strapped us into our aircraft. They

View from the tanker during inflight refueling of the U-2. Photo courtesy of Lockheed Martin Co.

hooked up the connections, checked our pressure suit and oxygen connections and tested everything to ensure it all functioned properly. Steve was scheduled to take off first, with me and then Chuck following at 30-minute intervals. Steve was strapped into his U-2, waiting, radio on, ready to copy his authentication of the execution order from SAC Headquarters. The Navigation Team planned his celestial navigation calculations for a 6:00 a.m. takeoff. The execution order didn't come. We waited and waited and waited. Thirty minutes went by, the limit upon which preplanned celestial readings were considered useable. They gave Steve my charts and planned celestial as it was for 30 minutes later in the day. The domino affect took place. Having given my charts to Steve, they then appropriated and gave me Chuck's charts and started re-planning Chuck's flight. And like most bad dreams, every 30 minutes of delay in the execution order our charts were shuffled forward. Old military descriptions of this three-ring circus comes to mind, "hurry up and wait," "situation normal all ____ up", etc. We went through the total cycle twice and were arguing over whether to start a third cycle at 10:00 a.m..

I let our Operations Officer know that we had now been on the flight line for almost six hours. I thought combining the delay with our planned flight time would mean that we would exceed SAC regulation crew rest requirements. I suggested we notify SAC Headquarters we were aborting for crew rest. Little consideration was being given to the Navigation, PSD and Maintenance teams that had been on duty in excess of 24 hours.

I was sitting in a lounge chair in the PSD van when I saw our Operations, Maintenance and PSD guys milling around the three U-2s lined up on the flight line. What was going on? Wouldn't you know, the execution order came right when we were ready to pack up our bags and go to Waikiki Beach.

I tried to tell the Detachment Commander saying, "It's too late." But by then this gaggle had its own momentum and it was going to grind on no matter what. I was informed in plain language that regulations are only a guide to the Commander, not the inviolable law. So, Steve launched without celestial charts. Thirty minutes later I followed Steve, also minus the celestial charts. Steve, Chuck and I dead reckoned our way across the beautiful blue Pacific Ocean. It was a clear day with no clouds, no haze and no fog. Were we ever glad to see Wake Island over our plane's nose about 250 nautical miles ahead. We experienced a big boost to our confidence in our flight planning based upon the forecast of high altitude winds.

The earth is mostly surrounded by water. We saw a lot of water that day. Four hours out of Hawaii, Steve radioed me he had picked up the Wake radio beacon and it was right on the target. Steve could not talk to Chuck, the third and last guy behind us; the two of them were separated by 425 nautical miles. I was in the middle and could talk to either of them so I relayed messages for the three of us. Steve reported he had passed Wake Island. I could make out the speck of black in the ocean on the horizon 200 plus miles away. It was indeed Wake Island. I passed Wake and radioed both Steve and Chuck that we were all about five hours out of Hickam. We had eight more hours to go to reach Clark AB. Chuck radioed back to me, "Keep your comments to yourself, thank you very much." We were three tired and bored U-2 pilots and had eight hours to go.

Three hours later, Steve communicated to me that he had turned on his radio beacon to allow the KC-135 refueling tanker to home in and rendezvous with him. His next report was that he was in radio contact with the tanker and was starting his letdown for mid-air refueling. The procedure was to descend to 25,000 feet and put on the U-2

"Gust Control." That action raised the flaps and ailerons up a couple of inches and reduced the wing and tail loading. It provided greater safety in rough air. It also allowed the maximum indicated airspeed (IAS) limit to be increased from 160 knots to 220 knots IAS. I heard Steve report to the tanker that he was at 25,000 feet and holding 200 knots IAS. That was good news.

I heard the tanker report they had Steve in sight and were coming up on his left side. They would advise him when their airspeed and altitude were stable for him to slide over for refueling. The minimum airspeed of 200 knots IAS was required for the KC-135 to maintain a stable platform at 25,000 feet altitude to conduct midair refueling. It was also a major safety factor during refueling for the U-2. I heard the tanker crewman report he was ready and the boom operator said his boom was engaged in Steve's aircraft; the refueling process began. About two minutes later I heard the boom operator report that Steve had a full fuel load. Steve was instructed to reset his aircraft's fuel counter. Steve disconnected from the tanker and thanked them for their service. He was over Guam and heading for Clark AB.

We planned the refueling to end over Guam. In that case we would need fuel and could land at Andersen AFB on Guam and get fuel there. The tanker called me and instructed me to turn on my radio beacon. The tanker was coming toward me at a closing rate of over 800 MPH for rendezvous and refueling. After letdown from 70,000 to 25,000 feet, the tanker looked beautiful as it pulled up close to me just off my left wing. I slid into position for refueling and reminded myself of the tanker bow wave. That bow wave was not visible but it was there. It is similar to the upheaval of water behind a speeding power boat only in my case there was upheaval of air behind the tanker. When my U-2 slid in behind the tanker it acted like a surfboard; it first catches a wave and then is riding it. I had to throttle back almost to idle as the U-2 caught the tanker's wave. We used our speed brakes while refueling as that would give us better aircraft control. During refueling, the pressure from the tanker boom and the flow of fuel helped keep the U-2 from over-running the tanker. The U-2, in my mind, felt like it wanted to do just that.

It seemed like only a second later the tanker boomer radioed me that I had a full load. The tanker pilot eased his aircraft to my left, wished me well and turned back to refuel Chuck. The refueling for Chuck went without any problems. Following Chuck's refueling, the tanker turned toward Clark AB. The tanker had our ground support crew on board and they had to get to Clark before Steve to prepare for his arrival. It was not to be. Steve, Chuck and I encountered a tail wind of about 30 knots that gave us ground speed of 450 knots. The tanker had about a 100-knot head wind. We would arrive at Clark AB and land before the tanker and our support guys.

I could see the sunset reflecting off the cloud cover below us. On arrival at Clark radio beacon at 20,000 feet altitude, I initiated an approach pattern letdown. I was going to position myself for a Ground Control Approach (GCA) pickup on their radar and their guidance to Clark. They lined me up and set me up for landing. I broke through the overcast at about 1,000 feet above the ground. I could see the Clark runway directly in front of me and followed the GCA instructions to the landing threshold. When I crossed the runway threshold, GCA released me and I landed visually. To me, it was more of a controlled crash than a landing. There was a nice breeze down the runway so I was able to fly the wings and keep them level throughout my landing rollout. I was fortunate that

I continued to be able to fly the aircraft through the turnoff to the runway and onto the taxiway with the wings still level.

In my entire life I do not believe I have ever been that tired and that dehydrated. The Clark transient ground crew was there to help me get out of the aircraft and into the staff car that had been sent for me. I felt as if I was in a fog. The staff car delivered me to a crowded and dimly lit room; someone handed me a beer. That was the last thing I remembered.

The next day we were tasked for our first overflight of North Vietnam. The detachment commander, navigators and maintenance teams arrived the same night in the KC-135, the same aircraft that refueled our flight of three U-2s over Guam. Those were long reconnaissance flights—the flight from Clark AB to North Vietnam and back to Clark. The flight included three hours deadhead time to NVN two hours over the target area and then another three hours deadhead time back to Clark. We flew these missions over NVN over a period of about four days. The Philippine Government then became aware we were flying out of their territory and ousted us and our U-2s. We were declared "Persona non-grata"; they gave us four hours to get off their sovereign territory, another political crisis in the making.

We made our Philippine imposed four-hour deadline and flew the three U-2s, support personnel and all our equipment back to Andersen AFB, Guam. There was no space in the Bachelor Officers' Quarters (BOQ) so the officers in our detachment were installed in two vacant four-bedroom family houses. Andersen had space in its Non-Commissioned Officers' (NCO) quarters for all our maintenance, PSD and other support personnel. It seemed like we stayed there forever but it was only about a week or 10 days. One significant occurrence came to me during that time. Cassius Clay beat Sonny Liston for the World Heavyweight Boxing Title. The reason I remembered that was because I bet Steve Heyser $5 that Clay would win. We gathered around the radio that night to hear the fight broadcast over Armed Forces Radio. I collected my huge winnings from Steve!

In a couple of days we received an execution order to move the detachment to Bien Hoa Air Base in the Republic of South Vietnam. Steve, Chuck and I ferried the birds to Bien Hoa which was about 20 miles north of Saigon. It was a clear day with light winds as we flew over the Bien Hoa radio beacon for approach and landing. Several times from my plane I called "Ben Ho" on the radio but received no answer. An English-speaking voice finally came on the radio and said, "Try 'Ben Waa'." I called "Ben Waa" exactly like that and right away a voice on the radio answered in English. I never understood why they didn't answer to "Ben Ho." I guess it was a French thing; if you don't say it to their liking, they don't answer.

A week after we arrived in Vietnam several members of the detachment were invited to meet the US Ambassador in Saigon. The Ambassador informed us that there were about 15,000 military personnel in South Vietnam. They were in an advisory capacity throughout the country. He told us we were the only independent unit there made up entirely of Americans. We were warned to be careful of what we said and what we did. He said we must be armed at all times and travel only in groups of two or three. We should never get into a position where we would be vulnerable to attack; we should never allow ourselves to be isolated from our unit. The Ambassador said they had found that the entire cadre of barbers on Tan Son Nhut Air Base was Viet Cong at night and friendly barbers during the day.

I drew a .45 caliber pistol because I had qualified expert with it. Chuck, being the hunter among us, had a carbine. Bob Spencer wanted something heavier and drew a Thompson submachine gun. We joked with him saying, "We didn't need to carry our weapons as long as you and your Tommy were with us."

The next day we started flying U-2 photographic reconnaissance missions over all of North Vietnam right up to the borders of China, Laos, Cambodia, Thailand and South Vietnam. Within a month we had mapped most of Southeast Asia (SEA).

Our Intelligence Briefer informed us the Viet Cong were everywhere around our airfield. To avoid ground fire on our landing approaches, we adjusted our landing patterns so we would arrive over the field at 3,000 feet or higher above the ground and then spiraled down so our ground track was within the perimeter of the base. We planned the touchdown point at the first taxiway down the runway, approximately 2,000 feet from the end. Every so often while I was there, the Viet Cong would lob a mortar shell onto the base but nothing was ever hit.

The U-2 pilots were quartered in Vietnam in two bedroom trailers with two men to a bedroom. The trailers were located close to the base Control Tower. I was always apprehensive about that because I thought the highly visible Control Tower would make a good target for mortars. That was where we lived, though. After I had rotated back to Davis Monthan AFB the Viet Cong destroyed several B-57s sitting on the ramp not too far from our U-2s and trailers. Everyone ate in the same mess hall in a barbed wire fenced compound. Our Officers' Club was primitive with only a bar, a few lounge chairs and a chessboard. We did receive first-run movies though; a new movie was shown every night at no charge. Jim Qualls and I played chess and drank MiG-5s (a drink consisting of two shots of Scotch and one of Drambouie) until we didn't care who won. Jim usually won. With a few MiG-5s under my belt, I didn't much care about anything.

Going to church was a unique experience. There was no chapel in the compound so we walked about a mile to a church in a small village. I worried at first about walking out in the boondocks to go to church. Our Intelligence Briefer informed us that almost all hostilities were suspended on Sundays. I gave him a little smile and asked him if the Viet Cong knew we do not fight on Sundays. I never understood the attitude of the Viet Cong. Supposedly they were Communists and by definition did not believe in God. Why was Sunday any different kind of day to them? I guess everyone needs a day off occasionally, even the Communists.

Victor L. (Vic) Milam

Del Rio, Texas
Wife: Louene

My Scariest U-2 flight

I was returning to Bien Hoa Air Base, Vietnam after a flight over North Vietnam. Everything was normal until about four and a half hours into the flight. I was still North of DaNang Air Base headed south at about 70,000 feet altitude. With no warning, I suddenly lost all pitot static instruments. Airspeed went to zero; vertical speed indicator dropped to the bottom of the dial and stayed there. The attitude indicator tended to float.

I immediately disengaged the autopilot knowing that it functions with information from the pitot static system. My dilemma was to let down, keeping my airspeed within what we called the "chimney".

At the cruise altitude of the U-2, the difference between stalling the bird and exceeding its limiting Mach was about eight knots indicated airspeed. I was trying to stay between the stall buffet on low side and high speed Mach buffet on the other with no instruments to help, only the feel of the aircraft. My only option was to start descending. I was most thankful then that I was just North of DaNang rather than over North Vietnam where I had just been for the previous couple of hours.

It was almost impossible to avoid looking at the instruments in my situation in order to fly the airplane. But looking at them was somewhat less than productive since they were totally useless. I knew I had to ride the Mach buffet because getting my bird into a stall buffet would probably be disastrous. If the U-2 stalls at those altitudes, recovery is unlikely before the tail comes off the airplane. The airplane is unstable at these altitudes and tends to continue further into the Mach buffet or stall attitude buffet if it should get into either one.

Trying to maintain a Mach buffet was a real "seat of the pants" pilotage challenge for me. A little too much nose down meant to pull back on the yoke which caused more buffet. Then coming out of that into no buffet, I had to nose down again or risk a stall. I had retarded the throttle but could not risk lowering the gear or going into the gust position. It would add too much turbulence and hamper my feel for how the airplane was flying. I had to get lower first and I was sweating bullets as it was. After what to me was an agonizingly long time, I was able to descend to a more favorable altitude. I then lowered the gear and extended the gust to give myself a larger airspeed envelope in which

Victor L. Milam (center) with crew chiefs, preparing for a flight.

Victor L. Milam, 1968.

Saigon street scene.

to fly. Still no instruments, but I could tell by the rush of air noise and feel of the airplane that I was within a safe flying airspeed.

This condition continued until at 17,000 feet when everything suddenly jerked back to proper indications. I continued to Bien Hoa Air Base and made a normal landing.

There was really nothing to write up for post flight. In talking with Maintenance personnel, it was decided that somehow moisture had formed in the pitot static system. The moisture then had moved into a position to freeze, thereby causing me to lose pitot static instruments. I had never had that happen before or since.

Of the Air Medals and two Distinguished Flying Crosses I received for being at the right place at the right time, I thought this incident was more deserving that any other was. However, it was not reported and I was just thankful to get the bird and myself down safely.

James K. Rogers

Sumter, South Carolina
Wife: Marge

The First Flight

My first U-2 flight was simply flying at low levels accompanied by a chase aircraft to verify I was not trying to kill myself or anyone else in the process of learning this new plane. My instructor pilot was in the chase plane, a U-3A, the military version of the Cessna 310, known as the Blue Canoe. Another instructor was on the ground in a chase vehicle monitoring my touchdown control and landing technique. I simply made numerous touch and go landings to prove I knew what I was doing to land this difficult aircraft safely.

The second flight, a solo, was a tad different. There was no chase plane to monitor my progress, and I wore the partial pressure suit. I climbed to 50,000 feet altitude and shut the engine off. It became very quiet in the cockpit, and the pressure suit inflated as it was supposed to do. I must have resembled the Michelin Man in the television tire commercials. The next step was to glide to 30,000 feet and restart the engine. In our training manual this was described as a "confidence maneuver." In reality the U-2 is a safe aircraft. Most of the flying time was at an altitude of 70,000 feet or greater. If the engine quit up there, we had almost an hour to determine where to land should the engine fail to restart.

The one disadvantage for the pilot of the U-2 was its capability to fly for over twelve hours without refueling. I flew a dozen flights from Laughlin AFB, Texas to Cuba and returned to Laughlin. When we moved our operations to Barksdale AFB, Louisiana, flying time to/from Cuba was cut by at least three hours. At the end of those missions, I staggered out of the cockpit, climbed down the ladder to the tarmac and stumbled around trying to return the circulation to my legs. After breathing 100 percent oxygen flying twelve hours seated in the tiny cockpit, I was ten pounds lighter due to loss of body fluids. Within a couple of days, my fluid levels returned to normal as did my weight. Thus began my penchant for a large gin and ice drink before dinner each evening, a tradition that continues today.

Vietnam

It was an interesting day over Hanoi, North Vietnam (NVN) in September 1964. We had been flying in that area for almost six months with absolutely no reaction from the enemy. This particular morning was around the time of the Gulf of Tonkin incident with the US Navy. Ed Perdue and I were both flying missions around Hanoi that morning when I heard Ed transmitting over Guard Channel. This channel was used only for emergencies and transmission could be received by any unit that had Guard Channel on their radio. I heard, "MAYDAY! MAYDAY!" I knew Ed and I were in the same general area, but we would never have made radio calls in the clear on any channel. After another painful minute that seemed like an hour, I switched to Guard Channel and called to Ed. "Ed, are you okay. This is Jim." He responded, "Yes, I am under missile attack, and I'm returning to base." I reported I was right behind him and headed out to the Gulf of Tonkin to vacate the area directly over Hanoi.

It was just two years following the loss of our U-2 over Cuba by a missile that shot down Rudy Anderson in October 1962. In Rudy's situation and our current one, the aircraft were not equipped with Radar Warning (RAW) devices to signal us of enemy tracking our aircraft in search mode. However, we knew the direction of the radar, the mode in which the radar was on, and the direction in which we should be looking to visually detect the incoming missile.

We learned two important things from this incident: Our intelligence on NVN's defenses was faulty. Up to that time we had no clue they possessed Surface to Air (SAM) missiles and there was no reason why aircraft were not equipped with the RAW gear. We were grounded from flying over NVM for ten days until the radar warning gear was installed on all our aircraft.

The only reason Ed did not get shot down that morning was that he was flying his target route by dead reckoning (magnetic heading and time). The area was completely covered by low clouds which denied him the ability to visually track his target. It was time for his turn to a new direction, and it was in the turn when he looked back in the direction he had been flying and saw the missile screaming vertically past him.

A month before this incident I had a flight over Hanoi that led me in the direction of China to the north. The route was an extension from Hanoi to my next turning point just south of China. I was worried about the weather on this mission, and it was very similar to the one Ed flew a month before with surprising results. The area was covered with low clouds estimated to be 70,000 feet below my flight altitude. As I left the Hanoi area and approached the China border, I was very careful to watch the time and heading on that segment of my flight. Within thirty seconds of my time to turn almost 180 degrees to the south, I noticed a break in the clouds ahead. I continued for another fifteen seconds when I recognized from my map of NVM the town on the border near China. I was more than a little relieved to know my dead reckoning navigation was on time and target.

After the Fall

Until the Gulf of Tonkin incident on August 2 and 4, 1964, US personnel in Vietnam were strictly advisors supporting ground and air troops of the South Vietnamese (SVN) government. An example of the support we provided was with the A-1C Skyraider two-seat propeller aircraft, formerly a Navy bird from the Korean War era. It had sufficient

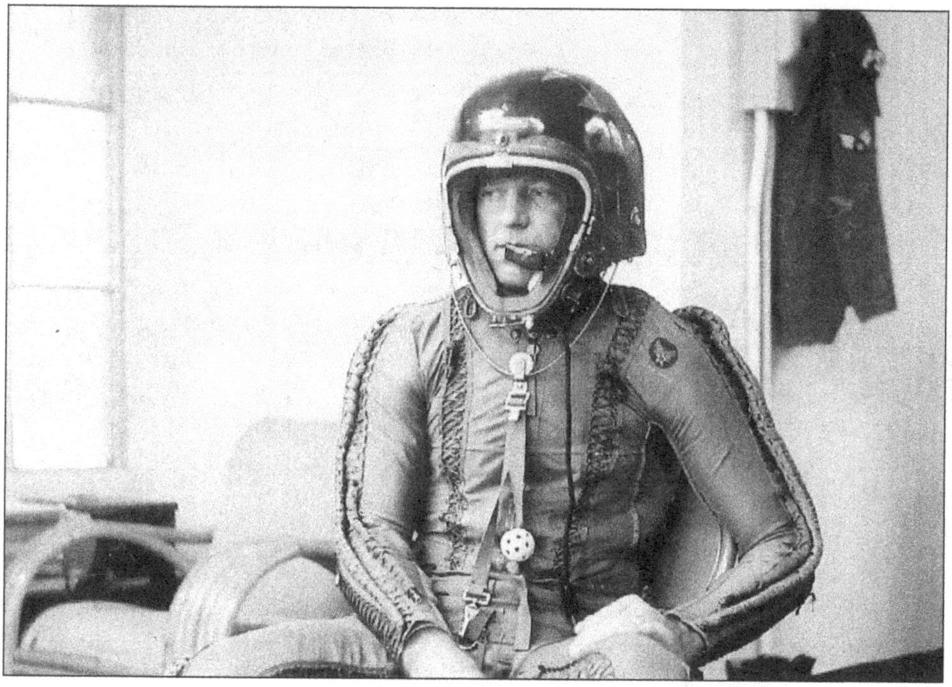

Jim Rogers in the dressing room, prior to a flight.

Saigon, October 1964.

US Embassy, Saigon, 1964.

Saigon street scene, 1964.

capability to give ground troops some air suppression. The A-1C aircraft were on a lend/lease program (a politically correct term for donated by the US) with the SVN government. A SVN Air Force pilot in training flew the aircraft with a USAF pilot in the instructor seat. The USAF pilot was considered the primary pilot, and if necessary, fired the guns and dropped any bombs.

Once a week Roger Herman, Vic Milam, Tony Martinez, our operating location commander, and I would jump into a van available for our use and drive to a great little restaurant near Bien Hoa on the Mekong River called Le Plage. It became a favorite place for many in our unit as an escape from the base chow hall. Thanks to the French influence, the food was exceptional and the *escargot* appetizer delicious, even if it did take a bit of effort to appreciate the first time.

On one of our trips to this particular restaurant, we were waiting for our meal when a big black Mercedes roared into the parking lot. Two guys with machine guns came running into our dining area and quickly scanned the restaurant. Actually at that time of day, there were very few diners. The gun carriers turned on their heels, returned to their car and sped away at the same speed they arrived. It all happened so quickly, we were completely surprised and had no idea what had taken place.

Within ten minutes the same black sedan returned to the parking lot, and General Nguyen Cao Ky, the SVN Air Force Commander, exited the vehicle and entered the restaurant. He and his bodyguards were seated in an area isolated from other diners at a specially arranged table with several bottles of liquor. General Nguyen was a dashing young officer who was already becoming well known to the local populace as a political figure. He was a flamboyant individual and dressed the part in his customized uniforms and flight suits. He was certainly the epitome of the word "class."

General Nguyen, most likely a regular at the restaurant, commanded and received preferential treatment from the entire restaurant staff during his twenty-minute lunch. It was quite amusing and interesting for the four of us to witness the spectacle. When he left the restaurant, he nodded in our direction and smiled as he passed by. We were in civilian dress, but we obviously stood out as Americans.

The Tribal War

In the fall of 1964 a tribal war erupted between the NVN forces and the Montagnard tribesmen who inhabited the central highlands of SVN. The Montagnards, aided by SVN forces and US advisors, hated the invading NVN troops who entered SVN via the Ho Chi Minh Trail. Equipped with short barreled twelve-gauge shotguns, the Montagnards fought the Viet Cong in the jungles of SVN. During nightly fights between the two forces, we were kept entertained with gunfire around the base and the occasional shoot down of an aircraft with small arms as it landed at Bien Hoa. The victims of the gunfire were SVN aircraft, several CIA planes and even an occasional A-1C were hit by snipers using small arms to shoot them down in the traffic pattern. It was all relatively low key until the base commander at Bien Hoa, Colonel "Wild" Bill Bethae from South Carolina received intelligence information that the NVN forces were planning a big "pow wow" in the jungles near Saigon. He marshaled every aircraft available for attack and killed many of the Viet Cong leaders attending the meeting. Within a week following the attack, flyers were found in Saigon offering a bounty on Colonel Bethea's life by the Viet Cong. Wild Bill retired in South Carolina a few years later, still quite healthy. I

U-2 detachment personnel, Bien Hoa AB, October 1964. 4028th Squadron Commander Lt Col Tony Martinez is standing far right. Jim Rogers is seated far left in the first row.

South Vietnamese Government building, 1964.

Woman herding water buffalo.

Pilots' trailer, Bien Hoa AB, 1964.

Typical family home, Vietnam 1964.

came away from this tour of duty with a souvenir of one of those discarded twelve-gauge shotguns. However, the gun was illegal in the US, so I gave it to a friend in Ecuador.

Office of the White House Press Secretary . . November 26, 1962

THE WHITE HOUSE

REMARKS OF THE PRESIDENT

AT PRESENTATION OF OUTSTANDING UNIT

AWARD TO

4080TH STRATEGIC RECONNAISSANCE WING

OF THE

STRATEGIC AIR COMMAND

HOMESTEAD AIR FORCE BASE, FLORIDA

Gentlemen, I want to express our great appreciation to you on behalf of the people of the United States, to all of you who have taken part in the activities which have made it possible for the United States to defend its security in very difficult times.

I may say, gentlemen, that you take excellent pictures, and I have seen a good many of them, and beginning with the photographs which were taken on the week-end in the middle of October which first gave us conclusive proof of the build-up of offensive weapons in Cuba. Through the days that have followed to the present time, the work of these two units has contributed as much to the security of the United States as any unit in our history, and any group of men in our history.

We are an open society and all that we have is, in a sense, available to the world. We are in a struggle, although we do not wish it we accept it, with a closed system. Therefore, the ability to detect those developments which directly threaten our security of those nations associated with us -- this ability is -- essential to our survival, to the maintenance of our security and vital interests, and, in a very real sense, to the maintenance of peace.

So I think that you gentlemen can take every satisfaction in what you are doing, what you have done, and in what you will do. We are very much indebted to you. We are particularly indebted to Major Anderson, who was a member of one of these Wings, who was the only casualty of the last few weeks, but who is symbolic, I think, of the willingness of a good many Americans to take great hazards on behalf of their country. We are very much indebted to you all.

END

Family And Community

"One of the greatest gifts that life can give to anyone is the very special love that families share."
Craig S. Tunks

Military Wives

It was just another harried Wednesday afternoon trip to the commissary (grocery store on military bases). My husband was off teaching young men to fly. My daughters were going about their daily activities knowing I would return to them at the appointed time, bearing among other things, their favorite fruit snacks, frozen pizza, and all the little extras that never had to be written down on a grocery list. My grocery list was in my 16-month-old daughter's mouth, and I was lamenting the fact that the next four aisles of needed items would have to wait. I was extracting the last of my list from my daughter's mouth, when I accidentally hit an old man with my cart.

This man had no appreciation for the fact that I had 45 minutes left to finish the grocery shopping, pick up my 4-year old from tumbling class and get to school, where my 12-year old and her carpool mates would be waiting.

I knew men didn't belong in a commissary, and this old fellow was no exception. He stood staring blankly in front of the soap selection, as if he'd never had to choose a bar of soap in his life. I was ready to bark an order at him when I realized there was a tear on his face.

Instantly this grocery aisle roadblock transformed me into a human. "Can I help you find something?" I asked. He hesitated, and then told me he was looking for soap.

"Any one in particular?" I continued.

He said he was trying to find his wife's brand of soap. I started to loan him my cell phone to call her when he said, "She died a year ago, and I just want to smell her again."

Chills ran down my spine. I don't think the 22,000-pound Mother of all Bombs could have had the same impact on me. Tears welled up in my eyes, and my half-eaten grocery list didn't seem so important; neither did fruit snacks or frozen pizza.

I spent the remainder of my time in the commissary listening to a man tell the story of how important his wife was to him: He told me how she took care of their children while he served our country. He was a retired, decorated World War II pilot who flew missions to protect Americans. He still needed the protection of a woman who served him at home.

My life was forever changed that day. When my husband works late or leaves before dawn, I try to remember that sense of importance I felt that day in the commissary.

Sometimes the monotony of laundry, housecleaning, grocery shopping and taxi driving leaves military wives feeling empty; that kind of emptiness is rarely fulfilled when our husbands come home and don't want to or can't talk about work. We need to be reminded at times of the important role we fill for our family and for our country. Over the years, I've talked to a lot of military spouses about how special they are and the price they pay for freedom, too. The funny thing is that most military spouses don't consider themselves different from other spouses. They do what they have to do, bound together not by blood or merely friendship, but with a shared spirit whose origin is in the very essence of what love truly is. Is there a difference? I think there is. You decide for yourself.

Civilian spouses get married and look forward to building equity in a home and putting down family roots. Military wives get married and know they'll live in base housing or rent some place. Their roots must be short so they can be transplanted frequently.

Civilian spouses decorate a home with flair and personality that will last a lifetime. Military wives decorate a home tempered with the knowledge that no two base houses have the same size windows or same size rooms. Curtain sizes have to be flexible and multiple sets are a plus; furniture must fit like puzzle pieces.

Other spouses have living rooms that are immaculate and seldom used. Military wives have immaculate living room/dining room combos. The coffee table has a scratch or a broken leg in the move from Germany, but it still looks pretty good.

Other spouses say goodbye to their husbands as they leave for a business trip and know they won't see them for a week. They are lonely, but can survive. Military wives say goodbye to their deploying spouse and know they won't see them for months, or a year, or longer. They are lonely, but will survive.

Some spouses, when a washer hose blows off, call Maytag and then write a check for having the hose reconnected. Military wives have to cut the water off and fix the hose themselves.

Spouses get used to saying "hello" to friends they see all the time. Military wives get used to saying "goodbye" to friends made the last two years.

Other spouses worry about whether their child will be class president next year. Military wives worry about whether their child will be accepted in yet another school next year and whether that school will be the worst in the city...again.

Other spouses can count on their husbands' participation in special events, such as birthdays, anniversaries, concerts, football games, graduation and even the birth of a child. Only military wives count on each other because they realize that the flag has to come first if freedom is to survive. It has to be that way.

Certain spouses put up yellow ribbons when the troops are imperiled across the globe and take them down when the troops come home. Military wives wear yellow ribbons around their hearts and they never go away.

A lot of spouses worry about being late for Mom's Thanksgiving dinner. Military wives worry about getting back from Japan for Dad's funeral.

Other spouses get emotional watching the television program showing an elderly lady putting a card down in front of a long, black wall etched with many names. The card simply says, "Happy Birthday, Sweetheart. You would have been sixty today." A military wife is the lady with the card, and the wall is the Vietnam Memorial.

I would NEVER say military wives are better than other spouses, but I will say there is a difference. I will say without hesitation, that military wives pay just as high a price for freedom as do their active duty husbands. Perhaps the price they pay is even higher. Dying in service to our country isn't nearly as hard as loving someone who has died in service to our country and having to live without them.

God bless our military wives for all they freely give.

Author Unknown

Buddy Brown.

Buddy L. Brown
Knoxville, Tennessee

Oildale Secret

The first orders for the U-2 came from the CIA for 20 aircraft. Building 82 at Lockheed in Burbank, California was straining with an order for 29 more U-2s pending. The Air Force needed a larger and more secure assembly building. There was nothing in Burbank suitable or available. A former potato warehouse in Oildale, my hometown, was available for lease. It was almost new, windowless and adaptable to assembly work. The warehouse also had the advantage of direct access to the Bakersfield Airport for delivery via an Air Force C-124.

Like all Skunk Works projects, it required the utmost in security precautions. The new Oildale facility would be called Unit 80 and would have no signs to identify its ownership. All parts were fabricated in Building 82 in Burbank and trucked to Unit 80 in Oildale.

The first five or six U-2s were assembled at Burbank and flown by C-124 to the Nevada test site. Thereafter, Unit 80 assembled and delivered some 50 U-2s via C-124 to Bakersfield Airport. The C-124s arrived in the dark of night and taxied to a revetment in a remote corner of the airport.

Production began in the spring of 1956, and ended by September 1957 with a peak production of eight aircraft per month.

Security at Unit 80 was never breached and in late 1957, everything was transferred back to Burbank. Neither the Air Force nor the Agency nor Lockheed ever admitted knowledge of activity at Unit 80. However, in 2002 an Oildale TV station reporter and Minter Field Air Museum representatives dug through piles of records. They made many telephone calls and invoked the Freedom of Information Act to put together the true story about what took place at Unit 80. The story about Unit 80 and the U-2 was broadcast on TV and reported to residents of Bakersfield and Oildale.

A few months after that report, I received a call from Major General Jim Whitehead, himself a former U-2 pilot and a member of the aviation board at the museum in Bakersfield. He explained that he had learned I was from Oildale. To celebrate some events that had been planned in the Bakersfield area, the General invited me to Bakersfield for some interviews and local TV appearances. The highlight of the event for me was the invitation to be the guest speaker at the Founders Banquet. I accepted the invitation and in February 2003 spent five days in Oildale.

I spoke at the banquet given in my honor and began my discussion by saying, "I can't believe, me, a guy from the little town of Oildale, to be honored like this. It is something I'll remember forever." It was a great trip; I met many WWII vets, some old school mates and had a visit with my sisters, one of whom is a retired minister with 27 years in the pulpit. I pointed out now that the secret was out, the people of Bakersfield and Oildale should be proud of their contributions during the Cold War.

John Harvey

(Deceased January 15, 2007))

The following was submitted by John's widow, Lilas.

> John received orders for Laughlin AFB, Del Rio, Texas in the summer of 1954. He and I remarked, "Why is it we always seem to get these remote bases?" Before Laughlin, we were at Hunter AFB, Savannah, Georgia with the B-47s. One of our friends in Savannah had a cousin who was a postman in Del Rio. There was no base housing at Laughlin at the time and rentals in town were few and far between. Through our friend's cousin, all the postmen in Del Rio were alerted to be on the lookout for a house for a colonel, his wife and four daughters. We arrived in Del Rio one afternoon at 5:00 PM and stopped for dinner at a café on Main Street. When the waiter took our order, he inquired where we were going. John answered that he was newly assigned to Laughlin AFB. The waiter replied, "You must be the new colonel with your wife and four daughters. All the postmen in the city are trying to find you a house." We thought that was a beautiful way to be introduced to our new assignment.
>
> After a few months, we were assigned to a house on base. We needed some unpainted bedroom furniture—two bunk bed sets for the girls. We were referred to Ricks' Furniture Store on Main Street in Del Rio. With our four daughters in tow, Pam age 10, Leigh age 8, Lindsey 6 and Jane 3, we visited the furniture store. We had finished picking out the furniture when a clerk approached us and asked, "Do you have a little blonde haired girl?" When we replied that we did, the clerk said, "You better come with me." At the front of the store there was a display of children's furniture. Sitting on the potty chair was Jane, waving to the huge crowd outside the store window. The spectators laughed and waved back. The *Del Rio News Herald* reported the following day Colonel John Harvey's arrival at Laughlin and Del Rio was upstaged by his three-year-old daughter, Jane's big splash at Rick's Furniture Store.

The Val Verde County Library in Del Rio conducted a fund raising program and our Officers' Wives' Club offered to participate. Zina Worley, wife of Colonel John Worley, and I volunteered to organize the Wives' Club contribution. We auctioned off some artwork and one of the sergeants at Laughlin, an artist himself, donated some of his work as a gift. The sergeant offered to help with the sale, but at the last minute he had to decline because he had to participate in a GI party. Both Zina and I were outraged that he made the commitment to help us and then said he had to go to a party. Zina and I begged our husbands to try and get him to ditch that party so he could help with our auction. Both husbands said they couldn't help us. Zina learned a few days later that a GI party was really an "all hands on board clean up of the barracks" and no absences were permitted.

One hot 110-degree summer day, our four children joined a group for a 25-mile horseback ride to one of the Del Rio ranches. There were no horses left for the sergeant leading the group, so he rode a donkey. When they all departed, he announced in a loud voice, "There will be no slouching in the saddle and no Coke breaks." I drove alongside for a few miles pretending to take pictures, but it was really to ensure nobody passed out from the heat. They finally arrived at the ranch, and the sergeant prepared a delicious stew for lunch. Of course, no one knew until they finished eating that it was rattlesnake stew.

A sudden rainstorm blew in, typical of those hot summer days. I called John and asked him to get a base bus to rescue all the children. He was very reluctant but

Welcoming the first group of Taiwanese student pilots to Laughlin AFB. Left to right: Major Chan Hia, unknown USAF officer, Major Mike Hua, Major Shia, Col John Harvey, Major Gen Wang, Col John DesPortes, Major Yang, Major Tiger Wang.

he finally gave in. John arrived with the bus and offered the children shelter on the bus, but they were only worried about the horses getting wet!

When we first moved on base, we had one of the temporary duplex houses. Base housing at Laughlin was located in what had been scrub brush fields and home to a variety of wildlife. It wasn't long before we realized we had an invasion of field mice in our attic, behind the walls and occasionally inside the house. Their antics sounded like a non-stop bowling game. We became accustomed to their racing up and down the Venetian blind cords inside the rooms. One day I had a coffee party at our home and some of the women sat on the floor. I noticed something beside the couch that looked like pink bubble gum. On closer inspection, I saw newly birthed mice rolling out from under the couch!

There were a number of stories that surfaced during and after the construction of the base housing. When the fields were cleared prior to construction, a number of rattlesnake nests were disturbed. We had so many rattlesnakes slithering up on the warm sidewalks and roads; we walked with our heads down looking for coiled snakes. We even learned bold techniques such as throwing a rock aimed at their heads. Fortunately, I don't recall ever hearing anyone being bitten by one of those rattlesnakes.

The black widow spiders, too, lost their prime real estate when the field was cleared. They just built new nests over the doors of the houses. We learned to look up prior to entering the door to be sure a spider wasn't swinging down on its web.

John and Lilas Harvey at their farewell party at Laughlin AFB.

The road to the back gate of the base was temporarily opened and I decided to use it one morning. I was in a rush to pick up our maid who lived in town. I use the term "road" loosely here; it had recently been graded out of the scrub fields. I took Jane, our youngest still in her nightgown, with me; I had thrown on some old clothes and had not put on any makeup. In my haste, I did not realize the road was wet from an early morning thunderstorm. Right at the back gate, my car sunk into mud so deep, I couldn't move it. I was totally humiliated to be stuck there and to look so unkempt. It took two cranes to get us out. My John came out and laughed at my predicament. What an embarrassment.

We moved into our new base house, but we had to furnish our own grass. The people of Del Rio generously furnished us with grass from their own yards as well as shrubs and trees. Right after many of us had finished planting the plugs of St. Augustine grass, we had one of those Texas rains. The newly planted grass came loose and went floating down the street. All our neighbors came running out with plastic sacks and wheelbarrows to retrieve the precious grass plugs.

Just to give an idea of the intensity of those infamous rainstorms, I was the honoree at the Officers' Wives' Club welcoming coffee party. At the very moment I was trying to get out of the car at the Club, a huge rain cloud burst over the base. It delayed my arrival for a short while. I was told the runway had several inches of water and there were waves with whitecaps on them. This particular storm was captured by a photographer and was filed by the base historian.

In October 1960 movie star John Wayne came to the area to film *The Alamo*. He had requested permission from the Base Commander, my John, to use the runway for his own plane. As a "thank you," Wayne invited my John and me to dinner with his wife, Pia, and their children at their temporary home in Brackettville. I was amused at the number of people who knocked on their door while we were having dinner to get a glimpse of the celebrities. The whole family was understanding and gracious about the intrusion. Wayne gave us a pass for our car to come watch the filming of the movie. I filled up our station wagon with at least 12 people and we drove to Brackettville to the movie site on a private ranch. That was certainly an interesting occasion for all of us.

President Dwight Eisenhower visited Laughlin in July 1962 and met with President Lopez Mateos of Mexico. The occasion was a celebration to open the Amistad Dam that spanned the Rio Grande between the two countries at Del Rio. Our house was selected as an emergency location should President Eisenhower suffer any health problem while he was at Laughlin. We were the only ones at the time with a king-size bed; they were so new we couldn't even find a king-size bedspread. I sewed two double bedspreads together to cover our king-size bed. Eisenhower's advanced team arranged for the special red telephone installed on the bedside table with a direct line to the White House.

Considering the entourage that accompanies the President now, it was interesting that President Eisenhower had no aides with him, only a female secretary. The President walked down the stairs of his airplane and was greeted by a great contingent of military and civilian dignitaries. My John followed behind the President and could hear him asking the secretary each time he was introduced, "Who in the hell is this? And this one?"

Our children's horse drill team wanted to greet President Eisenhower riding their horses at a full gallop with flags waving. It required permission from the White House and the President. Eisenhower was so concerned for the children, he did not approve the full gallop because he was afraid someone would be hurt. He did approve of the horse drill team with flags waving, but the horses could only walk.

President Eisenhower met the President of Mexico in the small town of Ciudad Acuña, across the Rio Grande from Del Rio. In preparation for the two presidents' visit, Ciudad Acuña freshly painted all the buildings and paved the entire travel route.

The town of Ciudad Acuña had little industry and depended on tourism for much of its economy. There were few paved streets and utilities, such as electricity and water, were in short supply or non-existent in some areas of Ciudad Acuña. A local dentist, Dr. Ramon Ortiz, offered his large home with a swimming pool for the meeting. Much to our surprise, when a review of the meeting site was conducted, planners discovered there was no water in the pool. Prior to the two presidents' meeting, Laughlin sent water trucks to fill the pool.

My John told me many of his on-the-job stories of those early days at Laughlin. One such story was about shooting the birds in the hangars because their droppings corroded the metal on the airplanes. There were occurrences of the maintenance technicians being the target of occasional droppings as they worked on the airplanes in the hangar. I can only guess that the sound of gunshots must have created quite a show in the hangar.

Joe Kerr, a resident of Del Rio, invited my John to his ranch to observe "real" ranching in action. The action they were watching was cattle roping. John didn't know at the time that "greenhorns" like him were ranchers' entertainment and their kind of ranch humor. Joe and some of the other fellows there chided John into roping a calf. Being a good sport but completely out of his element, John did rope a calf over and over again. After all that "real" ranching, John's clothes were dirty and torn and he was a disheveled mess. With Joe accompanying John to the gate at Laughlin, the guard asked the disheveled occupant for his identification, which he didn't have with him. He said, "I'm Colonel John Harvey, the Base Commander." As you might imagine, the guard didn't believe him and he called his commander to come identify John and his guest. I'm sure the guard never forgot that day and he probably made it an amusing story in the retelling. I know for sure my John never forgot the incident."

James S. Long

James Long is Chairman of the Board, Laughlin Heritage Foundation Museum. Del Rio, Texas

But what does he do?

My sister, Mary Kay Long, was taking her friend, Jane, daughter of Colonel A. J. Bratton, home one afternoon from school to the family residence on Laughlin AFB. They stopped the car at the main gate and a young Air Policeman (AP), noting an unregistered vehicle with two cute girls, stuck his head into the driver's window. He demanded identification. While Mary Kay was retrieving her driver's license, Jane passed her military ID across to the policeman and said, "I think this will help." The AP grasped the ID, scanned it briefly and quickly returned it. He abruptly withdrew his head knocking his hat off. He retrieved his hat, stood at attention and saluted smartly. Mary Kay was very impressed with the attention they received. As they drove off, she asked Jane, "What does your Dad do?" Jane replied, "He's the Wing Commander!" Mary Kay persisted, "I know, but what does he *do*?"

Wetbacks on the Ramp

Shortly after the Lockheed U-2s arrived at Laughlin AFB, my cousin, Warren Long, who was with the Army Corps of Engineers, was assigned to do survey work on the flight ramp. He was accompanied by an escort officer when he worked in close proximity of the classified aircraft. While Warren was occupied with his surveying, the escort officer noticed some individuals crossing the ramp and exclaimed, "Well, I'll be damned! Here we are with the most sensitive aircraft in the Air Force inventory and those illegal aliens are right in the middle of them!"

Who fired those shots?

My father, Stillman Long, and I were returning about dusk from a hunting trip northwest of Brackettville, Texas, approximately 30 miles east of Laughlin. It was during the Christmas holidays. We were driving our Jeep station wagon when we had some engine trouble on US Highway 90 near the end of the Laughlin runways. I volunteered to walk to the gate and call for a mechanic while my Dad remained with the Jeep and our rifles. A carload of kids passed and tossed out some fire crackers setting off a series of loud bangs. I arrived at the main gate of Laughlin, explained our situation to the guard, and he allowed me to call the mechanic in Del Rio, seven miles away. As I was making my call, a sedan arrived at the gate with two men in the rear seat armed with submachine guns. They demanded of the guard, "Who fired the shots?" I volunteered that I had seen that it was only kids with fireworks. The driver then asked the guard, "Who is he?" They seemed satisfied with the answer and drove out the gate to US Highway 90 only to return a short while later.

With my call made and the mechanic on his way, I walked back to the Jeep. I told my Dad about the fireworks incident and the guys with submachine guns. He said, "I guess that's why those guys over there have been watching me with their field glasses." Sure enough I saw the vehicle parked on Laughlin property that my Dad had seen.

Photographic Security

As an aviation fan and avid model airplane builder, I had built several of the Hawk Company's Lockheed U-2A models after the full-scale aircraft arrived at Laughlin. I was proud to be the first civilian to get one of the new model U-2s. I had the idea to place the models on the sidewalk at our house to simulate the ramp. I hung one from a pecan tree nearby with monofilament fishing line in a flight position. After I took a number of 35mm color slides, I sent them off to Kodak for processing in Dallas where I sent all my film for development. After an unusually long time, the slides were returned with special markings on the box. A special notation showed that it had been examined by Kodak security department. It then occurred to me that the photos had looked realistic enough on first glance for a censor to examine them!

I remember the date and time vividly, June 28, 1957. A high school classmate who lived near the Del Rio Municipal airport called me and hurriedly explained that a jet aircraft was landing, probably a Navy Crusader. I figured he had it all wrong, but I told him I would come pick him up on the way to the airport to catch a look. When we arrived at the airport, we saw a bunch of people running to the northwest part of the airport near Gulick Hill. From where we stood, we could only see a large silver object on the ground. We then drove toward Gulick Road and the hill near what we now understood was a crashed airplane. It appeared to have occurred only moments ago.

We left the car and ran towards the still unidentifiable aircraft just as a USAF H-19 helicopter landed at the site. We crossed the fence and were within 50 to 60 feet of the aircraft when the security force exited the helicopter. They ordered everyone back 50 feet beyond the fence and within a few moments we were told to move back 100 feet. The final order was for everybody to get completely out of the area.

The Laughlin fire truck crossed the runway and started up the slope to the crash site. The fire truck passed a number of people who had slowed to a walk. A puff of black soot escaped the exhaust as the driver accelerated to pass through the fence without slowing.

We jockeyed for position as close to the aircraft as we dared. What we observed that day remained with me even now. The fuselage was upside down and the pilot was still strapped in his seat. We took note of the tail number of the aircraft and my friend remarked, "Do you see anything funny about the tail number? It is all sixes and nines!"

We were still spellbound by the activity, and I saw Mr. Frank Gulick, the owner of the property where the crash occurred. He was taking pictures with his movie camera. I felt certain that his camera, or at least the film, would be taken from him. His niece later confirmed the camera and film had been confiscated.

After we were ordered away from the area by the security force, I took my friend home. I later returned with my Brownie Hawkeye camera and took a photo of the wreckage. The film was processed, but I never showed it to anyone until the early 1990's when I had it enlarged for a 4080th SRW reunion.

Patricia McIlmoyle
Venice, Florida

My Thoughts

When my husband was flying the U-2 all over the world I never worried about him. I believed he was the best of the best of pilots, I thought! At the end of this story you will understand I feel different. It is never too late to change our hearts and minds.

Did other wives in the Squadron really put jar lids filled with vinegar or some concoction under the crib legs to keep spiders, scorpions or earwigs from getting into our child's crib. I did that! Did military people earn the same salaries in their rank? Was I rich or poor? Wherever else in a same development would we get the same design of housing, a huge commissary, lovely parks, brand new swimming pools, nice ceramic and art classes, all kinds of athletic games? Those perks were exceptional. Weren't mothers all around outside to help monitor their children and the neighbors' children? Our Clubs were the best in food and shows. Didn't some of the men get up with their head covered (so we wouldn't recognize them) as we watched their "button" moving in circles imitating a whistle? The act was called "The Whistling Midgets". I had a ball! What talent we were exposed to. Didn't we have the best of imitators and also the best of dancers, whatever their act might be? In another way, didn't I take my sick children to the doctor; didn't he say to me that the children were okay and that they had the Fifth Disease because they missed their father when he was on TDY? Did I believe that? Was that true?

Were our experiences and adventures not so sophisticated as we have today? Did any other families have picnics underneath the bridges around the base area? We were afraid of the bats that would come flying out at us. Wasn't it like going to a zoo to take our littlest ones to the back gate to watch bunny rabbits bouncing around looking for food? Did you hear of one or more little boys sitting down on the street curb with the sharper edge of a dinner knife in one hand? They were swatting a rattlesnake on the head and they did not get hurt.

Were you there on base when the men were flying over Cuba? I put duct tape all around my windows so nuclear dust would not harm my children. I doubt, when I think about it, that Russia would nuke Del Rio. Who would want two young kids to sleep in her bed when their Dad was on TDYs? I wanted that! Did I ever get drunk at the Club and get sick? I did but it wasn't good for me. We drove back home through the back gate because my spouse did not want the guards to see me "toss my cookies." Did your children get up in the morning when it was still dark? Their father was home from a flight but they wanted breakfast so they went to the frig. The older one poured KoolAid (whatever became of milk?) onto his and his sister's cereal.

Were you one of the women who came to this church meeting that one friend had? A crowd of members in the group came to that insignificant mini-meeting. How did my friend manage to serve homemade pie to so many people? Well, she was an Air Force wife and everyone there had an adequate piece of pie and all the coffee they wanted.

Do some of you remember the singing group at most bases and especially the Women's Chorus we had at Del Rio? Our super director and artistic pianist were the best in talent. Did we have fun? Yes!

Some family, relatives and friends would visit us on-base but were disturbed by sounds of the jets revving up their engines so early in the mornings. Did those jet screams bother you? Not me!

Might you remember one cute Captain's wife who sewed an outfit for herself for the luncheon's fashion show? Showing off her outfit and seeing her bounce around the table were wonderful to me. She was the epitome of a pretty officer's wife. What about those lovely teas we would go to at some hostess' home? I will never forget those times. Whoever would get their children in their new Volkswagen bus and with another family drive clear to Breckenridge Park in San Antonio for a picnic? It was three hours away! I have had that experience.

Well, to get back to what I think of all of us and our husbands' careers, I find that my thoughts are different now. I liked all the events we have had and the good times. But, flying and working in support of that Squadron seems scary to me when I hear or read these stories. My heart tells me that these men were handsome, good husbands, good fathers and superb airmen. But, now I think they also are brave.

I am the wife of … a US Air Force Cold War Reconnaissance Pilot.

Clifford B. (Cliff) Melton

(Deceased November 1, 1980)

The following was submitted by Cliff's widow, Virginia.

> Cliff was an engineer by education and was assigned to the Field Maintenance Operation of the 4080th SRW.
>
> When Cliff was assigned to Laughlin, we rented a house in Del Rio. Our next door neighbors on one side were Bob and Barbara Ingram, on the other Rudy and Jane Anderson. Bob and Barbara's daughter, Stacy, was about the same age as our daughter, Joyce, and they became friends. Our sons played with Rudy and Jane's boys.
>
> During the time Cliff was with the 4080th SRW at Laughlin, we had three young children, Joyce, Wes and Bill, who was born in Del Rio. Our kids were involved in a variety of activities. I became a volunteer, mostly because I had already driven them to their functions. I was Cub Scout leader with Wes and Bill and a Brownie leader with Joyce. The boys were also into sports and played Little League baseball.
>
> I was a home economics major in college and enjoyed teaching my daughter and the Brownie Troop to sew. One of the Brownie projects was to sew a Barbie dress using a pattern that I made for each girl. They sewed the dresses by hand and later I took their carefully sewn clothes and finished them on the sewing machine so they would not come apart. Shortly after they finished sewing the dresses, we had a Father/Daughter Banquet. The girls brought their Barbie dolls with newly created outfits to the banquet. The dolls were set on the table and held the place cards for the dads.
>
> While we were in Tucson, Joyce's high school cooking class made cookies for the men in Vietnam. We wrapped and sent them to Cliff for distribution to the fellows at his base. Each of the men who received the cookies wrote thank you letters to the girls.

Clifford B. Melton, Laughlin AFB, 1966

William T. (Rody) Rodenbach II

Riverside, California
Wife: Barbara

Memoirs of a U-2 pilot's wife

Charles Dickens said it best in the opening of his book, *A Tale of Two Cities,* "It was the best of times and the worst of times." Rody received transfer orders from the 71st Strategic Reconnaissance Wing at Larson AFB, Moses Lake, Washington in June 1957 to join the 4080th SRW at Laughlin AFB, Del Rio, Texas. That wasn't such bad news. For two years we had enjoyed living at Larson in a nice little house on Doolittle Drive. Many of our friends previously stationed with us in Bitburg, Germany also transferred to Larson. They were the Bedfords, the Mohans, and the Bellingers. The Dixons lived a couple of streets away, which was a safe walk for our daughter, Janie, to play with her best friend, Diane. We all had two or more kids. On a freezing, snowy night our fourth child, Chuck, was born at the Larson AFB Hospital on January 17, 1957. You have heard it all before, I'm sure. It was time to leave for the hospital, labor pains were three minutes apart, but the car would not start. Bill opened the hood and I got behind the wheel to turn the key; we finally got it going. This was the *best of times*, a new baby boy, a new assignment and a new adventure.

We were pleased to hear that many of the Larson AFB families would be with us in Del Rio. It was especially nice for the wives and the children to transfer together, as an extended family, from one location to another. Most of us were many miles from close relatives so these great friends became "family." While living in Washington State, Rody and I couldn't have been much further from our roots in Connecticut. The children of

Barbara Rodenbach and dance partner in the production of *Olé*.

our Air Force friends were babies in Germany, toddlers in Moses Lake and now they looked forward to attending school together in Texas.

We took our annual leave in the summer to spend time with family. We drove to Connecticut from wherever we were stationed. Our families were overjoyed to learn that the kids and I would be spending the summer with them at the family cottage in Madison, Connecticut, on the shores of Long Island Sound. Rody made a wooden car bed for five-month-old Chuck to ride in the back seat of the car. I painted it blue and made a mattress for the combination bed and playpen. This was many years before secured child seats and seat belts. The children and I took turns riding in the back seat with Chuck and we referred to his bed as "the box." More than once when we stopped for gas or at rest stops, strangers would ask the kids what they had in the box. Our kids innocently replied, "Our baby brother." There were more than a few surprised looks from those same strangers. The box worked well for giving Chuck a safe, comfortable place for sleeping and playing under the watchful eye of his back seat companions.

Rody took on the packing of our household goods at Larson and then endured the white glove treatment of inspection before checking out of base quarters. After clearing the base, he drove the long trip back East to pick us up and move us to Texas.

We had heard that Del Rio was no paradise. However, that wasn't enough to prepare me for the long drive into that part of the country. The children and I had never been to Texas; consequently, it was hard for us to grasp how really big the state was and how long it took to drive through it. The children frequently asked their Dad if they were *still*

William T. (Rody) Rodenbach II.

in Texas. We drove farther south, each day hotter than the previous one. Our car did not have air conditioning and all four kids were cramped, tired and cranky. The rolling hills and tall trees of the eastern landscape were replaced with mesas and numerous species of cacti. The terrain became very flat and barren; tumbleweeds rolled across the road in front of our car. We could see for miles and miles with not a hill nor even curve in the otherwise straight as an arrow road. I felt as though we were driving to the end of the earth and within a few more miles, we were going to fall off.

Del Rio, Texas

Base housing had not been been built by the time we arrived at Laughlin. We had to find houses or apartments to rent in town. Many of us found houses in a dated development not far from the base on Kennedy Drive. Some of our Moses Lake group settled nearby and others were scattered around town.

Now to the *worst of times* category. We had barely emptied packing boxes and arranged the furniture when Rody had an appointment at Lackland AFB Hospital in San Antonio, approximately three hours away by car. I had assumed it was a physical exam related to his new flying job. I was not prepared for him to be admitted into the hospital for surgery on both ears. I suddenly felt overwhelmed as he drove off and left us in this unfamiliar place for four weeks and without a car.

While Rody was confined to the Lackland Hospital, the children and I spent those hot August afternoons on the shaded carport catching a slight breeze. We had not even had time to buy an electric fan or plastic wading pool for the kids. I filled the biggest pan I could find from the kitchen and sat little Chuck in it while the three older kids played and sprayed themselves with the garden hose. At night I opened all the windows hoping for some breeze and lower temperatures to cool off the house. In the morning I pulled the shades in hopes of trapping the slightly lower temperature for a while longer.

I was so grateful to have friends like Joe and Ann Nemo who lived three houses down from us on Kennedy Drive; Millie and Buzz Curry lived nearby as well. They were all family. They checked on the kids and me and drove me to the base commissary for groceries. We were all one-car families then; the guys usually car pooled to the base leaving a car for the wives to go to the commissary or to ferry the kids to sports activities. In those days, neighbors helped neighbors.

I laughed when I recently looked at those photos I had taken of our kids posed in front of the Kennedy Drive house. The children were not standing on grass, but instead they stood on sandy soil where prickly things grew and fire ants built hills. Scorpions and huge roaches were also in residence.

Capehart Base Housing

All of the Moses Lake families who lived around Kennedy Drive moved a year later into the completed Capehart base housing. What a joy it was to have a brand new house with all new appliances, a lawn landscaped in soft, green grass and new trees and shrubs. The term "tree" was really a misnomer; they were newly planted sticks that would take many years before they grew to provide shade from the Texas sun. Rody and neighbor, Phil Chase, solved that problem by cutting down three big cottonwood trees that grew along a stream out in the desert around Laughlin. Phil said he knew the cottonwoods to be excellent transplanting trees for this location regardless of the fact that they didn't have roots. Cottonwood trees are known to be resilient but horticulture experts recommend transplanting with a rootball. These adult trees were planted along one side of the house and by the patio in back. The next morning base photographers were in our yard taking pictures of this overnight "miracle" on Arantz Drive.

The Wing Commander and two US Senators came to see the new housing area. They asked if we would allow them to tour our house. We were honored to be asked especially when we learned one of the visitors was Senator Capehart, the very man who sponsored the Congressional Bill for construction of the housing on military bases. The visitors were very impressed with our fully leafed out cottonwood trees. These were the only adult trees in the entire housing area.

The other famous visitor to Laughlin was President Dwight Eisenhower, who was driven through our new housing area in his motorcade. I'll always remember seeing him standing in the convertible waving to us. I read that Senator Homer Capehart and President Eisenhower were very good friends.

The U-2 Spy Plane

The move to Laughlin didn't seem much different from all the previous ones. Rody was happy in his new job. He was checking out in a new plane, and enjoying the new assignment. The two older children were enrolled in Eastside Elementary School in Del Rio, and the two younger ones were at home with me. I don't remember hearing rumors at Moses Lake about the reason for the transfer to Laughlin, but Rody and the other pilots knew they were going to fly the new U-2 spy plane. The project was called Dragon Lady and everything surrounding it was secret. Wives were not told anything, because as one Colonel put it, "If the women know, it won't be classified for long."

It wasn't long before everyone on base was aware of the mission. Rumors started to fly, and we noticed the black planes with long wingspans parked on the ramp. I had totally forgotten about the day back at Moses Lake when Rody came home for lunch. That was very unusual for him to come home during the day. He usually grabbed a fast lunch at the base cafeteria. That day I asked what brought him home as he hurried to the bedroom; he explained he had to go into town for an appointment. When he came out, he was dressed in civilian clothes. He said he couldn't tell me about it right then, but said, "Don't be concerned. I don't know much about it myself so we'll both know later."

It was long after we moved to Del Rio and after the security was lifted on the U-2 that he told me the two men he met at Moses Lake were from the CIA and they came to talk to him about flying the plane for the Government. He learned the flying job would require him to be away from his family of three and soon to be four children for extended periods of time; he declined the offer.

Laughlin was a well-known training base for pilots. I should have been able to put it all together, but I was never a "had to know everything" military wife. I kept busy with our home, children and my own volunteer projects. As it turned out, Rody was at Laughlin to fly the U-2, not for the CIA, but for the Air Force.

This was becoming *the best of times.* From my point of view we had great housing, convenient shopping at the commissary and base exchange, a hospital and Officers' Club. When I was asked to write what it was like to be the wife of a U-2 pilot during the late 50's and early 60's, I was sure I would have to decline. So many years have passed. However, once I turned the pages of my saved copies of the Laughlin Officers' Wives Club newsletter, known as the *LOW JET,* I recalled such pleasant memories of happy social events I had attended.

Both the Officers' and Wives' Clubs were the glue that kept us socially and actively connected. Considering how remotely situated Laughlin was from a city with theaters, a choice of restaurants and cultural opportunities, it was important to have active clubs. I looked forward to the monthly Newcomers Coffee gatherings and luncheons. We socialized and established friendships with many of the women through the club.

Once a month and on special holidays, the club would hold a big theme party. Each squadron would take a turn sponsoring the party, such as Casino Night, Ship Wrecked party and Valentine dinner dance. Anyone with an ounce of talent could count on a full-time non-paying job in the entertainment. One outstanding party at the club was St. Paddy's Night with the talent of John Quinn. He wrote, casted, directed and performed in the show.

Not long after we moved on base, I joined the Laughlin Players, a Little Theater group. I helped the enlisted men and women put on talent shows at the NCO Service Club. I was dancing in a show one time when a local dance studio owner and volunteer, Helen Marie Jones, stopped in. She had just finished writing a Mexican musical called 'Ole', and she was looking for dancers. She invited me to join her show and I was honored to accept. The show was a success at Laughlin. Helen Marie offered the show for Del Rio and Ciudad Acuña residents at La Macarena. I thought the show was so funny. Imagine a troupe of gringos performing the Mexican Hat Dance and the Flamenco to the Hispanic audience. It was such a success that we were asked to continue the show for two more nights.

Those five years spent at Laughlin were definitely the best of times. It was long enough for us to feel part of the community and a closely knit family on base. In all honesty, the long separations from our guys were the worst of times.

Rody left the U-2 program in the summer of 1962 when he was reassigned to Command and Staff School in Montgomery, Alabama and we bid a sad farewell to our many friends at Laughlin.

Rody's Flameout

On September 16, 1958, Rody was on a training mission in the U-2 when he experienced an engine flameout at a critical altitude. Following proper emergency procedures, he called "Stargazer" for assistance in fixing his position and informed controlling agencies of his difficulty. His UHF radio would not respond after repeated efforts to contact any ground station.

Rody then turned off all electrical switches and descended to a safe airstart altitude. He had enough to deal with, but the canopy and his faceplace frosted over during the descent. Rody managed to clear a small area in the faceplate by rubbing his nose against the inside and successfully flew the aircraft on instruments.

The first airstart attempt was successful, but he was without hydraulic pressure. He continued on to Laughlin and lowered the landing gear by the emergency system. After penetration a GCA straight-in approach was requested. Three miles out, he realized he could not reduce airspeed. He attempted two more landings trying to reduce the airspeed without drag devices and managed to bring the aircraft down on the final try by lowering the engine RPM past the idle setting. The drag chute deployed and he completed a safe landing.

Investigation revealed a faulty speed brake hydraulic line had failed resulting in complete loss of the hydraulic system.

Rody was named the 4028th SRW Pilot of the Month in October 1958 for his skillful handling of the flight emergency.

Memories of Bill Rodenbach (then 11 years old)

My first rattlesnake roundup was in one of the base hangars. A guy stood inside a big box giving a lecture as a bunch of rattlesnakes slithered around his feet. I listened to his speech the whole time but wondered why the snakes didn't bite him.

Our house on the base was beside the playground and our large side yard was the site of many football games with Eric Chase, Gene Smith, Don Schweikert, Ricky Waters, and Chuck Wilcox. When we played football for Del Rio Junior High, our moms carpooled to pick us up after practice and brought us back to the base.

We caught the school bus down the street from the Colonels' houses. I think it is part of the golf course now. The Del Rio public school bus picked up students along the way and then left the base by way of the back gate.

I mowed yards on the base to earn spending money. One of my customers was the U-2 pilot who was shot down over Cuba. I learned what had happened when I saw the moving van outside his house.

Dad and I drove many of those three-hour trips to San Antonio for me to go to the orthodontist. In the summertime on the way home, we stopped at a river and swam, and then bought a watermelon for 25 cents. What a treat. Our car didn't have air conditioning so we had a canvas bag full of water on the outside of the car to use in case the car overheated and to drink if necessary. The water from the canvas bag didn't taste good and I didn't drink it unless it was absolutely necessary.

Memories of Jane Rodenbach (then 9 years old)

After we moved to Arantz Drive, we heard a lot about rattlesnakes being found around the houses. There was a story that the brand new fence surrounding the housing area was snake proof with a fine mesh on the lower part of the fence. Unfortunately, the housing was built on Rattlesnake Hill and it appeared the snakes were fenced inside!

One Halloween I returned home after Trick or Treating unexpectedly and was surprised to be hosed down in our driveway by Bill and one of his friends. I was dripping in my wet costume. I reached for the screen door and heard the rattle. There was a snake coiled up between the inside door and the screen door. I let out a big scream that got the attention of my brother and his friend and we all went for help.

The best part of being an Air Force dependent, especially at Laughlin, was the freedom to walk by myself to the swimming pool, to the movie theater, to the new library with its wonderful children's section or to visit friends close by. I loved going to the stables for horse riding lessons and trail rides. To me the base was like a safe little village.

Jennifer Rodenbach (then 5 years old)

I don't remember a lot about those days, but I do have a vivid memory of one morning watching my Dad as he got ready for work. To me he looked so patriotic and handsome in his uniform. I watched as he pinned on his rank and wings to his uniform shirt. It needed something more. I ran to my bedroom and brought my little American flag attached to a stick and put it in his back pocket as he walked out the front door. I'm not sure how far he went before the flag was discovered.

Chuck Rodenbach (then 2 years old)

I was the youngest member of the Rodenbach crew at Laughlin and the one who was transported to Texas in "the box." Because I was so young, I remember very little of those days. I liked riding my bike in our driveway, the only place I was allowed to ride. One day I felt adventurous and went a little farther and got lost. All the houses looked alike. I was so happy to see Mom coming for me on the back of a neighbor's motor bike.

Royal Air Force U-2 Pilots

Royal Air Force U-2 Pilots

Through agreement between the United States and the United Kingdom, the following pilots were trained in the U-2 aircraft.

Martin Bee
Michael G. Bradley
Richard Cloke
Basil Dodd
David E. Dowling
Harry Drew
John W. McArthur
Robert T. Robinson
Charles Taylor
Christopher Walker
Ivan B. Webster

Martin Bee

Royal Air Force
Croydon, England
Wife: Lilleba

My RAF training began at the RAF College Cranwell (similar to the US Air Force Academy) in 1955-1958. My first solo was on the tail wheel Piston Provost and then the Vampire jet. After receiving my pilot wings, I flew fighters, Hawker Hunters, Gloster Meteors and English Electric Lightnings. In 1960 we were the first Mach 2 squadron in the RAF.

My selection for the U-2 came out of the blue. One day my Station Commander, Group Captain Bird-Wilson instructed me to go to London for an interview. At the Ministry of Defense some senior officers talked in circles about going to the US, but they never told me the full story until a few days before I boarded the Cunard liner for New York. My guess was that the selection criteria included tail-wheel and high performance experience. I had certainly had no recce (reconnaissance) experience.

My period of service on "secondment" to the CIA began in 1964. (Secondment meant I was loaned to the CIA.) I traveled to New York by Cunard passenger liner with Squadron Leader Basil Dodd. Our flight planner/navigator, Alistair Sutherland and our doctor, Squadron Leader Nigel Mills, joined us a month or two later.

In the 1960s the RAF had about 100 personnel serving on "exchange" duty with several US air operations and, in turn, the Americans served on reciprocal "exchange" duty in the UK. The RAF personnel serving on the U-2 program had rather different orders than the other exchange personnel. We were never part of the regular 100 exchange personnel and were forbidden to meet up with them. Our initial month of training was

Martin Bee in pressure suit at Lake Meade for parachute training, 1964.

Parachute training at Lake Meade, Nevada, 1964. Martin Bee is in the harness.

Left to right: Lilleba Bee, Al Rand (CIA U-2 pilot) and Martin Bee in the UK, 1967.

Martin Bee at RAF Duxford Imperial War Museum beside a U-2, 1995.

with the USAF at Davis Monthan AFB. Gerald McIlmoyle was among the many I met through my instructor, George Bull.

We made six flights in the U-2A at Davis Monthan and then moved to Edwards AFB where we flew the much more powerful U-2C, U-2G, U-2F and U-2H which were owned and operated by the CIA from 1964 to 1968. We were still considered part of the RAF there but we seldom wore our uniforms.

Like our USAF counterparts, we traveled several times for pressure suit fittings to the David Clark Company in Worcester, Massachusetts. I was told the Clark Company manufactured women's undergarments prior to getting into the pressure suit business. As a gift on departure, we each were given a 1960 bra, which they also made in profusion.

One morning our Commander, Lt. Col. Miles Doyle called me to his office. He told me the following day we expected the Senate Armed Services Committee and some RAF VIP visitors arriving at Edwards to be briefed on our operation. I was selected to fly a demonstration for them to show the high performance of the U-2 and finish with some Field Carrier Landing Practice (FCLP) – touch and go landings.

I flew a U-2G, a modified U-2C fitted with a slightly beefed up landing gear, a flap setting increased from 35 to 50 degrees and a tail hook. With a standard training fuel load of 400 US gallons, the aircraft would weigh a little under 16,000 pounds and have a thrust available of 17,000 pounds at full throttle. However, full throttle could not be used at takeoff because it was far too much "oomph" for a fragile aircraft and airspeed and "G" limits could be exceeded in seconds.

For the Senate and RAF VIP demonstration I made a normal "gated" reduced power takeoff, lifting off at about 90 knots and accelerating quickly. I rotated the aircraft to about an 80 degree climb angle, and selected gust control. I added full power slowly, and activated the fuel dump producing an air-show style twin contrail of fuel vapour from the mid-wing fuel dump points. I held the airspeed at 170 knots, going nearly vertical in a corkscrew climb. It took only one minute to reach 10,000 feet. Without the vapour trail, the aircraft would have been barely visible to the onlookers at the runway edge.

I had to get the aircraft back to the airfield before the VIPs lost interest. I made a quick stall check at 10,000 feet to ensure that both wings stalled symmetrically and that the wing tank fuel was balanced evenly. Back in gust control with landing gear down and airbrakes out for maximum drag, I brought the bird down at 220 knots indicated airspeed. I made checks for a FCLP touch and go using the USN deck landing mirror system set up on our runway.

On finals at 90 knots with flaps at 50 degrees, the mirror "meatball" was picked up and held as a glide path reference. I slowly reduced airspeed to 82 knots as I approached the runway threshold. At about 20 feet the USN Landing Safety Officer (LSO) called "Cut One" at which point I retarded the throttle to idle. Moments later the LSO called "Cut Two" and I activated the spoilers. I eased back on the yoke a little further and the bird stalled at about a foot above the runway. Simultaneously the aircraft settled onto the twin main gear wheels and the solid rubber tail wheels. Now the fun started! I had to keep the wings level for the touch and go without the aid of the pogos by using deft aileron movements. With speed brakes retracted, flaps raised to take off position and elevator trim reset, the throttle was opened slowly to takeoff power. This time in a sedate fashion, I turned downwind for a final full stop landing.

I made the final landing again from a standard mirror approach with the LSO calling height above the runway from the mobile chase vehicle. Instead of using the speed brakes this time, I deployed the tail parachute at a foot or so above the runway. The U-2 immediately slowed and settled on to the runway. Thanks to a light headwind, I rolled quickly to a stop, wings level and tips off the ground. The ground crew refitted the pogos, and with one man sitting on each wing to keep the wings bent down slightly to ensure that the pogos made contact with the runway, I taxied the U-2 back to the ramp.

In the climb, the view ahead is nonexistent. Pitch attitude is obtained from peripheral vision with much time spent looking at the airspeed, RPMs and the turbine gas temperature (TGT). Watching the TGT was critical to limit the increased hot temperature allowed at that particular high power setting and avoiding damage to the engine. The controls felt decidedly slack as the U-2 sat in a close vertical attitude on 17,000 pounds of thrust. The aircraft went up quickly, but came down slowly. It was like a glider, and had little drag. Landings required full attention to detail as the undercarriage track is less than a metre. The U-2 requires a two-point "tail dragger" style attitude at touchdown to avoid porpoising back into the air. Popping the drag chute just above the runway at one foot set up a perfect landing attitude.

As I reflected on my U-2 experience some 40 years later, I am extremely happy I was a young pilot in my 20s at the time these demos were flown. Very few had the opportunity to experience the overwhelming feeling of sheer power, spectacle and fun, unlikely to be permitted these days.

Richard (Dick) Cloke

Royal Air Force
King's Lynn, Norfolk, England
Wife: Gillyan

I joined the Weather Reconnaissance Squadron (Provisional) 4 at Edwards North Base towards the end of 1967 and I started flying the U-2 early in 1968. I think I was the first Brit not to check out at Davis Monthan. My conversion was all conducted on North Base's 6,000-foot runway.

Now for some highlights (and the lows).

On an early transition flight with full fuel, I flew one of our older C models known to buffet at altitude. Sure enough it happened to me and instinctively, I throttled back far enough to cause a flameout, the only one I ever had.

On another C model flight while at altitude, I punched in the next heading and started to complete the green card. As I wrote, the autopilot tripped out. When I looked up, I had about 120 degrees of bank. I recovered without too much difficulty. After landing, the camera boys were surprised to see the unusual view of the sun in the tracker camera.

During "tropical" tests on the new R model at McCoy AFB, we had a lot of problems with the liquid oxygen system. I believe it was because the system was taken from the SR-71. We didn't have the skin heating factor, and, as a result, the oxygen gauge was prone to give erroneous readings. There's nothing like the oxygen showing zero to make 70,000 feet seem a very long way up. Returning from one of these tests, I let down, dumped fuel and ran into a wave of thunderstorms. I had difficulty finding McCoy in the heavy rain

Left to right: Andy Cumming (flight surgeon), Harry Drew (pilot), Dick Cloke (pilot and detachment commander) and Rod Booth (flight planner).

(Florida does not look anything like the Mojave!) and finally landed with only 15 gallons of fuel remaining. That was close.

In October 1969 I flew an R model from North Base to Kinloss, Scotland. About half way into the 12-hour flight, I turned my head to the left and my helmet locked in that position. I later learned a ball bearing had broken and jammed. The next few hours were very interesting, especially when it came to landing in typical Scottish weather of heavy rain and wind. It was a bit inconvenient with one's head stuck half left!

Later two of us Brits ferried U-2s from Upper Heyford, UK direct to North Base. My flight lasted 13 hours 55 minutes. With pre-breathing time added, plus a 30-minute hold on the runway waiting for the weather to clear for takeoff, we spent well over 16 hours in our pressure suits, half again as long as usual.

One special highlight was the carrier qualification. We had T2 training at Pensacola Naval Air Station, and mirror landing practice at North Base. We carried out our qualification aboard the aircraft carrier, USS *America*, a day after the Lockheed test pilot qualified the R model. The training must have been spot on because the carrier work was really straightforward.

In December 1968 I was climbing out of Edwards North Base for a high level sortie when there was a loud bang and the canopy disappeared. To cut a long story short, I dumped fuel and landed on the lake bed because the aircraft had developed an unusual heavy wing. At touchdown the yoke was at 90 degrees to the normal position. Subsequent

Dick Cloke in the cockpit of the U-2R at Edwards North Base, approximately 1969.

investigation revealed that one transfer pump had stuck in the 'on' position, continually transferring fuel to one wing. What I should have done was to dump all my wing fuel until only the collector tank fuel remained. At the time, I wondered whether the canopy had caused any airframe damage, although an airborne check did not reveal any signs of damage.

The subsequent inquiry concluded that the canopy was not locked correctly at takeoff, though my Mobile Officer and I were absolutely certain that it was.

Thirty years later, I had retired from the RAF, and was working for British Aerospace. In April 1999 I received a phone call out of the blue from a USAF major in Korea. He was conducting an inquiry into the loss of a U-2 canopy in flight, and had somehow learned of my experience. It happened that my loss of a U-2 canopy in flight was the first such loss, and over the years there had been several similar incidents, as well as incidents during pressurization checks on the ground. Modifications were recommended as a result, but exoneration was 30 years late as far as I was concerned! Ah well …

Republic of China Air Force U-2 Pilots

Republic of China Air Force U-2 Pilots

Through an agreement between the Republic of China and the United States, the USAF trained ROCAF pilots to fly the U-2 reconnaissance aircraft. Laughlin AFB at Del Rio, Texas and later Davis Monthan AFB at Tucson, Arizona trained the pilots from Taiwan. The training experience for the Chinese pilots was a combination of exposure to a new aircraft, new culture and for some, most significantly, a new language. The U-2 was a difficult aircraft for the best of pilots to master and for an added challenge, all training material was in English. Due to the ROCAF pilots' culture to present a positive appearance, they would often reply "yes" when asked by their USAF instructors if they understood the material.

A local school principal in Del Rio met weekly with the Taiwanese pilots to help improve their English skills and their understanding of American slang. The Chinese pilots were told that local citizens thought they were Hawaiian. USAF families "adopted" many of the ROCAF pilots and introduced them to American traditions and customs.

The following ROCAF pilots trained in the U-2 aircraft and returned to Taiwan where they flew reconnaissance missions for their own country.

Shi Chu (Gimo) Yang
Huai Sheng Chen
Tai Yu (Tiger) Wang
Chih Yao Hua
Hsi Chun (Mike) Hua
Chang-di (Robin) Yeh
Lee Nan (Terry) Ping
Liang The Pei
Li Yi (Jack) Chang
Hui Chia Yang
Chen Wen (Pete) Wang
Tse Shi (Charlie) Wu
Jai Chuang (Terry) Liu
Ching Chang (Mickey) Yu
Jen Liang (Spike) Chuang
Rung Pei (Tom) Hwang
Chung Li (Johnny) Shen
Tao (Tom) Wang
Peo Wei (David) Lee
Denny Huang
Chen (Joe) Wei
Chu Chien
Hung Ti (Andy) Fan
Hseih (Billy) Chang
Mike Chu
Chris I
Mory Tsai

Gen Lee Po Wei (David).

ROCAF T-33 squadron. Top row, far right, Robin Yeh.

Major General Jude B.K. Pao with P-51 Mustang.

Black Cat pilots. Left to right: Simon Chien, Chris I, Bob Birkett (USAF), Tom Wang, Mike Chu, Joe Wei and Mory Tsai.

Andy Fan.

Mory Tsai standing by U-2.

Colonel Tom Wang

Johnny Shen, Chih Yao-Hua, Tom Wang, David Lee, Andy Fan.

Mike Chu.

Robin Yeh with General Chiang Kai Shek.

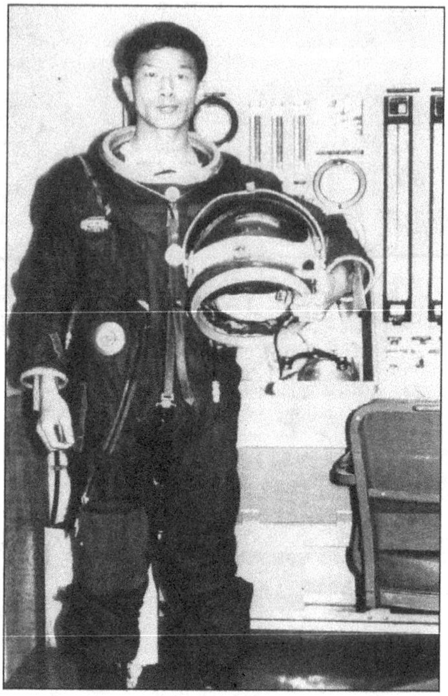

Andy Fan.

Black Cats.

Black Cat pilots, left to right: Johnny Shen, Tom Wang, Gimo Yang, Spike Chun, Tiger Wang, Andy Fan, Terry Liu, Denny Hung.

Standing, left to right: David Lee, Terry Liu, Johnny Shen, Spark Chung, Denny Hwong. Seated, left to right: Tech Rep, Andy Fan, Bob Erickson, Tiger Wang.

General I. Fu-En with Mory Tsai.

Left to right: unknown, Jack Chang, David Lee, Robin Yeh, Mory Tsai.

Black Cat pilots, U-2 in background. Left to right: Joe Wei, Mike Chu, Tom Wang, Simon Chien, Mory Tsai, Bob Birkett (USAF).

1990 ROCAF Reunion for Robin Yeh and Jack Chang, seated in middle row; Gimo Young is center in dark jacket.

2005 4080th SRW Reunion, left to right: Mory Tsai, Jack Chang, Robin Yeh and Andy Fan.

2005 4080th SRW Reunion, left to right: Robin Yeh, Jack Chang, Margaret Hua, Mike Hua, Chris I, Keiko Yeh, Pauline I, Robert (Gimo) Yang, Helen Shen, Andy Fan, Mory Tsai, Johnny Shen, Joe Wei.

Recommended Reading

Bromley, Linda Rios, *Freedom Flight, A True Story of a Republic of China Air Force U-2 Pilot*, (Solihull, UK: Helion & Company, to be published in 2012)

Davis, Larry, Perry Manley & Don Greer, *U-2 Spyplane in Action (Aircraft No 86)* (Carrollton TX: Squadron/Signal Publications, 1988)

O'Leary, Michael & Eric Schulzinger, *Black Magic: America's Spyplanes, Sr-71 and U-2* (Osceola WI: Motorbooks International, 1989)

Pocock, Chris, *The U-2 Spyplane: Toward the Unknown, A New History of the Early Years* (Atglen PA: Schiffer, 2004)

Polmar, Norman, John D. Gresham & Tom Clancy, *DEFCON-2: Standing on the Brink of Nuclear War During the Cuban Missile Crisis* (Hoboken NJ: John Wiley & Sons, 2006)

Index

Due to frequent changes in rank, to avoid confusion only names appear in this index, no ranks.

Related titles published by Helion & Company

Secrets of the Cold War. US Army Europe's Intelligence & Counterintelligence Activities against the Soviets during the Cold War
Leland C. McCaslin
ISBN 978-1-908916-91-4

Abolishing the Taboo. Dwight D. Eisenhower and American Nuclear Doctrine, 1945-1961
Brian Madison Jones
ISBN 978-1-907677-31-1

Black Tuesday over Namsi. B29s vs MiGs – The Forgotten Air Battle of the Korean War, 23 October 1951
Earl J. McGill, Lt Col USAF (Ret.)
ISBN 978-1-907677-21-2

Jet Age Man. SAC B-47 and B-52 Operations in the Early Cold War
Earl J. McGill, Lt Col USAF (Ret.)
ISBN 978-1-907677-46-5

HELION & COMPANY
26 Willow Road, Solihull, West Midlands B91 1UE, England
Telephone 0121 705 3393 Fax 0121 711 4075
Website: http://www.helion.co.uk